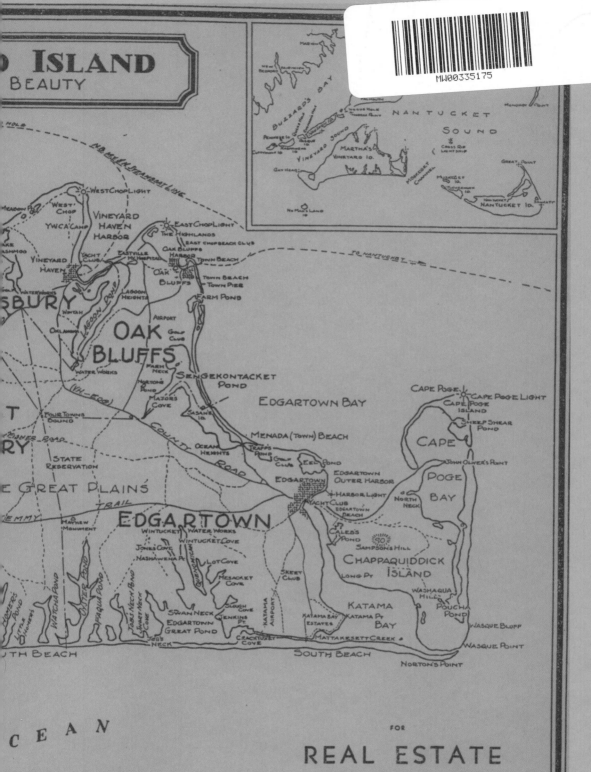

ISLAND
BEAUTY

FOR

REAL ESTATE

ANYWHERE ON MARTHA'S VINEYARD

SEE **DONALD SWIFT**

MAIN STREET   VINEYARD HAVEN MASS
PHONE   VINEYARD HAVEN 23

6737

19 Ⓒ 37 BY DONALD SWIFT

The History of Martha's Vineyard

The History of Martha's Vineyard

How We Got to Where We Are

Arthur R. Railton

Commonwealth Editions
Beverly, Massachusetts
Published in association with
Martha's Vineyard Historical Society

Excerpts from *War Within and Without: Diaries and Letters of Anne Morrow Lindbergh*, copyright © 1980 by Anne Morrow Lindbergh, reprinted by permission of Harcourt, Inc.

Library of Congress Cataloging-in-Publication Data
Railton, Arthur R.
The History of Martha's Vineyard : how we got to where we are / by Arthur R. Railton.
p. cm.
Includes bibliographical references and index.
ISBN-13: 978-1-933212-00-5 (alk. paper)
ISBN-10: 1-933212-00-4 (alk. paper)
1. Martha's Vineyard (Mass.)—History.
2. Martha's Vineyard (Mass.)—Biography. I. Title.
F72.M5R35 2006
974.4′94—DC22   2005029782

Cover design by John Barnett.
Interior design by Joyce C. Weston.
Printed in the United States of America.

Endpapers: In 1937 Donald Swift, a Vineyard Haven real estate man, gave this map to potential buyers. Peaked Hill in Chilmark, at 311 feet, is the highest point. There are "Cranberry lands" at Lobsterville, but no airport anywhere.

Published in association with the
Martha's Vineyard Historical Society by
Commonwealth Editions
266 Cabot Street, Beverly, Massachusetts 01915
www.commonwealtheditions.com

In loving memory of Marjorie
(1918–2000)

*Without her, there would
have been nothing.*

Contents

Acknowledgments

This book would never have been written except for Gale Huntington, who in 1978 asked me to take over as editor of the *Dukes County Intelligencer,* the quarterly journal published by the Martha's Vineyard Historical Society. He had recently retired as editor and George Adams, reporter on the *Vineyard Gazette,* helped by Alison Shaw and Janet Holladay, published the next three issues. George had moved off-Island, turning the responsibility back to Gale. It was then that he called me.

I had known Gale for many years, having rented his Chilmark camp every summer since the 1950s (still do). My wife, Marjorie, and I had just moved to Edgartown after my retirement, and Gale knew I would need something to do. He assured me that the Society would find a replacement within a year. I agreed to do it for a year. Nearly thirty years later, I am still the editor.

I began researching Vineyard history, an activity to which I quickly became addicted. I filled notebooks with data garnered in the graduate libraries of the Universities of Virginia and Michigan (plus the William Clements Library at Michigan). Two of our sons teach at those schools, and we visited them twice a year. While Marge spent the day with our grandchildren, I roamed the history stacks. When Marge died in 2000 I started to write this book, publishing a chapter at a time in the journal. It has had a long gestation.

During those years I have been helped by many Islanders: James Richardson III, Tom Hale, Bob Hughes, Bailey Norton, "Young Bob" Jackson, Charlotte Hall, Margot Willkie, Craig Kingsbury, Richard Burt, Mary Beth Norton, Dorothy West, Howard Andrews, Edwin Ambrose, Harry Butman, Frank McKay, and others, each knowledgeable about some phase of Vineyard history. Of great help with research were Eulalie Regan and Helen Gelotte, who struggled with microfilms of the *Vineyard Gazette,* seeking an obscure news item I needed.

I would have been lost without the help of Catherine Merwin Mayhew, the Society's genealogist, who unscrambled family relationships.

Others at the Society were always eager to help. Linsey Lee's oral history program was especially useful. The tedious task of selecting illustrations was done by Jill Bouck, Dana Costanza, Keith Gorman, and Susan Wilson. I am grateful for their hard work and especially for their patience with me.

Throughout the months of converting the journal articles into a book, the staff at Commonwealth Editions has been most cooperative. My thanks to Webster Bull and especially to Ann Twombly, who caught many errors before they were printed.

My son Stephen, a professor of English, has been especially helpful. His copyreading has been indispensable. Jean McCarthy has helped at various times with proofreading.

Through our many years together, my wife was my main support, in my writing and in my living. I have dedicated this book to her.

Finally, I thank my Aunt Jane, who started it all when she came to Edgartown in 1920 as a summer chambermaid at the Colonial Inn. Two years later, she married Everett C. Fisher, a quintessential Islander born on Chappaquiddick. They lived on School Street in Edgartown and she invited me, seven years old at the time, to vacation with them. From then on, I spent some part of most summers on the Island. Thank you, Aunt Jane.

If I have omitted the names of others who helped, it has not been intentional. I apologize. To all, named and unnamed, my deepest thanks.

The History of
Martha's Vineyard

1

From the Beginning to the Dutch Rebellion

Summer people are not new to Martha's Vineyard. They roamed over its hills and valleys more than ten thousand years ago. But they hadn't come to vacation at the beach; there was no beach. The ocean was seventy-five miles to the south and almost as far to the east. They were hunters, not bathers, chasing wild animals for food.

The Vineyard was not yet an island. So much of the earth's water had been frozen in a mile-thick ice cap that the ocean level had dropped low enough to uncover one hundred thousand square miles of continental shelf. The Vineyard's higher land, deposited by glaciers thousands of years earlier, was a tiny "bump" rising above that vast plain. Large mammals such as mastodon, caribou, and moose (perhaps even the wooly mammoth) roamed across the tundra, chased by those summer people on the hunt.

Summers were not warm. The southern edge of the melting ice cap was still only a few hundred miles to the north. Winds blowing across thousands of miles of ice drove cold air south, chilling the Vineyard even in summer. Great quantities of water running from the melt flowed to the sea, creating river beds and valleys. On the Vineyard, the southern terminus of the glacial flow thousands of years earlier, the melt had left undulating moraines, huge boulders, and thick beds of gravel.

Cold though it was, the climate was warming, very slowly. As the climate changed, so did the population. The caribou and moose moved north, and the mastodons and mammoths became extinct. Deer, elk, and smaller mammals took their places. Temperate-zone plants and trees began to flourish; fish of many varieties swam up from southern waters. Those summer hunters found their lives less harsh as food became more abundant. About eight thousand years ago, they began staying all year.

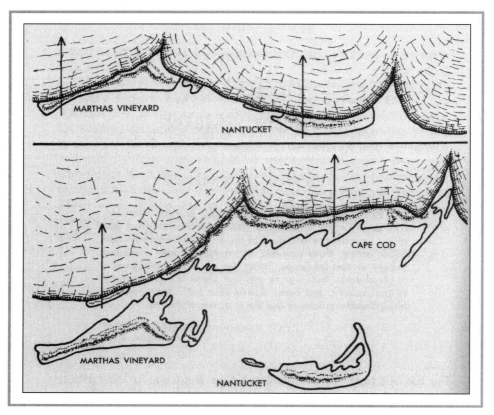

Top: When the mile-high glacier began retreating, it dropped gravel and boulders brought
down from the north to form the Vineyard's high ground.
Bottom: As the ice melted, the sea level rose to create the islands.
(From Barbara Blau Chamberlain, *These Fragile Outposts*)

As the ice melted, the ocean level rose. The lowland that had connected the Vineyard to the continent became soggy, delta-like. Then,
about six thousand years ago, the rising ocean became high enough to
surge across those coastal wetlands, turning the high ground into islands.
One of those islands is now Martha's Vineyard.

Through thousands of years, ocean tides, at first gently, then with
increasing velocity, scoured the sea bottom, creating channels and "holes,"
such as treacherous Woods Hole, with its bewildering currents that swirl
around the Labrador boulders left there by the glacier to bedevil mariners.

By five thousand years ago, the ocean had stopped rising and the coastline stabilized. Barrier beaches, formed by wind and tide, created shallow
saltwater ponds, along the shores of which those Vineyarders, now year-
rounders, built their wigwams. The ponds provided ample food; there was

shellfish in abundance. Life became easier. The residents had more leisure time and, as many have discovered since, this was a good place to live.

We know this story in part because of shell middens, trash heaps left behind by those early settlers that date back nearly five thousand years. These shell archives are still being uncovered by the surf and by excavators digging foundations for today's settlers.

An unknown hunter, about fifteen hundred years ago, invented the bow and arrow, which made killing wild animals easier. Nature was generous. It provided food and filled their spirits; its beauty brought them joy and contentment. The Island, with its gentle hills and shallow ponds, surely was a heaven on earth.

From the thick beds of clay the inhabitants dug raw material to make utensils and pots for cooking and storing their food. They began to develop agricultural skills, and from gardens on the fertile plains they harvested squash, beans, and maize.

In their dugout canoes they speared blackfish, occasionally even whales. Often those large ocean mammals, trapped in the shallow waters, washed up on the beach, providing vast quantities of food and oil for all to share. Fire became a tool to burn off the dense undergrowth that covered the land. The tangled jungle of trees and vines was cleared, so there was more land to farm and to hunt. With plentiful food, their numbers grew. By one thousand years ago, there were three thousand Wampanoag on the Island, members of the tribe that inhabited much of southeastern New England.

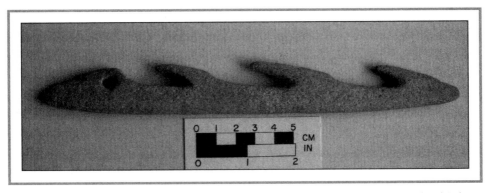

A Wampanoag bone or antler harpoon found on the southern shore of the Island. The Vineyard's earliest fishermen hunted whales and other sea mammals near the coastline in dugout canoes. Numerous harpoons dating back six hundred to one thousand years have been found in archaeological sites on the Island. (MVHS Collections)

Protected by the narrow moat of salt water, their Island was a most peaceful place. And for the next six hundred years, it was theirs—theirs alone.

Then, on May 21, 1602, a huge vessel with tall masts and billowing sails dropped anchor off Cape Poge, the northeastern tip of the Island. It was not the first such vessel the natives had seen, but the others had sailed past, far out on the ocean. This was the first to stop, the first they could see close up. It was gigantic, frighteningly so. Filled with wonder and concern, they anxiously watched from behind bushes and trees. The next morning, a few men left the ship and came ashore but saw nobody. It was, as one journal keeper wrote, "a disinhabited Iland."

But it was not "disinhabited." There were three thousand Wampanoags there, many of them watching and wondering from their hiding places. Who were these light-skinned men? What were their plans?

The vessel was the *Concord* from England, and its master was Captain Bartholomew Gosnold, an explorer and entrepreneur. He had crossed the ocean seeking a place, a certain place that had been glowingly described by Giovanni da Verrazzano, the famed Italian explorer, after his voyage of 1524. As David B. Quinn, an English historian of early American voyages, wrote in 1983: "Gosnold in 1602 hoped to find the happy and beautiful bay with its many islands where Verrazzano found rest and Indian friendship in 1524, though Narragansett Bay was to prove strangely elusive."

It is now generally accepted that Narragansett Bay was the special place described by the Italian explorer, the place that Gosnold had come to find. Once he found it, he planned to set up a trading post with the natives and swap trinkets for furs. He came close, but he never did find Narragansett Bay; he settled instead for what is now Cuttyhunk, or so conventional wisdom tells us.

On board the *Concord* were thirty-two men, many more than the usual crew. Only twelve of them were mariners. The rest were "adventurers," eager to get rich in the New World. The ship had two captains: Gosnold, who was in command and would leave the ship to spend the year running the planned trading post; and Captain Bartholomew Gilbert, who would sail the *Concord* back to England, returning in the fall with winter supplies for the adventurers.

It was a grand plan. And Captain Gosnold on that lovely May morning was tempted to settle on Cape Poge as the place. A "place most pleasant," wrote Gabriel Archer, the journal keeper, so agreeable and verdant that

4

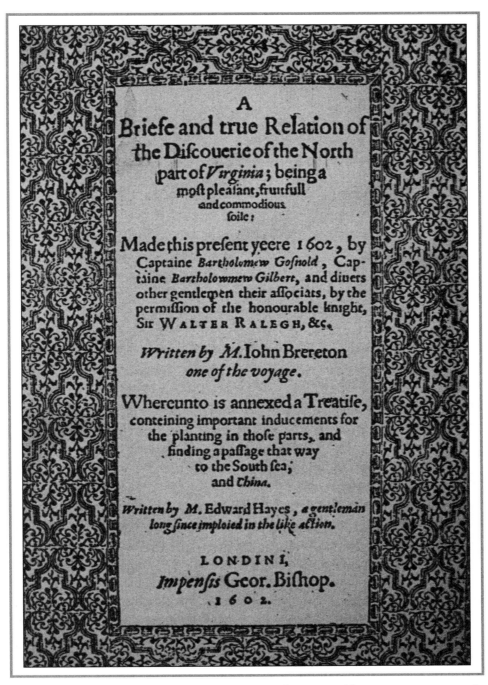

The title page of John Brereton's 1602 book describing Gosnold's voyage. Brereton and Gabriel Archer documented the *Concord*'s voyage with detailed descriptions of the Island's flora, fauna, and inhabitants—possibly to promote investment interest in overseas trade and settlement. (MVHS Collections)

Gosnold named it "Marthaes Vineyard," honoring his infant daughter, Martha. Archer recorded the events of those two memorable days, May 21–22, 1602:

> Coasting along we saw a disinhabited Iland which so afterwards appeared unto us: we bore with it, and named it Marthaes Vineyard. . . . The place most pleasant; for the two and twentieth, we went ashoare, and found it full of Wood, Vines, Gooseberie bushes, Hurberies, Raspices, Eglentine, etc. Heere we had Cranes, Hearnes, Shouler Geese, and divers other Birds which there at that time upon the Cliffes being sandie with some Rockie stones, did breed and had young. In this place we saw Deere, heere we road in eight fathome neere the shoare, where wee tooke great store of Cod, as before at Cape Cod, but much better.

When Archer wrote those words more than four hundred years ago, he was the first, but certainly not the last, to describe the Island as a "place most pleasant."

Gosnold liked to name places. A few days earlier, while the *Concord* was anchored inside a sandy hook of land to the north, he had gone ashore. The men who stayed on board did some fishing, catching many large, tasty codfish. So large and so tasty were they that when Gosnold returned, he named that hook of land "Cape Cod."

Now, a few days later, off Cape Poge, they again "tooke great store of Cod, as before at Cape Cod, but much better." Had Gosnold not already used the word, he might have named the place "Cod Island," instead of the more mellifluous "Marthaes Vineyard."

In the morning Gosnold decided it wasn't the place after all, and the *Concord* sailed west, coming to anchor in the sound off today's Lambert's Cove. On the beach they saw thirteen "fast-running Savages, armed with Bowes and Arrowes, without any feare." Again a small party rowed ashore—this time, no doubt, more cautiously. But there was no need for concern. The welcoming Indians, who probably knew of the earlier visit to Cape Poge, "brought Tobacco, Deere skins and some sodden fish . . . in great familiaritie." Archer wrote, "This Iland is sound, and hath no danger about it."

Captain Gosnold still was not satisfied. He had not found the place. They continued to sail west. Passing some colorful cliffs, he named them "Dover Cliffs" after those in England, but that name, unlike the others,

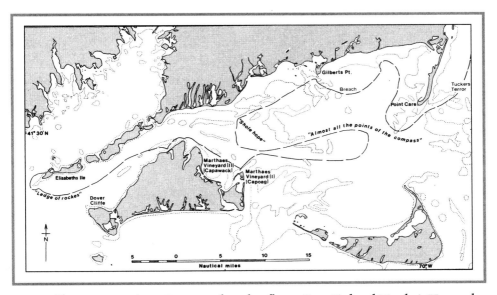

Gosnold's course in 1602. He went ashore briefly on Cape Cod and Martha's Vineyard, finally building a fort at Cuttyhunk of the Elizabeth Islands. He had intended to stay through the winter, but when his men refused, the Cuttyhunk settlement had to be abandoned. (From David B. Quinn and Alison M. Quinn, *The English New England Voyages, 1602–1608*)

does not survive. (Nobody knows who first called them "Gay Head Cliffs," an inspired choice.)

When the *Concord* rounded a chain of islands that ran to the northeast, they found themselves in what Archer called "one of the stateliest Sounds that ever I was in." Gosnold, too, was impressed. He named the westernmost island "Elizabeth's Isle," honoring his sister; the name has since been transferred to the entire chain.

Going ashore on that island, Gosnold found a small freshwater pond behind the barrier beach. In the middle of the pond was a small island, a secure site for their trading post. "We stood awhile," Archer wrote, "like men ravished at the beauty and delicacy of this sweet soil." Captivated by its beauty, Gosnold declared that this was *the* place.

While the men unloaded the *Concord*, they were visited by Indians, Wampanoag, men much taller than they, nearly naked, their olive-colored skin glowing in the sunlight. From the mainland these Wampanoag had seen the tall masts and paddled over to investigate. Like those on Martha's Vineyard, the Indians were peaceful, friendly.

Gosnold took the smaller pinnace and sailed along the shores of the "stateliest sound," today's Buzzards Bay, and saw more Indians, many more. He was pleased: there would be plenty of hunters to trade with, plenty of furs to take back to England in the fall.

For six weeks his men worked, building a house and fort that would be their trading post. More Wampanoag came to trade furs for cloth and trinkets. Gosnold had indeed found the place.

Soon it was time for the *Concord* to sail back to England. But some of the adventurers who had promised to remain with Gosnold to operate the trading post were having second thoughts. There had been a frightening encounter one week earlier. Four of the English, away from the settlement catching crabs and other shellfish, were assaulted by four Indians. One man, hit by an arrow, was seriously wounded. A few days before, the English had found a Wampanoag canoe and put it aboard the *Concord* to take back to England. The surprise attack may have been in retaliation.

The second thoughts multiplied. More men joined the doubters, claiming that the meager supplies would not last until the *Concord*'s return. So few agreed to stay with Gosnold that his grand plan had to be abandoned. For some it was a great disappointment; there were "many true sorrowful eyes" when the *Concord* departed, leaving a house and a

Woodcut by Sidney Riggs, a Vineyard artist, of how he imagined Gosnold's *Concord* must have looked under full sail. (MVHS Collections)

fort in the middle of the pond—and, no doubt, some bewildered natives.

Why, the Indians surely wondered, did these pale-skinned strangers, with sharp tools and shiny weapons, work for weeks to build these structures with smooth boards and iron nails, unlike anything they had ever seen, and then leave, taking only some furs, sassafras roots, and cypress logs? Strange people!

Had the men stayed, Cuttyhunk would now be a national shrine: the first English settlement in America. Jamestown and Plymouth would be denied their glory. Cuttyhunk would be the nation's birthplace. Instead of praising pious Pilgrim fathers, we would be honoring Gosnold and his adventurers, men who came seeking freedom of enterprise, not freedom of religion. There would be no paintings of sober-faced believers walking through the snow to church, no Thanksgiving turkey.

During the next forty years, other ships stopped at the Vineyard. Captain Edward Harlow in 1611 kidnapped two Vineyard Indians, Epenow and Coneconam, and took them along with three others from the mainland to be sold as slaves in Spain. Epenow was "a goodly man, of a brave aspect, stout and sober in his demeanor." But there were no buyers for Indians in Spain, where they had a reputation for being poor slaves. With an abundance of well-tested Africans on the auction block, buyers weren't interested in the Americans.

So Epenow and the others ended up in a London sideshow, billed as "Savages from the New World." Sir Ferdinand Gorges, one of the backers of Gosnold's voyage, owned the sideshow. He wrote that Epenow had learned enough English words "to bid those that wondered at him, 'Welcome! Welcome!'" Sir Ferdinand was a leading promoter of the New World, and with good reason. He had something to sell, having obtained settlement rights to Maine and the islands south of Cape Cod, including Martha's Vineyard.

Epenow knew more English than Sir Ferdinand realized. A clever man, he quickly spotted the English appetite for riches and was able to convince Sir Ferdinand that on his native island, Martha's Vineyard, there was gold—lots of gold. Gorges persuaded the Earl of Southampton, who had also been a backer of the Gosnold voyage, to outfit another ship to sail to America. This time, the goal was not to set up a trading post, but to find Epenow's gold mine. Captain Nicholas Hobson, who had been with Harlow when Epenow was kidnapped, was picked to head the adventure partly because he was so convinced by Epenow's story that he invested one hundred English pounds of his own money in the venture. In 1614, with Epenow and two other Indians on board, the ship sailed off to find El Dorado.

Soon after the ship arrived at the Vineyard, Epenow managed to escape during a bloody confrontation in which a number of Vineyard Indians were killed. Captain Hobson returned home empty-handed, without gold and without Epenow. When Gorges was informed of this, he wrote, "Such are the fruits to be looked for by employing men more zealous of gain than fraught with experience how to make it."

Captain John Smith described the futile adventure this way: "They spent their victuals and returned with nothing." Captain Smith (who, years later, claimed to have been saved from death by Pocahontas and thus created one of this country's cherished myths) had briefly visited the Island in 1615 and was so enamored of the place that he promised himself that he would return and create a plantation there. He died before he could make his Vineyard dream come true.

Captain Thomas Dermer, who had been with Smith on that 1615 visit, returned to the Island in 1619. He met Epenow, who "gave mee very good satisfaction in everything almost I could demand." There was no attempt to punish Epenow for his trickery. He had outsmarted the English fair and square, it seemed.

The following year Dermer went back to the Vineyard to trade with the Indians. With him was Squanto, later the friend of the Pilgrims. Serious violence broke out. Governor Bradford of Plymouth described the Dermer visit in *Of Plimouth Plantation*:

> [Dermer] came to the Isle of Capawack [Martha's Vineyard] (which lies south of this place on the way to Virginia) . . . Squanto with him, where he, going ashore amongst the Indians to trade, as he used to do, was betrayed and assaulted by them, and all his men slain, but one that kept the boat; but himself got aboard sore wounded, and they [would have] cut off his head . . . had not the man rescued him with a sword. And so they got away, and made shift to get into Virginia, where he died; whether of his wounds or the diseases of the country, or both together, is uncertain.

Bradford explained the unexpected Indian violence by stating that they thought Dermer had come to revenge the killing of two Europeans by Indians on the Cape a year earlier. Certainly, the violent attack was not typical of previous (or later) meetings between the English and the Wampanoag.

Perhaps that violence discouraged further visits to the Island by the English. In the next twenty years, none was recorded. Then, in 1641 or 1642, a Welshman came with a different purpose. He hadn't come to find riches. He was the Reverend Roger Williams, who had sailed to the Island from Providence Plantations, the settlement he founded on Narragansett Bay after being expelled from Massachusetts for his strong antiestablishment views. He opposed making church attendance compulsory and church membership a requirement for voting. He opposed levying taxes to pay ministers, although he was a minister himself. In his view, church and state should be kept separate.

After he arrived on Narragansett Bay, Williams became the Indians' best friend. He was critical of English monarchs who gave grants of land to the settlers, land that belonged to the Indians. It wasn't any king's to give, Williams said. He admonished the settlers: "Boast not proud English of thy birth and blood. Thy brother Indian is by birth as good."

No wonder he had been kicked out of Massachusetts.

From Providence Plantations Williams often sailed to nearby islands, spreading his religious message among the Indians. On one such mission, he stopped at the Vineyard, probably at Gay Head. He mentioned the visit in a book that was published in 1643 in London: "The Indians of Martins [Martha's] Vineyard, at my late being amongst them, report generally, and confidently of some Islands, which lie off from them to Sea, from whence every morning early, certaine Fowles come and light amongst them, and returne at Night."

His book was about the Indian language and lifestyle. Williams was fluent in Algonquian. That quotation is from a chapter on Indian names for birds. But Williams hadn't sailed to the Vineyard to watch the birds; he had come to spread the word of God, his Anabaptist God. As a result, perhaps, Gay Head had the Island's first Baptist church. That was in 1693, many years later, but the seed he planted had flourished. The Indians chose to become (and remain) Baptists. Williams's visit in 1641 or 1642 made him the Island's first missionary.

When he sailed over from Providence Plantations, there already was a settlement of English at the eastern end of the Island, far from Gay Head—or so some believe. About 1636, according to the believers, a ship heading for Virginia from England anchored off today's Edgartown and sent a party ashore for freshwater and berries. The Atlantic crossing had been long and stormy, causing sickness and death among those on board.

Highly imaginative drawing by Theodore de Brys of Gosnold's meeting
with the Indians in the New World. The artist depicted a fleet of vessels,
but the *Concord* had sailed alone. (MVHS Collections)

Some of the men who went ashore, on solid land at last, decided to stay.
The settlement has never been documented and to many it remains a fic-
tion known as the "Pease Tradition," after its supposed leader, John Pease.

According to that tradition, the Englishmen, coming ashore at today's
Pease's Point, walked south along the western shore of Edgartown harbor
looking for a sheltered spot in which to settle. They soon came upon some
sandy bluffs that formed a bowl protected from the wind and warmed by
the sun. There they settled. The place is now called Green Hollow. The
men lived in caves they dug in the bluffs; they later built crude houses.
Soon they became friends with the natives, who helped them survive.

There is another version, which says that John Pease and his brother,
Robert, stopped at the Vineyard on a voyage from Salem, their first home
in the colony, to Enfield, Connecticut, where they planned to resettle.

They liked the Island and John, with a few others of the group, decided to stay, while Robert continued on to Connecticut.

There are no surviving records to authenticate the Pease settlement, except one, and that is not contemporaneous. It is on a stone placed years later in the oldest cemetery in Edgartown, on Tower Hill. That first cemetery is far from where the Thomas Mayhews, the family generally accepted as the Island's the first settlers, lived on what is now South Water Street in Edgartown.

In the 1600s grave markers were usually simple fieldstones without inscriptions, so they provide no data to settle the Pease versus Mayhew dispute. But the location of the Tower Hill cemetery is relevant because it is adjacent to Green Hollow, the site of the supposed Pease settlement. It certainly is not a location that Mayhew would have picked for a cemetery, but it did make sense for those in Green Hollow.

The inscription on a stone placed there years afterward would seem to support the Pease position: "This is in place of the oldest gravestone on Martha's Vineyard. . . . Sixty rods southeast from this grave may be seen the ruins of the cellar of the House of the first white settlers who came to the Island 1630."

The grave marker is that of Robart Stone Sr., a transient mariner who died while his vessel was in Edgartown Harbor in 1689. The original marker had been defaced and was replaced at some unknown date by one containing the above quotation. It too was broken by someone. A second replacement now rests atop it. The deliberate defacing of the two older stones only adds to the mystery of the Pease Tradition and Green Hollow.

A thorough examination of the Pease Tradition was written by the Reverend Hebron Vincent in 1889 and published in *The Dukes County Intelligencer* in November 1962. Vincent, a careful researcher and historian who was a descendant of one of the Pease settlers and hence an interested party, argues that the settlement did occur, citing the fact that the names Pease, Trapp, and Vinson (Vincent), all original settlers, have survived on the Island.

Whether the Pease settlement occurred continues in dispute, although the theory is gaining support despite what Dr. Charles E. Banks wrote in the early 1900s in his *History of Martha's Vineyard*. He flatly declared it to be false. In doing so, he disputed not only the Reverend Vincent but also the Reverend Joseph Thaxter, the Island's religious leader after the American Revolution. In 1814, when the Reverend James Freeman of Boston

Another imaginative painting of Gosnold and the native Americans, this one by William Wall. Like de Brys, Wall was a romantic fantasist with little research to support his work. (Courtesy of the New Bedford Whaling Museum)

was writing a history of New England, he wrote to his friend Thaxter, asking about the Island's first settlers. Thaxter replied:

> It is beyond a Doubt true that several years before the Mayhews had a grant of the Island there were a Number of Families settled on the Island. . . . I am confirmed in this by the Division of the Town—the Mayhews and their associates had 25 shares and others were called half-share men. These made the Number of Shares 42—those it is presumed were settled here when the Mayhews obtained the grant.

Thaxter cited Thomas Mayhew's great-grandson, the Reverend Experience Mayhew, who supported the settlement, as his authority: "Experience Mayhew must have had evidence of the Fact, otherwise it is presumed he would not have said it."

The first Mayhew to settle on the Vineyard was Thomas Mayhew Jr., who arrived in 1643 with a few others from the Watertown, Massachusetts, area. He was twenty-one years old. His father had sent him to form the first "authorized" settlement. As far as is known, neither he nor his father had been on the Island before. It was a bold move, fraught with uncertainties.

The elder Mayhew had come to Massachusetts from England in 1630, probably on the historic Winthrop fleet. He had been hired to manage a farm and trading post owned by Matthew Cradock of London on the Mystic River just outside Boston. Furs and deerskin were the principal exports of the farm. Cradock also owned fishing stations along the coast. It was a profitable enterprise. When the previous manager had been arrested for making blasphemous remarks about the king and the church, Cradock fired him and sent Mayhew to take his place. Although he never came to America, Cradock had been the first governor of the Massachusetts Bay Colony and was a major investor in New England. While governor, he defined the colony's purpose: "The mayne end of our plantation [is] to bring the Indians to the knowledge of the gospell."

That lofty purpose was written long before Cradock sent Mayhew to the colony to manage his business. It seems unlikely that he gave his new employee that as his goal. But the principle was adopted by Mayhews in the years that followed. Five generations of the family were involved in bringing "Indians to the knowledge of the gospell," the last being Zacchariah, who died in Chilmark in 1806.

At the time Cradock hired Mayhew, the Puritans, in control of the Massachusetts Bay Company, sent John Winthrop to the colony as its resident governor. He and about seven hundred colonists sailed from England in the spring of 1630 in five ships, arriving at Salem two months later. Thomas Mayhew Sr., heading for his new job, is believed to have been on one of the ships.

He settled in Medford in a house owned by Cradock close to the farm he was to manage. It is not certain whether Mrs. Mayhew and their son, Thomas Jr., came with him. She died at about this time, but there is no record of where or when.

A year or so later, Cradock and a man named Edward How financed a gristmill on the Charles River at Watertown, one of the first such mills in the colony. Mayhew represented Cradock in the undertaking. In late 1634 Mayhew went to London, probably to report to Cradock, but while there he did more than talk business. He wooed and married his second wife, Mrs. Jane Paine, the widow of a wealthy London merchant.

Widow Paine must have been a courageous woman. It is unfortunate that we don't know more about her (or about the first Mrs. Mayhew, for that matter). This well-to-do widow gave up her comfortable life in London to move to the primitive colony of Massachusetts. London was lively with theater and society. It was the era of the Globe Theatre and Shakespearean drama. She and her two young children left all that behind for a great unknown. It was a brave move that not only says something about her, but also tells us that Thomas Mayhew must have been a man of great charm.

The new Mrs. Mayhew soon had reason to doubt her decision. Shortly after they arrived in Massachusetts, Cradock fired her husband. The reason could not have been trivial. Whatever it was, it so angered Cradock that he wrote to his friend Governor John Winthrop of Massachusetts on January 13, 1637, to complain. In vitriolic language he told Winthrop of Mayhew's "most vyle bad dealings." He listed no details, but it is clear that there had been a serious breach of trust:

> The greyffe [grief] I have been putt to by the most vyle bad dealings of Thomas Mayhew hath & doeth so much disquiet [to] my mynd, as I thank God never aney thing did in the like manner. . . . Good sir, lett me intreate your self & those in authority there to make some course that Thomas Mayhew may be answerable ffor that estate of myne which . . . hath come to his hands. . . . When it shall appeare hoe [how] he hath dealt by me, you & all men that shall see it, if I ame perswaded, will hardley thinke it could be possible that a man pretending sincerity in his actions could deal so viley as he hath & doeth deale by me. . . . Lett me cravve your favour & the courts so ffarr as you shall see my cause honest & just.

There is no record that Governor Winthrop made Mayhew "answerable ffor that estate of myne." Mayhew, like Cradock, was the governor's friend. He was also a partner with the governor's son, John Winthrop Jr., in an importing business. (Its dealings may have been part of the problem.) The governor could not have been eager to punish his friend in Massachusetts to please another friend in faraway London.

That was not the only complaint the governor received about Mayhew. A few months earlier, in a letter criticizing Mayhew's behavior, Cradock had written: "Yf Mr. Mayhewe doe realley approove his Integrity I shall desyre to Contyneue him in my imployment. . . . I ame perswaded when ever wee parte he will not fynd one so willing to doe him good as I have beene and ame." He sent his "servant Jno. Jolliffe" to the colony to investigate, believing that he was not making enough profit on his large investment. Forgotten, it seems, was the lofty principle of bringing "Indians to the knowledge of the Gospell."

There is other evidence of Mayhew's failure to run Cradock's operation in a businesslike manner. The Reverend Roger Williams of Salem, not yet expelled from Massachusetts, wrote to the governor to complain about a lawsuit he was facing. He had owed Cradock fifty pounds for "commodities receaved from Mr. Mayhew," with the understanding that payment would be made when he sold his house in Salem. As soon as the house was sold, Williams said, he paid Mayhew. Now he was being sued for that amount plus damages. He asked the governor to help him.

We don't know the exact date, but it seems that Cradock fired Mayhew early in 1635. With his pregnant wife, Mayhew moved out of Cradock's house to the new village of Watertown, where their first child was born in June 1635.

Mrs. Mayhew must have had further doubts about her decision. Watertown was even smaller, just a tiny cluster of houses around the grist-mill. Mayhew soon became a leading citizen. When the village named its first officials in 1636, Mayhew was one. For as long as they lived there, he held public office, sometimes several at a time, and received six large grants of land from the town.

He built a small cottage for the family, which now numbered six. To support his growing family, Mayhew bought Edward How's half of the gristmill. Cradock owned the other half. It is hard to believe that Cradock, who had written so angrily to the governor about Mayhew, would agree to accept him as a partner. But he may not have known about the change. Communication was slow.

Two years later, perhaps when he did find out who his new partner was, Cradock sold his half to Mayhew for £240, holding a mortgage for the full amount. In 1640 Mayhew sold the mill, with Cradock's mortgage still on it, to the deputy governor of Massachusetts, Thomas Dudley, a political enemy of the governor. Cradock was still unhappy about his lack of profits. He wrote to Governor Winthrop to thank him for cutting his taxes, adding: "I greyue [grieve] for my owne Losses. . . . They have been verry heavey and greate."

In the next few years the tiny Mayhew cottage became more crowded when two more daughters were born. The family now totaled eight. It isn't clear where the income was coming from to support such a flock—perhaps from Mrs. Mayhew's inheritance. Mayhew wrote to Governor Winthrop in March 1640, explaining his problems. Apparently, the colony ("Countrey") owed him money that he needed so that he could pay his taxes. He asked for immediate advice:

I am to pay my owne Rate [tax] and some 5 li [pounds] for other men that
I owe it unto and although that I have had bills due from the Countrey
[colony] one yeare and 7 monthes synce for 70 and od pownds I must
now have my [household] goods solld except I pay out this money: which
seeing I have mony to re[ceive] from the countrey methinkes it is verry
hard measure. I cannot see equitie in it. . . . I desire your worshipps
advice per his bearer which is the Constable. . . . Mony is verry hard to
gett uppon any termes. I know not the man that can Furnish me with it.
. . . I delight not to compleyne [complain].

The following June the town of Watertown "agreed that Mr. Mayhew
shall enjoy the 150 acres of land on the south side of Charles River by
Watertown Wear [weir]." The land was across the river from Mayhew's ten-
acre homestead and included a freshwater pond with a herring run. We
don't know whether this agreement was related to his financial problems.

Now controlling land on both sides of the river, Mayhew built a pedes-
trian bridge, the first across the Charles River, and charged tolls to those
using it. There were objections by the villagers and the dispute was turned
over to the governor. After two years the governor's council ruled that a toll
bridge could not be privately owned. It must belong to the town. In
exchange for the bridge, the council ordered the town to grant Mayhew
another three hundred acres of land.

Mayhew's neighbor was John Oldham, the founder of Watertown and
a clever man with land grants. He had gone to England and received the
rights to the area between the Charles and the Mystic rivers, including
Watertown. Like Mayhew, he was involved in business with John Winthrop
Jr., now the governor of Connecticut.

Perhaps Oldham's land dealings inspired Mayhew to seek his own. We
don't know that, but in 1641 Mayhew began to negotiate for the rights to
settle the islands south of Cape Cod. In October, for forty pounds, he
bought settlement rights from the Earl of Stirling, who claimed ownership
of Long Island and all islands to the east, including the Vineyard. This
claim was challenged by the Dutch, then in New York. Settlers from Lynn
had gone to Long Island with a Stirling grant sometime earlier and had
been forced to leave. It seems strange, if he was aware of the Lynn settlers'
experience, that Mayhew would have believed Stirling's agent enough to
pay him forty pounds. But he did, and one witness to the agreement was
Nicholas Davison, Cradock's agent in the position once held by Mayhew,
which suggests that Cradock might have been involved.

A few days later Mayhew bought from Richard Vines, the colonial agent for Sir Ferdinand Gorges, a second charter to settle the islands. Gorges, you will recall, was the man Epenow had tricked into sending a ship to find gold on the Vineyard. The second grant was needed because Gorges owned rights to Maine and all islands (not named) off New England. Mayhew was playing it safe, making sure he had authority from both claimants.

Mayhew could now buy land from the Indians and settle on that land. He wasted no time in becoming the Vineyard's first real estate developer. Even before he had visited the place, it seems, he began to sell lots, or at least options to buy lots. Among the early buyers was the same Nicholas Davison, Cradock's agent, who had witnessed Mayhew's signature. We don't know when Davison bought his land (or perhaps was given it by Mayhew), but it must have been one of the early transactions. In 1654 he owned two large tracts on the Vineyard, one of which was a working farm with livestock. In that year he swapped "his sheep, cattle, and land in Martha's Vineyard" to buy the old Mayhew homestead in Watertown from Mayhew.

Even after that swap, Davison still was a major landowner on the Vineyard, holding "the land (1000 acres) which he received of Mayhew for the Oldham Farm" in Watertown. Considerable mystery surrounds these dealings. Watertown records show that after Oldham's death Cradock bought his farm. Why Mayhew wanted it enough to give Davison one thousand acres for it is only part of the mystery.

There is no list of who came with Thomas Jr. on that first trip to the Vineyard in 1643. Nor is there any record that Mayhew had already bought from the Indians the land his family settled on. There was a general belief at the time that because the Indians were not "using" the land (by English standards), the colonists had a God-given right to use it themselves. Only when the natives protested did the English feel obligated to negotiate its purchase.

Whether the land had been bought from the Indians or not, the first lots were laid out in today's Edgartown along the waterfront from Starbuck's Neck on the north to Tower Hill on the south. Indians on the Island, then totaling about three thousand, did not put up any resistance. Nor, it seems, did they show much interest.

The Indians did not object, believers in the Pease Tradition claim, because that earlier English settlement, under John Pease, had shown them that the pale-faced men who arrived in large ships would do them no harm. As Thaxter mentioned, Mayhew gave half shares to the men who had not bought land from him; they were assigned less desirable lots, but they did get land as a gift from Mayhew. That would have been a way for him to prevent any conflict with the earlier Pease settlers and even with the Indians. It made sense to have the Pease group (assuming it existed) on his side rather than in opposition. With so much land, he had nothing to lose.

No record confirms this; it is speculation. Many years later a few accounts were published about those early years, but they were written mostly by Mayhews and describe their missionary work and Indian conversions; they do not go into the practical problems of land ownership, nor do they tell us anything about harsh winters, near-starvation, sickness, or death.

And so those first years remain a mystery. It is no wonder that the Pease Tradition survives.

The senior Mayhew moved from Watertown to the Vineyard in 1646 with his second wife and five children. In that year Thomas Jr. married a woman named Jane, who may have been his stepsister, Jane Paine. (I believe she was.) If so, the bride's mother, the former Mrs. Paine of London, now Mrs. Mayhew of Martha's Vineyard, had no grand English cathedral in which to watch her daughter marry. The tiny Edgartown settlement had no church building, no social life. She had given up London for this!

Nor was there any government until seven years later, when a committee of Mayhews was chosen by the elder Mayhew to run the village. A couple of years later he dissolved the committee and took total authority upon himself, appointing the village officials—family members all. With no more than twenty English families in the settlement, little government was needed. The Mayhews would handle everything: church, courts, and taxes.

The grant from Gorges had stated that Mayhew would form a government in his settlement similar to that of Massachusetts, where there was a touch of democracy. But that was not done. Nobody complained—at least, not at first. Some years later, when the Mayhew "aristocracy" had become so deeply entrenched as to be arrogant, there did occur a nonviolent rebellion that demanded equal treatment for all.

Demands for equality for all, of course, referred only to the English; nobody even thought about equality for the Indians. There is no record of the tribe's complaining. Perhaps the Pease group had created so much trust that equality was not an issue. It is more likely that the Indians, totally unfamiliar with the English concept of private ownership, could not imagine what was happening. When they found out, it was too late. Mayhew was careful not to stir them up. He knew that he had to get along with the natives, at least in the beginning. With thousands of Indians and a handful of English, any other course would have been foolhardy.

Supporters of the Pease Tradition claim there had been a record of their settlement and of their dealings with the Indians. It had been kept in a black book that mysteriously disappeared when John Pease died; there were rumors of a Mayhew conspiracy. With nothing in writing, we are left with only speculation.

The first published record of the Mayhew settlement (although Mayhew's name was not mentioned) was in October 1643 in the journal of Mayhew's friend Governor Winthrop. He wrote: "Some of Watertown began a plantation at Martin's [Martha's] Vineyard beyond Cape Cod, and divers families going thither, they procured a young man, one Mr. Green, a scholar, to be their minister, in hopes soon to gather a church there. He went not."

Winthrop's description of "one Mr. Green" is confusing. The Reverend Henry Green was the minister in Watertown. Could it have been his son? It matters not, as young Green decided to take the church in Reading rather than chance it on the Vineyard.

With no minister "to gather a church," Thomas Mayhew Jr. took on the task. Though not educated as a minister, he must have been well suited. Within a few months, an Indian, Hiacoomes, began attending his services, standing shyly in the back of the room. Mayhew, pleased to have an Indian in the congregation, invited him to his house. Hiacoomes soon became a Christian, which prompted his family and the other Indians to label him "the English man" who had abandoned his heritage. His family cast him out.

His conversion was important to history. It inspired young Mayhew to focus his energies on bringing the "savages" to Christ. Some years later Thomas Prince wrote of that inspiration in *Account of Those English Ministers*:

> But [Mayhew's] English Flock being then but small, the Sphere was not large enough for so bright a Star to move in. With great Compassion, he beheld the wretched Native perishing in utter Ignorance of the true GOD, and eternal Life, labouring under strange Delusions, Inchantments and panick, Fears of Devils, whom they most passionately worshipped. . . .

21

GOD, who had ordained him an Evangelist for the Conversion of these Indian Gentiles, stirred him up with an holy Zeal.

Thomas Mayhew Jr. had found his calling: he would become a missionary. His first convert, Hiacoomes, taught him to speak Algonquian and he began preaching to the natives in their language, becoming the first of five generations of missionaries in the Mayhew family.

Acceptance of his Christian message was helped by a serious plague that devastated the Indian population. Among those who had been attending Mayhew's preaching the disease was less virulent, and Hiacoomes and his family were untouched, as Prince noted: "At last the Lord sent an universal sickness, and it was observed by the Indians, that they . . . did not taste so deeply of it, but Hiacoomes and his family in a manner not at all."

When Governor Winthrop learned of Mayhew's missionary work, he urged him to move to Connecticut, where his son, John Winthrop Jr., had formed a settlement. The governor suggested that Mayhew should take the Vineyard's "praying Indians" with him. There were many more Indians in Connecticut than on the Vineyard: he would be able to accomplish much more of God's work. Mayhew went to Boston to discuss it but turned down the suggestion.

The Reverend John Eliot of Roxbury, also a missionary, urged young Mayhew to write to a missionary group in London about his work. Mayhew did so, describing how his prayer-healing had brought many Indians to Christ. He also told of one Indian who, after being cured by Mayhew's prayers, had reverted to his native religion. Mayhew wrote that he told the other Indians: "God will kill him . . . and so it shortly came to passe." His letter was published in London in 1649, along with one from Eliot.

The letters from Mayhew, Eliot, and others aroused so much interest that Parliament set up a corporation to raise funds to convert the "savages" in the colony. The Reverend Henry Whitfield, then a pastor in Guilford, Connecticut, was called to London to help with the fund-raising. On his way to Boston to board a ship for England, headwinds forced his vessel to stop at the Vineyard. He met young Mayhew and attended a prayer meeting for the Indians. So impressed was Whitfield that when he arrived in England, he persuaded his new employers, the Society for the Propagation of the Gospel, to put the young missionary on its payroll, along with Eliot. The two men became the first paid missionaries in New England.

In 1650 young Mayhew received his first pay: twenty pounds a year. At Eliot's suggestion, he was given many books along with his pay (the Vineyard's first library). His salary was soon doubled, and Hiacoomes and other Indians were added to the payroll as preachers and teachers, becoming no doubt the most prosperous members of the tribe. In 1654 the society built an Indian school, the Island's first schoolhouse. Missions had become a major activity.

The work was seen not only as a way to save the souls of the Indians, but also (perhaps more important) as a way to make them more willing to accept the English way of life, to give up their land peacefully, and to abandon their "savage" traditions, their nakedness, their worship of thirty-six gods, and even their belief that witch doctors, not prayer, could rid them of sickness.

To fund the work, Parliament authorized collections in all English parishes as well as in the army. Ministers went from house to house with collection baskets each Sabbath to solicit those who had not attended services. The money was used to buy farms, and the rental income from them was sent to the colony for mission work. This was not the first time such solicitations had been made. Earlier the Crown had ordered collections in all parishes to build an Indian college in Virginia. One thousand acres were set aside for its campus, but the college was never built and the money disappeared into unknown pockets, according to the late historian Francis Jennings, once of Chilmark.

With its funds increasing, the society decided to revive the dream of a college education for Indians. It would send them to Harvard College to be trained as ministers. They would return to their tribes and bring their brothers and sisters to Christ. But Harvard, then a young college, had no room for them (or so it said), so the society built a separate building as the Indian college, the first brick building on the campus.

Six Indians selected by Mayhew and Eliot made up the first class. Two were Vineyarders: Joel Hiacoomes, the son of Mayhew's first convert; and Caleb, the son of Sachem Chesschamuck. (Two years later, while Caleb was still in school, the elder Mayhew "bought" from him much of the northern part of the Island.)

In 1656 the six enrolled in a Cambridge preparatory school to begin their education. They were taught to read and write Greek, Latin, and English, as well as their own language. (The written language was created phonetically by missionaries.) It was an ambitious dream, too ambitious. Of the six, only two made it to the senior year of college. They were the two Vineyard Indians, Joel and Caleb.

23

An amazing accomplishment it was: two Martha's Vineyard Indians in Harvard's senior class, along with the sons of the leaders of the colony of Massachusetts. They were not treated as equals, of course, but they were there, at Harvard College. The contributors in England must have believed it a miracle

But the miracle had a short life. Near the end of his senior year, Joel Hiacoomes went to the Vineyard to visit his family. As he was sailing back to Boston, a storm drove the vessel aground off Nantucket. All on board were lost.

That left only one Indian student, Caleb, who became the first and only graduate of the Indian college, which was discontinued after that class. Earlier the first floor of the new brick building had been turned into a print shop, where in 1663 the first Indian-language Bible was published. (The building was later torn down and its bricks reused.)

Caleb's name was listed among the graduates in Harvard's Class of 1665 as "Caleb Chesschamuck, *Indus*." The names of the others, all from the colony's leading families, are listed alphabetically; Caleb's name is separate, at the bottom. He graduated with them, but he, the *Indus*, was not one of them.

Thomas Mayhew Jr. had hoped his son Matthew would be one of the graduates (Eliot's son was), but after attending Corlett's preparatory school in Cambridge at the expense of the missionary society, Matthew dropped out. He had no desire to be a minister. His talent lay elsewhere, as we shall see.

Tragically, soon after Caleb graduated, even before he would leave Cambridge, he died of consumption, a disease common among Indians who took up the English lifestyle. His death, along with Joel's, denied the Vineyard the services of two Harvard-educated Indian leaders. History would have been different had they survived.

Thomas Jr. did not live to see his two protégés in college. A year after they entered preparatory school, he had sailed for England to settle a dispute over his wife's inheritance. Her father had left a large estate in England that was being threatened by legal actions. Thomas Jr. and his wife's brother, also named Thomas, left for England to protect their inheritance. Traveling with them was a young Indian who lived with the Mayhews, no doubt as an indentured servant. Their ship left Boston for England in November 1657 with fifty on board. It never reached port.

The elder Mrs. Mayhew had now lost both her son and her son-in-law.

Her six grandchildren were fatherless. She must have been wondering more and more about the wisdom of her move to the colony. The Mayhew home was overwhelmed with grief, as were Island wigwams, where with grief came questions. The third converted Indian had died; first it had been the Harvard students Joel and Caleb, and now it was the missionary's young servant. What kind of a God would do this to three young Indians who had put their faith in Him?

Great Harbour, as the village was called, again had no minister; the Indians had no missionary. At the society's urging, the aging governor agreed to take over. He had no religious training, nor did he speak the Indian language. He explained how he handled that in a letter to his friend Governor Winthrop: "I can clearly make knowne to them by an interpreter, what I know my sellfe."

The man making Mayhew's thoughts "clearly" known to the Indians was Peter Folger, the Island's first teacher. His father, John Folger, was one of the settlers from Watertown. Both father and son had worked in Mayhew's gristmill there. Peter was hired to teach the Indians to read English, or at least to read the English Bible, and he was fluent in their language, a skill that the governor found useful. When Mayhew bought Naushon Island from the sachem Quaquaquinigat for two woolen coats, it was Folger who did the bargaining.

Paid by the society as a teacher of the Indians, Folger became Mayhew's real estate agent. In 1659, when some off-Island men wanted to buy Nantucket, Mayhew sent Folger to negotiate. He sold all Nantucket (Mayhew kept one lot) to Tristram Coffin and his partners for thirty pounds plus two beaver hats. For another five pounds, they got adjacent Tuckernuck Island. The buyers liked Folger so much that they gave him a half share in their venture and he moved to Nantucket to be an interpreter and to run a gristmill.

While this was going on, there were occurrences in England of great importance to Mayhew, although he wasn't yet aware of them. In 1660 the Puritan Commonwealth was ended and King Charles II, an Anglican, was restored to the throne. He promptly disbanded the Puritan missionary society. But he was soon persuaded that the missionaries were good for England. A new society, more to his liking, was formed and the work went on, its message changed only slightly, though on the Vineyard not at all.

Folger's work as Mayhew's agent had long-term consequences. One of the men who bought Nantucket (and the wife of another) was a Baptist, the "cult" of dissidents. The sect appealed to Folger, who had long criticized the established church for its intrusion in government. He became a Baptist. In Nantucket, where he was town clerk, this led to a falling out. He refused to turn the town records over to the anti-Baptist Coffin, who wanted to use them to check voter qualifications. Arrested, Folger was held in jail for a year and a half. When released, he moved to Rhode Island, where the antiestablishment Roger Williams did things more to his liking.

The Royal Commissioners in Hartford, agents for the new society, sent the Reverend John Cotton Jr. to the Vineyard as minister of the English church and missionary to the Indians. Cotton learned the Indian language and was soon preaching to the natives as well as to the English. His stay was brief. In 1667, after a falling-out with Mayhew, he left and moved to the parish in Plymouth.

It wasn't difficult to have a falling-out with Mayhew. He ruled the Island as his fiefdom. He accepted no outside control, no higher authority. His only off-Island connection was the missionary money he received from faraway London. The Vineyard, his island, was ignored by the colonial governors and he liked that.

In 1664, when the English took New Amsterdam from the Dutch, Charles II gave New York, New Jersey, and the islands to the east, including the Vineyard, to his brother, the Duke of York. Mayhew was pleased. When Indians boarded a wrecked ship near Tarpaulin Cove in the Elizabeth Islands in November 1667 and stole its cargo, he decided this was a chance to establish a friendly connection with New York, which he preferred over one with Massachusetts. He reported the theft to the acting governor, Richard Nicolls, the military man who had led the takeover from the Dutch. Colonel Nicolls ordered Mayhew to "compell by force of arms or otherwise [the Indians] to make restitucions."

No doubt Mayhew wished that he hadn't informed New York. He had no desire and no means to compel, "by force of arms or otherwise," the Indians on Naushon Island to make restitution. When a similar event occurred two years later, he made no report. A ship had been wrecked on the shores of the Vineyard and forty hogsheads of rum and other items were taken from it by Indians. New York's new governor, Francis Lovelace, somehow learned of the incident and demanded an explanation. What was Mayhew going to do about it? Rum was not something Indians should have, especially not forty hogsheads of it.

Mayhew was slow to respond. Six months later, on May 14, 1670, he sent his grandson Matthew, then twenty-two years old, to New York with an explanation. In his message, Mayhew asked Governor Lovelace which colony his Island now was under, New York or Massachusetts. Lovelace replied that the Vineyard's "Inhabitants are from henceforth to have directions of their Government from this place." To be sure there was no misunderstanding, he ordered Mayhew to come to New York to discuss the matter.

This time Mayhew decided he had better go himself, and he took Matthew along. For a week they stayed at Fort James, the governor's headquarters, discussing the matter of governance. The two men became friends, or so it seems: when Mayhew made several requests, all were granted. One of these was that he, Thomas Mayhew, be made "Governor for Life" of Martha's Vineyard. He also asked that a large tract of land he had "purchased" from the Indians on the western end of the Island be designated a manor in the English tradition. The Manor of Tisbury was created, named for the English village where Mayhew had been born. (Manors were in vogue, several having been created along the Hudson River under the Dutch.)

Governor Lovelace then designated Mayhew and his grandson Matthew as "Lords of the Manor of Tisbury," with authority to collect rents from all who lived within its bounds. Included in those bounds were most of today's Chilmark, a part of the present West Tisbury, plus the Elizabeth Islands and a few small islands in Monument Bay off the mainland. Not included was today's West Tisbury village, where two years earlier, with Mayhew's approval, four off-Islanders had "purchased" considerable land from the Indians. Two of the four buyers had settled there. The others had bought the land for speculation. Mayhew proposed that this settlement in mid-Island, then called Middletown, be named Tisbury Village, separate from the Manor of Tisbury. That was done.

During that congenial New York meeting, Great Harbour was also renamed. It would become Edgar Towne. The historian Charles Banks, after reading the minutes of the meeting, said that the new name had been proposed by Governor Lovelace, in hopes of pleasing his boss, James, the Duke of York. Edgar, James's four-year-old son, would be in line to be king if his father took over the throne after the death of the childless Charles. Mayhew liked the idea. It would be the first Edgar Towne in the world and would have a special place in the heart of the possible future king.

It may have been a wise move politically, but it came to naught. There would be no King Edgar. Even before the meeting, the boy Edgar had died, but the news had not yet reached New York. Today there is only one Edgartown in the world. Had Edgar lived to be crowned, there would have been many.

Two years later, in August 1673, the Dutch recaptured New York from the English. Mayhew's new friends had to leave the city. On his island problems were building and not only because of the Dutch taking over New York.

The "place most pleasant" that Mayhew loved was changing, becoming less pleasant. At least that was true for some Vineyarders who were weary of being ruled by the autocratic Mayhew and saw their chance. With the Dutch in New York, the reign of the Governor for Life might be ended. So they hoped when in 1673 the Dutch Rebellion began.

2

From the Dutch Rebellion to the American Revolution

Ιt is called the "Dutch Rebellion" not because the rebels were Dutchmen, but because it was triggered by the Dutch fleet taking New York back from the English in 1673. It was, Vineyarders who were weary of the autocratic Mayhews thought, a good time to rebel. The Dutch might be more sympathetic than the English had been.

Dissension had been increasing. The Mayhews were running the Island as their fiefdom, appointing all officials, holding no elections. Their rule was not tyrannical; it was more like a benevolent monarchy, but that did not suit the rebels. They wanted some say in the government.

With the English gone from New York, the anointment of Thomas Mayhew as "Governor for Life" by Governor Francis Lovelace, agent of the Duke of York, had become invalid. Or so the rebels thought. It was time to take action.

There were only forty English families on the Vineyard and more than half of them joined the rebellion. Two issues topped their list of grievances: taxes and the court. Taxes were unfair, they said, because taxpayers had no say in how their money was spent or in how much they had to pay. Officeholders were exempt from taxation, and as most were Mayhews, the tax burden fell mainly on non-Mayhews. Similarly, court officials were all Mayhews. Non-Mayhews did not get fair trials, the rebels claimed. They hadn't come to America to be ruled by a "royal family," especially not by one headed by a former mercer from Southampton, Thomas Mayhew.

Two very different men led the rebellion. One was Thomas Burchard of Edgartown, who had come to the Vineyard in about 1650. During his first years in Edgartown he had been a favorite of Governor Mayhew's and was appointed town clerk, the first such. The two men soon had a falling-out. Burchard was forced out of office and shortly began opposing Mayhew.

The second rebel was Simon Athearn, the political leader of Tisbury—the village in the middle of the Island that later officially became West Tisbury. Younger and more aggressive than Burchard, he was inclined to be abrasive. The governor was scornful at first. Athearn was young enough to be his grandson, just an annoying kid. Athearn's social standing was against him: he had come to the Vineyard as an indentured servant to Nicholas Butler of Edgartown. Butler was one of the wealthiest settlers and a friend of the Mayhews. (Athearn's situation wasn't unusual; half the early immigrants to New England came as indentured servants.) Clever and ambitious, Athearn had not come to the New World to be a servant for life. He had bigger plans. While Athearn was working for the Butlers, he and Mary, a granddaughter of his employer, fell in love. In 1665, when his indenture was up, they married. She was only thirteen, and he was twenty-one. The Butler family could not have been pleased, for they surely had other plans for Mary. (Later they came to agree with their brash son-in-law and joined the rebellion.)

When Governor Mayhew returned from New York in 1671 to announce he had been made Governor for Life and Lord of Tisbury Manor, Athearn was furious. As Lord of the Manor, Mayhew could collect rents from landowners like Athearn. Athearn and his family lived in (West) Tisbury on twenty acres, not far from Tiah's Cove, which he had bought from Josias, an Indian sachem, and Benjamin Church for ten pounds. Athearn would now have to pay rent to the Mayhews, in addition to taxes to the governor.

Athearn and Burchard were rebels, but they were not revolutionaries. They wanted to settle the issues peacefully. So they asked the governor to join in their petition to have the Vineyard made part of Massachusetts rather than New York. They preferred Massachusetts because it was more democratic and closer geographically. (Mayhew disagreed, and for the same reasons.) They wanted Mayhew to continue as governor for only another year, after which they wanted an election. As one would expect, Mayhew opposed any change; too much democracy was not something he favored. And he knew that he might very well be voted out of office.

Among the names of the twenty landowners who signed the petition were Norton, Skiffe, Pease, Butler, Arey, Luce, Smith, and Trapp, all well-known Island names even now. The governor turned down their request. He had just been made Governor for Life; why should he give it up? He would have to be overthrown, something the rebels had no intention of doing.

Despite Mayhew's disapproval, they sent the petition to Governor John Leverett of Massachusetts, an act that the historian Charles E. Banks called the "Vineyard's Declaration of Independence." Even though the petition would seem favorable to him (it asked that he accept the Vineyard as part of his colony), Governor Leverett turned them down in a note signed by his secretary. It wasn't something he could do anything about: "[The] differences betwixt your selves and your Ancient and long continued Governour [Mayhew] . . . is very grievous to us, but how to help wee know not. . . . You understand [it is] his Majesty's pleasure whether to Establish your own Govern't or to settell you under sum other of [the] Collenyes in these parts. . . . [signed] Edw. Rawson, sec. to the governor of Massachusetts."

There was a good reason why Leverett did not wish to be involved. Tension between the Indians and the English was building, and a dispute over who was governor of a tiny island off Cape Cod must have seemed unimportant to him.

Legal efforts having failed, the rebels formed a "rump" government—a futile gesture. It was not a government in any sense, merely a face-saving protest, which collapsed the next year when the Dutch and English signed a peace treaty that put the English back in New York. Mayhew's friends were back in power. The rebels realized that any hope they had to change things was gone.

Governor Mayhew retaliated against the rebels, charging some of them with crimes. The court, of which he was chief magistrate, levied fines on them. A number left the Island, believing they would be harassed. Simon Athearn was arrested and told he would be taken to New York for trial.

Mayhew's retaliation did not please some very important persons in Boston. The Reverend Increase Mather, the pastor of North Church, wrote disapprovingly in his diary on March 19, 1675: "At Martin's [Martha's] Vineyard diverse honest people are in great trouble, their estates sequestered by reasons of Mr. M—— [Mayhew] complaining to the governor of New York."

Simon Athearn, facing trial in an unfriendly court in New York, in a less-than-admirable moment made a plea bargain, swearing that he had been only an innocent participant in the rebellion; he had been led astray by Burchard. His affidavit read: "Simon Athearn, desiring by way of petition that whereas himself was by the Authorities, reputed one of the Ringleaders in the late resisting of the Government, that being led and induced thereunto by others, the Governor and Assistants would so look uppon him and judge him accordingly; testified uppon oath that Thomas Birchard was a principall instigator of him, whereby he was induced to act in the opposition of Authoritie."

It was not Athearn's proudest moment. Mayhew's court fined him ten pounds and agreed not to send him to New York for trial. He was allowed to pay half the fine with "neat cattle" and to postpone payment of the other half until the "Court shall demand it." It was a slap on the wrist, nothing more.

Burchard, who had induced the "naive" Athearn to rebel, remained on the Island until 1683, when he moved to the mainland. By then he was eighty-eight and no doubt wanted to spend the rest of his life with his daughter. There is no evidence that his rebellious behavior brought any sanctions from the Mayhews.

Athearn continued to complain about the Mayhews. He wrote to Governor Edmund Andros of New York, charging them with malfeasance. Vineyard court records were so messy that he wanted his own land titles to be recorded in New York: "I verily believe did your honnor know the broken Confusednesse of the records on Martin's Vineyard, your honnor would See it nessessary for all to take a better title."

He was fearful that when he died the titles would be contested and the Mayhew court would deny his heirs their inheritance. He implied that Mayhew was treating him differently from others because of his rebel activities. The exact meaning of the charge is unclear: "I once delivered Six Shillings in money to Mathew Mayhew for my part of the acknowledgement, but it hath not been used with others to buy fish. Others had their mony restored to them again; but I had never mine to this day." He then described problems he was having with his Indian indentured servant, telling us a lot about how the natives were being treated by the English at the time:

> I have received rong [sic] in the loss of my Servant. . . . I took a naked Indian boy to be my apprentice fower [four] years . . . to provide him sofitiant [sufficient] food & rayment [raiment] during his Service & at the end of his Service to give him Sofitiant duble [double—that is, two sets of] upparrell & one good young Cow for his service, but after about a yeare there came an Indian of the boy's kindred & . . . caryed away my

boy, but Sum days after, the Indians brought him again. . . . [Later when] I went from the Iland the boy run away also, but soone after, the Indians brought him. . . . The boy [told] my wife that if She would lett him goe every Satterday and Com on Munday then he would tary till I com whom [home], but my wife Said no. You . . . Shall go to meeting [church] with me and do as your Master hath apoynted you, but quickly after, my boy run away. . . . Near a month [later] I cam Whom. my boy was then at whom, the Indians having brought him two days before. . . . I gave the boy two boxes on the ears with my fist . . . the boy run away agin. . . .

I complained to Mr. Mayhew our Governor and the justis I had!! The boy was to return to me but I not to requier anything for loss of time (because I strook him twice and if I strook him so again he should be free) . . . when Green Indian Corn was eatable, my boy run away again and hath been gon ever Senc. . . .

I said that if my boy would not Serve me, I would Sell him; Unto which Richard Sarson, an assistant [Mayhew's son-in-law], answered, my Indentur was unlawfull. . . . It hath been Mr. Mayhew's Judgment [as justice] that no Master Should Strik his Servant & that if the Servant is not willing to abide, the Master should let him go.

Athearn told the governor that because of Mayhew's actions some English settlers were planning to leave the Island. The governor's failure to allow them to provide for their religious and educational needs was a major factor:

If things be not mended divers of the inhabitents will remove their dwelling to go where they can. . . . I beseech your honnor . . . that we may be delivered from all rible rable and notions of men. . . . [We are] butt about 38 Englishmen on the Island able to bare arms and the Indians a multitude. . . . I beseech your honnor to give order that each town build them a meeting house and call them and maintain them a Minister able to divin the word of God aright that we may be kept from profainness, herressy and vice. And a Schoolmaster to teach our children. . . . We are kept very few in number and poor in estate.

He told about Jacob Parkins of Holmes Hole, who could not read or write. Thomas Daggett, a justice of the court, had stolen his goat and sheep, Parkins claimed, and nothing was done. Justice Daggett's wife was Hannah, the governor's eldest daughter, who, we learn from Athearn's complaint, was an influential and formidable woman: "Jacob Parkins . . . presently [met] Dagget's wife, Mr. Mayhew's daughter (which woman the people of Martin's Vineyard very generaly call the deputy Governor) she being very displeased."

Although these problems seemed major to Athearn, they were trivial compared to what was happening on the mainland. In June 1675, the same year Athearn wrote to Governor Andros, Indians attacked Swansea, near Plymouth, and King Philip's War began. (Philip was the name the English had given Metacomet, a son of Massasoit, the Wampanoag chief who had aided the Pilgrims.) The attack came after the English had executed three Indians charged with killing a Christian Indian, who had been, it was claimed, an English spy inside Philip's court. Violence by both sides followed for two years. The historian Francis Jennings called it, per capita, the most killing war in history. Yet Vineyarders seemed unaffected and uninvolved, perhaps even unaware of the intensity of the slaughter.

Many "praying Indian" villages, the lifework of the Reverend John Eliot of Roxbury, were pillaged by "pagan" Indians from the western end of the Massachusetts colony, who were angered by the way the English were destroying their heritage and taking their land. Only four of fourteen villages of Christian Indians survived.

Major fighting ended when the Rhode Island hiding place of King Philip was revealed to the English by another Indian, one of Eliot's converts. The English surrounded the place, trapping Philip. When he tried to escape, Philip was shot to death by an Indian serving in the English force. His body was barbarously dismembered. A severed hand was given as a souvenir to the Indian who had killed him. His head, impaled on a pole, was carried triumphantly to Plymouth, where it was exhibited for twenty-four years. His wife and child were sold as slaves.

It was not a time to be squeamish, or, it would seem, to be proud of being a Christian.

The Vineyard's only involvement in the war occurred when some inhabitants became concerned about the guns owned by Gay Head Indians. A disgusted Matthew Mayhew wrote later: "An Evil Spirit possessed too many of our English whereby they suffered themselves to be unreasonably exasperated against all Indians . . . [demanding] the disarming of the Indians, for whose satisfaction Capt. Richard Sarson, Esq., was ordered with a small party . . . to Treat [negotiate with] the Indians on the West end of Martha's Vineyard."

When Richard Sarson married the widow of the missionary Thomas Mayhew Jr., he was appointed to the court and made a captain in the militia. Moving into the Mayhew family, he, like Daggett, became a right-hand man of the governor. When he told the Indians at Gay Head he had come for their guns, they refused to give them up. Governor Mayhew, they said, had persuaded them to swear allegiance to the English king and because they had done so, they feared an attack by mainland Indians. They needed guns to protect themselves and the English on the Island from any attack from the mainland. Convinced, Mayhew had let them keep their guns and even sent them more ammunition. Apparently Sarson wasn't aware of that longtime arrangement.

Neither guns nor ammunition was needed to repel any attack by mainland Indians. The closest the war came was Providence and Plymouth. When it ended in August 1676, prejudice was strong against the Indians. There were also strong feelings against the missionaries. Praying Indians had been killed and their villages burned in a war started because one of them had become a spy against his nonpraying brothers. What had conversion accomplished? It seemed only to generate hatred and hostility.

This anti-Indian feeling did not develop on the Vineyard. The "Evil Spirit" that Matthew wrote about later seems to have been overstated. Missionary work continued on the Island. The missionary at the time was John Mayhew, son of the first missionary, Thomas Jr., who had been lost at sea years earlier. John was twenty-one years old when he started. His pay was ten pounds a year, but after the death of his grandfather Governor Mayhew, who was also being paid as a missionary, it was increased to thirty pounds.

Governor Mayhew was ninety years old when he died in 1682. He had lived a long, productive life and had made the Vineyard a comfortable, secure place—if not for all, at least for most. His strong, gentle rule of the Indians had brought a peaceful coexistence, but nothing more. Little effort had been made to educate them or to improve their living conditions. Instead, a steady erosion of their quality of life, as was occurring throughout the colonies, was taking place on the Island.

When John Mayhew died in 1689, nine years after his grandfather, the Indians were without a missionary. The next Mayhew in line was John's son, Experience, but he was only sixteen, too young for the work. For the next five years, the Lord's work had to be carried on completely by Indian ministers.

With the death of the governor, his grandson Matthew, after years of understudy, took political control, thus assuring continuation of the family's power. Like most colonists, he did not believe in democracy. Years later, in his book about the Indians, he echoed the conventional wisdom of the day: "The Government of this People [the Indians] was the best of all Governments, Monarchy." It would have been foolhardy of him to try to lead a march to democracy a century before the Declaration of Independence. He would have marched alone.

Matthew became ruler of the Island at age thirty. All courts and public offices continued to be controlled by the Mayhew family. The only change was the absence of the patriarch, Thomas Mayhew, who had governed for forty years. The Dutch Rebellion had changed nothing.

When Governor Thomas Mayhew died, the title died with him. Governor Andros in New York named Matthew Mayhew to be chief justice of Martha's Vineyard, but not its governor. He continued to be "ruler of the Indians." He was paid twenty pounds a year by the missionary society for "ruling" them, hardly work that a missionary society should be paying for. Matthew's brother Thomas received ten pounds annually as ruler of the Indians of Chilmark. The third brother, John, the English missionary, was paid ten pounds a year at first and then thirty pounds. The Mayhews ranked high in the missionary society's budget.

In 1683 the Duke of York sent Thomas Dongan to New York to replace Governor Andros. Dongan, an Irish Catholic, was one of the most successful and popular governors, a welcome change from the much-disliked Andros. One of the first things Governor Dongan did was to call a meeting of representatives ("elected representatives," he ordered), from New York, Martha's Vineyard, and Nantucket to approve a "Charter of Liberties." It was an early, tiny step toward representative government.

There is no record of who represented the Vineyard. If, as Dongan had ordered, an election had been held, it would have been the first in Island history. Elected or not, someone did go; most likely it was Matthew Mayhew.

The Charter of Liberties, a liberal document for its time, called for an end to religious prejudice, especially against Catholics (the Duke of York, Governor Dongan's boss, was a recent convert to Catholicism). It also decreed that landowners must vote on tax levies, something that no doubt pleased Simon Athearn. An assembly would be elected and would meet every three years. The charter, noble though it was, didn't last. When the Duke of York was crowned King James II in 1685, he declared it invalid.

During Dongan's first year, 1683, the "royal" counties of Kings, Queens, Dukes, and Duchess were created. This royal family connection continues. Twenty years later, about 1700, when one of the Mayhews tried to have the name changed from Dukes County to "Mayhew County," the effort failed, and so the Island remains one of the royal counties.

When the Duke of York became King James II, New York became a royal province. Governor Dongan invited Matthew Mayhew and his wife, Mary, to visit its capital, New York City. The two men may have met at the charter assembly two years earlier, but it would have been Mary's first visit to New York, perhaps her first trip off-Island. They stayed in the governor's mansion at Fort James, probably the fanciest residence in the colony. Mary, with little if any experience in such a setting, must have been intimidated. Worries about protocol, what to wear, and rules of etiquette and conversation no doubt made the visit a nervous one for the unsophisticated young woman.

Dongan hadn't invited them for conversation. He had a plan, a bold plan. He had created the "Mannor and Lordship of Martyn's [Martha's] Vineyard" and made Matthew "Lord of the Mannor." (Martha's Vineyard was called "Martyn's Vineyard" in New York, for reasons unknown.) As Lord of the Manor, Mayhew would be expected to deliver to the governor "six Kentalls [672 pounds] of merchantable fish, if Demanded, on the 25th of March yearly, in full of all Rents, Services and demands."

About two weeks later, while Lord and Lady Mayhew were still luxuriating at Fort James, they were told that Dongan would buy the just-created "Mannor of Martyn's Vineyard" for two hundred pounds. Not included in the sale were all lands granted or willed to Matthew by his grandfather Thomas Mayhew and his father, Thomas Mayhew Jr. Also excepted were Edgartown, Tisbury, "Nashawakemmuck, Quanaimes, . . . Half of Kaphegon, Nasha-queedse and 2 lotts in Edgartown about 80 acres." What Dongan was really buying was Gay Head and Nomans Land.

Mayhew would pay Governor Dongan each year seven lambs and two mink skins for being allowed to keep the exceptions. Dongan made Matthew his agent to run the manor. It was a friendly game, and everybody won.

When the Mayhews got back to the Vineyard, they discovered that the friendly game was flawed: Gay Head, the land Matthew had just sold to Dongan, was not his to sell. It had never been bought from the Indians. To correct the error, two years later, in 1687, Matthew and the sachem Joseph Mittark (Mataack) sailed to New York, where Governor Dongan paid the Indian thirty pounds for Gay Head, the same land for which he had earlier paid Matthew Mayhew two hundred pounds. Joseph Mittark, who no doubt was overwhelmed by all this, was the son and heir of Mittark, who had died in 1683. The elder Mittark had become a Christian, which displeased his family deeply. He then moved to Edgartown, but he returned some years later to become minister in Gay Head. The sale of the land caused a near-revolution in Gay Head: it was claimed that the old sachem Mittark had said his family's land could never be sold.

The rather suspect real estate deal provided the Athearns with fresh ammunition. Simon Athearn's oldest son, Samuel, was going around town talking about it so vituperatively that Matthew sued him for slander, demanding four hundred pounds in damages: "Complaint by Maj. Matthew Mayhew against Samuel Athearn, that Athearn did publickly, maliciously, and purposely to defame the sd. Major Mayhew . . . at a tavern in Edgartown, did say to sd. Matthew Matthew, 'You, to cheat Colonell Dongan, after you had sold the land to him, [did] make a deed to Capt. Skiffe, and antidated or dated it before that of Colonel Dongan, to cheat him.'"

Dongan's creation of the "Mannor of Martyn's Vineyard" made possible what much later became the town of Gay Head (now Aquinnah). Without it, that western tip of the Island would probably never have survived as a separate entity. It would have been merged into Chilmark, and the separate village might never have come into existence.

When Dukes County was created in 1683, Matthew Mayhew appointed himself county registrar of deeds, county treasurer, clerk of the county court, and county sheriff (he gave up the sheriff's job soon after), all in addition to already being chief justice of the county court and "ruler" of the Island and the Indians. In court sessions he was surrounded by family. The other judges were his brother Thomas III, his stepfather, Richard Sarson, and his uncle Thomas Daggett. Court sessions were strictly family affairs.

When he decided to build a new county jail in 1698, Matthew Mayhew put himself and his brother-in-law Benjamin Skiffe of Chilmark, an opponent of Athearn, in charge of the project. There was little happening that the Mayhews didn't control. They were still the Island's "royal" family.

In England, where the ruling family was as genuine as any royalty can be, the unpopular Catholic monarch, King James II, had no living son (his one son, Edgar, for whom Edgartown was named, had died as a child), so his daughter, Mary, ascended to the throne when he abdicated in 1688. She had married William of Orange, a member of the Dutch royal family, and the reign of William and Mary began. Both Mary and William were Protestant.

The change was welcomed in Massachusetts, where King James was strongly disliked. In 1685 he had formed the Dominion of New England, combining Massachusetts Bay and Plymouth colonies. He appointed as governor the unpopular Edmund Andros, former governor of New York. The Vineyard was made part of the Dominion.

King James's abdication triggered a citizens' uprising in Boston. Governor Andros was arrested and jailed before being deported to England for trial. He had been very unpopular for his support of the Catholic Church in strongly Protestant Massachusetts. (In 1700 a law was passed ordering all Catholic priests to leave Massachusetts.) Evidence indicates that Governor Dongan was in Boston at the time, trying to sell his Gay Head "manor" before his ownership could be declared illegal by the new English rulers.

When Andros was arrested, some of his supporters pirated a vessel off Cape Cod and sailed it into Holmes Hole, stealing provisions from a vessel there. They continued on to Tarpaulin Cove, where they did more mischief. Andros escaped from his Boston jail and headed for Rhode Island, where, the story says, the Tarpaulin pirates planned to pick him up and take him to France to join the deposed King James in exile. There is no proof of this, but the story was widespread at the time. Andros was soon recaptured and sent to England, where he was released. In 1692 he came back to the colonies when he was appointed governor of Virginia, where he was a very well-liked and successful governor.

The Vineyard rebels, still eager for change, were pleased when William and Mary became joint monarchs. The Mayhews were less pleased. Their friends Andros and Dongan were out of power and in disgrace. The new king sent Henry Sloughter to be governor of New York; Dongan had been forced out by a rebellion not unlike the one in Boston. Simon Athearn, seeing another opportunity to force change on the Island, wrote to Governor Sloughter in 1691, his letter dripping adulation:

When tidings first came to us of the Revolution we may truly say (we were like they that dream) scersly [scarcely] believing so wonderful a deliverance. . . . God have to be pleased to give us such gratious soverans—a King to be a nursing father & a queene to be our nursing mother. . . . We pray your ayd to settell the maintenence of the work of the ministrie on Martains Vineyard . . . for want of this settelment comes much disorder, both of contention among the people and the ministrie often left vacant . . . [there] being about fifty eight English inhabitants familys on the Iland & most pore. Four of the rich Justices of the Peace . . . all of one family, [do] what and how thay please to raise money on the people, without an assembly, the Justices estates being rate [tax] free . . . the people are at a low ebb. . . . We hope to be defended in our rights against Colonal Dongan's purchas [of Gay Head].

Governor Sloughter must have wondered why he was being bothered by some rebel on a small island many miles away. Athearn also asked that something be done about the sale of liquor to Indians: "The wholl trade of disposing any strong liquers to the Indians of the vineyard [must] be stopt, which is a thing of so evil consoquent in drunkenness, Eydlness [idleness] & selling theire corn for nought, which brings them into poverty and stealing for hunger."

Athearn was writing to the wrong man. New York's governor had nothing to do with the Vineyard anymore. It and Nantucket had been put under the jurisdiction of Massachusetts, whose new governor was an American, Sir William Phips, who had been knighted in gratitude by King James II after he found a sunken Spanish galleon in the Caribbean and shared its gold treasure with the king. Phips was a mystery man. Born on a Maine farm, close to Indian country, he never went to school. As a young man he walked to Boston, where he found work and soon became manager of a shipyard. He took up treasure hunting, married a wealthy widow, and with the help of his friend Increase Mather was appointed governor of Massachusetts.

Matthew Mayhew refused to recognize the authority of Governor Phips or to accept the fact that the Island, his island, was part of Massachusetts. He and his grandfather had always preferred New York's rule, distant and indifferent as it usually was.

Despite Mayhew's objections, somehow in 1692 Simon Athearn (Tisbury) and Joseph Norton (Edgartown) went to the General Court of Massachusetts (the state's house of representatives) as representatives of the

Vineyard. How the two men attained that position is a mystery. They apparently were the first public officials not appointed by a Mayhew. It seems unlikely that Mayhew would have named them when he was so opposed to accepting the state's authority.

Mayhew held his ground. He refused to take the chief magistrate's oath to uphold the laws of Massachusetts. Governor Phips had to do something; he couldn't allow the rebellion to continue. He asked Wait Winthrop, owner of Naushon Island (then a part of Chilmark), to administer the oath to the recalcitrant Mayhew. The two men met in Woods Hole. Mayhew was unwavering. Winthrop was upset: "I met Mr. Mayhew at this place [Woods Hole] . . . told him I had his Excellency's order to administer the oaths to himself and the other officers. . . . He utterly refused . . . but said he knew not but his brother [Thomas III, another justice] might, which he should encourage; and so went home in his canoe. . . . [I] resolved [not to] expose the Government as well as myself to contempt amongst such a crew as I understand are these."

Thomas III refused also. Matthew, standing firm, sent Winthrop some papers "proving" that the Vineyard was still under New York rule. A short time later the Mayhew brothers relented and took the Massachusetts oath. In the next election Matthew was chosen to represent Edgartown at the General Court. Nobody was elected to represent Tisbury. Somehow Athearn was denied reelection. Matthew Mayhew had ways of accomplishing such things.

Being out of office didn't quiet Athearn. He wrote to the General Court in 1694, proposing that Chilmark and Tisbury be combined as one village, a move Mayhew opposed because it would lessen Edgartown's size and population advantage:

> I proposed to Major Mayhew yesterday that Tisbury & Chilmark be made one for ye better carrying on all publique affairs there. It being absolutly den[ied] showeth your supplicant humbly praying this honorable house, that an act might pass, that all the lands on north side of Chilmark & on the westerly of Chilmark including all west end of marthas vineyard be made payable in all publique tax and rats [rates] To the Town of Tisbury. . . . The end of this motion is to heal our being cut in pieces, and to insure us all into a compotent Township to . . . worship God & serve our King & Country which is the prayer of your most humble supplycant, Simon Athearn.
>
> [P.S.] major mayhew is only a representative for Edgartown.

Throughout his life Simon Athearn was a confusing figure; sometimes he was shrewd and decisive, at other times irresponsible and erratic. He was often called into court to answer charges by both Indians and English. One time he would sue Indians for trespassing on his land; another time he would be defending himself against Indian charges that he was trespassing on theirs. Some English neighbors charged him with stealing their sheep and cattle. He faced charges of slander and assault. He was, in the surviving records at least (records kept by his adversaries), a chronic troublemaker.

In one incident he entered a schoolroom where his daughter was a pupil, making disparaging remarks to the children about their schoolmaster, Thomas Pent, "counseling them to forsake him." He grabbed a pen from a pupil and wrote "the teacher's name in a mock verse" that did "blemish, blast and stayn" his reputation, Pent later claimed in a suit. The teacher demanded one hundred pounds for damage to his reputation. The court agreed but levied only a trivial fine. It seemed to consider Athearn so unstable that a gentle slap was enough.

Despite such inexplicable actions, when elections were held he regularly won office. His reputation was so high that when Judge Samuel Sewall came to the Island as an agent of the missionary society, he regularly met with Athearn and enjoyed his company and conversation. Athearn deserves a much more thorough treatment than there is space for here.

Experience Mayhew became twenty-one in 1694 and was put on the missionary society payroll. Although there had been no paid English missionary for five years, the work had continued, according to Matthew Mayhew, writing in 1694: "[Indian] Children are taught to Read and many to Write; in one of their Towns the last winter, viz. 1693, Thirty Children were at School, Twenty more at the same place of the same time, accidentally, being not supplied with Books, could not attend it."

Although not college educated, Experience Mayhew was an effective missionary, fluent in Algonquian, a language he had learned as a child. He soon became the colony's authority on the Indians, earning great respect and influence in Boston. His influence was helped, no doubt, when he married Thankful Hinckley, a daughter of the former governor of Plymouth Colony, who had lost his office when Plymouth was merged into Massachusetts Bay Colony in 1691.

Judge Sewall of Boston was appointed by the missionary society as one of its six commissioners in 1699. Within a year he was made treasurer, responsible for paying the missionaries and "rulers," most of whom were on Martha's Vineyard. Sewall's interest in the Indians was genuine, and his contribution became of great importance to Island history. A sensitive man, he carried a strong feeling of personal guilt for his role in sending the Salem "witches" to the gallows in 1692. In 1697 he stood up in Boston's Old South Church while a "bill of error" he had written was read to the congregation. He was the only judge in the trial, which had sent twenty persons (fourteen of them women) to their deaths, to admit his error and to ask God and the people for forgiveness.

That experience no doubt gave him great empathy for the Indians. His diary entry for October 14, 1699, indicates his deep concern: "I meet with the Governour, Lt. Govr., Mr. Increase Mather, &c. about the Indian Affair, which is the first time. The Lord make me faithfull and usefull in it."

The Indians needed someone like Sewall. They had been ignored while Athearn and the Mayhews argued over matters that had nothing to do with their true needs. As desirable land was taken from them, they were forced onto less fertile, less usable land. Without political power, they were an ignored underclass. Their numbers steadily declined.

A year after his appointment and before he had visited the Island, Sewall urged Sir William Ashhurst, head of the London missionary society, to create a reservation for the praying Indians of southern New England. Converting them to Christianity was not enough, he argued. They needed land, secure land: "Upon which for any English-man to encroach, should be accounted a crime, and it will be a vain Attempt for us to offer Heaven to them, if they take up prejudices against us, as if we did grudge them a Living upon their own Earth."

In the spring of 1702 Judge Sewall made his first trip to the Vineyard to see what the society was getting for all the money it was sending there. On the way to the ferry in Falmouth, he stopped in Barnstable at the home of the former governor of Plymouth, Thomas Hinckley, who was Experience Mayhew's father-in-law. Thankful, the governor's daughter, now Mrs. Mayhew, had just given birth to their third child and had written a letter to Sewall from the Vineyard, extending her good wishes. It was a pleasing (and politically wise) introduction to the Mayhew family, who depended upon the financial support of the society. Sewall and Experience Mayhew soon became close friends.

Sewall's ferry ride to the Vineyard was pleasant: "Go to the Ferry-house . . . at little Wood's hole. . . . Embark and have a good passage over in little

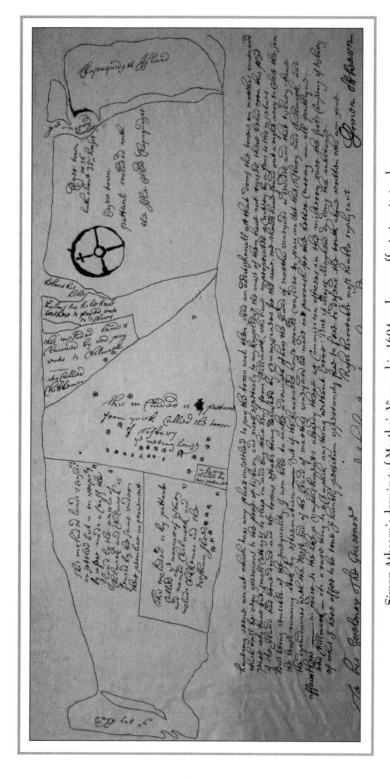

Simon Athearn's drawing of Martha's Vineyard in 1694 makes no effort at cartography.
Rather, it is his rough interpretation of how the Island was divided into towns.
(Courtesy of the Massachusetts State Archives)

more than an hour's time. Refresh at Chase's [tavern at Holmes Hole], from thence ride to [West] Tisbury." He stayed with Sheriff Ebenezer Allen and his wife, who kept an inn in Chilmark on the south shore, an area known as Quansoo. At supper they were joined by Matthew, who had come up from Edgartown, and Experience Mayhew, as well as the Reverend Josiah Torrey, both of whom lived nearby. After the meal, Sewall wrote: "Have a very good chamber and bed to lodge in. One of the best in Chilmark."

The next day Sewall visited "Exper., whose wife lyes in of a son." Experience Mayhew's diary entry describes a busy day:

> Then ride to the Gay-head Neck, to Abel's Wigwam, where was pleased with the goodness of his house, especially the Furniture, demonstrating his Industry, *viz*, Two great Spinning Wheels, one small one for Linen and a Loom to weave it. When Abel came in from his sowing of Wheat . . . he gave us very good Milk and Water to drink. As came back, saw an English House of Harry, but he not at home. . . . Abel says there are Fifty-Eight houses in the Gay-head Neck. Major [Matthew] Mayhew says 'twill entertain 58 more, and less than forty Rod of Fence takes it in—1000 Acres.

Sewall met the two Gay Head schoolteachers, both Indians, one being the Anabaptist preacher Jonas Hassaurt. The next day, April 8, 1702, Sewall talked (through an interpreter, probably Experience) with several other Gay Head Indians, one of whom, Stephen, like Jonas, had fallen from grace, a fact that concerned Sewall: "I try to convince Stephen of his Anabaptistical Errors; Jonas and he have a Church of about 30, ten [of them] men. . . . Gave Japhet two Arabian pieces Gold, and Stephen two pieces 8/8 to buy Corn. Mr. Exper. Mayhew proposes . . . that some Short Treatise be drawn up and translated into Indian to prevent the spreading of the Anabaptistical Notions."

Although Stephen was Anabaptist, Experience thought highly of him, as he wrote later in *Indian Converts:* "I cannot but judge that he acted according to the Dictates of his Conscience . . . and not out of any . . . base and sordid Ends. . . . The last time I went to see him, he professed his good Opinion of those People and Churches from whom he differed."

Sewall had dinner that night at the home of Simon Athearn and was surprised to learn that "his wife, [was] not [yet] 14 when he married her." The following day, before sailing back to Woods Hole, he learned about

Maſſachuſee PSALTER :

A S U H,

Uk-kuttoohomaongaſh

D A V I D

Weche

WUNNAUNOHEMOOKAONK

Ne anſukhogup JOHN,

Ut *Indiane* kah *Engliſhe*
Nepatuhquonkaſh.

Ne woh ſogkompagunukhettit
Kakoketahteaekuppannegk, aketamunnat,
kah wohwohtamunat Wunnetuppantam-
we Waſſukwhongaſh.

John v. 39.

*Natinneakontamook Wuſſukwhonkanaſh, newut-
che ut yeuſh kuttunnantamamwoo kuttabtom-
woo micheme pomantammooonk ; kuh niſh
naſhog wauwaonukqueniſh.*

BOSTON, N. E.
Upprinthomunneau *B. Green,* kah *J Printer,*
wutche quhtiantamwe CHAPANUKKEG
wutche onchekehtouunnat wunnaunchum-
mookaonk ut *New-England* &c 1 7 0 9.

The title page of the *Massachusetts Psalter, or Psalms of David,*
written by Experience Mayhew in the Wampanoag language
in 1709. (MVHS Collections)

the various Indian dialects: "I perceive by Mr. Exper. Mayhew and Japhet, 'tis hardly feesible to send any [Indian preachers] to the Eastward [to Maine] to convert the Indians, their Language is so different."

Four years later Judge Sewall again visited the Island, this time to see what could be done about those "Anabaptistical Notions." He had been a divinity student at Harvard (although he never became a minister) and was an out-and-out Puritan. He didn't believe in observing the holy days of Christmas or Easter—that would be papist. Baptists, he was sure, had been misled by the Devil, and Indians should be protected from them. Unlike Experience Mayhew, Sewall could not accept their point of view.

On this second visit, he didn't meet Experience, who was in Barnstable, where his wife, Thankful, gravely ill after childbirth, was staying with her parents. Two weeks later she died. Experience had become a widower with three small children, one of them a mentally retarded son.

When Sewall got back to Boston, he wrote to London, urging that Gay Head be purchased by the society to become the "Recess" for Indians that he had proposed years before: "Gayhead Neck is the Westernmost end of the Island. . . . This Neck affords a convenient Recess for the Indians, that they may live comfortably and inoffensively."

No doubt he and Experience had talked about the plan to buy Gay Head. They were close friends. Some years later Sewall made that obvious in his diary: "July 22, 1709: In the evening, Mr. Mayhew and I bath ourselves in Charles River behind Blackston's Point."

Action was quickly taken on the Gay Head purchase. The missionary society began negotiating with Thomas Dongan, now the Earl of Limerick. Dongan, you will recall, had bought Gay Head from Matthew Mayhew in 1683 for two hundred pounds and paid another thirty pounds to the sachem Mittark when it was discovered that the Indians, not Mayhew, owned Gay Head. Dongan had apparently never visited Gay Head, but he still owned it in 1711 and was happy to sell it.

Matthew Mayhew died in 1710, a year before the society bought Gay Head. He is believed to have been buried in the family homestead lot on South Water Street, Edgartown, alongside his grandfather, the governor, and grandmother. Gravestones nearby mark the graves of Matthew's son (also Matthew) and his family, but no stones mark those of the governor and his grandson. The site was recently marked by a plaque in the lawn close to the sidewalk on South Water Street about two hundred feet south of Cooke Street.

Although the Island had been affected little by King Philip's War, that was not the case during the French and Indian Wars, a long series of wars, mostly in Europe, between 1689 and 1763. The colonies became involved at times, when the British ordered the colonial militia to stop the threat by the French (whom they were fighting in Europe) to take over Massachusetts and New York with the help of Indians (hence the conflict's name). The war was between the French and English, with some Indian involvement.

Vineyard men, many of them Indians, were sent to fight in Canada. Towns were also assessed special taxes to pay for the war. Nicodemus Skuhwhannan of Gay Head was one who fought. He died at Port Royal in Nova Scotia in 1710, the first Vineyard man known to have died in any war. We know of his death from Samuel Sewall's diary and Experience Mayhew's *Indian Converts*. While on the Vineyard in 1714, Sewall went to Chilmark to talk to Benjamin Mayhew about the fence the Indians were putting up to keep English sheep from wandering onto their land at Gay Head. When he visited Gay Head, Sewall learned of the Port Royal death, quite inadvertently: "He [Mayhew] is promis'd that his so doing [finishing the fence] shall not alter any Lease he has of Sam. Osowit for about 10 or 12 Acres just within the Neck. [I gave] to Sarah Japhet, widow, 12s [12 shillings], to help Fill her Land. Bethiah, Nicodemus's widow, who died at Port Royal, is her daughter, and dwells with her. Bethiah has one son, of 22 years old, who is helpless by reason of Sickness; have one Servant 17 years old."

Nicodemus's death in Nova Scotia is also mentioned by Experience Mayhew in *Indian Converts*. He writes about Japheth, a converted Indian, son of the dead man: "After the Death of his Father, who dy'd at Annapolis Royal [Port Royal], after the Place was taken in the Year 1710, his Mother being left a Widow, went to live with her Father where he before was; and his Grandfather dying not long after, *viz.* in the Year 1712, his Mother, Grandmother, and himself, were left to keep House together."

Nicodemus should be recognized. He is the first Island man known to have been killed in a war. Other Islanders may have died during that protracted conflict, but we have no record of their deaths. Only because Sewall and Experience mention it do we know of this one.

After Matthew Mayhew died in 1710, his brother Thomas III took over the job of "ruling" the Indians and the Island. His rule was short-lived, as he died five years later. With the two brothers gone, the Mayhew family's control began to decline. A brother-in-law, Benjamin Skiffe of Chilmark, became the leader of the government, such as it was. Matthew and Thomas had married Skiffe sisters so the government was still "in the family," although the family name had changed.

Experience, the nephew of Matthew and Thomas, had remarried in 1711. His second wife, Remember Bourne, was, like his first, a member of an influential Massachusetts family. Still being paid as a missionary to the Vineyard Indians, Experience was spending even less time on the Island and more time doing society work on the mainland. Occasionally, he was sent to inspect missions in various praying Indian villages, but mostly he stayed in Boston, translating Biblical tracts into Algonquian. He was very much a part of Judge Sewall's social circle, and at the judge's suggestion he began writing *Indian Converts*. That book, for which he is best known, was published in 1727 and is a collection of biographies of Vineyard Indians whom the Mayhews had converted through the years.

Experience's absence from the Island raises the question of what the paid missionaries were expected to be doing. By this time there were very few "savage" Indians yet to be converted remaining on the Island. Several Indian settlements had organized churches with Indian ministers paid by the missionary society; others were Anabaptist congregations whose ministers were paid by the Indians themselves.

In a letter to Sewall the London head of the missionary society urged him to get "the missionaries to visit the Indians in their abodes and not to meet them only at monthly services." The Mayhews did not often visit Indian wigwams, if they did at all, scattered as the settlements were, from Gay Head in the west to Chappaquiddick in the east. It is not known how often—or whether—they attended Indian prayer meetings. The Indian teachers and preachers had long since taken over.

The society concentrated its attention on Gay Head, the largest Indian settlement. At the others, the Indian preachers did the Lord's work. That was especially true on Chappaquiddick, the second largest. The Mayhew missionaries had moved from Edgartown to the center of the Island in (West) Tisbury, and the society's attention moved with them. Sewall, during his infrequent visits, spent most of his time at Gay Head, pursuing his "recess" plan.

Sewall came to the Island more often than any other Bostonian. He was very familiar with the ferry service, such as it was. On his first visit in 1706 he and his fellow commissioner Bromfield had problems. After their visit to Gay Head, they left Holmes Hole by ferry for Woods Hole, but their boat was becalmed and carried by the falling tide to Tarpaulin Cove, where they spent the night: "Sept. 9, 1706 . . . embark'd with a scant wind; put in to Tarpoling Cove: Mr. Bromfield not yielding to go to Cushnet." Even then Vineyard and Nantucket Sounds were important north-south waterways, and Tarpaulin Cove on Naushon was the usual harbor of refuge. A tavern had been built there to take care of sailors awaiting favorable wind and tide. There were no anchoring fees, but marine etiquette allowed gifts to harbor masters, as we learn from Governor John Winthrop. During a 1702 stay on Naushon Island at the house of his father, Wait Winthrop, the governor wrote in his diary: "September. 1702. Here arrived an English ship from Nevis. Ye Master whereof sent Father a dozen and a half of Oranges."

Many shoals and confusing currents made the two sounds treacherous. There were, at the time, no official charts published by the government, so each mariner made his own. The oldest one extant that we know of was drawn by Joshua Benjamin in November 1717.

Maintaining the Indian churches and schools on the Vineyard was a major drain on the London society. Some way had to be found to increase income. The society came up with a bold plan: it would lease out part of Gay Head. In September 1713 Commissioners Sewall and Penn Townsend were told to assign lots to the Indian families, setting aside a large section to be leased to others, Indian or not:

> Competent and Convenient Portions of this Land [to be] assigned unto the Indians . . . to be Inhabited and Cultivated by the Indian Families. Each of the Families to know their own Allotments. . . .
>
> That part of the Land which will remain after the Indians have their Portions alloted . . . shall be Leased out unto Tenants, at such Rates and for such Terms, as by the Agents may be thought most Reasonable, that there may be something of a benefit Revenue from thence towards the Support of Schools, and other good Interests among the Indians of that Island. . . . What Revenues doe arise . . . Will be wholly applyed for their Benefit.

It was a huge undertaking. To divide the Indian land fairly would be a challenge. Sewall didn't begin working on the plan until the following spring, when he made a trip to the Island to start the process. His diary tells us more about the ferry service and provides our first report of a physical handicap that would become very well known much later:

April 5, 1714: . . . Went to the Ferry [in little Woods Hole]. . . . In our Passage we were becalmed, and the Tide [was] against us . . . were 2 hours getting over. Were fain [forced] to row to the west side of Oakakemy [Lambert's Cove], where we landed, the Sloop coming to an Anchor. Our Horses were forced to leap into the Sea. . . . [We] found Thomas Paul, a Lame Indian, on Horseback with his Net on his shoulder, to catch Fish by Night. Upon my speaking to him to Pilot me, he left his Net and did it very well. We were ready to be offended that an Englishman, Jonathan Lumbard, in the Company, spake not a word to us, and it seems he is deaf and dumb.

This entry tells us a great deal. The ferry was a sloop, large enough to carry several passengers and crew, plus at least two horses. Yet it was small enough to be rowed when the wind collapsed and the falling tide (flowing west toward Gay Head) carried them into Lambert's Cove. They had intended to land at Holmes Hole. At the cove they anchored close to shore and pushed the horses overboard. The men probably went ashore in a skiff. It was getting dark. An Indian intending to fish was on the beach. He was Paul, for whom Paul's Point was named, riding a horse, the first mention we have of Vineyard Indians owning horses. He guided them to Sheriff Allen's inn. It had been a long day; no wonder Judge Sewall was "indisposed" the next morning.

Sewall's reference to the deaf-mute Jonathan Lumbard, "who spake not a word," is our first record of that genetic condition on the Island. Lumbard was born on Cape Cod and moved to the Island about 1690. He was born deaf, as were two of his seven children. Neither deaf child married, but the trait recurred in later generations and became most common on the western end of the Island. The story of this phenomenon is told by Nora Groce in *Everyone Here Spoke Sign Language.*

Sewall spent the next day, a quiet Sunday, at Sheriff Allen's recovering. On this trip he did not meet with Simon Athearn, who was in failing health; he died early the next year. After the deaths of Matthew Mayhew and Simon Athearn, the Island's conflict level soon subsided. Simon's son, Samuel, occasionally questioned the government, but with a much lower voice than his father had. The Reverend Josiah Torrey of (West) Tisbury, Athearn's son-in-law, usually met with Sewall on his Island visits so the family involvement continued, but at a less confrontational level.

While Sewall was resting at Sheriff Allen's, Experience Mayhew sent

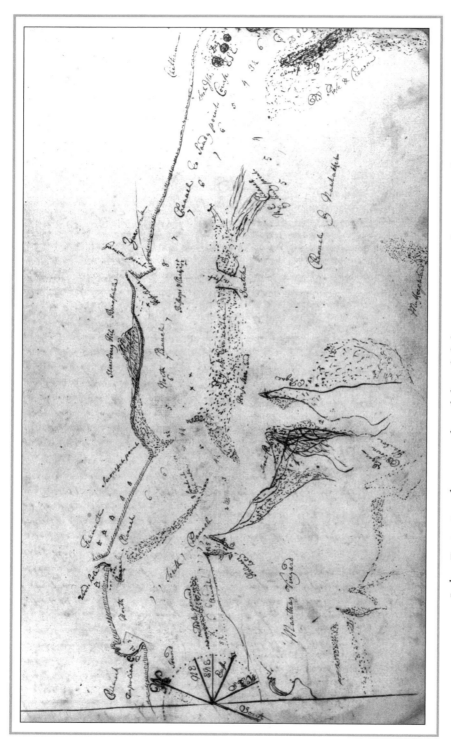

Joshua Benjamin, a first mate who sailed regularly between Boston and Virginia, made a crude chart of Vineyard waters in 1717, probably the oldest such in existence. The Vineyard is at bottom left, with Tarpaulin Cove (then part of Chilmark) above it. He emphasized, as a mariner would, the shoals between the Vineyard and the mainland, top. (Courtesy of the William Clements Library, University of Michigan)

word to Gay Head, telling the Indians to gather the next morning. Sewall's diary entry reads: "Mr. Mayhew writes a Letter in Indian to Saul, which I subscrib'd, to notify the Indians of the Gay Head to come together something before Noon. I would speak with them after Mr. Mayhew's Lecture."

At Gay Head, on Monday, April 7, 1714, about one hundred Indians assembled to listen to Sewall (no doubt as translated by Mayhew). He told them of the plan, his plan, to provide a "recess" for them, a place where no Englishman would be allowed (except for any who might lease the section that came to be called Gay Head Farm).

When he finished, Sewall asked how many could read. There was a long pause. Finally, two young men were brought forward. Sewall handed one of them his "Psalm-book with red Covers," which the young man read from. When he finished, Sewall gave him the book as a present. Sewall did not seem pleased. He sounded disappointed when he wrote that after his question, "at last, only two were produced." Hardly enough, he seemed to be suggesting, to repay the society for its thirty years of mission work.

Sewall's dream of a recess for Indians had a lasting impact on Island history. Had the society not bought Dongan's "mannor" for that purpose, the land would have been inherited by his nephew, who intended to make it his private hunting preserve, a move that would have greatly changed Gay Head. The head of the society, Sir William Ashhurst, was pleased that Dongan's nephew was out of the picture, but for a religious reason, as he wrote in a letter to Sewall: "He being a Papist and a person of no great prudence, he would certainly have made the poor Indian inhabitants very uneasy, if not wholly disposed of them."

Sewall's plan to assign each Indian family on Gay Head a parcel of land was not carried out. The Indians opposed it, preferring to keep the land in common, as they always had. Each family would "borrow" as much land from the tribal holdings as it needed. Nobody owned any land, nobody inherited any. No fences and no property lines: that was the Indian way.

Sheriff Ebenezer Allen, in whose inn Sewall usually stayed when he visited the Island, had an inside track on leasing the land not included in the recess. Those six hundred acres at Gay Head were leased to him for ten years at fifty pounds a year; the rent money was to be used on behalf of the Indians, thereby reducing the drain on the society budget. Sixteen Indian families lived on the leased acreage in the northeast section of Gay Head; they would have to move. A condescending letter, dripping with "love," was read to them. The change, the letter said, would make them happy:

The commissioners love you and seek your good in everything. We direct that 16 families of you now on the land that we have leased to Mr. Ebenezer Allen, to remove unto that land which we think most suitable to be inhabited by the Indians. . . . Every penny of the money received of Mr. Ebenezer Allen, or of any other, is all laid out only to make you a happy people. We shall use all the care of kind fathers . . . to look after you, who love you like their children.

The Indian population, those "children" so loved by the commissioners, had been steadily declining. In 1690 a virulent fever had killed many of the converted. Matthew Mayhew, in his book *Brief Narrative of Indians* (1694), wrote that "of more than 100 Adult Persons [Indians] that dyed not less than three-fourths were of the Sober Religious Professors; that it was by the English inhabitants vulgarly taken notice of." Mayhew seemed to be saying that the Christian God had not protected the Indians who had accepted Him and that some English tried to use that fact to stop spending money on missions.

By 1700 only one thousand Indians still lived on the Island, one-third the number who were there when the English arrived only sixty years before. The white man had taken much of their land and his diseases had taken many of their lives. Matthew Mayhew, the first of his family to turn away from mission work, was wrong to imply that the missionaries had failed. Their work was to save souls in the hereafter, not to save lives in the present.

For thousands of years, the Indians had survived, supporting their families and living healthy, rewarding lives. They were a proud and caring people, deeply devoted to their children. That pride began eroding as the land, their source of sustenance, was taken from them. With diminished self-esteem, increasingly they turned (were even encouraged, some say) to seek solace from alcohol. Some English saw alcohol dependency as a way to encumber Indians with debts, debts they could pay off only by selling land or by servitude.

Daniel Gookin, an early historian of the Indians, described it as another communicable disease brought by the white man: "They had drunk water before the English came . . . and their taste for alcohol had been acquired from the white settlers." Court cases described the illegal selling of alcohol to Indians. David Silverman wrote in *The New England Quarterly:*

Tavern owner Robert Cathcart of Tisbury was called before Dukes County magistrates several times for selling alcohol to Indians. Not coincidentally, he also sued numerous Indians for unpaid debts, purchased land from natives on a number of occasions, and died in 1718 with 117 natives owing him a total of £168, 8d. So too Samuel Athearn . . . [was] formally charged with selling Indians drink during the 1720s and . . . [brought] seventeen suits for Indian debt.

Unpaid debts often brought long sentences as indentured servants, which made Indians slaves for years to work off their debts. As indentured servants, they were property that could be sold. The buyer agreed to house, feed, and clothe the servant for the term of the sentence. When the time was up, the Indian was freed and given two sets of clothes, one for work, another for church, but during the term of servitude they had few, if any, rights.

Indian children, though not guilty of any crime, were sometimes sold into servitude by their parents to pay off debts. The Vineyard author James Athearn Jones told how it worked in his family: "It was my grandfather's custom, and had been that of his ancestors . . . to take Indian boys at the age of four or five years until they had attained their majority. . . . During my minority, we had three of these little foresters in our house."

For crimes considered to be petty thievery today, the court would sentence Indians to long servitude. Silverman noted:

> On the Vineyard in October 1734, Dinah Sissetom of Sengekontacket was found guilty of stealing three bed sheets from the house of John Daggett. . . . [She] was bound out by the Dukes County Court for a full three years. Similarly, Martha Job of the Vineyard was sentenced to two years of service in 1747 when she pleaded her inability to pay 45 shillings as damages for stealing a silver shoe buckle from Simeon Butler of Edgartown.

Very much longer was the sentence in a suit brought by Matthew Mayhew, chief magistrate, against his Indian servant girl, Hannah. He had accused her of stealing corn, linen, woolen goods, and money from his house in 1690. His court found her guilty and authorized him "to make sale of her for the terme of thirty yeres in any part of these Maisto dominyons [Majesties' dominions] or Elsewhere." So for thirty years Hannah was a slave off-Island. The money paid by the person who bought her went to Judge Mayhew.

Indians received long sentences for such questionable crimes as steal-ing sheep that had wandered onto their land, where the grass was appar-ently greener. For this kind of theft the Indian Wahommo was sentenced to five years' servitude; "Sam, the sone of Piamco, an Indian boy [is] to be sold . . . for seven yeres for stealing Sertayn Sheepe." One of the judges in the trial, Thomas Daggett, bought Sam's indenture and the boy became his slave for seven years.

Indians received far harsher sentences than whites for more serious crimes. When an Englishman, Andrew Newcomb, was charged with killing his son, Andrew, in 1688, despite strong evidence against him, the grand jury ruled, "We declare it Ignoramus," and he went free. The next year Pommatoock, an Indian, was found guilty of killing "Sarah, an Indian mayd of Tysbury." It was "Ordered that pommatoock, Indian, shall be exe-cuted ye 26 : of Septemb'r 1689, for murder don in, or about, 1664, while he is dead, dead, dead."

Punishment for sexual misdeeds also fell much more heavily on the Indian. In 1711, when Samuel Osborn of Edgartown was found guilty of fathering a child born to Mercy Norton, he was sentenced to pay "one shilling and six pence per week" until the child was three years old; then the payment would drop to one shilling per week for four years, "if said child shall so long live." Contrast that with the sentences two Indians received that same year for a similar crime that did not even involve a child. Abel Ossoowit and Elizabeth Pomit were found guilty of "being in bed together." Abel was sentenced to "six stripes" with a whip, to pay a fee of four pounds, and to give bond for his good behavior until the next ses-sion in March; "and the said Elizabeth is adjudged to suffer Corporal pun-ishment by whipping the number of four stripes, and to pay fees of Court £4 and to stand committed until sentence be performed."

Curfew laws applied only to Indians. An Indian found in Edgartown "halfe an hower after the sunn is Sett" would be whipped unless he gave an acceptable excuse to the court.

In 1720 there were only eight hundred Indians on the Vineyard, living in six villages. The largest of them was Gay Head, where, as Experience Mayhew reported to London, there was an Anabaptist church, "but the number of people belonging unto this is very inconsiderable."

The "ruler" of the Indians, paid by the missionary society, was now Zaccheus Mayhew, who had taken over when his father, Thomas Mayhew III, died in 1715. Thomas III was described by the Reverend William

Homes of Chilmark in his diary: "He was a man of good sense, considering his education, and seemed to be piously inclined, though he did entertain some singular opinions in religion." It is unfortunate that Homes didn't go into more detail about those "singular opinions."

Experience Mayhew's regular reports to the society tell us a lot about the occupations of Indians. Success was measured, it seems, by how close they came to "becoming English." In one report he wrote:

> There are yet but few Indians . . . that have houses of the English fashion. . . . Some have learned trades; . . . there are several weavers, one or two house carpenters, one wheel wright, who is so good a workman as to be frequently employed by his English neighbors. There are several tailors and one, if not more shoemakers, and one blacksmith, who . . . made his bellows and other tools; and one cooper, *viz.*, William Charles, who is a good workman. . . . This shews that . . . the Indians are capable of learning such callings as English men follow.

When Experience finished writing *Indian Converts* in 1724, the London missionary society did not have the money to publish it. A Boston bookseller, perhaps encouraged by Samuel Sewall, recognized the value of the work and sold subscriptions to it prior to publication. When he had sold three hundred at ten shillings each, the book was published in 1727. It contains lengthy biographies of those Indians, men, women, and children, who were converted. Its subtitle reads: "Some Account of the Lives and Dying Speeches of a Considerable Number of the Christianized INDIANS of *Martha's Vineyard* in *New-England*."

Sewall had suggested the book's theme to Experience, saying the "dying speeches" of those converted should be preserved. Thomas Prince wrote the final chapter, "Some Account of Those English Ministers." The ministers he praised were the four generations of Mayhews: Thomas Sr., Thomas Jr., John, and Experience. The book greatly increased the reputation of Experience and the fame of the Mayhews.

Many of the Indians memorialized in the book had died unhappy, despite their conversion and hope of a better life in the hereafter. Increasingly, they were victims of poverty and the addiction to alcohol. Belatedly recognizing what was happening, the colony of Massachusetts created a guardianship program to oversee the Indians. Three "Guardians of the Indians" were appointed on the Vineyard. (One was Zaccheus Mayhew, son of Thomas III, and himself a paid missionary.) The Indians did not

INDIAN CONVERTS:
OR, SOME
ACCOUNT
OF THE

LIVES and Dying SPEECHES of a considerable Number of the Christianized *INDIANS* of *Martha's Vineyard*, in *New-England.*

VIZ.

I. Of Godly Ministers.
II. Of other Good Men.
III. Of Religious Women.
IV. Of Pious young Persons.

By *Experience Mayhew*, M. A. Preacher of the Gospel to the *Indians* of that Island.

To which is added,

Some Account of those *ENGLISH* MINISTERS who have successively presided over the *Indian* Work in that and the adjacent Islands. By Mr. *Prince.*

Acts x. 34, 35. *I perceive that GOD is no Respecter of Persons: but in every Nation he that feareth him, and worketh Righteousness, is accepted with him.*
Acts xv. 8, 9. *Giving them the Holy Ghost, even as he did unto us: and put no Difference between us and them, purifying their Hearts by Faith.*
Mat. xxviii. 19, 20. *Go ye therefore, and teach all Nations, &c.*

LONDON,

Printed for *Samuel Gerrish*, Bookseller in *Boston* in *New-England*, and sold by *J. Osborn* and *T. Longman* in *Pater-noster-Row.*
M.DCC.XXVII

Experience Mayhew's best-known work is *Indian Converts,* a lengthy account of the Christianized Indians on Martha's Vineyard. It tells many stories of the Indian men, women, and children who were converted. (MVHS Collections)

welcome them. A petition sent by Gay Head Indians in 1749 to Massachusetts authorities makes their feelings clear:

> We want . . . that we may have our fields, which the Guardians have let
> out. . . . We are more Poor [than] Ever. . . . We have not liberty to Pasture
> our Cretures, only as we Buy, or Hire Pasture. . . . It was not so before
> . . . by the Guardians we are Deceived. . . . The number of all the souls
> are about 165 and the number of our Cretures are about 400 (we know
> not the number of our sheep). What shall these Cretures do for Pasture?
> we have none only as we buy it. . . . We have been with the Guardians to
> seek for money but they give no money, or other things.

The Chappaquiddick Indians were also unhappy. In 1760 some complained to the Massachusetts government that English "squatters" were
moving onto Indian land illegally, sometimes making token payments for
land to the Indians living there, who were not allowed by law to sell land.
Nine English houses had been built and the owners were burning up the
Island's scarce supply of firewood. The Guardians, despite their title,
seemed unable or unwilling to do anything to protect the Indians.

Experience Mayhew died in 1758, leaving a sizable estate. He owned
land in Deerfield, Massachusetts, and a large tract on Quansoo, where he
had lived. His will divided nearly one thousand pounds among three
daughters. His son, Zacchariah, the principal heir, asked the missionary
society to pay for his father's funeral and gravestone at Abel's Hill Cemetery in Chilmark.

Zacchariah applied for his father's job as a paid missionary. Like Experience, he had not been educated to be a minister. The London society,
low on funds, did nothing for a number of years. Finally, in 1767, nine
years after Experience died, Zacchariah was added to the society payroll,
where he stayed until he died in 1806.

When the Revolutionary War began, all payments by the society to the
colony were stopped, but a group in Boston was formed to continue paying the missionaries. In 1779 Zacchariah, as part of his salary, was given the
rights to Gay Head Farm, now eight hundred acres. It consisted of the six
hundred acres that had originally been leased to Sheriff Allen and two
hundred acres that Allen had persuaded the society to add. The society
had received almost no money from Allen, who stopped paying rent after
a year or two. In 1789 he claimed that the neighboring Indians were so

troublesome that he was forced to leave the farm, and he was given £233 as compensation. Sheriff Allen had a special place in the heart of Treasurer Sewall, it would seem.

The Mayhew family influence on the Island declined greatly with the death of Experience, but off-Island the family's fame was strong. After he graduated from Harvard, Experience's youngest son, Jonathan, was named pastor of Boston's West Church (Congregational). There he built a reputation for his doctrinal liberalism, being one of the first to reject the Trinity in favor of Unitarianism. As such, he was shunned by many. Not one Boston clergyman attended his ordination, where his aging father, Experience, delivered the sermon. It is sad that Experience died before his son's reputation peaked. He was, however, still alive when, at only thirty, Jonathan was awarded an honorary Doctor of Divinity degree by the University of Aberdeen in Scotland. The father must have been proud.

Today Jonathan is considered to be a founder of Unitarianism and Universalism, but during his life he became best known for his views on individual freedom. His election-day sermons (a church tradition at the time) were intensely political, defending the right of free men to revolt against tyranny. Many credit his fiery sermons with being the sparks that ignited a feeble fire that later burst into flames as the American Revolu-

The Mayhew homestead on Edgartown Harbor, photographed by John Chamberlain in 1898. This house was most likely built around 1720 by Micajah Mayhew, the great great-grandson of Governor Thomas Mayhew. (Courtesy of Joanne Coffin Clark)

tion. He did not live to see the conflagration he had ignited; he died at age forty-five in 1766.

President John Adams, an Arminian like Jonathan, called him "the father of civil and religious liberty in Massachusetts and New England." He is without question the Island's most distinguished native, born and raised in Chilmark, the youngest son of the Indian missionary Experience Mayhew. What conservative Vineyarders at the time thought of this hothead we do not know.

For nearly a century the Island's power center had been in Edgartown. It was now moving westward, along with the population. In 1720 Chilmark began a campaign to relocate the county seat to (West) Tisbury, the geographical center of the Vineyard. The proposal met strong opposition from Edgartown, as expected, but residents of Chilmark and Tisbury united to petition the General Court to make the change.

Edgartown responded with its own petition. These two documents provide a description of the Vineyard in the mid-1700s that sounds very familiar today. Up-Islanders argued that Edgartown, at the eastern end of the Island, was not the place to have the county government. It was inconvenient for many. Furthermore, "parking" was a problem and ferryboats didn't go there: "That part of Edgartown where the Courts are Held now is Poorly furnisht with Pasture or Hay to Keep Horses, etc. Moreover yr Petrs [petitioners] further Inform yr Excellency & Hon'rs that The Ferry for Transporting People from the Vineyard to the Main Land is in Tisbury."

Edgartown responded, hitting hard on the two complaints in the up-Island petition, that there was plenty of "parking":

> They further assert that that part of Edgartown, where the Courts are now held is poorly furnished with Pasture or Hay to keep Horses, & to which we answer that they don't generally attempt to put up their Horses, & so it is possible that some time when they have desired it they may have found the less provision there, but it does not appear that they have any Reason to Complain, there being several Persons that live near who Declare they have ever been ready to take proper Care of their Horses & never Refused any when applyed to for Twenty years past, and are still ready to furnish them with good hay at one Shilling pr night at March Court and Pasture at eight pence pr Night at October Court.

Edgartown supporters argued that the absence of ferry service was not a problem. Most who came to the Island on county business came from

Nantucket, Boston, or Rhode Island, and the packets from those places dropped them off only a few steps from the county building: "People from Boston, Rhoad Island & Nantucket (to which places our Trade is almost wholly confined), can come within 20 Rods of the Court House by Water, whereas in case the Courts were held in [West] Tisbury, they would be obliged after Landing to Travail 6 or 8 miles."

Edgartown was also more hospitable to Indians, especially to those awaiting trial (from the petition, we learn that the prisoners are expected to provide their own firewood and food):

> The Indians who often have occasion to attend Courts are now much better accommodated [in Edgartown] than in case the Courts were held at [West] Tisbury, for here they can within call of the Court furnish themselves with plenty of Shell Fish for Provisions, whereas they would be obliged to spend their money therefore . . . or suffer hunger; and now when any of them are in Gaol others easily furnish them with fire wood, which they have a great plenty of on Chappaquiddick, which lies near the Court House.

Should an attack occur while court was in session in (West) Tisbury and the sheriff was there, Edgartown would be defenseless: "Likewise as we are liable to be ransacked by Privateers or the like . . . in case the Courts were held in [West] Tisbury our danger hereof would be very greatly increased for if an enemy knew when our Courts were held and that they were held there (as they might easily inform themselves), they would doubtless Choose such a time to Plunder us."

Finally, Edgartown argued demographics. The population was changing. There was no more vacant farmland. Those who came now would be not farmers but entrepreneurs who would set up shop in Edgartown. And there were other arguments:

> Altho' the other two Towns [Tisbury and Chilmark] have Increased faster than we for some time past yet there is no Rational prospect of their doing so in the Future; for the Island has now as many Inhabitants as the Land will comfortably support; . . . any further increase of Inhabitants . . . must be supported by whaleing, Fishing & seafaring business, and as there is no other safe harbour except this [Edgartown] . . . this must be the Place for Carrying on such business. . . . There sailed from this Town the Summer past, nineteen Masters of vessels and upwards of fifty Sailors.

Disorders arise often among the sailors who live in the Harbor and some of them have been obliged to be committed to Gaol, which now can very easily be done and the Prisoner be delivered immediately when ever the wind suits for sailing; whereas it would be vastly incommodious to send them up Eight miles from the Harbour and when the vessel was ready to sail to wait till they could be brought back again . . . and if it should here be objected that Holmes hole Harbour is more used than this by Coasters and Foreigners it may be very easily answered that it is much easier to sail into this Harbour (a thing which they frequently do when they are under apprehensions of a storm, that harbour being much Exposed to a North East wind).

The controversy was intense. In 1764 a compromise was reached in Boston: a second courthouse would be built in (West) Tisbury. Alternate court sessions would be held in each village, but county functions other than courts would stay in Edgartown. It was a clumsy solution and it was discontinued in 1807.

While Edgartown and Tisbury fought over the county seat, Gay Head

Illustration of the Towanticutt Assassination Attempt from *Pious Indian Chiefs*
by Experience Mayhew

was being ignored. The missionary society still owned the land, but it was losing interest in the Vineyard Indians. The colonies were becoming increasingly defiant and talk of a revolution was being heard in London. When the Revolutionary War began, all missionary payments from England were stopped, but they had already become of little value. Indians were no longer "savages." A major change was under way: the Indian population on the Island had even started to increase, as the historian Richard L. Pease noted: "In Dukes County [in 1764], 313 Indians, 86 in Edgartown, 39 in Tisbury and 188 in Chilmark [Gay Head and Naushon included] . . . about that period, they began to intermarry with negroes in consequence of which the mixed race has increased in numbers, and improved in temperance and industry."

Pease wrote that twelve years later, at the start of the American Revolution, the number of Indians, many of mixed heritage, had increased by 40 percent, to 440. Intermarriage of Indians and blacks was further encouraged in 1790 by laws passed in Massachusetts and New York banning intermarriage of blacks and whites, while allowing blacks and Indians to marry. Intermarriage didn't need any encouragement. The mixing of the races was already increasing sharply when the law was passed, as Pease's numbers show: "[In 1776], there are of pure Indian and of the mixed race about 440 persons—75 in Chabbaquiddick (not more than one third pure), 25 at Sagechantacket (not more than one fifth pure) about 40 at Chilmark (about one half pure), 24 at Nashawakenker [Naushon] (about three-quarters pure), about 276 at Gay Head (about one quarter pure)."

As the numbers of "colored" increased, so did their problems. That same year, 1776, a petition was signed by 37 of the 276 Gay Head Indians, asking the General Court for help. The petition stated that an Indian, Elisha Amos of Tisbury, had persuaded a few Gay Head Indians to sell him their land rights. When he died, he willed the land he had bought (about two hundred acres) to a family member, who then sold it to a non-Indian. This was contrary to the Indians' belief that land was not owned. It was borrowed, used, and returned: "When any one Died, his share [of land] immediately fell into the hands of the whole and his Children, if any were left, have no addition [to what they already have] by reason thereof . . . . We have always supposed that no one had any right longer than they lived."

There were other problems, one of them critical, they said. Their petition to the General Court read:

The gravestone of the Reverend John Mayhew, who died in 1688, located in West Tisbury, as sketched by the historian Charles Banks. (From Charles E. Banks, *History of Martha's Vineyard*)

We are much burthened . . . at Gayhead, *viz:* a very considerable number of Negros and Mulatto's that have . . . built them Houses and setled amongst us, which we have not been able to prevent; some of the Indian Women that formerly resided at Gayhead have lately returned with a very considerable number of Mulatto's, as they say, Children, Grandchildren and even Great Grandchildren. . . . If they cannot be prevented from settling amongst us, [it] will greatly impoverish if not entirely Root us out.

We therefore beg that your Honours would . . . do that for us which Shall in your wisdom appear proper.

There were good reasons why this was happening, and why it would continue. There was a shortage of men among the Indian population, so many of them having gone to sea, and a similar shortage of women among blacks, as the slaves being imported were mostly male. Not allowed to own land themselves, black men marrying Indian women had access to their wives' tribal land. Furthermore, their children would be free. There was nothing that the General Court could do to change things.

Furthermore, it was a poor time for Gay Head Indians to be asking for help with their problems. There were more important worries in the colony. Only one hundred miles away, shots had been fired, shots "heard round the world." The Indians may not have heard them, but the sounds of the muskets had drowned out their complaints.

That week General George Washington was marching most of his army south from Cambridge to occupy New York.

On April 15, 1776, the petition was quickly disposed of by the General Court. It ordered that three Guardians be appointed to look out for the well-being of the Gay Head Indians, who had for years been opposed to any guardianship.

Judge Samuel Sewall's dream of a recess for Indians at Gay Head had vanished behind the smoke of muskets fired to bring freedom to Americans—not to all Americans and certainly not to the first.

3

Nervous Neutrals and Reluctant Rebels

When news of the shots fired at Lexington and Concord reached the Vineyard in the spring of 1775, there were no patriotic outbursts, no drums rolling. Nor were there any such happenings in the villages on Cape Cod. Instead, a sense of worry, of uncertainty, settled over the people. What was coming? they wondered.

Those who lived on Cape Cod and the Islands depended on the sea. It was all very well for those "embattled farmers" crouching behind stone walls to fire on the British as they marched back to Boston, but on the ocean there were no stone walls. Britannia ruled the waves. Who would protect the mariners? Certainly not that hotheaded Sam Adams or his embattled farmers.

The issues that had brought Adams and his rebels to the boiling point had never meant much to Vineyarders. They had never seen British redcoats marching through their villages demanding housing. Such "nuisances" as duties and taxes didn't bother mariners. They had their ways of getting around them. Five-sixths of the tea consumed in Massachusetts came in illegally, according to Governor Thomas Hutchinson. On the Vineyard it was probably closer to six-sixths. Sailors could avoid paying the tea tax, but they couldn't avoid His Majesty's warships.

It is no wonder that Vineyarders had little enthusiasm for the rebellion, isolated and vulnerable as they were.

Years later, Colonel Beriah Norton stated the case forcefully when he was in London seeking restitution for the Island's war losses:

> It is a matter even of public notoriety that the inhabitants of Martha's
> Vineyard did at the commencement of the Rebellion in this Country

make the most explicit declarations that they would not be concerned with either party in the Controversy, because by their local situation they were equally exposed to the resentment of both: they were on the one hand directly opposite and near to, as part of the Province of Massachusetts Bay, where the Inhabitants could annoy them at pleasure; and on the other, were liable from their insular situation to every incursion either from King's Ships or Privateers.

Colonel Norton described the Islanders as neutral, on neither the colonies' side nor England's. Nervously neutral they were, with good reason. The English navy, along with thousands of soldiers, was based in Newport, Rhode Island, only thirty-five miles away. His Majesty's warships regularly sailed in Island waters. Vineyarders watched the tall, powerful ships, their cannons ready to be fired. They knew how vulnerable they were. Neutrality was their best course.

Not all Vineyarders were neutral. Some were on the side of the English, preferring the known to the unknown. They were not alone in that. John Shy, a historian of the Revolution, estimates that one-fifth of all colonists remained loyal to the Crown; two-fifths were for the rebels, and the rest were undecided.

The Vineyard's most outspoken loyalist was William Jernigan of Edgartown, the representative to the General Court. In a memoir written late in his life, he described how he was threatened by strong-headed Edgartown patriots for his position against the rebellion. Most of them, he said, were young men, noisy and riotous, especially in the middle of the night, but they were not a majority.

Even the hotheads in Boston were not demanding independence, not at the start. They weren't in revolt against the king, only against a Parliament that was interfering with what they thought were their freedoms. It had ordered them to pay duties on many of life's necessities. They were rebelling against laws that allowed soldiers, without a warrant, to search their homes and to be housed in those homes without consent of the owners. These were the legitimate complaints of colonists who considered themselves free men. That was why they had come to the colony. Their fight was with the Parliament, where they had no voice, no representation.

The rebellion had been born in 1763 when Parliament voted to tax the colonists to pay for maintaining an army in the colonies. James Otis from Barnstable on Cape Cod, the king's advocate general in Boston, resigned his post to become counsel for the Boston merchants who were opposed to the tax. It was Otis who coined the expression "no taxation without representation," a battle cry that would last for years.

In 1765 Parliament levied an even more unpopular tax: the Stamp Act, which required that stamps be bought and affixed to all printed materials, including legal forms, invoices, and even playing cards. This tax hit the professional class, the lawyers and businessmen, very hard, and it united them in opposition. It was, some say, the beginning of an organized revolt throughout the colony. The justices of the courts were so strongly opposed to it (affecting as it did most of their work) that it was rarely enforced. So widespread was the evasion that the next spring Parliament repealed it.

But England still needed money. In June 1767 Parliament passed the Townshend Acts, which set duties on glass, paint, lead, paper, and tea. The duty on paint might have found some support on the Island, where a paint mill was operating in Chilmark. In 1764 a man named W. Whitwell learned that his father, a minister involved in Indian missions, was going to Gay Head to preach. He wrote to him, asking a special favor: "Have just time eno [enough] to inform you of my desire to have a barrel of yellow & red paint from Gay-head, & will pay whatever Charges may accrue from the same. Please to let the barrel be filled [?] with Red & [?] with Yellow; if it can't be procured, fill it up with such Colours as you can get. Yr. dutif. Son, W. Whitwell."

Paint, as described by Whitwell, was not the liquid it is today. It was a dry powder of finely ground colored clay. Different colors could be shipped in the same barrel, as he proposed. The powder was later mixed with oil for use as paint. Most of the Chilmark paint was sold off-Island to be used for coloring oilcloth, a floor covering.

Boston's rebel Sam Adams had no interest in protecting a tiny paint mill on the Vineyard. He was opposed to the Townshend Acts as a whole on principle. Encouraged by his friend James Otis, he drafted a letter for the General Court to send to all the colonies. Governor Bernard, the king's appointee, called the letter a "treasonous" act, one urging the other colonies to disobey a law. He ordered the General Court to rescind it at once. A vote was taken and the legislature refused, ninety-two to seventeen, to rescind.

Two of the seventeen "loyal rescinders" were from the Vineyard: William Jernigan of Edgartown and Matthew Mayhew of Chilmark. James Athearn of Tisbury, the Island's third representative, voted with the majority.

Governor Bernard was so upset by the defiant vote that he dissolved the General Court, giving the rebels an issue around which to gather. The ninety-two who had opposed the governor were "raised to sainthood," wrote the historian Robert Middlekauff in his book *The Glorious Cause,* while the seventeen loyalists, including the two Vineyarders who voted to rescind, were attacked as enemies of the people.

More united than ever, the colonies voted to embargo all English goods until the Townshend Acts were repealed. Jernigan, one of the two Vineyard loyalists, explained his vote in a memoir written much later. He phrased the issue differently (writing, at times, in the third person):

> In the year 1768 at the time when that most importent Question was before the House, which was, "Shall we or Shall we not, ingage in a war against our Mother Country" (or words to the same effect) in order to obtain our Liberties and Indipendance; he [Jernigan] then considering the matter to be very siours [serious?] in our infant state and doubtfull on our side, all circumstances considered at that time, and the Particular situation of the Vineyard, gave his Vote in the negative with the 17, acting according to his best skill and judgment for the good of the whole, and he did not run with the current, nither with the 92.

Jernigan was claiming that what he had done was what was best for the Island. He cited another example of how he was looking out for the Island's interest: his action in opposition to an Island militia. When the General Court was debating an act that would require every town to form a company of militia, men who could be called upon to serve in the colonial army when needed, Jernigan successfully argued for exempting the islands. He said that the Vineyard and Nantucket, isolated and vulnerable as they were, could spare neither the men nor the money: "[He] used his best skill & judgement to have the Vineyard & Nantuckett, being two islands in the midst of the sea, to be exempted from all melisha [militia] laws whatever . . . which has saved to each Island more than $1000 per annum and in case of war I am in hopes will save our towns [from reprisals]."

William Jernigan (later spelled Jernegan) was one of the Vineyard's most influential men. Despite the loyalist beliefs from which he never wavered, he was elected to public office many times. He died in 1817, nearly eighty-eight years old.

Recriminations against loyalists such as Jernigan were urged by the rebellious James Otis and Samuel Adams. They encouraged the formation of the Sons of Liberty, an activist group that, among other things, harassed some of the seventeen rescinders. We can't find evidence of any action against the two Vineyarders, Jernigan and Matthew Mayhew.

As the rebels intensified their action in Boston, more British troops were sent to dampen the fires. The presence of these additional troops led to confrontations, and on March 5, 1770, three colonists were killed by English troops (two more died later of their wounds) when a belligerent, stone-throwing mob confronted the soldiers. The shooting, called the Boston Massacre, caused such a citizens' uprising that the governor sent the English troops out of the city and onto islands in the harbor.

To lessen the growing tension, Parliament repealed most of the Townshend Acts, keeping the tax on tea. That tax was more a political than an economic issue, especially on the Vineyard, where ships came and went with no customs officer to enforce the law, making smuggling a way of life. Elsewhere in the colony, smuggled tea was common; it was brought in mostly by the Dutch, always keen to find ways to make money in trade.

To save the East India Company from bankruptcy, a likelihood increased by the Townshend Acts embargo, the British Parliament passed the Tea Act of 1773. It gave the company a virtual monopoly on the colonial tea market and remitted some previous duty the company had paid. The Tea Act was much misunderstood by colonists and soon such hotheads as Sam Adams were using it to incite revolt.

The first load of East India Company tea arrived aboard the ship *Dartmouth* in Boston on November 28, 1773. Public opinion was stirred up by Sam Adams and others in meetings held in Old South Church. Driving the rebellious cause was not so much the tea tax as the brazen manner with which the colonies were being treated by Parliament. Taxes could be levied as it wished, despite the fact that the colonies had no representation in the body.

The *Dartmouth* was thought to be in such danger as it awaited unloading that the governor ordered it to be tied up at Griffin's Wharf with an armed guard placed aboard. That guard was overwhelmed on the night of December 16 when a crowd of thousands, after being fired up by Sam Adams in a mass meeting, stormed the wharf and demanded that the *Dartmouth* and two other ships carrying tea, owned by the East India Company, be sent back to England.

As every schoolchild knows, the Boston Tea Party occurred when about fifty men disguised as Indians stormed the ships and dumped 342 chests of legal tea into the ocean. Similar tea parties took place in New York and other ports. Parliament responded with the Intolerable Acts, which closed the port of Boston until the ruined tea was paid for.

As the historian Mary Beth Norton pointed out (in private correspondence): "It is ironic that Americans today regard the Tea Party as a protest against higher taxes [when] it was actually against a monopoly and *lower* taxes, which the patriots feared would make legal tea so cheap that people would start buying it again."

The Tea Party is often cited as the spark that ignited the American Revolution. The fire started slowly. It was not until a year later that delegates from all the colonies met in Philadelphia to decide what to do; should they unite in revolt? The meeting in September and October 1774 was called the Continental Congress, a rather inflated name for a gathering of representatives from thirteen weak, thinly populated colonies along the eastern shore of the continent. Few delegates were in favor of going to war. They knew there was no chance to win against the world's most powerful nation and feared what retaliation it might bring. Instead, they urged colonists to boycott all British goods.

In November 1774 Vineyarders decided it was their turn to make a decision. Delegates from each town met in (West) Tisbury and passed a series of declarations, each taking a slap at the English, but it was a plea more for reconciliation than for independence. The twelve declarations ended with high praise for the king:

> By the Emigration of Our Ancestors . . . into parts . . . inhabited only by wild Beasts and Savages in human form. . . . (After a fair purchas hereof of the Indian Propriators). . . . Are now with but verry Little if any Expence to the Crown or People of Brittain become a verrey Valuable Part of the Dominions of the Brittish Monarch. . . .
>
> 11thly: With regard to non Importation, non Consumption and non Exportation of goods, wares and Merchandizes, we Earnestly recommend to the People of this county a Strict Conformity of their Conduct & Practice to the . . . Advice of the Late Grand American Congress.
>
> 12thly: And Finally . . . that no Tax be imposed on them but with their own consent, Given Personally or by their Representatives. . . . By Imposing Duties on commodities Imported here from Brittain for the Single purpose of Raising a revenue . . . [they] Have Taxed us without our Consent. . . .

And that Great Brittain and her Colonies may be blessed with an happy Union and harmoney . . . and that King George the Third, our most Rightfull Sovereign, both for himself and his Subjects may Long and hapily reign over the People of his widely Extended Empire: And that his Successors on the Brittish Throne . . . may be Protestants of his Illusterous Race . . . under whose wise, mild and Righteous Goverment their Subjects shall enjoy great Peace and hapiness is Our most Earnest Prayer to the Supreme ruler of the Universe to which we wish every Britton and Every Brittish American would Sincearly & Devoutly Say A Men.

It certainly was not a call for war, not even for revolt. The Vineyarders were playing a waiting game, hoping that a boycott of British goods would be enough to bring the controversy to an end. All they wanted was a chance to live peacefully, as they had been doing for generations.

But that was not to be. In retaliation for the continuing embargo, Parliament passed the Restraining Act of 1775, thereby closing the North Atlantic fishing grounds to all New England fishermen and prohibiting New England from trading with any nation except England.

Such an act, if enforced, would bring disaster to New England and its fishing ports, such as those on the Vineyard. In England serious opposition to the act was quick in coming. The English had become dependent upon New England fish, and they didn't want their supply stopped. Edmund Burke, the British philosopher, spoke against the measure in Parliament: "For some time, Mr. Speaker, has the Old World been fed from the New. . . . When I know that the Colonies in general owe little or nothing to any care of ours . . . when I see how profitable they have been to us, I feel all the pride of power sink and all presumption in the wisdom of human contrivances melt and die away within me."

As Tom Paine wrote later in *Common Sense,* trading with the colonies could not be stopped as long as "eating is the custom in Europe." Both sides may have been eager to end the rebellion without bloodshed, but feelings had become too heated for that.

Early on the morning of April 19, 1775, blood was shed in a sudden skirmish, lasting only minutes. But as Ralph Waldo Emerson wrote later, the shots were "heard round the world." A column of British troops marching from Boston to Concord to confiscate an ammunition depot was confronted by a small, unorganized group of rebels on Lexington Common. The gunfire, the start of the long war, seems to have been almost accidental.

The Americans, faced with overwhelming British strength, were already dispersing. But the British were ordered to fire, ill-advisedly it now seems. Eight Americans were killed, ten others were wounded. One British soldier was wounded.

The British troops then continued on to Concord. Another armed confrontation took place at Concord's North Bridge. British and Americans were killed in a disorderly, impromptu exchange of gunfire. The British then searched the town for the arms they had come to seize. There was plundering and several buildings were set afire. Only a small amount of ammunition was discovered. Both "battles" were insignificant, in retrospect, except to the dead and wounded.

But the war had begun.

(Among those fighting at Concord bridge was a chaplain from Medford, the Reverend Joseph Thaxter. Before the war had ended, he left the army and came to Edgartown to begin his forty-year reign as the village pastor.)

Marching back to Boston in formation, the British met disaster. Hundreds of American patriots lined the road, crouching behind stone walls and firing at the marching men. By the time the British column reached Boston, it had suffered nearly three hundred casualties. The Americans, despite the protection of the stone walls, had one hundred casualties.

Inadvertent and almost accidental though it had been, that day's action aroused the entire colony, creating, as Thomas Jefferson wrote to a friend, "a phrenzy of revenge." Governor Thomas Gage, the king's new leader in Massachusetts, saw the action as a direct attack on the Crown and placed the colony under martial law.

On the Vineyard, the feeling of neutrality was changing. Another meeting of town delegates was held in Tisbury to decide what to do. The colonial rebellion was not going to end peacefully, as they had hoped. An incomplete document in the Martha's Vineyard Historical Society archives indicates that Islanders no longer considered themselves neutral. Their concern now was defense, but who would protect them?

> There was a very large majority in favour of appling [applying] to General Court at Boston for soldiers. . . . All our arms were particularly inspected & now the minds of many were sounded amongst the young men to see who would Join the Volinteer Corps of Edgarton. We soon found the number of active young men, say 12. Some had call afterward to leave and go [to] sea but their number was soon replaced.

Twelve "active young men" could hardly defend the Island against the British navy. Money and men were needed. The General Court, after receiving the Island's request for soldiers, named Joseph Mayhew of Chilmark to head "A Committee of Safety for Dukes County." He was ordered to report to the legislature on how much money could be raised. Only one of the Island's three villages, Tisbury, replied to Mayhew's inquiries: "Tisbury reported that . . . they were under great Difficulty with respect to raising Money for that purpose as they have great occasion for Money to procure a necessary supply of Bread, Corn, and Money was very scarce amongst them thro' the failing of the whale-voyages last year, and thro' their having no Market for the Oyl they have since obtained."

The Island's plea of poverty rested on its declining whaling industry. From 1770 to 1775 the Vineyard had twelve active whaleships, which employed 156 seamen. Annually, an average of twelve hundred barrels of oil was produced. The Island ranked fifth in Massachusetts in whaling, far below Nantucket, Dartmouth, Wellfleet, and Boston (New Bedford took over later).

Mayhew reported to the General Court that the Island had neither the men nor the money to defend itself. Meanwhile, the shooting was drawing closer. His Majesty's sloop *Falcon* had been patrolling for a year out of Tarpaulin Cove on Naushon Island, just across Vineyard Sound. It was enforcing the act that prohibited the colony from trading with any nation except England. Its cannon was heard often, reminding Vineyarders of their vulnerability

The Historical Society has a copy of a *Falcon* log that covers about two months of that period. In one month it "brought too" fourteen vessels, seizing several as prizes and impressing eight seamen to replace some of its own crew who had deserted. The vessel often sailed into Holmes Hole. One day, while in the harbor, it fired a cannon and seized two suspicious vessels. No longer were Vineyarders able to feel safe.

All prospects of a negotiated peace had vanished. The battle at Bunker (Breed's) Hill made that clear. Unlike those at Lexington and Concord, that battle was not inadvertent. Both sides were ready. Americans were dug into entrenchments on the hill when the British redcoats came charging up, bayonets flashing. When it was over, the Americans were forced to retreat and the British occupied the hill, at great cost to both: more than one thousand British and four hundred Americans killed and wounded. The war had become deadly serious.

A few weeks before Bunker Hill, the Second Continental Congress had met in Watertown. Beriah Norton of Edgartown and James Athearn of Tisbury were there as delegates. Chilmark did not send a representative. The congress voted to form a Continental Army, and it chose Colonel George Washington of Virginia to command it.

It also voted to supply coats for local militiamen in all the towns. Edgartown's quota was thirty-six coats, Tisbury's thirty-two, and Chilmark's forty-four. It is unclear why Chilmark, with the smallest population, was to get the most coats. But it didn't matter; there is no record of the coats ever being received or of there being a need for them. There were no local militia units on the Island, according to William Jernigan, as we have seen.

Militias were not simply a defensive home guard. They were a reserve force that could be called up when General Washington needed more men. There was no public support for such a commitment on the Vineyard. Nor was there any way to recruit the more than one hundred men needed to fill the coats that had been authorized. Most men of military age were at sea, even with a war going on.

Their seagoing activities were sometimes illegal and thus brought suspicion and serious charges against both the Vineyard and Nantucket. There were persistent rumors that some vessels sailing from the islands were taking provisions to the British. The Massachusetts General Court in December 1775 claimed:

> Supplies of provisions, more than are necessary for internal consumption and for such voyages as may be prosecuted . . . have been lately shipped from this and the neighboring colonies for the islands of Nantucket and Martha's Vineyard, and there is great reason to suspect that the inhabitants . . . [have been] supplying our enemies with such provisions. . . . And the Select-Men . . . of each Town on Martha's Vineyard are directed forthwith to make strict enquiry into the importation of provisions into their respective towns since the 28th of September last, and of all provisions now in said towns, and to make returns thereof on oath to the Court. . . . And the inhabitants of this colony and of the other United Colonies are desired to withhold further supplies of provisions, fuel and other necessaries from said islands.

This was serious. If the united colonies complied with the request, the Vineyard (and Nantucket) would be without many necessities. Both were dependent on imported grain, butter, and cheese, the basic foodstuffs that provided most of the calories in colonial diets.

The Vineyard pledged to stop those few who were trading with the enemy. The General Court voted to annul its action, but only so far as the Vineyard was concerned. Nantucket was not included:

> [Having learned] upon inquiry . . . that it doth not appear that many of the inhabitants of the island of Martha's Vineyard ever had a disposition to supply the enemy with provisions, and . . . that they were suspected of corruptly doing the same, and such measures having been taken as (in all probability) will prevent the enemy from being supplied from that island, and the inhabitants thereof must suffer while under the aforementioned restraint, Therefore, Resolved, that the order of this Court . . . so far as it respects Martha's Vineyard only, be and hereby is annulled.

Nantucket, still subject to the embargo, strongly denied providing the British with any provisions.

On the Vineyard there continued to be great concern about how the Islanders could possibly repel an attack. With the few men and arms they had, residents would quickly be forced to surrender. Outside help was essential. On March 8, 1776, Tisbury petitioned the General Court "to see if they will grant us A further Supply of Men, Arms & Ammunition for the Defence of the Island against any Invasion." A reply to their petition was slow in coming.

That spring, the colonial congress authorized the arming of ships to intercept and capture any vessel carrying supplies to the British. These were the privateers, legalized pirates, who were required to post bonds and to take their conquests to "prize" ports. For Vineyarders and other mariners, privateering offered a way to make a profit patriotically.

The capture of enemy vessels by self-appointed patriots had been taking place for some time without any authority. What may have been the first naval "battle" of the Revolution was one such action at Holmes Hole in April 1775. Charles E. Banks describes it, citing *History of American Privateers* by Edgar McClay (1894) as his authority:

> What was probably the first naval skirmish of the Revolution took place . . . in one of our harbors, probably Homes Hole, as the party was under the command of Captain Nathan Smith. In a whaleboat, mounted with three swivels [small cannon], and a small crew of volunteers . . . he under-

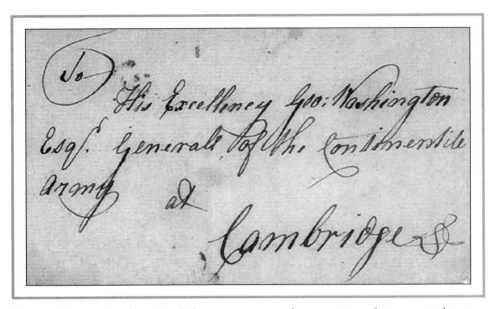

Captain Wemyss Orrok, an English mariner, wrote a letter to General George Washington in Cambridge, asking that his personal property, taken by the Americans who had captured his vessel near the Vineyard, be returned. Orrok was taking provisions to the British troops in Boston when it happened. (MVHS Collections)

took the capture of the armed schooner *Valante*, a tender of the British cruiser *Scarborough*. . . . After a struggle, the enemy struck colors and the victorious Captain Smith brought his prize into safe harbor.

That was a year before the Massachusetts colony legalized privateering. A year later a well-documented act of illegal privateering by Vineyarders involved Captain Wemyss Orrok of London. His ship, the *Harriot*, had been driven onto the shoals between the Vineyard and Nantucket during a fierce gale in early March 1776. Orrok normally carried goods between London and Jamaica, but for this voyage he had been unable to find a Jamaican cargo. He agreed instead to take a load of provisions to the British troops in Boston and was heading there when he ran aground. After a day or two on the shoal, he managed to get the *Harriot* off with little damage. While he was anchored in safe water, awaiting a favorable wind and tide to continue to Boston, his predicament became known in Edgartown. A sloop loaded with armed men and accompanied by several smaller craft sailed up to the *Harriot*. The men demanded that Captain Orrok surrender his vessel. He refused, shots were exchanged, and the captain was wounded. The Edgartown men took him and the *Harriot* into port as a prize of war.

The Vineyard Historical Society has a letter Captain Orrok wrote to General Washington describing his capture. It is addressed "To His Excellencey Geo. Washington Esq., Generale of the Continentile Army at Cambridge." Orrok stated that Beriah Norton of Edgartown had agreed to take the letter to Washington, then in Cambridge. (Somehow it ended up in the Historical Society. It may, of course, be a copy, but it looks like the original.) Orrok wrote:

May it Please your Excellency,

Having this opperturnity by Colonel Norton; I must beg leave to trouble you with this letter—Tho an intire Stranger, I flatter myself you will take compassion upon me when you hear of my preasent situation, which I must beg leave to lay before you.

I have been a constant trader from London to Jamaica for this some years back and no freight offering this voyage out, I was prevailed upon to take a Cargoe of Coals, Porter, etc., by Messrs. Morse & Company, the Shippers, for Boston where I was to be immediately Discharged, & from thence to proceed for Jamaica.

But unfortunately for me, was Drove upon Nantuckett Sholes, but Got off with Very little Dammage—soon after, I was attacted by an armed vessel from the Vinyard—and I being Not willing to part with my property without makeing some defence—But being unfortuneately Wounded, was oblidged to submit to superior force.

I am very Weak at preasent but as my wound is not Mortale I hope to have the Honner of waiting on you personally in a few weeks—At preasent I have the greatest reason imaginable to expect (without your Excellency interfiers on my behalf) that my private property which consists of a few [illegible] & some other trinkets which was intended for sale in Jamaica and likewise my wearing apparell which they are fully determined to Plunder from me. At Preasant I have nothing at my Command.

Should your Excellency be so very obliging to permit me to Depart for Jamaica, I should not so much regret they [*sic*] loss. But if it is my lot to be Detained here [in Edgartown] I would wish to appear a little Deasent, but that I cannot doe without your Excellency will take compassion upon me & send orders for them to restore what they so ardently wish to keep.

I beg your pardon for giving you all this trouble but can see no way of my having redress but by this method. I shall patiently relly upon your goodness.—I sincerly wish you health & happyness. I remain your Excellencys Most Obediant humble Serv't, Wemyss Orrok

What Orrok didn't know was that even had he made the trip to Boston, he would have received little help; the city was in disarray as the British occupiers prepared to leave.

There are no records to conclude the Orrok story. The fact that his letter remained on the Vineyard suggests that it never left the Island, and that Colonel Beriah Norton never took it to Cambridge. If Orrok's captors eventually set him free without the *Harriot* (which had been taken to Dartmouth as a prize), we hope they gave him his "wearing apparrell" so he would "appear a little Deasent" as he made his way to Jamaica.

Privateering was profitable, legal or illegal. The prize was divided among the owners of the capturing vessel and its crew. If the captor was a bonded privateer, the division was controlled by law. But in the case of the *Harriot*, the armed men had no official status. The law had not yet been passed and letters of authority (marque) were not yet being issued, nor was any bond required. There were no rules. The prize belonged to those who captured it.

The *Harriot* capture was piracy, nothing more. The men involved were just an excited bunch of armed men eager for profit. The fact that the *Har-*

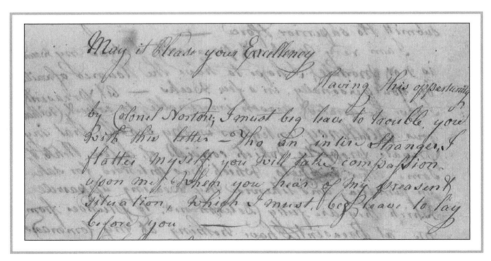

The opening paragraph of Orrok's pleading letter to George Washington.
(MVHS Collections)

riot was said to be carrying provisions to the British made it fair game, they claimed. The sloop they used to capture the *Harriot* did not belong to them. It was a transient vessel from New York whose captain agreed to take them out to do battle. The Edgartown men did all the fighting, and they afterward disputed the sloop captain's claim to his share of the prize. We don't know how the dispute was resolved, but it is clear that profit was the men's motive, not patriotism.

That was usually the case in privateering. And why not? Money was scarce and any way to make it was welcome. English naval vessels harassed mariners, preventing many from working at fishing, at whaling, and in coastal trade. Americans saw nothing wrong with retaliation.

Money was so hard to get that on April 30, 1776, Thomas Cooke petitioned the General Court to abate the taxes owed to the colony by the Vineyard, listing four reasons:

> 1st: [When these taxes were assessed] the town had 1000 tons of whaleships . . . at this time, not one Vessel in any employ except one to the Eastward [to Maine] for Lumber.
>
> 2nd: Because a great Number of Pilots that used to have Almost constant bu'ness [business] in Piloting Vessells that frequented [the] Island in abundance, is entirely lost.
>
> 3rd: Because diverse Publick Houses in different Harbours of sd County, purpose to entertain Ship's Company, etc., was profatable, in consequence . . . their yearly income was set on sd County by the Assessor & enlarged their proportion of Taxes at the Valuation, which at this time [is] useless.
>
> 4th: The great expense the Inhabitants of sd County are at, by reason of obtaining Supplies from the Main Land, which it convey's in small Cedar Boats, said Island being incapable to produce not more than one half of a Supply for its inhabitants who are general seafaring Men & poor.

Cooke's petition tells us that the Island was producing only one-half the items it needed. It has often been stated that the Vineyard was self-sufficient during these years, but Cooke contradicts that assertion.

There also are contradictions in the role Islanders actually played in the war against England. William Jernigan, as we have seen, persuaded the General Court to exempt the Vineyard and Nantucket from enlisting a company of militia, saving "each Island more than $1000 per annum and in case of war I am in hopes will save our Towns" from retribution.

This document lists some of the 1776 Vineyard militia men, with their signatures, "in the service of the Massachusetts Bay Colony for the defense and protection of the Sea Coast," although the colony had declared its independence from England. (MVHS Collections)

After the war Colonel Beriah Norton stated, when he sought restitution from England for the losses Vineyarders suffered in Grey's Raid in 1778 (details of which are in the next chapter), that no Islanders were ever called up to serve in the colonial army. Norton's statement: "When Troops were levied in every other place to serve against the King, not an individual was raised upon that Island [Martha's Vineyard] for that service."

There were two seacoast-defense companies on the Island in 1776, totaling about 150 men. Such companies, unlike militia, were not subject to being called up to serve in Washington's army. They were a defensive force. Two seacoast-defense companies were not enough to repel an invasion, so, as we have seen, Islanders in the spring of 1776 petitioned the General Court to provide militia from the mainland. The state sent about one hundred men, who made up a third company of militia. The Islanders began to feel a bit more secure.

In July 1776 the Declaration of Independence was signed. The thirteen colonies were now officially at war with England, a war they seemed unlikely to win. The British had a trained army in addition to the Royal Navy; the colonies had a motley crew of poorly trained militiamen who served a few months and then went home. Washington's Continental Army had relatively few regular soldiers, and there was not enough time to train the militia because of their brief tour of duty, only ninety days.

For help the Americans turned to France, England's longtime enemy. France, itself a monarchy, had no enthusiasm for encouraging rebellions against a king, but it was willing to make an exception. Damaging England was more important than principle. But the help must be secret, undercover. Despite having money problems of his own, the French king, Louis XVI, authorized one million *livre* for the Americans. A sham organization was created to transfer the money and arms in secret. Silas Deane of Connecticut went to Paris as the agent for the colonies. He and his French counterpart soon managed to manipulate the accounts so that not just a little of the money ended up in their pockets.

With the British navy controlling Vineyard waters, the state Board of War stationed lookouts on one of the Island's hills to sound an alert when an enemy warship approached. It also provided six whaleboats and three cannon. A feeling of security was building among Vineyarders.

That feeling was short-lived. When the English drove Washington's army out of New York and took control of the Hudson River, the Americans suffered many casualties. Washington called for more militia. Each town was ordered to send men. The off-Island militia protecting the Vineyard was recalled. The Island, as usual, petitioned for special treatment:

> We are much alarmed at the Dismission of the soldiers which ware alowed as a Defence for our Island as the Kings Army is so near us [in Newport]—and as we find . . . we are called upon to tack [take] one quarter of our men and send them . . . to join the Continental Army. . . . Your Petitioners humbly pray that your honours would . . . Tack [take] one thought on our auwful Surcumstances—and grant that we may be Released as to Rasing our Men to go of [off] the Island on any ocation.

The General Court granted the request, but it added a bit of advice: "Removal of stock, &c, to the main-land is recommended."

That advice came as a shock to Vineyarders. How would they survive if their livestock were removed? Thirty-five Chilmark residents, who owned thousands of sheep, signed a petition to the General Court, declaring they would have to move if their sheep were taken away. The lengthy document stressed what the Island was doing to support the rebellion. The colony's privateers depended upon Vineyard harbors for provisioning and refitting. If they were forced to leave with their livestock, British forces at Newport, "no further than twelve leagues" away, would move in:

> If nothing better than this can be done with the stock belonging to Marthas Vineyard, in what a state of wretchedness must the owners thereof be reduced! For if that stock be removed where will they find pasture or Hay for it? And if for want thereof they are obliged to sell it, where will they find Buyers who will give them anything near the value thereof? And in this way the People of this Island would be likely to suffer almost a total loss of their Stock.
>
> They would suffer also . . . the loss of their Houses and lands, which they must depart. For without stock they will not be able to till it. And if this Island be forsaken by its inhabitants, it will . . . in all Probability be taken possession of by the Enemy.

The thirty-five petitioners regretfully pointed out that all the men in Chilmark did not support the rebellion; many were still loyal to the king and not eager to take up arms:

> There are yet (we are sorry to find ground to say it) some here who have manifested at least a Doubt of our being in the Right, in taking up arms

and fighting against the Forces of the King of Great Britain, and they with others have openly expressed a Belief that Britain will conquer & subdue America, and have labored to infuse such a belief into others. . . . There is a considerable number of men here who appear to be very Doubtful which side will finally overcome . . . and who therefore chuse to be as stil and inactive as possible . . . and are accordingly averse to doing anything towards the Defending of this Island by arms.

That was, as we have seen, the position of William Jernigan of Edgartown. But that spirit was weakening as the situation worsened. Shortly before the Chilmark petition, there had been a report of fighting on Naushon Island, the first such report. A sailor on the British ship *Diamond* in January 1777 wrote of the conflict, mistakenly thinking the skirmish had occurred on Martha's Vineyard. But it was on Naushon, probably at Tarpaulin Cove:

> We sailed for New-York on the 27th of November [1776] on a cruize. We put into Martha's Vinyard and sent our boat on shore with a flag of truce. The rebels let the boat come within gun-shot and then fired upon them and wounded one man in the boat; to revenge this insult, we landed our marines and a party of sailors under fire from the ship; the rebels posted themselves on a hill and fired very briskly from behind the rocks and bushes; however, we drove them off the island. We had in the action one man killed and one wounded; the rebels lost four killed and many wounded. We got some plunder such as oxen and poultry; then burnt their houses and barns, etc. From thence we sailed to Rhode-Island.

That letter was published in *Naval Documents of the American Revolution*. Another letter, written to Sir Peter Parker, commander of the British fleet at Newport, by John McCartney aboard the H.M.S. *Ambuscade* and published in *Early History of Naushon Island* by Amelia Forbes Emerson, places the encounter on Naushon. After describing many of the same details given in the sailor's letter, above, he gives a graphic report:

> [We] drove all the Rebels, now grown pretty numerous, from off the Island into some small vessels on the other Side with the loss of 4 or 5 of their Men killed. Their villainous Conduct in firing at a Flag of Truce intitled them now to all the Horrors of Rebellion, which was immediately put into Execution by setting Fire to every thing that would burn, so that naught House, Barn, Hay nor Indian Corn that could be met with escaped

the Flames, nor did the live Stock share a better Fate for what could not be carried off was Shot.

When Lord Howe in New York learned of the overreaction by his men, he wrote to Sir Peter Parker in Newport of his shock. The English troops should have been more understanding, he wrote: "I rather suppose they are of a Class wholly uninformed in such Distinctions [as not firing on a flag of truce]. . . . It is my earnest desire that . . . every requisite facility be given to promote [an understanding of why it was done]."

Another report in *Naval Documents of the American Revolution* lists forty-nine American prisoners held in Newport who were exchanged for captured British sailors on January 17, 1777. Six are listed as being from Martha's Vineyard:

Josiah Stelton, Seaman, *Wolf.*
Dan Kenney, Master, *Greenwich Packet.*
Thos. Coffin, Master, *Sea Horse,* brig, Seamen John Green,
    Emanuel Decker and Emanuel Coffin, on the same vessel.

Of the six, Thomas Coffin is the only one we can find as a possible Vineyard resident at that time. The Coffins were an important family in Edgartown and the capture and later the exchange of Captain Coffin for British prisoners must have been major news, but again we find no confirmation. The document doesn't describe the details of his capture.

Vineyard harbors were sometimes used as temporary places to hold prize vessels until they could be taken to a port and turned over to a prize officer. These harbors were not always secure havens, as we learn from a report in March 1777 in the *London Chronicle,* a newspaper with little rebel sympathy: "Letters from Rhode-island say that two of our frigates, belonging to the squadron there, being on a cruise, looked into the harbour of Martha's Vineyard Island, where they saw a large ship which they took to be a prize carried in, and also another vessel, a sloop; on this they stood as close as they could and in the evening cut them both out and brought them safe off without the loss of a single man."

British warships roamed the coastal waters freely and the Americans needed a counterforce. They had no illusions that they would ever be able to match Britain's fleet. Instead, what they could assemble would be, like the privateers, a guerilla force, intercepting the flow of supplies to British bases on the mainland. At first they were state-owned. One of the first was the Connecticut state ship *Oliver Cromwell,* which spent several weeks in Vineyard harbors trying to enlist a crew.

It was not an easy task to sign up mariners. They preferred privateering to serving on a naval vessel. There was more money to be made on privateers with less discipline and danger, preying, as they did, only on unarmed merchant vessels. Privateers from either side were welcomed by Vineyard farmers and merchants, who sold them provisions. One such transaction was recorded when the American privateer *Clarendon* stopped at Edgartown in the winter of 1776–77 and paid William Daggett one pound, 10 shillings for "Fresh Meet at Marthes Vinyard."

Gradually, as Vineyarders began moving away from their neutrality, some of the younger, more eager patriots began harassing loyalists. William Jernigan was one such victim. Jernigan, one of the seventeen "disgraced" representatives who had voted on the king's side in the failed attempt to rescind Sam Adams's letter, was proud of his loyalty to the king. It was reported that "Jernigan and his son, Thomas, had sung and danced when they heard that the British Troops had landed at New York." Overzealous Edgartown patriots retaliated one night in January 1777. Years later Jernigan described the episode (at times his report slips into the third person):

> On the Night preceding the 30th of January in the year of our Lord 1777, between the hours of one and two o'clock in the morning, I, William Jernigan, then being up with his daughter Sally in his arms, his wife Mary then being very unwell, Ebenezer Smith then coming into said Jernigan's House, informed him that his House was surrounded with fifty or sixty men with guns, swords and clubs, and he, the said Jernigan, was ordered forthwith out of his own House amongst those armed men in the ded [dead] of the night and ordered to march with them to the House of Peter Norton, Esq., about four miles through the woods and when we arived at Mr. Norton's House, he, being then in bed, asked what is the matter?
>
> Some of the Company answered that the said Jernigan and his son Thomas sung and danced when they heard that the British Troops had Landed at New York; the said Jernigan then answered that there was not one word of truth in the Report and that it was a ley [lie], &c.
>
> And then some of the armed men insisted that the said Jernigan should write and signe a Papper, which he did; but I never heared of it

afterwards. The armed men then fil [file] out among themselves and desappeared, etc., and the said Jernigan returned to his own House about seven o'clock in the morning. But what must [be] the anxiety of his wife and children at the time to have him carried off by force of armes in the ded time of the night, &c.

Certainly, as Jernigan wrote, it must have been a very frightening event, not only for himself, but even more so for his wife and children. He named the nine men who led the posse: "Samuel Look, Samuel Daggett, Stephen Cunneham, Zaphaniah Chase, Timothy Chase, George West, Ebenezer Roger, Elijah Butler Jr., and William Daggett." He also listed eight more who were in the mob "and a number" who saw what happened and would testify.

A few weeks later the Connecticut navy brig *Defence* sailed to the Vineyard seeking recruits after failing to fill its complement in New London. It isn't known whether any of those enthusiastic rebels signed up. The brig's commander, Lieutenant Samuel Smedley, had been optimistic: "I have therefore Got the Brig Ready for Sea so that there is Nothing Wanting but Men, which there is No Chance of Getting here [New London]. We have not More than forty Men now belonging to the Brig & but few Seamen Amongst them, but Shall not be Detained any on that Account As I think there is Great Prospect of Getting our Complement at the Vineyard soon."

The war became very real for Gay Head residents in September 1777, when some of them took part in a deadly gunfight, according to a journal kept on the H.M.S. *Cerberus*: "At 6 AM saw a sl[oop] off Montock [Montauk] weighed and Gave Chace. . . . At 2 PM at Gay head . . . at 4 Run the Chace on shore who prov'd to be a Schooner, Loaded Wt Rum, Sugar & Warlike Stores, Anch'd within Gun shott of her & kept a constant fire upon a Body of Arm'd Men lurking about the Beach while our Boats went & Burnt the Vessell, had 1 Man kill'd & 1 Wounded, [?] past 6 weighed & came to Sail."

Although the British journal makes no mention of it, testimony given on the Vineyard in 1817 in a totally different context indicates that there was a Vineyarder killed in the skirmish. He was Sharper Michael, who was struck by a musket ball fired from the *Cerberus*. Sharper was a black man who lived on Squibnocket and had gone to the beach to see what the shooting was all about. If that 1817 court testimony has been interpreted correctly, Michael would have been the first Vineyarder to be killed in the Revolution.

British privateers sailing into Vineyard harbors seeking fresh food and water usually received a friendly reception, but not always. One of those unpleasant episodes was reported in a Boston newspaper:

> [From] a Gentleman of undoubted Veracity, who arrived in Town last Sunday from Martha's Vineyard, we learn that the British Pirate [privateer] Ship . . . *Ambuscade,* of 32 Guns . . . lay at Anchor in Holmes's Hole. . . . [The captain] sent several Flags [of truce] on Shore begging that his Crew might be supplied by the Inhabitants with fresh Provisions. . . . He was refused, receiving an Answer that they had no Traitors there, nor should they be provided with any Thing, but what they got at the Point of a Bayonet and Mouth of the Cannon.

The Vineyard Historical Society has in its archives a somewhat different account of the *Ambuscade* episode than the one described in the newspaper. When Captain McCartney of the privateer sent a party ashore requesting supplies, Colonel Beriah Norton, head of the Island's defense committee, was notified. Norton sent back a message to the captain, explaining that the Island was suffering from shortages of food and supplies and couldn't be as generous as he would like. He hoped the captain would understand. Then Colonel Norton added:

> As to a Small matter for Capt. McCartney's Table, the Committee will Present him with Three Sheep & doz. or Two of Fowls Tomorrow at 10 oClock at the Landing where his Boat has Landed this day. Expecting Capt. McCartney will not make any further demands on these People as there Case is extraordinary. . . . Sheep on this place are but Indifferent as they have no winter keeping. If this is Agreeable, Capt. McCartney will please to return an answer by the Boat.

The Island didn't have a surplus of "fresh Provisions" to sell, either to friend or to foe. The embargo the British had placed on Martha's Vineyard and Nantucket had forced residents to rely on a black market. Entrepreneurs in Connecticut and Long Island would load small boats with flour, corn, and wood and sail to the islands during the night to avoid capture by the British stationed in Newport. They charged exorbitant prices for the provisions. It was not an easy time to be an Islander.

The war would be brought home to Vineyarders in ways other than food shortages. Occasionally the Island became a haven for sailors whose vessels had been captured and destroyed—or, as often happened, had been wrecked. For example: "A privateer sloop of 6 guns was sent this day [into Newport] by the *Unicorn* [a British warship], who took her yesterday near Martha's Vineyard, on which Island she run another of the same force on shore, and burnt her. Crews of both escaped."

The American privateer *Hampden*, setting out on a long cruise, ran ashore at Cape Poge in October 1777 and "soon bilged" in the surf. All hands, along with guns and stores, were saved by Edgartown residents. Another brig, the *Fox*, did the same a week later.

There were other ways that the war kept drawing closer to Vineyarders. Local men were being recruited to serve on war vessels. The Vineyard's maritime history made it a fertile place to find able seamen. In June 1777 Marine Lieutenant John Trevett, aboard the twelve-gun American navy sloop *Providence*, wrote: "We are under sail bound to the Vineyard to get a few men. [Stopped] at [New] Bedford and pressed one John Scranton, one of my townsmen. . . . Sailed for Old Town [Edgartown], arrived the next day & got what men we could; lay there 2 days and then ran for Sandy hook."

In December a large privateer, beginning a five-month cruise with a crew of 125 and twenty cannons, did the same thing: "Rhode Island privateer ship *Marlborough* anchored in Tarpaulin Cove on the evening of 25 Dec. and the next day put into Holmes Hole . . . seeking seamen. She returned to Martha's Vineyard on 29 December to recruit more men before departing on her Cruise on 2 January 1778."

General Washington, after his impressive victory at Saratoga in October 1777, had moved his army into Valley Forge for the winter. But the war at sea couldn't take the winter off. A British fleet anchored in Holmes Hole in February 1778 while en route to Boston from Newport. It was carrying provisions for the convention troops in Boston waiting to be shipped back to England. They were the 5,700 men of Burgoyne's army who had surrendered at Saratoga. Under a convention of war (hence the term "convention troops") they had been marched to Boston to be sent back to England and were under oath not to return to fight. The English wanted to be sure Americans had no excuse to attack the unarmed mercy fleet carrying provisions for prisoners of war. Frederick Mackenzie, a British officer in Newport, detailed the precautions taken:

The Transports for Boston . . . are to go, over the Shoals, as it is termed here, to Boston; that is, they are to go between Martha's Vineyard and the Main, and so close around Cape Cod, into Cape Cod harbour. . . . If they were to go round the Nantucket Shoals, they would be in danger, as light ships, of being blown off the Coast this boisterous season. All the transports go as Cartel ships and the utmost care has been taken by Lord Howe to take out of them all Cannon, Arms and Military Stores. Not even a Cutlass is allowed to be taken on board. All this is necessary to prevent the Rebels from having any pretence for detaining the troops or Molesting the Ships. There are 2000 barrels of Flour on board . . . to be landed for the use of the Convention troops. . . . If the troops are permitted to embark [for England] immediately, the flour is to be sent back here for the use of the troops on this Island [Rhode Island], who have been served with [hard] Biscuit for five weeks past.

The trip would be a slow one. Three weeks after the fleet left Newport, it was still anchored in Holmes Hole. Such were the problems of sailing, especially in Vineyard and Nantucket sounds, with their strong tidal currents, shoals, and contrary winds. Newport got the news of the long delay from two men who had arrived from Sandwich: "These men say that the ships for Boston sailed from Holmes's hole in Martha's Vineyard only two days ago, having waited there for many days for a fair wind to take them over a particular part of the Shoals."

The presence of so many enemy vessels and sailors, unarmed though they were, in Holmes Hole must have given Vineyarders much to talk about.

Two days after the men from Sandwich arrived, two more visitors sailed into Newport: "9th March: Two men came in yesterday in a small boat from Martha's Vineyard." The journal tells us nothing about why the two men from the Vineyard had sailed to the British naval base at Newport or what news they might have carried. The matter-of-fact tone suggests such trips to the mainland were not unusual.

France, encouraged by the diplomatic skills of Benjamin Franklin as well as the British defeat at Saratoga, made known its support of the colonies when it signed a treaty of alliance with the Americans in February 1778. The action told England that the colony was recognized as an independent nation, the first such recognition. France's move forced the

British toward conciliation. They had no desire for the "minor" rebellion to turn into a war with France. Americans, sensing that victory was now possible, turned down the British overtures.

The news from France was especially welcome at Valley Forge, where a cold winter and food shortages had brought on depression. France's alliance was something to celebrate. Washington ordered an extra ration of rum and banquet tables were set up. The troops, their spirits lifted only in part by the rum, paraded before a reviewing stand where George and Martha Washington sat with the army's newest and youngest general, the Marquis de Lafayette. Washington, showing a "countenance of uncommon delight and complacence," rallied the soldiers, showering praise on Louis XVI and ending with "Huzzah! Huzzah! Long live the King of France!" For the first time Washington seemed to believe that the war could be won. The powerful French fleet would destroy the British, cut the enemy's supply lines, and bring victory. So certain was Washington that he told his brother the odds were now one hundred to one in his favor.

Expecting the French navy to attack, the British were ordered to leave Philadelphia and join the other British troops in New York. There was no feeling of panic, no rush—plenty of time for farewell parties. The redcoats had been enjoying the social life in Philadelphia among the overwhelmingly loyal upper class. Before leaving, the army hosted "a magnificent entertainment to grace his [Sir William Howe's] departure," with a banquet, a fancy dress ball, and fireworks. They were celebrating a retreat, it would seem. But celebrate they did.

Washington's plan had been for d'Estaing, the French admiral, to sail into Delaware Bay before the English realized they were coming. The stronger French fleet would destroy the surprised enemy, perhaps ending the war. But the plan failed. By the time d'Estaing got there, the British fleet was gone.

The French fleet seemed to be in no hurry, as it took eighty-seven days to cross the Atlantic, twice the normal time. Even with their prolonged partying, the British had no need to hurry out of Philadelphia. The French admiral, whose attitude throughout the entire campaign seems to have been tentative, blamed his slow voyage on poor winds and the time he needed to train his new crews in their battle stations.

The English now were consolidated in their two bases in the northeast: New York and Newport. Newport was the more vulnerable. On an island (the original Rhode Island) in Narragansett Bay, it was being blockaded by a large rebel army under General John Sullivan on the mainland. All fresh provisions had to come by water, from Block Island (three to four hundred wildfowl, delivered daily), Long Island (grain and wood), the Elizabeth Islands (lamb), and even, it is said, occasional shipments from the Vineyard and Nantucket. The people in all those places needed the money. Patriotism was put aside.

Fearing a British invasion of Naushon Island to get food, the Island's owners decided to move their livestock to the mainland. When the British learned of the plan, they sent some transport ships over to purchase the animals (or at least some of them) before they were moved. Frederick Mackenzie, the English officer in Newport, wrote in his journal on May 9, 1778:

> The transports from the Elizabeth Islands arrived last night in the Seconnet passage. The troops have been very successful and met with no opposition. The two transports have brought 884 Sheep and Lambs—150 of them were bought from such of the Inhabitants as were well affected [loyal] and willing to sell them. The rest, being the property of noted Rebels, were taken without payment. The party has also secured about 1000 more sheep and lambs on a small Island under the protection of the *Unicorn* until the transports can return for them. The whole were taken from Nashawn Island, which is the largest of the Elizabeth Islands. . . .
>
> A Company of Rebels were posted upon it [Naushon], but they retired upon the appearance of our fleet. Our people burnt the Barracks they had occupied and destroyed two pieces of Cannon. . . . An officer and 40 men are to return immediately for the remainder of the Sheep.

The entry reveals the guidelines the British used when paying for confiscated items: loyal residents were paid, rebels were not. It also makes clear that the war was drawing closer to the Vineyard. Frank Moore, in *Diary of the American Revolution,* quotes a news account published on May 31, 1778, which confirms that closeness: "Last week, a party of British troops from R.I . . . made a descent upon . . . Bristol and Warren . . . plundering and destroying all they could lay their hands on. . . . Another party from the same place, consisting of 150 men . . . landed at the mouth of Fall River . . . to burn Tiverton and the mills."

Flames from those fires must have lighted the western sky that night and Vineyarders no doubt slept uneasily, wondering if they would be next. Little did they know how much closer the war would be in a few months.

Frustrated by finding no English ships in Delaware Bay, d'Estaing sailed to Sandy Hook, at the entrance to New York Harbor. Across that sandy spit of land, on which the British had mounted some cannon, the French admiral could see the enemy ships lined up, ready for battle. This will be, the Frenchman thought, the decisive battle, the one he had crossed the Atlantic to wage and win. His larger ships with greater firepower would destroy the English, who would be unable to escape from the harbor. Meeting with his captains and pilots to plan his attack, he was told that their greater size was actually a disadvantage: the men-of-war were too large to enter the harbor. They drew too much water.

He refused to believe it and offered any pilot who would take his ships inside the harbor a huge bonus. (The story says it was to be his own money.) No pilot took up his challenge. Still unconvinced, d'Estaing sent some small boats out that night to sound the depth of the channel. They came back with the news that the pilots were right. There wasn't enough water for his ships to enter the harbor. The British fleet was safe inside.

A council of war was held by the French admiral and American aides of General Washington. (The two leaders themselves never met face-to-face.) It was decided that the French fleet, with its four thousand soldiers on board, would sail to Newport and attack the English naval base there. The attack would combine the French troops with the five thousand Americans under General Sullivan already there, in addition to soldiers that Washington would send under forced march from New York. The Americans would cross over to Rhode Island from the northeast at Howland's Ferry while d'Estaing's marines would storm ashore from their ships on the southwest. It would be a classic pincer attack, with the cannon of the warships pounding the Newport defenses to protect the advancing troops. All that firepower would surely bring victory, and perhaps end the war.

In London, the British were worried. And no wonder. The entry of the French had changed everything. King George wrote to Lord North from Windsor Castle, for the first time expressing doubt about victory. Negotiation was now his goal: "We must content ourselves with distressing the Rebels and not think of any other conduct until the end of the French, which if successful will oblige the Rebels to submit to more reasonable [terms] than can at this hour be obtained." Parliament began debating whether to abandon the war in order to concentrate on defending the West Indies, Florida, and Canada to prevent the French from taking them over. The great power of England was trembling.

Admiral d'Estaing, now with his third chance to destroy the English fleet, arrived off Point Judith at the mouth of Narragansett Bay on July 29, 1778. The troops General Washington had sent from New York were still on forced march in eastern Connecticut. The attack had to be delayed until they arrived, which gave the British time to move their soldiers from the northern end of Rhode Island to Newport, where they dug strong defensive positions.

The two allied commanders, Sullivan and d'Estaing, agreed to attack on August 10; by then Washington's troops would have arrived. For unexplained reasons, Sullivan sent his troops across to Rhode Island one day early, August 9. The Frenchman was furious. His ships were not yet in place to land the four thousand men for the pincer maneuver. Frantically, he tried to speed the movement, but a thick fog blanketed the bay. By the time the marines were ashore on Rhode Island, the fog was so dense that neither commander knew where the other was. The allies, ready to attack, had to wait for the fog to lift.

When it cleared the following morning, a lookout atop the mast on d'Estaing's flagship spotted a fleet of British warships approaching from the south. It was Admiral Howe, coming from New York to defend Newport. Told of the approaching enemy, d'Estaing recalled his marines. He was concerned about being trapped inside the bay, unable to defend himself. He sailed his ships into open water to prepare for a naval battle with the British fleet. The American soldiers on Rhode Island were shocked to see the French depart, not knowing the reason. As the French warships sailed past Newport, they fired twenty-five hundred rounds of cannon into the British dug in there. No major target was hit, later reports showed.

The two fleets were still jockeying for battle positions south of Point Judith when darkness fell. Both sides went into defensive positions until daylight. During the night a powerful northeaster, perhaps a hurricane, pounded the coast. The two fleets were battered: both suffered great damage, though the French were hit harder. D'Estaing's flagship, the *Languedoc*, was dismasted and its rudder lost, and it wallowed helplessly in the huge waves. Finally, during a lull in the storm, the ship was towed to a safer spot.

For the third time d'Estaing had lost his chance. He sent a messenger ashore to inform General Sullivan that he was taking the fleet to Boston for repairs, and with him would go the four thousand soldiers Sullivan had been counting on. The attack on Newport had to be abandoned. Seeing the French warships sail away to the east, Howe took his fleet west to New York. Both sides needed repairs.

Washington's almost sure victory had not been won. The joint attack, so filled with hope, had failed. General Washington wrote to his brother:

> The whole [story of Rhode Island] may be summed up in a few words and amounts to this, that an unfortunate storm (so it appeared, and yet ultimately it may have happened for the best) and some measures taken in consequence of it by the French Admiral, perhaps unavoidably, blasted in one moment the fairest hopes that ever were conceived; and, from a moral certainty of success, rendered it a matter of rejoicing to get our own troops safe off the [Rhode] Island.
>
> If the [English] garrison of [Newport], consisting of nearly 6000 men, had been captured, as there was, in appearance at least, a hundred to one in favor of it, it would have given the finishing blow to British pretensions of sovereignty over this country.

Although Vineyarders did not know it, they, too, had a major stake in the Newport struggle. If that battle, carrying Washington's "fairest hopes," had gone as he had expected, Grey's Raid, the most traumatic event in the history of Martha's Vineyard, would never have taken place.

4

Grey's Raid: An Attack or a Shopping Expedition?

The ferocious storm that battered the English and French fleets as they prepared for battle off Narragansett Bay in late August 1778 did more than shatter the masts of European ships; it also shattered the hopes of Americans.

The French alliance had given birth to great expectations, as beleaguered Americans allowed themselves to dream of victory. But d'Estaing's failures so shattered their dream that an ugly backlash developed; the French were accused of cowardice and deceit. There was even violence. General Sullivan, the brash, inelegant Irishman who led the rebels blockading the English base on Rhode Island, wrote a critical letter to Admiral d'Estaing, who then was sailing his storm-damaged fleet to Boston, having left Sullivan without naval support. The Frenchman was insulted. Who was this commoner, this Irishman, who wrote to him this way? James Flexner wrote in his biography of Washington:

> From the first, d'Estaing and Sullivan had got on badly. The French courtier-admiral had complained that the short-set, ruddy, rough Irish American frontiersman "has shown towards me the manner of a commander to his servant; he styles himself my general . . . while [his] troops were good for a defensive, they had no qualities necessary for attack." The Americans . . . accused the French of being "thin, polite, and always dancing. . . ."
>
> After the French had sailed away, Sullivan insulted them in his general orders. . . . Lafayette took offense and insulted the American officers back, becoming, as he angrily reported to Washington, "more upon a warlike footing in the American lines than when I come near the British lines at Newport."

97

D'Estaing was a French count, a general in the French army, and an admiral in the French navy. He was not accustomed to insults. He had no desire to die for democracy. He was fighting for his king. A few years later in Paris, he was captured and guillotined by the revolutionists for doing just that—battling for his king. He had come to America to defeat the British, not to risk his men and ships for a piece of real estate called Rhode Island. He would take his damaged fleet to Boston for repairs no matter what General Sullivan thought.

Once the French arrived in Boston, the insults grew worse. Street fights broke out between d'Estaing's men and the patriots, who called the French cowards, unreliable allies, and worse. One such incident at a bakery became deadly. The French, always anxious to eat well, had set up a bakery to provide their sailors and marines with fresh white bread daily. Boston residents, who had been without white bread for years, became violent. Mackenzie, the Welsh diarist in Newport, wrote: "There have been some Riots at Boston, on account of the Scarcity of Wheat bread. The French Seamen are served with white bread, and the British Seamen on the American service receiving hard bread, or Indian corn [bread] only, assembled and forced some bread from the bake houses. A French Major and several others have been killed."

That was not what George Washington had expected when, at Valley Forge, he had called for "huzzahs" in praise of the French king Louis. Worried that d'Estaing might take his fleet and leave, he wrote soothingly to the Frenchman: "I most ardently hope, that my countrymen will exert themselves to give you every aid in their power, that you may, as soon as possible, recover from the damage you have suffered, and be in a condition to renew your efforts against the common enemy."

That same day General Washington wrote to Congress: "I will use every means in my power to conciliate any differences that may have arisen in consequence of Count d'Estaing's going to Boston, and to prevent a publication of the protest."

These were difficult days for General Washington. He had been so hopeful at Valley Forge, but now he began to resent the "foreign aid," French and German. As Flexner noted:

> Washington was very angry. He had no reason to love the French. They had been his enemies in his previous war and had incited the Indians to great brutality against Virginians. He could not doubt that France had

entered the war for no high-minded motives but because it was to her "interest" to weaken Great Britain. . . . [The German] Steuben was off junketing to Congress . . . to have most of the supervision of the army taken away from Washington and put in his own hand. In a fury, Washington wrote, "I do most devoutly wish that we had not a single foreign officer among us except the Marquis de Lafayette."

While d'Estaing was sailing to Boston, Admiral Howe, his ships quickly repaired in New York, had returned to Rhode Island, expecting to battle the French. When told they had gone to Boston, he set out in pursuit, knowing that d'Estaing was sailing under jury-rigging and would have slow going. He hoped to intercept the fleet before it reached the safety of Boston Harbor. But he didn't. The French were in Boston by the time Howe got to Massachusetts Bay. Aware that he would be bombarded by rebel batteries on the harbor islands if he tried to get into Boston, he returned to Rhode Island.

Admiral d'Estaing never again was active in the fighting in New England. When his ships were finally repaired (a slow process, which enabled the Frenchman to work his charm on many of Boston's high society, including Abigail Adams), he left New England on November 4, 1778, for the West Indies to fight the English. He was still fighting for his king, not the colonies. Before leaving Boston, according to a 1795 history, he published a manifesto to be distributed in Canada, reminding the Canadians of their former loyalty to France and urging them to rebel against the British.

A second English fleet was at Newport when Howe got there. It was carrying 4,300 troops under General Clinton and had sailed up from Whitestone, Long Island, to join the fighting. A powerful naval force with warships and twenty troop transports, this was the fleet that would conduct Grey's Raid on Martha's Vineyard.

The British and Hessian troops on board were eager for battle, but there was no enemy for them to fight. General Sullivan had withdrawn his diminished army from Rhode Island to the mainland, safe from English attack. Thousands of colonial militiamen had gone back to their farms, upset by the French departure. The war in New England seemed over.

With no battle in prospect, Clinton turned his fleet over to General Charles Grey and returned to New York. Before leaving, he ordered Grey to sail along the south coast of New England, ravaging villages and destroying the privateers in those ports that harassed the ships carrying supplies to Newport. But Admiral Howe opposed Clinton's order to pillage seaports, believing that it would encourage more rebellion, not hasten its end. He had given up all hope of reconciliation, a course he and his brother, General Howe, the retired army commander, both had favored. Reluctantly, he agreed to wait off Block Island with his fleet in case Grey needed help.

General Grey, on September 5, took the huge fleet under the naval command of Captain Robert Fanshaw into Buzzards Bay. By sunset the fleet was in Clark's Cove, south of New Bedford. Six companies of troops went ashore and marched into New Bedford during the night to begin their destruction. The troops had been on board ship for weeks and were eager to have something to do, especially pillaging. In two days they burned more than thirty buildings. General Grey described the results: "26 storehouses at [New] Bedford, several at McPherson's wharf, Crane's Mills and Fairhaven [were burned]; these were filled with very great quantities of rum, sugar, molasses, coffee, tobacco, cotton, tea, medicines, gunpowder, sailcoth, cordage, &c. Two large ropewalks [were burned]." Seventy vessels as well as many small craft were also destroyed. Smoke from the burning rum, molasses, and gunpowder blackened the sky, surely visible to residents of Martha's Vineyard, twenty miles away. Were they to be next?

General Grey reported to Clinton on the successes at New Bedford and Fairhaven in a self-serving manner:

> The Business was finished, and the Troops all re-embarked this Morning by 12 of clock, with the loss . . . of only 5 or 6 Men wounded, one of whom is since dead. The Stores destroyed were valuable, and the Number of Ships burnt about 70, Privateers and other Ships, ready, with their Cargoes in, for sailing. The only Battery they had was on the Fair Haven side, an enclosed Fort with eleven pieces of Cannon which was abandoned, and the Cannon properly demolished by Captain Scott . . . and the Magazine blown up.
>
> I cannot enough praise the Spirit, Zeal and Activity of the Troops you have Honored me with the Command of . . . also their Sobriety in the midst of Temptation, and Obedience to Orders, as not one House in Bedford and Fair Haven I think was consumed that could be avoided, except those with Stores. . . .
>
> I shall proceed to Martha's Vineyard for the purpose of Collecting

Cattle for Rhode Island, &c. Immediately after performing that Service, shall return with the Troops to Long Island. s/ Charles Grey

His plans for the Vineyard sounded peaceful enough, not like the destruction at New Bedford and Fairhaven. Its purpose, he wrote, was "Collecting Cattle." There is no mention of punishing the rebels for privateering. Fresh meat was needed by the garrison in Newport, where troops had been on short rations for weeks. A Hessian soldier stationed there wrote to his family in Germany on September 8, the day Grey's fleet headed for the Vineyard: "It is so sorry looking around us, as far as fresh vegetables and meat are concerned. . . . We shall hardly have anything here in a fortnight, since we are now having to live on nothing but salt meat, dried peas, and rice."

The British fleet also needed provisions. As he sailed for Holmes Hole, Grey ordered the rations cut by one-third. But he knew things would be better if his plans worked out. He sent word to the Newport commander to dispatch all the vessels he could spare to Holmes Hole to carry back the livestock he would collect on the Vineyard.

At noon on September 8 Grey's ships left New Bedford, crossing Buzzards Bay. But before all of them could make it through Quick's Hole in the Elizabeth Islands, the tide changed, forcing a number of ships to anchor in the bay to await a fair tide. There were other delays, and it was six in the morning of September 10 before the eleven warships and twenty troop transports were completely through Quick's. They soon were at Holmes Hole. Vineyarders must have watched nervously from the north shore as the huge armada sailed down the Sound.

Grey received advance word that morning of what was on the Island in an intelligence report, no doubt from a Vineyard loyalist. Here are a few excerpts from the report:

The number of farm animals: 600 oxen, steers, etc.; 560 cows; 13,000 sheep.

Militia, a Colonel, 5 captains, 600 men, mostly at sea.

Almost all the bread consumed on the Island is procured from Connecticut, their other supplies are brought from [New] Bedford & Boston. There is hardly any Timber of Size on the Island, and wood for fuel, or building vessels, chiefly brought from the continent.

The number of Inhabitants do not exceed 3500, exclusive of Indians of whom there are about 60 Familys who cultivate a little ground and are possessed of about 60 head of Cattle & 200 Sheep. . . . Few vessels [are] properly owned here, having formerly shared in those fitted out at Nantuckett & Bedford for whaling, as they do now in the Privateers.

On the afternoon of September 10 General Grey, aboard his flagship, the H.M.S. *Carisfort*, which was anchored off West Chop, studied the report, deciding what he would demand from the Islanders. While deciding, he sent several warships and transports north to ravage Falmouth, where, he had been told, there were many privateers. When they got there, so many local militia lined the shore of the narrow harbor that the English quickly left without doing any damage.

Another of Grey's pillaging expeditions also had to be abandoned, as he explained in his report to Clinton: "The Transports with the Light Infantry, Grenadians and 33rd Regiments were anchored without the Harbour [Holmes Hole] as I had at that time a Service in view for those Corps whilst the business of collecting cattle should be carry on [*sic*] upon the Island. I was obliged by contrary winds to relinquish my designs."

His plan had been to send those transports to Nantucket to destroy privateers and ships' stores. But as was often the case in those waters, the wind and the tide took over. Grey didn't mention in his report to Clinton that the real cause of the abandonment of the Nantucket mission was the foot-dragging by Captain Fanshaw, the fleet's naval commander. When the fleet arrived at Holmes Hole, the wind and tide were right for sailing to Nantucket, but Fanshaw insisted on first holding a meeting with the captains of his ships. When the meeting was over, the tide and wind had become unfavorable for a sail to Nantucket. Postponed until the next day, the raid was abandoned a few days later when Grey was ordered to return to New York at once.

Captain John André, Grey's aide-de-camp who was hanged in Tarrytown later as a spy, was on board the *Carisfort*. His diary tells us what happened next at Holmes Hole:

> In the evening a Flag of Truce with three Committeemen came on board. They professed the most peaceable dispositions and the utmost readiness to comply with the General's requisitions. General Grey ordered them ashore to direct the inhabitants to drive in their sheep and cattle, or that Troops should be marched thro' the Island; likewise to bring in their arms, or that the Colonel and Captains of the Militia should be sent [as] prisoners to New York.

The colonel whom André mentioned was Colonel Beriah Norton of Edgartown, who came aboard with two captains under the flag of truce. Norton had experience negotiating with the English. A year earlier, on September 9, 1777, as head of the Island's Committee for Defense, he had received a letter from Captain McCartney of the H.M.S. *Ambuscade*, then in Holmes Hole harbor. When McCartney had demanded provisions for his men, the diplomatic Colonel Norton, eager to conserve the Island's meager supplies, made an offering to McCartney of a number of fowls and some "indifferent" sheep. We don't know how the matter was resolved, but surely the captain accepted Norton's gracious offer and left the Island with the hens and "indifferent" mutton. Norton's adjective was no exaggeration. The Vineyard sheep were range animals. It was not until the early 1800s that fatter, more woolly Spanish merino sheep were imported into the colony, and it was much later before they were brought to the Vineyard. Until then, the animals that survived winters on the Island's grasslands indeed provided "indifferent" mutton.

Beriah Norton, the top-ranking military man on the Island, was getting accustomed to dealing with English officers, and they soon learned to respect his integrity. But the visit to the flagship *Carisfort* was his biggest test, his first face-to-face meeting with such a high-ranking officer as General Grey, who commanded not a single vessel but a huge fleet. Norton took with him to the meeting two other Islanders, one of whom was Joseph Mayhew of Chilmark. There is no record of the discussion, but it was obvious that Norton did not resist General Grey's demands. The meeting was brief and at its end, Norton was handed this written order by B. Symes of General Grey's staff:

> Beriah Norton, Colonel of Militia at Martha's Vineyard, is required to order the Militia of the Island to assemble at Day Light tomorrow morning, collect the horned Cattle, Milch Cows excepted, & Sheep in their Different Districts & proceed with them immediately to homes hole. They are expected at the appointed place precisely at two in the afternoon, in failure of which the Troops will March at that hour to collect them. The Militia are ordered to bring their armes, accoutrements and ammunition.

It was getting late in the day. To have livestock from all over the Island delivered to Holmes Hole by 2:00 P.M. the next day must have seemed an impossibility to Colonel Norton. During the night he was able to have

Grey's orders delivered to his five captains: "You are hereby ordered to muster your Company of Militia by Day Light tomorrow morning & Collect all the oxon & Sheep in your Destrect and Bring them with your armes, acutorment & ammunition to home's hole harbour By two oClock tomorrow, there to Receive further orders."

It must have been a frantic night on the Vineyard as the militiamen rode from house to house arousing residents and ordering them to drive their animals to Holmes Hole. No numbers were given; the order simply said, "Collect all the oxon & Sheep," and get them to Holmes Hole by 2:00 P.M.

A number of years later, while seeking restitution for the livestock taken by Grey, Beriah Norton described in detail his meeting aboard the *Carisfort*:

> On General Grey's arrival . . . I was one that immediately waited upon him, and I solemnly affirm that he did not at the time suggest in my hearing any intention of punishing the Inhabitants by military exactions. . . . He required that they should deliver up their arms (which were the same they had formerly used as a Militia under the King's Government) and this was instantly complied with.
>
> He also required a large quantity of Stock, Cattle and Sheep, these were also immediately collected at the landing, persons were appointed to take an invoice of them and appraise them and every formality of a contract was observed, nor was there during General Grey's continuance there a single circumstance which resembled depredation on Enemies or levying a contribution upon the Inhabitants. . . .
>
> The whole of this business was negotiated between the General and myself and I most sacredly declare that on the evening of the 10th of September on board the *Carisfort* Frigate, General Grey assured me that upon the Stock being delivered according to agreement, I might depend upon its being paid for in full or in part and that every justice should be done to the Inhabitants.

The following morning, September 11, 1778, about 450 troops from the 4,300 aboard the transports went ashore in Holmes Hole, setting up camp in the open area near Bass Creek (about where Five Corners now is in Vineyard Haven). Grey promised that the residents would not be bothered by the troops if his demand for 10,000 sheep and 300 oxen, plus hay, was promptly met.

Colonel Norton's order brought quick results. Before noon the next day livestock from nearby farms began arriving at Holmes Hole, creating much confusion around the harbor. For the next two days, flocks of sheep kept coming in. Controlling them became a nightmare. The tiny village was in turmoil, its downtown alive with the sounds of baaing sheep. By the end of the day, twenty vessels had sailed into the harbor from Newport and anchored close to shore, waiting to load the livestock.

It was a remarkable accomplishment, but General Grey was not satisfied. The number of weapons that had been turned in, 229 guns and not much ammunition, did not meet the number he knew was in the hands of the militia. He sent one regiment to Edgartown to pressure the inhabitants, and the men took Colonel Norton and his captains into confinement until all the weapons were turned in.

A warship and some troops were also sent to Edgartown to collect the tax money held in the county courthouse. The soldiers, happy to have something to do, busied themselves by destroying two small vessels in the harbor. There was no resistance reported.

For two days the frenzy continued. All the collecting was being done by residents. The English troops were present to intimidate, not to harass. Most of the sheep came from up-Island, but no troops had been sent there. In the owners' minds, they were selling their livestock. It was an involuntary sale, to be sure, but it was a sale nonetheless.

In Holmes Hole the men in charge began loading the animals onto the transports. The confusion began to subside. As each animal was loaded, a record was made of its owner, condition, and estimated weight. By the end of the day the transports were filled, and they left for Newport with orders to return immediately for the rest of the animals.

Soon after they left, a vessel arrived with orders from Lord Howe, who was still at Block Island. Grey was ordered to sail his fleet back to New York at once. No explanation was given. More than four thousand sheep were still in Holmes Hole. Grey ordered them loaded onto his ships. While that was being done, the troops that had been sent to Edgartown were recalled. By the evening of September 14, all the men and most of the animals were on board the ships.

A roll call revealed that two British soldiers had deserted. Residents were ordered to turn them in; otherwise, four Islanders, probably Norton's captains, would be taken to New York as hostages. By nightfall the two deserters had returned. Norton and his captains were released. All was ready for a departure in the morning. In a parting gesture, General Grey ordered a saltworks onshore destroyed and its store of salt confiscated.

Colonel Stirling, the officer commanding the troops onshore, told Colonel Norton to assemble all residents to hear a statement from General Grey that he would read. Several hundred villagers gathered in an open field near Bass Creek. Beriah Norton described the meeting: "He [Stirling] informed us that General Gray [*sic*] had directed him to inform us that we ware [were] to apply at New York for payment for the Stock they had received. I asked the Colo. if we had Best send a man in the fleet at that time for the payment, to which the Colo. replyed we might if we Chose, but recommended to us to wait a Little time before Applycation was made."

No Vineyarder was sent with the fleet, but shortly after it left, Beriah Norton sailed to New York to begin his campaign to obtain compensation for what had been taken. Just before Grey left, he ordered Colonel Norton to require that the inhabitants not merely be neutral in the rebellion, but also assist English warships by furnishing provisions when asked. (This commitment much later was used to block Vineyarders from being accepted into membership in the Daughters of the American Revolution.) In his journal Captain André wrote the terms that Norton was forced to accept: "A solemn injunction to abstain from taking part any more in the War or persecuting others for their political opinions; they were also bound to assist the King's ships with water or provisions whenever they should call upon them to do it."

It is unlikely that Colonel Norton put up much resistance to the pledge. He was not a firebrand. Like many Islanders, he was an accommodator. If selling fresh meat and vegetables to an English warship would keep the Island peaceful, that was fine with him, as it was no doubt with the other residents. But even if he had objected, there was little he could have done except agree. When a British warship entered port demanding provisions, armed resistance might be heroic—but futile.

The fleet, its ships now loaded, was scheduled to sail with the tide at six in the morning of September 15, 1778, but there were delays, as usual. It wasn't until sunset that they left. During the delay, two small vessels in the harbor were burned.

Colonel Norton watched the huge fleet sail away to the west, into the setting sun. He had reason to congratulate himself. His had been a major accomplishment. Little damage had been done, nobody had been hurt, no shots had been fired, and the Vineyarders would be paid for what had been taken from them. Norton wrote about it proudly in 1782: "When it is considered that the requisition for Ten Thousand Sheep and more than Three Hundred Cattle was made on the evening of the 10th of September, that the Stock was to be collected from the extreme parts of the Island and the whole business was effected by the Inhabitants alone, the Stock put on board, and the Troops re-embarked and ready to Sail on the 14th, I flatter myself. I need make no further observation."

He admitted that all the gunpowder had not been turned in promptly, which caused him and his captains to be jailed briefly: "The quantity of Gun-powder, which the General [complained was missing] was a few pounds belonging to an Individual, which was secreted for his own private use and the Proprietor of it at that time [was] off the Island."

Few documents written by Vineyarders who took part in the events of those momentous days have survived. The Martha's Vineyard Historical Society does have three statements that were written by Chilmark men. The purpose of the statements (which seem to be affidavits) appears to have been to determine how many sheep had been taken from individuals so that a fair compensation could be made. The first is from forty-year-old Moses Lumbert:

> I was Near the house of Simon Mayhew's in Chilmark in Company with Johnathan Allen when I see a large Drove of Sheep Driving in the highway or Road Leading from the Neck of Land Caled Squipnocket. Mr. Allen observed that those Sheep Might be from that Neck of Land [and] if they where he had Sheep at that Place & [they would] likely be among them. Your Deponant was of the Same mind having Sheep at the same place. . . . The Sheep was then Drove of[f] Towards the Harbour where the British Fleet Lay for General Gray, as the Drovers said, the Drovers to that flock being Four in Number, all belonging to Chilmark.

Lumbert claimed only that some of his sheep were "likely to be among them." His account affirms that owners did not know how many of their sheep were being taken. In the urgency of Grey's order, all available sheep were rounded up and driven to Holmes Hole. Any accounting of exactly whose sheep were being taken would have to come later.

The second affidavit adds a little more to our knowledge of the procedure. Not everybody's sheep were taken. In this case, sheep owned by Indians were separated from English-owned sheep, all being pastured on

Gay Head. This apparently was evidence of the uncertain status of Indians as citizens:

> I Francis Mayhew of Chilmark . . . do say that when G. Gray was at the
> Vineyard taking of[f] stock, cattle & Sheep, the Indians brought the
> Sheep off of the Gayhead and yarded them on Mr. Benjamin Mayhew's
> land . . . and took out the Sheep that they had in keeping and Drove
> them Back to sd Gayhead. I was Present at the yard when they took out
> their Sheep. . . . The rest of sd sheep [in] sd yard where [were] drove
> Eastward to go to sd. Gray.

The third deposition explains how the town of Chilmark determined how many sheep had actually been taken from it. All the sheep that remained in the town after Grey left were counted. Ownership of the animals was determined, no doubt by examining the earmarks, which were registered in the town. Among those who still had sheep was Sheriff Peter Norton: "I Nathanel Mayhew [state] that soon after sd Gray went from this place, people were yarding sheep in sd Town [Chilmark] in order to find what they had remaining . . . at a yard on M. Tilton's land where I saw sd Peter Norton's son take out a considerable number of sheep belonging to sd. Peter & his sons."

Nathaniel, while giving his deposition, was asked if he had ever been paid for the livestock taken from him. His response sounds a bit sarcastic: "I suppose I received part pay for one yoke of oxen."

General Grey did not give an exact count of what he had taken in his report to General Clinton, made only a few days after the raid. Round numbers were good enough for him. He summarized his four days on the Vineyard this way:

> On our Arrival off the Harbour [Holmes Hole, September 10], the Inhabitants sent persons on board to ask my Intentions with respect to them, to which a requisition was made of the arms of the Militia, the public Money, 300 oxen and 10,000 Sheep; They promised each of the Articles should be delivered without delay: I afterwards found it necessary to send small detachments into the Island and detain the deputed Inhabitants for a time, in Order to accelerate their Compliance with the demand.
>
> The 12th I was able to embark on board the Vessels which arrived that day from Rhode Island 6000 Sheep and 130 Oxen.
>
> The 13th and 14th were employed in embarking Cattle, and Sheep, on

A drawing of the Major Peter Norton house, ca. 1740. (MVHS Collections)

board our own Fleet, in destroying some Salt Works, in burning or taking, in the Inlets, what Vessels and boats could be found and in receiving the arms of the militia.

On the 15th, the Fleet left Martha's Vineyard and after sustaining the next day a very Severe Gale of Wind, arrived the 17th at Whitestone without any material damage.

I hold myself much obliged to the Commanding officer of the Corps and to the Troops in General for the Alacrity with which every Service was performed.

In a later report sent to General Clinton in New York, this one in Captain André's handwriting, there is a more precise account of what was destroyed and what was taken:

In Old Town Harbour [Edgartown], Martha's Vineyard:
1 brig of 150 tons burthen, burnt by the *Scorpion*. 1 schooner of 70 tons burthen burnt by ditto.
23 whale boats taken or destroyed. A quantity of plank taken.
At Holmes Hole, Martha's Vineyard:

4 vessels, with several boats, taken or destroyed. A salt work destroyed and a considerable quantity of salt taken.

Arms taken at Martha's Vineyard:

388 stand, with bayonets, pouches, etc., some powder and a quantity of lead, as by artillery return.

£1000 sterling, in paper, the amount of a tax collected by authority of the Congress, was received at Martha's Vineyard from the Collector.

Cattle and sheep taken from Martha's Vineyard:

300 oxen, 10,000 sheep.

The report failed to mention that 9 of the 388 rifles were on Grey's order given to nine unnamed men, three in each village, for maintaining order after the English left. When the three towns completed their careful counting of losses, the totals came to 10,574 sheep and 315 cattle, as well as 52 tons of hay to feed the livestock on the ships.

Thirty years later the continuous claims for payment by the residents had become a local joke—at least to the writer Edward A. Kendall, who after a visit to the Island in 1807 wrote: "In the rebellion, large numbers [of sheep] were taken, and paid for, for the support of the King's troops, but it is a common jest in the neighbourhood, that the number paid for far exceeded the whole number the island could have produced."

The Vineyard's contributions to the diet of the English troops may have seemed large when the sheep were being loaded at Holmes Hole, but in fact the supplies didn't last long. There were many hungry men to be fed and the food inventory had reached its lowest point, as the historian R. Arthur Bowler wrote: "For all its apparent success, Grey's expedition kept the army in meat for no more than two weeks. . . . There were still only four days' provisions in the storehouses when the British fleet arrived in New York harbor in January 1779 [four months later]."

But while it lasted, the fresh meat was much enjoyed. Sir Robert Pigot, commander of the British troops in Newport, wrote to General Grey and thanked him, mentioning the help given by a loyalist named Tupper in the raid:

Many thanks to you my dear General for the fine parcel of Sheep you have been so kind as to send us. Everything was ready for a second Trip [to the Vineyard by the Newport transports] the day before you appeared off [Newport], but the Convoy receiving orders to proceed to New York with the Cattle, our Motions were retarded till we could provide another armed vessel here. . . . I am glad Tupper the Guide was useful to you, he is a valuable man. . . . He tells me that if you would be so good as to give him one of the Sloops taken at Martha's Vineyard, he could get a livelihood by fetching wood for the [Newport] Garrison. . . . I send this by the Wood Fleet, an Article we are much in want of.

P.S. Pray are the sheep to be paid for? Mr. Leonard, the Commissary, thinks they are & that a Valuation was fixed upon them.

The question in the postscript indicates clearly that what Grey took was not thought of as plunder; it had been taken with the intent to reimburse the owners. Leonard, the commissary officer mentioned, had been with Grey at Martha's Vineyard and no doubt watched the inventory being kept as the animals were loaded.

Pigot was not the only person who was grateful for the Vineyard's mutton. Mackenzie, the Welsh officer at Newport quoted earlier, wrote of others who enjoyed the fresh meat:

The Historical Society has several woodcuts by Charles Banks, such as this one of British troops rounding up sheep during Grey's Raid. They are decorative but not accurate historically. (MVHS Collections)

[September] 14th: Very fine day. Wind N. The Stock brought from the Vineyard was partly landed on the East side of this Island [Rhode Island]. The vessels are to return for more, as soon as they are unloaded.

15th. Above 5000 sheep have been landed from Martha's Vineyard for the use of the troops on this Island. This will prove a seasonable supply as the Stock on this Island is nearly exhausted.

26th—200 sheep of those brought here from Martha's Vineyard have been put on board the *Princess Royal,* and *Culloden,* for the use of the Officers and men. [The two ships had just arrived from England, a voyage that had taken fifteen weeks. Fresh meat would certainly have been appreciated.]

Oct. 6th. . . . Each Commissioned Officer of the troops of this Island received a Donation of a Sheep, out of those brought from Martha's Vineyard.

Feeding the thousands of troops stationed on Rhode Island was a continuing problem. General Sullivan's colonial army on the mainland had blockaded the English base so completely that all provisions had to be brought in by boat. The blockade provided welcome income for some Americans. A few weeks after the English in Newport received the Vineyard sheep, Mackenzie, who was stationed there, wrote:

Oct. 9th. . . . A boat from Long Island came in this Morning with some Provisions to sell. . . .

10th. The Wood fleet from Lloyd's Neck, Long Island, came in this morning, under convoy of the *Fowey*. They have brought 534 Cord of wood. . . .

Nov. 27th. Two Block Island boats came in last night with 24 quarters of good beef, some Mutton, Cheese, pigs, fowl, etc.

Dec. 17th. The Block Island boats frequently bring 3 or 400 Sea fowl of different kinds. . . . [That business is] a great relief to the poor Inhabitants.

General Clinton, now at his headquarters in New York reading Grey's reports of success, was pleased. On September 21, 1778, he sent his own report on the raid to London. In it he explained that before going to New Bedford, he had planned to pillage New London, but the plan was abandoned owing to adverse winds and a scarcity of privateers in the port. He then returned to New York, sending Grey with the fleet to burn warehouses at New Bedford and to the Vineyard for provisions. Such coastal raids, he wrote, not only would provide provisions, but would send a message to "those poor deluded people": "I therefore left G. Grey with the troops, and directed him to move towards [New] Bedford. His success [there] was complete, and since that, at Martha's Vineyard, and I hope it will serve to convince those poor deluded people that that sort of war, carried to a greater extent and with more devastation, will sooner or later reduce them."

One of those "poor deluded people" was Colonel Beriah Norton, the Islander who had been most involved in the bargaining. But it was only a beginning. He spent most of his remaining years trying to collect full payment from the English for what they had taken. Within a few days after the raid, the selectmen of the Vineyard's three towns met to plan what action to take to get the money. They prepared a statement to be delivered to the General Court in Boston by Colonel Norton. The statement explained that when Grey arrived, residents had no choice but to comply with his demands, and consequently "our case is rendered deplorable by having neither sufficient beasts for draught or provisions for our support."

The message described their condition but asked for nothing specific, and it brought no action. A week later, September 26, 1778, another try was made. Colonel Norton, James Athearn, and Thomas Cooke signed a petition to the General Court stating that help was needed in the Holmes Hole area by "many persons with large families." Nothing was said about payment. It requested relief, not compensation:

> The late stop of the British troops have made in Depriving them of their stock has rendered the case of many persons with large families Truly deplorable. In particular near the Harbour of Holmes Hole where they landed who are not only Deprived of every article & necessary of life not having an Exchange of any kind of clothing for them or children and unless immediately assisted must unavoidably suffer extremely or perish.

The reason there was no mention of sheep may have been that the Vineyarders fully expected to be paid for them once they presented a bill to the English in New York. With that in mind, James Athearn was sent to New Jersey with a letter from the General Court that asked General Washington to allow him to go through the British lines and into New York to present the Island's claim for reimbursement.

Thomas Cooke, one of those asking the General Court to help Vineyarders after Grey's Raid, lived in this Edgartown house, now owned by the Historical Society and open to the public. (MVHS Collections)

General Washington seemed not a bit eager to become involved and forwarded the request to the Congress in Philadelphia, where it died for lack of interest. Thus, Athearn's trip to New Jersey, which Islanders hoped would present their claims to the English in New York, ended in failure.

Other problems occupied the attention of Vineyarders, some more important than their getting paid for livestock. A serious smallpox epidemic had broken out in both Edgartown and Chilmark. Tisbury, sandwiched between the two towns, was greatly concerned that the disease would erupt there. Late in December 1778 the town named a committee to determine whether transients wishing to go through Tisbury in their travel between Chilmark and Edgartown should be stopped at the town line. James Athearn was named to head the committee, but when he came down with smallpox himself, the blockade seemed useless. The disease was already in town.

The Revolution was now being fought in the south of the country, but there were occasional raids along the New England coast by a nondescript navy of British sympathizers, loyalists led by George Leonard of Boston. He had been given a fleet of ten vessels, castoffs from the British navy. He fitted them out at his own expense and regularly sailed along the south shore of the Cape, harassing ships and villages. It came to be called the Refugee Fleet, its sailors being refugees from the country and deprived of property and civil rights.

On one adventure Leonard used Edgartown and Holmes Hole as his base for several weeks. From there he raided Nantucket, taking quantities of sperm oil, whalebone, and coffee. Leonard was particularly pleased to harass Nantucket, as he had been in Grey's fleet when the Nantucket raid was aborted in 1778. He became well liked by Vineyarders and convinced them to sell fresh provisions and wood to the British at Newport. Some years later William Jernigan wrote about the Leonard fleet: "About the year 1779, a fleet of the British ships anchored in our harbour at Edgartown. Some of our People was then anxious to fire on them with our small arms. Wm. Jernigan [he often wrote in the third person] then and there interposed and used his influence with the People not to fire on them: if we did we should have our Houses burnt. At that time, they did us but little damage and went off with themselves."

This Refugee Fleet was protected by the pledge, mentioned earlier, that Colonel Norton was required to sign when General Grey left: "A solemn injunction to abstain from taking part any more in the War . . . also bound to assist the King's ships with water or provisions whenever they should call upon them to do it."

The Island's towns were still trying to put together an accurate count of the livestock and other items taken by Grey. For some reason, Chilmark was not pleased with how things were being done and it hired an attorney, Timothy Folger of Nantucket, to represent it. The other two towns were so upset by Chilmark's move that they told the English that the up-Island town's claims were greatly exaggerated.

With James Athearn sick with smallpox, Colonel Norton took over. He was certainly qualified to negotiate with the English. Massachusetts Bay gave him permission to travel to London to argue the case for remuneration, but he was required to post a bond to assure that he would not do any business with the enemy except to try to get a settlement. Going to England would be expensive, and the Islanders were not eager to pay to have Beriah Norton living in London at their expense for what might be a long mission. Norton solved the problem by agreeing to pay all expenses himself. He would be reimbursed when a settlement was reached; then he would get one-third of any amount received. If there was no payment, he would receive nothing. It was a bold move on his part.

In August 1780 he sailed to London to represent the entire Island. (Chilmark had returned to the fold.) He was there until the spring of 1782—a frustrating eighteen months. His petition was quickly turned down by the Board of Whitehall Treasury, but that didn't stop him. He became an active lobbyist, cultivating friends among the lords and ladies, no doubt charming them with his farmer's wit and dignity. He argued that, despite what General Grey claimed, Vineyarders had not put up a fight against the English. Furthermore, Grey had promised to pay for what he took: Norton could prove that by citing the alacrity with which ten thousand sheep were driven to Holmes Hole, which was certainly proof of their cooperative attitude.

The Treasury asked Sir Henry Clinton for his opinion. Clinton, you will recall, was the general who had turned the fleet over to General Grey in September 1778. Apparently, he sided with Colonel Norton: the Treasury overruled the Whitehall board and authorized the payment of seven thousand pounds, subject to the approval of the commanding officer of His Majesty's forces in New York.

It must have been an enjoyable sail back to New York for Norton. Now all he had to do was to make his case with Sir Guy Carleton, the New York commander. He did so in New York, knowing that there was money available if he could convince Sir Guy. He prepared twenty-one documents to support his position. Among the documents was a harsh criticism of General Grey for misstating the facts:

> The solemn injunction which General Grey refers to, to abstain from taking part in the War or prosecuting others for their political opinions has been religiously attended to; and . . . the King's Ships, Troops, and Garrison have been uniformly supplied with every article the Island affords. . . .
>
> At the time of [General Grey's] landing . . . not a man was armed, nor were any of them collected. . . . All remained quiet at home untill summoned by the General's order to bring in the Stock . . . which they faithfully performed. . . .
>
> It is very fortunately in my power to produce the most irrefragable evidence of this promise [to pay for the livestock] made by General Grey

from the Deposition of Mr. Leonard who acted as Commissary upon that Service. . . . For what purpose . . . was so particular an account taken of the number and weight of the Stock supplied and the value of each article ascertained . . . by persons appointed by the express order and direction of General Grey? Surely such conduct was by no means consistent with the Idea of a contribution to be levied upon the Inhabitants as a punishment for their disloyalty, but clearly evinced a deliberate intention at the time that compensation should be made.

On July 8, 1782, Colonel Norton was requested to go to New York, and Major General Peterson would convene a board "to hear what you have further to urge in favor of the Claim of the Inhabitants of Martha's Vineyard."

Colonel Norton presented his documents. Two weeks later Sir Guy Carleton ordered his paymaster to give Colonel Beriah Norton, "agent for the Inhabitations of Martha's Vineyard without deduction the Sum of Three Thousand Pounds Sterling being part of the Demand made by them for Cattle, Sheep & Hay furnished General Grey in . . . September 1778."

Norton had won. He had convinced the English to pay for what they had taken. It was a triumph for the farmer from Edgartown, who had defeated one of England's military leaders, General Grey (although not on the battlefield). To be sure, it was only partial payment, but the principle had been agreed to: England owed the Vineyard for what Grey had taken.

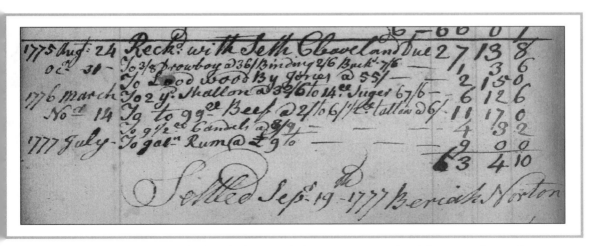

Colonel Beriah Norton dealt with the British during Grey's Raid and for years afterward sought restitution. The Historical Society has many of his papers, including an account book kept during the Revolution. (MVHS Collections)

Colonel Norton was still not satisfied. In October 1782 he posted bond and was granted permission to return to New York (still occupied by the British) to try to collect the remaining four thousand pounds. But nothing came of this visit. There were rumors that a peace treaty would soon be signed. Nobody wanted to jeopardize the prospects of peace. Norton came home, but he wouldn't give up the fight.

A year later, on September 3, 1783, the peace treaty was signed in Paris. The American Revolution was finally over. Signing the treaty for the United States were John Jay, Benjamin Franklin, and John Adams.

Early in 1784 Beriah Norton sold his farm for £458 and moved into a small house that he had recently purchased for £59. He would need the money for his continuing quest. In June 1784 he left the Vineyard for Boston to sail to London aboard the ship *Active*. On the vessel, he quickly learned, was a distinguished passenger, Abigail Adams, the wife of John Adams. She was sailing to London to join her husband after his successful diplomacy had ended the war. In her diary on the day the *Active* sailed, Mrs. Adams wrote, "Several of the Passengers called upon me, amongst whom was a Col. Norton from Martha's Vineyard, a Member of our Senate, a grave, sedate man about 50 years of age."

The farmer from Edgartown was moving up in the world.

5

After a Frustrating Quest, the Start of Something Big

When Beriah Norton of Edgartown boarded the ship *Active* at Rowe's Wharf in Boston on June 19, 1784, bound for London, he quickly discovered he had made a lucky choice of vessel. Also aboard was Abigail Adams, who was going to London to join her husband, John Adams, America's new minister to England. Traveling with Abigail Adams were her eighteen-year-old daughter, also named Abigail, and her two servants, a man and a woman. She was the most distinguished of the eleven passengers on the *Active*. Norton was making his second trip to London, as he continued trying to persuade the English to pay the balance they owed for what they had taken from Vineyarders in Grey's Raid in September 1778.

The *Active* left the wharf at noon the next day. As soon as the ship was outside Boston Harbor, the ocean swells brought distress to Abigail and others, as she wrote:"[The captain] sent word to all the Ladies to put on their sea cloaths and prepare for sickness. We had only time to follow his directions before we found ourselves all sick."

For the next two weeks, the turbulent ocean made her and the others miserable:

> To those who have never been at Sea or experienced this, ouch!, disspiriting malady 'tis impossible to discribe it, the Nausia arising from the smell of the Ship, the continual rolling, tossing and tumbling, contribute to keep up this Disorder, and when once it seazeis [seizes] a person it levels Sex and condition. . . . My maid was wholy useless. . . . Every Body on Board Sick except the Dr. and 3 or 4 old sea men. My [man] Servant as bad as any.

A cow, on board to provide fresh milk during the monthlong voyage, was severely injured by the ship's rolling. Since she was unable to stand, it was thought best to put her out of her misery. The ladies were asked whether they would object. The captain delegated Norton to make the inquiry. The women agreed, as Abigail Adams recorded: "Col. Norton was charged with the message and delivered it in form—upon which Sentance of Death was pronounced upon her; and she was accordingly consigned to a watery grave; but not without mourning, for we feel her loss most essentially."

When the ocean finally quieted and the passengers had somewhat recovered, Abigail and her servants cleaned the dirty and disorderly cabin and made puddings that the queasy passengers were able to keep down. In addition to herself, her daughter, and her maid, there was one other woman on board, another Mrs. Adams (no relation). The females had been given the "stateroom," a tiny saloon about eight feet square, which had been partitioned, probably by curtains, to provide some privacy. The men slept in the larger main saloon, just outside the ladies' cabin door. It was not a comfortable arrangement: "The door [to the women's stateroom] opened to the cabbin where the Gentlemen slept. We were obliged to keep open our Door or be suffocated and poisoned so that we only closed it to undress and dress and sometimes [we were] so sick that we fell from side to side in doing it."

As uncomfortable as the trip was, Norton realized that traveling in the company of someone as important as Mrs. John Adams was worth it. He sought her friendship, and she seemed to approve of this quiet man from the Vineyard. Later, he hoped, her acquaintance would open doors in high places.

Norton would need all the help he could get. On his previous trip, he had to spend a year and a half in London before winning his case. And the victory had been only partial. The Royal Treasury did authorize payment of seven thousand pounds from funds available in New York, the amount Norton and the Vineyarders were seeking, but when he tried to collect that amount in New York, the English commander there, Sir Guy Carleton, gave him only three thousand pounds as partial payment.

Norton took his one-third (the arrangement agreed upon with Islanders), and the remaining two thousand pounds were distributed to petitioning Vineyarders. Each got far less than he expected, which caused a general feeling of disillusionment with Norton's accomplishment. But

Norton himself had not made out well either. His one thousand pounds was hardly enough to reimburse him for his living expenses in London, not to mention the need to support his family in Edgartown during the eighteen months he was away. His precarious finances made him as eager to collect the remaining four thousand pounds for his share as he was for repaying the Vineyarders. (He was among those with claims, having lost two cattle and forty-five sheep in the raid.)

Norton's farm was on the road to (West) Tisbury, about one mile from the village of Edgartown. The house is shown on a map in *Letters from an American Farmer,* by Hector St. John Crèvecoeur, the French immigrant who ran a farm in this country at the time of the Revolution. The book is a series of letters he wrote to a friend in France about life in America. In one letter he described a visit he made to Martha's Vineyard. Norton had been one of his hosts: "Here, let me remember, the hospitable treatment I received from B. Norton, Esq., the colonel of the island, as well as from Dr. Mahew [*sic*], the lineal descendant of the first proprietor."

Crèvecoeur's stay on the Vineyard was brief, only a few days. At least one night was spent at the Beriah Norton farmhouse. The rather crude map of the Vineyard in his book identifies only three houses, the three places he seems to have stayed overnight: Beriah Norton's in Edgartown; James Athearn's in (West) Tisbury; and Dr. Matthew Mayhew's in Chilmark. Although Crèvecoeur's book was not published until 1782, his account of the number of sheep and cattle on the Island suggests that his visit came before Grey's Raid in 1778:

> A good ferry is established between Edgar Town and Falmouth on the main. . . . The number of inhabitants is computed at about 4,000, 300 of which are Indians. . . . The stock of the island is 20,000 sheep, 2000 neat cattle, besides horses and goats; they have also some deer, and abundance of sea-fowls. . . . The Indians there [on Chappaquiddick] appeared, by the decency of their manners, their industry, and neatness, to be wholly Europeans, and no way inferior to many of the [English] inhabitants. They often go, like the young [English] men of the Vineyard, to Nantucket, and hire themselves for whalemen or fishermen; and indeed their skill and dexterity in all sea affairs is nothing inferior to that of the whites.

Norton, in 1784 heading again for London, was no longer living in the farmhouse where he had entertained Crèvecoeur. He sold it shortly before leaving and moved his family into the village of Edgartown. The sale may

A vest of Beriah Norton, which he may have worn while
entertaining the famed French author Hector St. John
Crèvecoeur in his farmhouse. In *Letters from an American
Farmer,* Crèvecoeur mentioned visiting Norton's farm.
(MVHS Collections)

have been to provide money for his trip. He was so short of money that he
had to solicit financial help from some Edgartown men with claims against
the English. At least two of them, Peter Norton and Ebenezer Norton,
agreed to advance him ten pounds, but his account book shows they still
owed him their pledges years later.

Beriah Norton was very hopeful of collecting the four thousand
pounds the British still owed. The Revolution was over; the peace treaty
had been signed. And now he had this chance meeting with Mrs. John
Adams, whose husband had built a strong relationship with the English.
He was sure her support would be helpful.

Norton was fifty years old at the time, as Abigail Adams had estimated
in her diary. He and his wife, Anna (née Cosens or Cousens), had nine

children. Two of them were dead, one having died only a month before Norton left on this second trip. Six of the remaining seven were still unmarried and probably living at home. It was a big family to support. Although he had been a farmer earlier in life, he now listed his occupation as "weaver," a job title probably related to his retail business, which dealt mostly in textiles (although he bought and sold a great deal of alcoholic liquor as well). Norton was also running a "commission" business, buying off-Island goods on orders placed by Vineyarders. (The Martha's Vineyard Historical Society owns two account books he kept.) Before Grey's Raid the business prospered, but afterward there was a sharp drop in activity, as might be expected because Norton was in London so much of the time.

His expenses overseas were a financial drain on the family. In London he had to dress well, dealing as he did with members of Parliament and the Treasury. He had to have the right sort of address from which to operate. The cost of the voyage could not have been small. Although the ship's accommodations might seem primitive to us today, surely Abigail Adams, the wife of the new minister to Great Britain, was not traveling economy class.

Despite Norton's optimism, his second trip brought no success. We don't know how long he was in London, but he was back on the Vineyard in the fall of that year, 1784. And he did not give up. He returned to London the next year. We know he made that third "Voiage" because he says so in a letter to the Commissioners of the Treasury on July 15, 1785:

> Your memorialist [himself] on receiving the said £3,000 [in 1782 in New York] proceeded to the Island of Martha's Vineyard and distributed the same in just proportion to each one's demand and returned to New York in the Spring 1783 in full expectation of Completing the business but the peace taking place prevented a final Settlement at that time.
>
> Your memorialist has therefore been under the necessity of making a Second and now a third Voiage to England to Complete the Said business.

Also during the trip Norton wrote to Prime Minister William Pitt: "This being the third Voyage I have made to England for the sole purpose of settling the Balance on behalf of myself and of the Inhabitants of the Island of Martha's Vineyard, who entirely look up to me for Payment . . ."

After explaining how much was still owed to the Vineyard residents, he took a more personal, pleading tone in his letter to the prime minister: "The heavy Expences I have been at in coming to and returning from England to Martha's Vineyard, and the necessary Supplies which must be afforded to a distant and suffering Family, fill me with distress, and urges me thus to submit to you, Sir, the Case of myself, and of those on whose behalf I am empowered to intercede."

A year later he was still in London seeking restitution. The Martha's Vineyard Historical Society has two invitations Norton received in July 1786 from Lord Sydney and Colonel Symes to their homes for dinner. (Symes was one of General Grey's aides who had been present during Norton's discussions aboard the *Carisfort* in Holmes Hole in 1778.)

Norton may have been well received in London, but when he got back to the Vineyard empty-handed, he was treated as a pariah for having spent so much time and money in distant places with so little to show for it. It was an unfair judgment. He was paying all his own expenses, a drain on his finances that reduced his family to near-poverty. But Islanders showed little sympathy. In 1789, when the governor appointed him justice of the court, Thomas Cooke, a justice of the peace himself, was outraged, according to a deposition later taken for a lawsuit:

> I, Cornelius Norton . . . testify and say that I was in Company with Thomas Cooke Esqr., at his house Some time in November 1789 when said Cooke Brought on Some Conversation Respecting a Justice's Commission that was Come from the Governor for Beriah Norton Esqr., at which time Said Cooke appeared to be much against said Norton taking such Commission; and said, "if said Norton Should take . . . Said Commission, that he the Said Cooke would Put him in Gaol . . . and further Said that he would Distress him as much as Possable, for he, the Said Cooke, thought Said Norton to be a Bankrupt therefore not Suitable for Said Commission and the Said Cooke Seemed to Discover Temper on the occation.

The deposition was taken when Beriah Norton sued Cooke for slander, a case he won, being awarded one hundred dollars in damages. He served as a justice until a few years before his death. He also was appointed Edgartown's first postmaster on January 1, 1795, a post he held until 1819. The combined income from these two positions was small. The postmaster was paid a percentage of what he took in. Records in the Martha's Vineyard Historical Society (which may be incomplete) show that between April 1 and July 1, 1795, he collected only $33.60 in the post office.

Norton remained convinced that he could win restitution and even thought of making a fourth trip to England to get the four thousand pounds still owed. He petitioned Congress, then in New York, to pay for the trip. Congress turned the request over to John Jay, secretary for foreign affairs, who replied in legal terms:

> It appears to your Secretary that Martha's Vineyard being American ground, the enemy had good right, *flagrante Bello,* to take away all sheep and cattle they found there without paying anything for them. If however from Motives of Policy they gratuitously promised payment . . . it would not be proper for the United States to take any measures respecting it.
>
> If, on the other hand, this Promise or Contract is to be considered as being of legal obligation and not merely honorary & gratuitous, then the Memorialist has his remedy at Law. . . . National Interposition . . . should not be extended to such concerns and affairs of Individuals as . . . do not touch or affect the National rights.

One would think that Jay's opinion would have put an end to Norton's quest, but he did not give up. He went to Philadelphia in 1800 to meet President John Adams, a trip that caused the Vineyarder Thomas Butler to write to Ichabod Norton of Edgartown to enlist financial help for the traveler:

> Col. Norton is bound to Boston to Morrow with Capt. Jethro Worth [who ran a packet between Boston and the Island]. The old Gentleman seems to be much Crowded for a little Money. . . . He tells me he will make it his particular business to go to [Philadelphia] respecting our matters . . . and also [to meet] the President. To enable him to do which, I think you and I can do no less than give him one Dollar apiece. Which if you are disposed to do, you may send by my Son James. Your Friend, Tho. Butler.

In Philadelphia Norton had "Conciderable Conversation with the President" and later "had a full Hearing before the Committee." He got no money, but he never gave up. Nearly twenty years later, in 1818, only two years before he died, he wrote to President James Monroe, reminding him that when Monroe was governor of Virginia, he had been a guest in the Monroe home with "the Honor of Being Seated at the right hand of your Precious Lady." After introducing himself that way, he turned to his reason for writing:

Since which time, as well as During the whole of the Revolution war, my Station was Extreem Difacult and I have met with many, very many, Grievious Losses and Misfortunes whereby I am reduced to real Dependence as you may See by the Statement here inclosed—and as I am now about Petisioning the Secritary of war for Some assistence to Support me in my old age, I have thought it Posable that you Sir in your Goodness Might Condesent to Say Some thing in My Behalf.

He was no longer seeking remuneration for Vineyard residents. He was now pleading for himself.

It was a sad closing of a life that had been so rich, that had taken him to high places, where he met some of the leading men and women of the time. Now Beriah Norton was reduced to pleading for himself and his family. Nowhere is his desperation more apparent than in a letter he wrote to Mrs. Thankful Ripley, asking her and her son to delay their demand for payment of a note he owed her late husband: "I have lost more than $7,000 Cash, Lost my three Sons, one of which was 25 years & 5 months, under a Deranged State of Mind, at Great Expence. My wife Benn [been] helpless many years. My own late Misfortunes is Grevious. I beg of you, Mrs. Ripley with your Son, Capt. Ripley, to think & act on the above on Christain Prinsapel. I wish to see Capt. Ripley my Self whether he Does anything or not."

The final years of Norton's life were sorrowful. His wife was bedridden. Of their nine children, three sons and one daughter had died; two married daughters had moved off-Island, one to Maine, the other to Georgia; two other married daughters, Zoraida and Sarah, had lost their husbands and returned home with their children, dependent upon him. His youngest daughter, Ann Frances, never married, no doubt burdened with the care of her mother. With many expenses and little income, he had reason to write those pleading letters.

Beriah Norton lived to be eighty-seven years old, dying in December 1820. His wife, Anna Frances, lived only a few weeks longer, "having declined for a number of years and was helpless," the Reverend Joseph Thaxter noted in the church records.

A life that had seemed so promising had ended in despair.

Although most Islanders had little sympathy for Beriah Norton, there were some who might have if they had they known of his frustrations. They were the Island's Indians, who had themselves been seeking restitution for nearly two hundred years without success. What they had lost was much more than sheep and oxen. What they had lost was their way of life.

There was no way to compensate them for that.

By 1810 these original Islanders had ended up under social and economic pressures, segregated in several so-called Indian Lands. The Reverend James Freeman of Boston, a founder of the Massachusetts Historical Society and a friend of the Reverend Joseph Thaxter of Edgartown, visited the Island in 1807 and wrote a valuable description of Island life. Here are some excerpts from what he wrote about Gay Head and the Indians living there:

> It is destitute of trees; but there are many swamps, some of which afford peat, and others springs of good water. . . . There are no roads. The Indians have twenty-six framed houses and seven wigwams. The framed houses are nothing better than mean huts. There are three barns, and two meeting houses, which are small buildings, not more than twenty feet square. The number of families is thirty-four; and of souls, a hundred and forty-two; beside whom about a hundred Indians are absent . . . some of whom are children put out to service in an English family; and others whalemen. . . .
>
> Every native, whether he lives off or on the island, is considered as a proprietor; and every child born to him is entitled to a right, which is equivalent to the pasture of three sheep. No sheep are kept; but a cow is reckoned equal to six sheep; an ox to eight; and a horse to ten. . . . Nine men are pure [Indian], and still more of the women; the rest are intermixed, chiefly with negroes: the mixed race is better than the pure Indians. Almost all of them have cows; and a few of them, oxen; they own as many as twenty horses.
>
> A part of their land is every year let to the whites; and the income is appropriated to the support of their poor. The Indians raise very little corn, but have pretty good gardens. They annually sell a hundred or two hundred bushels of craneberris which grow in great plenty in their cranberry bogs. The rest of their subsistence is derived from fishing; and from the sale of clay. . . . Small as their numbers are, they have two preachers; one of whom is a Baptist; the other, a Congregationalist; and both of them, Indians. . . .
>
> There is one Indian house, and three wigwams in Chilmark; all the in-

Sampson's Hill meetinghouse on Chappaquiddick Island, where the Christian Wampanoag gathered to worship during the mid-1800s. This photograph was taken many years later, after the Indians no longer used it. (MVHS Collections)

habitants of which, except a woman living in one of the wigwams, have rights at Gay Head.

There were even fewer Indians on Chappaquiddick. The Reverend James Freeman also visited them:

On this island, they have a tract of land reserved to them, containing about 800 acres. They are much intermixed with white and negro blood, very few of them being pure Indians; and they have been improved in their industry and general habits by the intermixture. Several of them live in framed houses, are good farmers, and are tolerably neat in their persons and habitations. The old men only are farmers, and are assisted by the women, who sow and hoe the corn; the young men are seamen. . . . Their numbers, which are probably increasing, are sixty-five, of whom nine are strangers [off-Islanders] intermarried with them. The framed houses are ten; the wigwams, two.

At Farm Neck he visited another Indian village: "Near Sangekantacket, adjoining the lagune [Lagoon], at a place called Farm Neck, there was formerly a large town of Indians; and twenty persons of a mixed race still remain, who live in six houses . . . and retain near two hundred acres of land."

After stating that "there is one Indian family, consisting of five persons," at West Chop, Freeman described Christiantown: "In the northwest part of Tisbury there is a tract of land, called Christiantown, assigned to the Indians, who are placed under guardians. They consist of nine families and thirty-two souls, of whom one male and six females are pure; the rest are mixed, chiefly with whites."

All together in 1807 there were an estimated 330 Indians on the Island; compare this with the more than three thousand living there two hundred years earlier, when the English settlement began. What had been a proud, independent people was now only a remnant. The Reverend James Freeman told a sad story of how it had happened: "The Mayhews, however pious and benevolent, did not much benefit the Indians; but the English derived the most essential advantages from the ascendancy which was gained over their minds; they were disarmed of their rage; they were made friends and fellow subjects. . . . Their numbers dwindled away, their courage abated, and they sunk into a mean and depressed people." They had become, the English came to believe, so incapable of taking care of themselves that Guardians were needed to look after them, as though they were children.

From time immemorial, Indians had taken good care of themselves and of the land on which they lived. The men, who once had been skilled hunters, now had no place to hunt. Fences and the English concept of private property denied them access. With no place to hunt and few other marketable skills, many men became lost souls, reduced to sitting around feeling sorry for themselves, easy prey to the addiction of alcohol, which whites happily sold to them.

Something more than land had been taken from them. By intermarriage with other races, they had lost their "Indian-ness." As the Reverend Joseph Thaxter wrote early in the 1800s:

> The natives, by mixture with the Blacks, have lost, I believe, much of the Fox and acquired more of the Bear and Wolf. These perhaps have better capacities for learning. But the misfortune is that most of the blacks that come and marry among them are very dissipated. They are a most improvident gang. They go to Nantucket and enter the Whaling Business

and after a Voyage of Two or Three years often come home in Debt. In their absence, the Squaws scratch as well as they can and support themselves and [their] children as well as they can. Clams, Quahogs, Ells [eels], etc., afford them a subsistence and they are generally remarkably healthy.

Those squaws did more than "scratch as well as they can," keeping themselves and their children alive; they became active politically, especially at Gay Head, where they were Proprietors and as such had equal status with the men, something not known among whites. Two petitions submitted by the Gay Head Proprietors to Massachusetts Bay governors are evidence. One of them, dated 1749, was written in the Indian language; the second was written in English in 1776. The first was signed by thirty-two Proprietors, ten of them women. The second has thirty-seven signatures (some signed with marks), of which sixteen, nearly half, were women's.

They were not the only Indian women who were active in politics. In 1809 four of them on Chappaquiddick, Mary Cook, Elizabeth Carter, Hannaretta Simson, and Charlotte Matteson, petitioned the governor of Massachusetts to provide a school for their children. Some of the white residents of Edgartown supported their request and urged the governor to take action: "We are well acquainted with the [Indian] Women—they Belong to the first families on the said Island and are generally of good moral character. We consider that their Endeavor to have the Gospel Preached among them, and a School for the Education of their youth is a Laudable Pursuit and hope they may Succeed."

No doubt the Reverend Joseph Thaxter had encouraged this petition by the Indian women (and their white supporters). He had, early in his long life on the Island, recognized the weakness of the missionary teaching. Five generations of Mayhew missionaries had devoted themselves in a sincere and well-meaning fashion to preparing the "savages" for life in the hereafter. What was needed was preparation for life in the present. Thaxter wrote:

> I consider the instruction of these poor creatures an object of importance. . . . I have been acquainted with them for near 40 years and am fully persuaded that schooling the children ought to be the first object: preaching to them, the second. Were the missionary intrusted with a small sum to employ a school mistress, it would be productive of a great

good. It would not only benefit the children, but endear him to their parents and render his labors much more useful.

In 1836, at a ceremony memorializing King Philip, the Wampanoag tribal chief who had been killed in Rhode Island many years before, the Reverend William Apes, himself an Indian, was critical of the missionaries: "But must I say, and shall I say it, that missionaries have injured us more than they have done us good, by degrading us as a people, in breaking up our governments, and leaving us without any suffrages whatever, or a legal right among men."

The last of the five generations of Mayhew missionaries, Zachariah Mayhew, in 1791 had recognized the importance of education. He convinced the missionary society in London, which held title to Gay Head, to use the rental money from the eight hundred acres known as the Farm to pay for an Indian school. It was not a new idea. Years earlier, in 1714, when the land was first leased to Sheriff Allen, the Indians had been promised that "Every penny received of Mr. Ebenezer Allen, or of any other, is all laid out only to make you a happy people."

But that had not happened because nobody was collecting the rent, and so Allen and others used the land without paying. Later the Indians, unhappy with what was going on, took the Farm by force. The Reverend Zachariah Mayhew realized that something must be done. A school at Gay Head would stop the violence, he wrote to the missionary society: "There now appears a disposition in the natives in general to have their children instructed by having good schools among them. . . . If your hon'able Society should see fit to adopt such measures as to appropriate the Farm to the benefit of the natives, particularly for the instruction of their children, by having good schools among them, it is my opinion that it would be so pleasing to them as to prevent all future acts of violence."

Those activist Indian women, the Island's (and perhaps the nation's) first feminists, seemed to be getting action—meager action, but action nonetheless. Other Indian women, off-Island Indians, raised a much more sensitive issue, as a 1792 document by Jeremy Belknap of Boston indicates: "From the difficulties which [the Indians] experience in obtaining support, and from the sufferings which they endure by the want of food, we find that many arts are practised by the wives to prevent, as much as possible, the increase of children and the augmentation of their families.

An ambrotype of Deacon Simon Johnson (1817–89) of Gay Head,
one of the last Wampanoag ministers on the Vineyard. He followed in the footsteps
of the missionary Mayhews. (MVHS Collections)

Zachariah's death in 1806 had left the society without a missionary. For the first time in five generations, no Mayhew was interested in the job. The Boston missionary society that had been paying Zachariah asked Thaxter to recommend someone to replace him. Thaxter, a trusted friend of the Indians, saw a chance for a major change. He urged the society to hire Frederick Baylies, then a teacher of the Indians on Nantucket. Although Baylies was not a minister, the Boston society, to its credit, hired him as its missionary. He was expected to combine teaching with Bible study. That didn't satisfy the Indian women. Baylies wrote to the Boston society of the pressure he was under: "In my visits, my feelings are often hurt; the universal complaint is, 'Our children are suffering for want of a school, and we are not able to support one. Can you help us?'"

It was not a good time for education of any kind, Indian or English. The few schools that did exist were stingily financed and poorly attended. Pupils came when they had nothing better to do; discipline was weak. Tisbury, in 1783 and again in 1793, was sued by the state for failing to provide any public school for its children. As late as 1823 the village was spending four times as much to support the poor ($800) as to provide schools in its four districts ($200 in total, $50 per district).

There were few trained teachers. In 1793 William Butler, a farmer at Farm Neck, in northern Edgartown, took over as teacher in the small school there. He realized how unqualified he was for the job and was trying to improve: "It now appears to me that I make but small progress in my Studies. I have lately been applying myself to English Grammer [sic] . . . but find it hard & most impossible to confine my mind wholly to that noble Science." A few weeks later he suddenly "Left off running School," making no mention of who, if anybody, would replace him.

Towns that were not eager to pay for schools for the white children felt absolutely no obligation to educate the Indians. That was something for missionary societies. Baylies, paid by one, pushed ahead, establishing schools in the Indian Lands and staffing them with Indian teachers when he could find them. Among the first teachers he hired was Mrs. Betsey Carter, one of those four activist women on Chappaquiddick who had petitioned for a school in 1809: "On the 30th of August [1818] Betsey Carter, a woman of colour, opened school at Chabaquiddick, to continue 8 weeks. . . . She has over 20 scholars and gives good satisfaction."

At Gay Head, Baylies was pleased with the reception his new school was being given by the natives:

> The Indians . . . chose a committee of seven to agree with a woman to take charge of the school, etc. On the 28th, the school was opened. On the 3d of July I visited it. There were present 30 scholars from 5 to 16 years of age; 2 only could read in the Testament and they but poorly. The

mistress, who was a coloured woman, told me 36 had attended and that 4 could read. . . . The scholars conducted themselves handsomely and appeared very decent.

Baylies opened a third school, this one taught by a white woman, at Christiantown. There were thirteen pupils for her first term of only six weeks. All together, in Baylies's three schools there were ninety-seven Indians in attendance. Though the terms were brief and probably little serious studying was required, the Indians were in school.

Paid $350 a year by the English missionary society, Baylies was making the first serious effort at teaching Vineyard Indians to read and to write English. He also supervised Indian schools in Nantucket and Rhode Island. About two hundred Indians attended his five schools, some for as many as sixteen weeks a year.

On the Vineyard there was little money for educating anybody. Residents were struggling to feed themselves, as they tried to recover from Grey's Raid. They had lost ten thousand sheep and had little hope of full payment. Gradually they rebuilt their flocks. By 1800 wool once again was the Island's leading moneymaker. Writing in the first decade of that century, the Reverend James Freeman computed the number of sheep on the Island and how important they were to the Island economy:

> Eleven thousand seven hundred pounds of wool have this year [1809] been purchased for exportation; the same number of pounds are annually manufactured [on the Island] into stockings, mittens, and cloths, chiefly flannels and blankets; making the whole twenty-three thousand four hundred pounds. [Since] sheep . . . yield a pound and a half of wool annually, there must be then fifteen thousand six hundred sheep.
>
> The number of pairs of stockings knit for sale by the women of the island in a year are about fifteen thousand; of mittens, three thousand; and of wigs [caps] for seamen, six hundred. The stockings, which bring fifty cents a pair, and the mittens, one third of that sum, are sold to the traders on the island, and in New Bedford, and paid for in goods. A pound of wool makes two pair of stockings.
>
> The wool, which is not manufactured [into clothing here], is principally purchased by persons who come for it from Connecticut, and who also carry away poquaus [?] and dry fish; they pay for it [the wool] about thirty cents a pound.

Freeman's computation indicates that the Island had by 1809 recovered from its livestock losses in Grey's Raid. His figure of 15,600 sheep on the Vineyard was about the same as before the raid. He also lists other means of making money on the Vineyard, mostly by manufacturing in Chilmark and Tisbury, where there were streams to provide power. Edgartown had only the wind to turn its machinery. The entire Island had the sun to turn ocean water into salt, helped by wind power that pumped the water into the vats:

> To prepare the wool for the manufacturers there is in Chilmark a carding machine, at which 5,000 pounds are carded annually. Connected with it is a fulling mill at which in the year 1805, 3,200 yards of cloth were pressed. . . . There is in Tisbury another mill at which about 700 or 800 yards are pressed in a year.
>
> Besides these mills there are, for the grinding of corn, four windmills in Edgartown, one of them on Chappaquiddick; one windmill and three watermills in Tisbury; and five watermills in Chilmark. These watermills are very small and grind only two or three bushels of corn in a day. . . .

Amelia Watson made this watercolor of a Chilmark pasturage in the 1880s. It is unknown what this scene had looked like before the English arrived with their sheep in the 1700s; there no doubt were more trees and bushes. (MVHS Collections)

There are in Edgartown three sets of salt works, containing 2,700 [square] feet; and in Tisbury five sets, containing 8,900 feet. This manufacture is increasing and probably in three or four years there will be more than double the number of feet.

The other manufactures are not of much importance. There are tanners, sadlers [cordwainers] and hatters . . . and mechanicks, as many as are necessary. The rest of the inhabitants are either seamen or farmers. In Edgartown the young and middle-aged men are seamen and are employed in fishing and foreign voyages and sail principally from other ports. The elderly men are employed in cultivating the land. The same thing may be said of Holmes's Hole. But in other parts of Tisbury and in Chilmark . . . a majority of the inhabitants obtain their subsistence from tilling the soil.

Much of this changed during the War of 1812, a war that was strongly opposed by New England and especially by the Vineyard, where the economic losses were serious. The Embargo Acts cut off shipping to the mainland and ended the export of Island wool. Much Island food had to come from the mainland, and prices skyrocketed when it had to be brought in surreptitiously both to avoid British warships and to get around the embargo. In 1813 things were so bad that Tisbury sent a memorial to the Congress, stating how the Island was suffering:

In consequence of the War with Great Britain many of [our residents are] destitute of employment by being deprived of their real Occupations and the present high price of bread . . . nearly double the Usual price. They see with infeigned Sorrow, Vessels dayly carrying Bread stuff (under British Linners) out of the United States to the ports & Countries under the controul of the British Nation & their Armies. In return we see the Manufacturers of Great Britian filling our ports & Towns thereby aiding our enemies as well as drawing out precious Metals (now so much wanted in our Country). . . . We request that the Nonimportation Law be strictly and rigidly enforced against Great Britain which will we believe alleviate many of our Citizens in the price of Bread and find Employment for our own Manufacturing Citizens.

Again in 1814 Tisbury petitioned, this time asking that the embargo on coastal shipping be lifted: "Our Oil, Salt, Wool and other domestic Articles and Manufacturers are cut off from their usual markits of New York &

Connecticut their being no markit within our limmitts. . . . Deprived of the Necessaries of life and Employment for our Fisher and Small Craft . . . [we] ask that Embargo Act be so modified that wee can have a communication by water with . . . New York & Connecticut." The embargo was quickly eased when Nantucket residents told Congress that it was threatening them with starvation.

Food and money were the major concerns of Vineyarders during the war, but there was another, more mental than real. They felt vulnerable. And the federal government agreed when it ordered the customs collector Thomas Cooke in Edgartown to transfer to a Boston bank the bonds he was holding for customs owed, lest they be stolen by a British invader.

There were other reasons to be apprehensive. Cannon fire was regularly heard along the south shore. Rebecca Smith, a teenager living at Pohoganut, wrote in her diary between April 1813 and March 1814 of hearing distant cannon fire ten times. Here are two of those entries:

> April 20, 1813. A dead silence reigns throughout this mansion, all is still save the roaring of distant cannon. . . . America once happy land is now involved in war; America, methinks I saw your blooming sons fall in battle. . . .
>
> July 18, 1813. A stately ship is now full in view. . . . She is a "74" [a large warship with seventy-four cannon] by her majestic appearance. . . . As I sat viewing the stupendious barque from the top of the house, my ear was suddenly saluted with the report of deep toned cannon from the ship. . . . I espied another ship of equal bigness. . . . A continual roaring salutes my ears.

Although this sensitive, poetic girl lived in remote Pohoganut, on the south shore, she was not isolated from the news. Her father was the county registrar of deeds and he had his office at home. Visitors arrived almost daily, bringing the latest news along with deeds to be registered. She makes frequent mention of their reports, including one of an English privateer in Edgartown. Here are a few more of her entries:

> June 6, 1813. I have just been informed that the Frigate *Chesapeake* is taken. Uncle [the Reverend Joseph] Thaxter was at Boston, was an eye witness, saw the battle fought and the conquering enemy bear away the prize. Mr. B. Luce is here and tells the same.
>
> July 7, 1813. Mr. Jabez Smith is here this evening. He brought a News

paper which gave an account of the defeat of Gen. Dearborn's army. Thus, thousands of our country-men have lost their lives by this ungenerous and cruel war. . . .

July 22, 1813. Melancholy news from the South. Richmond is taken and plundered.

September 28, 1813. I am this day informed that the United States Brig *Enterprise* captured the Brig *Boxer* on the 5th instant after an action of 45 minutes. Both Captains killed and buried side by side.

October 20, 1813. The all accomplished Mr. Lev [Leavitt] Thaxter has been here this morning, informs us that there is an English Privateer in Old Town Harbour [Edgartown]. Yesterday they burnt one of the Smacks belonging to Mr. Fisher and Mr. Coffin.

If Leavitt Thaxter's report was correct (and there is no reason to doubt it), that was the only "invasion" of the Island during the War of 1812.

There was much privateering by both sides. Islanders served on many of the armed vessels that harassed British shipping. Many of them were Indians, and Thomas Cooke, as Guardian of the Indians of Chappaquiddick, wrote to the privateer owners, telling them to send any prize money due to Indians to him; he would be sure the money went to their families. He also wrote to whaleship owners, asking that money owed to Indians on their vessels be sent to him.

When the war ended in December 1814, shipping activity soon recovered. Thomas Cooke Jr. reported as customs collector that in the first nine months of 1816, 712 vessels entered Edgartown and Holmes Hole and that 100 of them were foreign vessels carrying imports. If the Vineyard was their first port of call, he was required to certify their arrival in the country before allowing them to proceed to whatever port their cargo was to go. He complained that because they did not pay duty there, he was not compensated for all the work the increasing activity required of him.

Thomas Cooke had a way of getting government positions. He was also one of the Guardians of Indians. Each town had these political appointees. There is little evidence that they did much to improve the lives of those they were supposed to be protecting. The system became so bad that Chappaquiddick Indians sent a petition to Governor John Brooks of Massachusetts in 1818:

> Under the Special Law passed January 26th, 1789 . . . the Governor was empowered to . . . appoint two white Persons and one Indian as

Guardians, to have the Care and oversight of the said Indians. . . . Guardians have Repeatedly been appointed . . . yet it has so fallen out at this time that one of the white Guardians, namely Samuel Smith Esqr. . . . shall Send up his Resignation; and that Isaiah Johnson, the Indian Guardian, for a Long time Past [has] been absent and is not Likely to Return . . . in Consequence of which your petitioners . . . are greatly injured by their white neighbours in that they neglect to keep in Repair the Partition Fence which separates their Lands from ours, which by Law belongs to them to keep in Repair, and their Cattle, Sheep, and other Creatures frequently Come into our Lands and Distroy our Corn, Rye and Grass.

The fence in question ran east to west, dividing the island of Chappaquiddick in half, the Indians being confined to the wet, boggy north side (except for a woodlot on the south side). The petitioners urged the governor to appoint Captain Valentine Pease Jr., "a Person in whom we Can Confide," and Ebenezor Cadody, an Indian, to fill the two vacancies. Elijah Stuart Esq., the third guardian, should be retained, the petitioners said.

The guardian system was indeed a failure. It never had protected the Indians from aggressive whites who found ways to take over their land, sometimes by purchase, sometimes not. The General Court seemed to go along. As the Reverend Joseph Thaxter wrote with disapproval and disgust to his friend and fellow Unitarian the Reverend James Freeman in 1823, for many whites cheating an Indian was not a sin:

> I think it extremely wrong for the Gen'l Court to give leave to any [Indian] to alienate their [property] Rights. Christiantown and Farm Neck have and must suffer sorely in Consequence of this Practice. A few Designing white men have acquired Property and the Natives [are] left to perish or live by begging. . . . When sick, their sufferings are beyond Description. . . . I fear those who have been benefited by buying their Lands have but little feeling for them. . . . I do fear that there are those who think it is no Sin to cheat an Indian.

Many Indian males, both young and middle-aged, tried to escape the system by going to sea. They were eagerly sought by ships' agents and masters to fill their crews. It was becoming harder to find whites willing to sign on for the long voyages. Pay for men of color was usually below that for whites, and they often finished a voyage with little or no money due them after deductions were made for what they owed for purchases from the slop chest and advances given at various ports of call.

We have no way of knowing how many of the Island's Indians and mixed-race men were mariners in the early 1800s. Nonwhites living in Indian Lands were not included in the 1850 federal census. But crew lists show that almost every whaler had men of color in its crew. Skin colors were recorded in a variety of tones, black, brown, yellow, negro, African, and Indian among them. The New Bedford Public Library crew lists of whalers owned in New Bedford, Fairhaven, and neighboring ports provide the following information about the skin colors of Vineyarders aboard those whalers:

> Edgartown: Total crewmen, 73. Of whom 4 were black and
>   negro, 3 were colored and yellow [probably meaning mulatto].
> Tisbury: Total crewmen, 85. Of whom 2 were black, 1 was negro,
>   1 was copper and 1 was Indian.
> Chilmark: Total crewmen, 44. Of whom 3 were black, 4 were
>   colored, 6 were Indian and 1 was copper.
> Gay Head: Total crewmen, 8. Of whom, 4 were Indian, 1 was
>   native, 1 was black.

Many of those men of color who said they were from Chilmark probably lived in Gay Head, which was then part of that town. Mariners gave their town of residence, but the officers decided on the color of their skins. Skin color was not listed in every case. The term "white" was not used; instead, white sailors were listed as "fair" or "light." Those two shades made up the largest number from every Vineyard town except Gay Head. Edgartown had 39 light- or fair-skinned mariners (of 73); Tisbury had 58 (of 85); Chilmark had 18 (of 44); Gay Head had none (of 8). The total for the Island: 115 of 210, or 55 percent, were fair- or light-skinned. This clearly was a subjective survey. How light-skinned Portuguese were categorized, or for that matter, any light-skinned minority, is unclear.

On whaleships men of color only infrequently made it to positions of responsibility, such as boatsteerer or officer. Conventional wisdom has it that Gay Head Indians were sought out as harpooners (a term rarely used by whalemen; the man who thrusts the harpoon into the whale was called a boatsteerer). The harpooning skill of Indians no doubt became accepted as fact after Herman Melville's novel *Moby-Dick* became popular, which was not until long after it was published in 1851. Melville's boatsteerer is named Tashtego, "an unmixed Indian from Gay Head." The Vineyard, Melville added, "has long supplied the neighboring island of Nantucket with many of her most daring harpooners." Melville's suggestion that "unmixed" Gay Head Indians (of whom there were very few by then) were sought out as boatsteerers could not have become widely accepted by the public until after the glory days of whaling were over. *Moby-Dick* was virtually unknown to the public before Raymond M. Weaver's biography of Herman Melville came out in 1921.

The New Bedford crew lists show no Vineyard Indian (of any of the various skin colors listed) as a boatsteerer. The Vineyard did have one black whaling master. It is not known how much, if any, Indian ancestry he had. He was Captain William A. Martin of Chappaquiddick, master on three whaling voyages between 1878 and 1890, two being made on schooners and one on a brig. Two of the three vessels were owned by Samuel Osborn Jr. of Edgartown. There may have been other whaling masters of color, but records suggest that nonwhites never advanced very high in the hierarchy.

For white Vineyard men, going to sea offered a chance to get rich, and it was the most popular occupation in the 1800s. The census of 1850 lists 686 males with the occupation "mariner," compared to 342 farmers, the second most numerous. It is said that the Vineyard had more whaling masters per capita than any other place, although no data are known to prove it.

As for numbers of ships owned, the Vineyard was far down the list compared to Nantucket, New Bedford, and several other ports. The peak years of Vineyard ownership were 1841 and 1842, when there were sixteen Island whalers in service. During those same years New Bedford had more than seventy, and Nantucket had twenty-five. Vineyard whalers with the longest and most successful records were *Almira* (15 voyages), *Splendid* (13), *Vineyard* (12), *Champion* (11), and *Mary* (10). All were active during the great whaling years, from 1830 to 1879.

In terms of sailings, that is, the number of times whalers left their home ports on voyages, the minor-league status of the Vineyard is obvious. Judith Navas Lund, in her masterly work, *Whaling Masters and Whaling Voyages Sailing from American Ports*, published in 2001, shows 5,146 departures from New Bedford throughout the history of whaling, 2,223 from Nantucket, 1,156 from Provincetown, and 1,116 from New London. Edgartown had 237, with 17 more from "Martha's Vineyard," no doubt meaning Holmes Hole and Menemsha.

Capital investment in whaling ships was small on the Vineyard, but there were many Island males who invested their lives. There were so many, in fact, that a major social change was engendered. With so many men away for years at a time, women were forced to take enlarged roles. Children were raised in what were essentially single-parent homes. The business of keeping up the house, paying the bills, and disciplining and educating the children all fell to the mothers. Unmarried women were also affected. They had fewer men courting them, fewer men with whom to socialize and to share the joys of young love.

More than half the Island's males between fourteen and nineteen went to sea and thus were isolated socially during those formative years aboard ships, living totally with men—some of them crude, cruel men. The dictatorial behavior and sadistic treatment by some whaling masters must have had a profound affect on the personalities of those young men. Inadequate diets, unsanitary living conditions, and irregular sexual experiences on ship and ashore certainly did something to them physically and mentally. They lived through those critical years without the gentility, grace, and courtesy they would be exposed to on land in a population half female.

There is a saying, "Send a boy to sea and get back a man." No doubt it is true, but what kind of a man? It is no wonder that whalemen turned to scrimshaw, sea chanteys, and dancing the sailor's hornpipe to add touches, however slight, of gentility to their totally male-oriented lives.

The shortage of males on the Vineyard perhaps caused young women to be drawn to religious meetings, the major social events at the time. The Island (along with other places) was undergoing a religious reformation. Young women seeking something to do flocked to nightly meetings held by evangelists. We don't know exactly when the evangelizing began on the Vineyard, but Rebecca Smith's diary may provide a clue. On August 2, 1813, she wrote, rather obtusely: "Mrs. Beetle informed me that there has been an eruption broke out amongst the inhabitants of the East side of Holmes's Hole, has been allmost as dangerous as those which issue forth from the burning Volcanoes, Vesuvius and Aetna."

The east side of Holmes Hole was known as Eastville and was where many newcomers, especially people of color, settled. Rebecca didn't detail what was "erupting," but it is likely that it was an outbreak of religious fervor. She would have been well informed about such happenings, since her uncle was the Reverend Joseph Thaxter, the minister of the Congregational church in Edgartown. His congregation would soon be decimated as scores of members were "born again," converted by the spellbinding Baptist and Methodist evangelists. Rebecca and her sisters, Hannah and Clarissa, often attended services at Thaxter's church and must have been disturbed to see so many of its members leave.

Baptist and Methodist societies (they were not called churches at first) date back to the late 1700s on the Island. There is little documentation of precisely when the first evangelist arrived. Jeremiah Pease of Edgartown, who was one of those who was "born again," said that the first Methodist to come was a black man, a former slave from Virginia who arrived in 1787. He was not a minister, but he did preach: "The first Methodist that visited this Island . . . was a coloured man by the name of John Saunders, who with his wife came to this town in the year 1787 and took up their residence in the village of Eastville. He preached to the coloured people at Farm Neck. . . . In 1792, they removed to the Island of Chapaquiddic. His first wife died. He married . . . Jane Diamond, who is now living and is 95 years old." (Pease wrote this in 1847.) Pease's account is confirmed by the journal of Mrs. Priscilla Freeman, who was a granddaughter of John and Priscilla Saunders. She wrote about her grandparents, describing her grandfather as a minister who came to a violent end on Chappaquiddick:

> He was a pure African, she half white. . . . They took passage with Capt. Thos. Luce [in Virginia] . . . in a small vessel ladened with corn, in which the Captain had buried them the night previous to sailing. . . . Arriving at H. Hole . . . they repaired to Col. Davises on the East Side and were invited to move into the little schoolhouse, standing a few rods east of the Colonel's residence. . . . Here, the minister's wife Priscilla died. After living 5 or 6 years in this place, he located at Chappaquidic, where he preached and became acquainted with [an Indian] Jane Dimon, and married with her; which exasperated the Indians there, on account of his African descent; and this . . . is supposed to be the cause of his being murdered in the woods.

During the years that followed various itinerant preachers—Baptist, Methodist, and even one evangelical Congregationalist—crisscrossed the Vineyard by horse and buggy, holding meetings in private homes and gaining important converts such as Judge Benjamin Bassett, who allowed the itinerant preachers to stay with his family. They traveled from village to village proclaiming their frightening, emotional warnings of damnation, unlike the ministers with their conventional and boring sermons heard in the established churches. Ministers like Thaxter intoned long sermons on verses from the Bible each Sabbath. The itinerants, very few of them well educated, were more dramatic, more interested in arousing their listeners' emotions than in teaching Scripture. Damnation and hellfire were all the verses they needed.

The Congregational church in Edgartown, the oldest church on the Island, was especially vulnerable. Its unemotional services, along with its aging pastor, bored many, especially young men, who, according to Pease, had lost their way and turned to sin:

> Intemperance prevailed to an alarming degree. Vice and immorality fol-
> lowed, with its train of evils too numerous to enumerate. . . . Inhabitants
> of this place . . . employed their evenings and I might say their nights in
> playing Billiards, Pitching dollars, Playing cards, and drinking. . . . I have
> known the aged but vigorous Mother to visit those places in the night
> and bring out her children (young men) from these scenes of dissipation.
> I have known fifteen men of good abilities and worth a handsome prop-
> erty enter into the business of retailing ardent spirits, who in a few years
> became intemperate, all of whom, I fear, found a premature grave.

The evangelists, despite their theatrical late-night meetings, had little success converting Pease's "sinners." They were having too much fun. The Methodists and Baptists opposed everything the young men enjoyed. Prayer meetings, which often ran past midnight, were disrupted by these sinners who, Pease wrote later, had come from

> all grades of Society who were destitute of vital piety. . . . Meetings
> [were] disturbed by throwing stones, mud, dead cats and the howling of
> dogs. . . . A Baptist preacher . . . was thrown from the table [on which he
> was preaching]. Such a scene of confusion, I presume, was never wit-
> nessed in any meeting in this town before or since. . . . The assembly was
> confused, some shoving, some pulling, multitudes rushing for the door.
> . . . One man struck [the preacher] with his fist and cried out, "Run, you
> Devil, or they will kill you."

In their early years Jeremiah Pease had actively opposed the evangel-ists. Standing faithfully behind his friend and mentor, the Reverend

Joseph Thaxter, he was so upset by their methods that one evening he, not unlike those he would become so critical of later, disrupted one of the meetings. He confessed his actions to a group of Methodists years later:

> One evening while he [the Methodist minister Steele] was preaching, he was seized with a trembling in consequence of which the house . . . shook and caused a great alarm among many of the Congregation. I heard the sound and hastened to the Meeting House, went into the Pulpit, took hold of the Preacher and offered to bring him out if any one would help me. But as none seemed disposed to assist, I retired, much enraged. . . . This rash act of mine, I have always regretted.

Brother Steele, as the regretful Pease came to call him, was the first Methodist to ignite the flame, the first to awaken the multitude. He was followed by John "Reformation" Adams, the most successful revivalist in Vineyard history. When Adams left Edgartown after two years, there were 160 Methodists, several times more than were in Thaxter's Congregational church, from which many had come, one of them being Jeremiah Pease. Adams, a nonstop worker for the Lord, built on what Steele had begun. His flair for dramatics brought the revival to a peak, not only in Edgartown but all over the Island.

What Mrs. Beetle had described as a volcanic eruption in Eastville ten years before was surely the beginning of a change in the Island's religious life that devastated the Congregational church and broke the heart of the aging Thaxter, who for nearly forty years had been the Island's spiritual leader. He was a bitter, old man when he wrote to his friend the Reverend James Freeman in Boston on February 25, 1823:

> In June 1821 a John Adams from New Hampshire came. He is an illiterate & weak man, his wife attends him & grasps a high degree of self confidence, not to say impudence. . . . He has a thundering voice & many curious agitations of body. He boldly affirms that he was sent by God to preach the Gospel in this place. . . . "I have a Message from God to you, don't you want to get Religion?" In this way they go from Town to Town & from House to House. They hold their Meetings Night & Day. . . . Adams is so loud as to be heard a quarter of a mile. . . . By such means as these, the whole Island has been thrown into a Flame. . . . Children are set against their parents & Wives against their Husbands.

. . . [When his converts] "come out," as they call it . . . born again, they immediately become self-confident & swell with spiritual Pride like a puff-Fish when the Boys scratch his belly. . . . Adams [Methodist] & Hubbard [Baptist] with their Wives ride about in their carriages . . . [and take] frequent collections & get as much Money in one Week as I have received for the last fourteen months.

That same month Rebecca Smith's sister Hannah wrote in her diary about what was tearing apart Uncle Thaxter's church:

February 8, 1823: There appears to be an uncommon stir in every part of the Island respecting religion, some for one denomination and some for another.

February 20: Jonathan Allen has returned from Edgartown. He informs us that Religion flourishes in the Vilage.

The next Sunday Hannah and her other sister, Clarissa, attended services in Uncle Thaxter's Congregational church. She remarked on the dwindling congregation: "We attended Parson Thaxter's Meeting. He had but few hearers Sunday Eve."

Even the remoteness of Pohoganut could not protect the Smith girls from proselytizing by "Reformation" Adams, as Hannah recorded in her diary:

June 2: Eleven o'clock. The Rev. John Adams and Lady are here—Mr. Adams Exhorts and prays with us. His prayer flows like a stream which, murmuring like the distant sound of signs and plaintive moans, creeps along the vale.

2 of the clock. Mr. Adams presents Clarissa and myself with a couple of Hymn books. He invites me to ride as far as Harrisons with him. I accept of his invitation. [Harrison is her brother, who lived a short distance away.]

It is unlikely that Adams gained any followers among the Smiths at Pohoganut. Their family relationship with Joseph Thaxter surely prevented it. But one of Thaxter's strongest followers, Jeremiah Pease, did succumb, as mentioned earlier. He attended a Methodist prayer meeting on October 1, 1822, and his life was changed. He gives no details in his diary, but on that date he wrote, "This day I hope will never be forgotton [sic] by me."

Pease didn't allow himself to admit to any exaltation over being born again. The entry is one we could slip past if we hadn't read what the fiery evangelist "Reformation" Adams wrote in his autobiography years later. Here are some excerpts (Adams used only initials to identify individuals):

> [September 28] In the evening, I conversed with J.P. He is very serious, and under true awakenings. He said that, when I first came to the island, if I had come to his house to talk on religion, he would have ordered me out. He would not suffer a Methodist hymn to be sung in his house. . . .
>
> [October 2] Wednesday I came back, and visited with J.P. Bless God! . . . He found peace the night before, and now preaches a free salvation. . . . He says he was like Saul of Tarsus. He never was seen at our meeting till of late, excepting once, when he helped take the preacher from the pulpit. Glory to God for another of the sturdy oaks of Bashan that is brought down!

The next Sunday, after attending the Adams meeting, Pease again was guarded in describing the joy that had come over him: "Oct. 6th. This was a very pleasant Sabbath to me." It is almost as though he didn't want to admit the change, momentous though it was. More than a month later he finally recorded that he had become a Methodist: "Nov. 28th. Became a Member of the Methodis [sic] Class." As much as Pease played down what had happened, it was a major factor in the history of the Island, as we shall see.

Reformation Adams left the Vineyard in 1824, at the end of his two-year assignment. With a quieter man replacing him, the Edgartown Methodists became less "wild," more conservative. As they cooled down, their membership continued to increase. They and the Baptists were soon numerous enough to build a church together. Some members were unhappy about the changes brought on as the fire cooled and asked the Providence Conference to reassign Adams to the Island. In 1826 he returned.

Again he aroused the Methodists. He traveled all over the Island, holding meetings and rekindling the fire. One night, while he was hurrying to a meeting in Chilmark, his horse stumbled and he was thrown to the ground and rendered unconscious. When he revived, he managed to get the horse back on its feet and make it to the home of a Chilmark follower.

Not long after, he began hallucinating; his mind became flooded with messages from God. He refused medical care. He was in God's hands, he said. After some weeks his followers forcibly bound his arms and legs and carried him from his room in Holmes Hole to Edgartown to be treated by Dr. Daniel Fisher. Two Methodist men sat beside his bed twenty-four hours a day to prevent him from getting up, as he continued to fight all treatment: "I did not believe in Doctor Fisher's medicine; for, while I was fishing for souls, he was fishing for money. . . . Wicked men . . . offered me medicine that I had no faith in . . . they tried to deceive me. They thought I was crazy."

In a few weeks he had recovered enough to return to his preaching, although his mind was still confused. He saw himself and his followers as characters in the Bible and gave each a Biblical name. Later, in his auto-biography, he made it clear that he firmly believed his hallucinating was God's way to inspire him. As his second term neared its end, he was con-vinced that God was ordering him to assemble his soldiers on a camp-ground where "God's forces will muster" and destroy the Devil.

For that battlefield Reformation Adams selected a site on West Chop. He paid twenty-five dollars to rent it for a week, hired carpenters to build a preachers' stand, and invited Methodist ministers from the Cape to deliver a weeklong onslaught on the Devil. On August 1, 1827, eight years before the first Wesleyan Grove camp meeting, he held a meeting on West Chop. Adams described it: "August 1st, our camp-meeting commenced and more than twenty preachers were present and not far from thirty tents were on the ground. The people came from different islands and many from the Cape, New Bedford and Boston. All parts of the Vineyard were represented. There was but little disturbance. . . . I exhorted a few times, preached once with freedom and prayed often. The care of the meeting . . . devolved considerably on me."

Among those attending was his prize convert, Jeremiah Pease. With ninety other Methodists, Pease sailed to West Chop from Edgartown. He wrote in his diary: "We set sail with a pleasant breeze. . . . Arrive at the West Chop in about an hour & twenty minutes. . . . There were about 40 very large Tents erected. On Sunday there was tho't to be about 4,000 peo-ple present."

One week later Adams left the Island, his tour of duty finished. He left without realizing what he had set in motion. He had planted an idea that would change the Island forever. That West Chop meeting infected the Methodists with camp-meeting fever. Most infected was Jeremiah Pease.

The West Chop Campground did not continue. But a few years later

Pease, remembering that first camp meeting, became the father of the Wesleyan Grove Campground. Late in May 1835, with the help of Bertrand Sherman, a Methodist from Nantucket, he spent several days at Eastville, where for years he had been the leader of the Methodist Society. The two men spent those days selecting the site that became today's Oak Bluffs Campground.

The choice was theirs alone. There were no meetings of Methodists, no discussions, simply two men making a decision. They chose a cool, shady grove of oak trees on the farm of William Butler of Farm Neck. For fifteen dollars and a pledge to pay for any damages that might be done to the trees or his sheep, Butler, himself a Methodist, agreed to rent it to them for a week's camp meeting.

Jeremiah Pease marked the spot for the preachers' stand between two of the tallest oaks. On each of the two trees a large lantern would be hung to illuminate the meetings, which would extend into the night. The land was cleared of huckleberry bushes for a circle of tents. Nine tent frames were built of wood, over which old sails were draped to form the communal tents shared by many worshippers. At meeting time smaller, private tents were put up outside the circle by individuals and families. Pease wrote in his diary on August 20, 1835: "Wind SW. Went to East Chop to clear ground and erect our tents for Camp Meeting."

Throughout the rest of his life, Jeremiah Pease never failed to take part in the camp meetings, spending the week in his tent and serving as an exhorter and a chorister for the flock. He never lost his faith in revivals. Years later, during the Reformation of 1853, revival meetings were held in Edgartown for one hundred nights in succession. Pease became so totally involved that his wife, not a born-again Methodist, became ill. When their son, Lieutenant William Cooke Pease of the U.S. Revenue Service, learned of his mother's illness, he wrote to his wife, Serena, in Edgartown: "I wish a Methodist Minister had never seen Martha's Vineyard. There is Mother sick again, just by their nonsensical pow wow—the whole Town seem to be running mad . . . and acting just like so many Block Islanders . . . they seem like so many raving Hottentots, and had better stay at home, read their Bible and learn wisdom, and not rush to that Methodist Vestry every night, and howl like so many Coyotes."

Lieutenant Pease, aboard his revenue cutter in the Pacific, could not have foreseen what his father had done. He had altered the history of Martha's Vineyard. Wesleyan Grove Campground became something bigger than anybody, Methodist or not, could have imagined. But Jeremiah Pease didn't live long enough to see what he had done. Walking along Edgartown's Main Street on the afternoon of June 5, 1857, he collapsed. That night he died.

It was just as well. He would not have been pleased with what followed.

6

Seeking God, Gold, Whales, and More

It was a time of unrest. After years of contentment, of satisfaction with their simple Island life, Vineyarders began to want more. There was not enough discontent to spawn a revolt, but enough to convince some residents that life could be better.

In northern and western Edgartown, unhappy residents petitioned the state in 1836 to let them form a separate town. They didn't think their interests were being served by the village establishment. Others, their families expanding, needed more farmland and, finding none, moved to Maine or Ohio, where land was plentiful and often free for the taking.

Other factors aggravated the unrest. Irish workers, mostly female domestics, began arriving in large numbers. With them came Roman Catholicism, a "foreign" religion—a threat from abroad, some thought.

An occasional fugitive slave from the South would escape from a coastal vessel in a Vineyard harbor, seeking help and raising ethical problems. Should escaping slaves be protected or sent back? The law was clear: send them back.

In 1848 gold was discovered in California, tempting many whalemen, their voyages getting longer and longer and less and less profitable, to seek a quicker path to riches.

Perhaps it was the growing unrest that moved Jeremiah Pease and other Methodists to seek a retreat, a secluded spot where they could get away from such problems, a place where they would be closer to God. Whatever the reason, in August 1835 a few of them created a campground where praying and preaching went on day and night as they sought salvation.

Camp meetings had been popular on the mainland for years. Jeremiah

151

Pease and other Island Methodists often attended them. The first one on the Vineyard had taken place some years before, when Reformation Adams held one on West Chop. It lasted only one season. Pease wanted a permanent campground where Vineyarders could revel each August in the glory of God. He and a group of other Methodists agreed on William Butler's oak grove, south of Squash Meadow Pond on East Chop, away from any village. And so Wesleyan Grove Campground came to be.

It was early summer. For a meeting to be held that August, as Pease intended, they would have to hurry. With Jeremiah Pease on that day of decision were Thomas M. Coffin, Chase Pease, Frederick Baylies Jr., the Reverend Daniel Webb, presiding elder of the district, and the Reverend James C. Boutecou, the Edgartown Methodist pastor.

Baylies and Coffin were two of the town's finest carpenters, and they agreed to build a preachers' stand and benches. They went to work the following week. With them was Henry Baylies, son of Frederick. Years later, he wrote about that week:

> A vessel was freighted at Edgartown with lumber, sails, etc., for the new camping-ground. Her cargo was rafted ashore on the east side of the [East] Chop. . . . It was a hard day's work to get the material ashore and up to the grove; but it was done, and the preachers' stand was partly constructed the same day.
>
> During the week, the stand was completed, seats were arranged, and some nine tent frames, built of rough joists were covered with superannuated sails of various patterns. While the men were thus employed, we two younger boys, John Wesley [Coffin] and myself, were employed in pulling up huckleberry brush within the "circle of the tents" and doubtless thought we had the hardest part of the work. . . .
>
> Water was obtained by sinking two barrels close to the edge of the Squash Meadow Pond. . . . These barrels furnished sufficient water for the first meeting. . . .
>
> [In] our party, camping on the ground this first week, were Thomas M. Coffin Esq., and his two sons, Sirson P., and John Wesley, and Frederick Baylies Esq., and his son Henry, the writer hereof, all of Edgartown. . . .
>
> This was the day of small beginnings.

Indeed, they were small beginnings. Hebron Vincent, a campground historian, described the first camp meeting:

The stand was a rough board shed of quite limited capacity, with a one-pitch roof, much in the style of some [fire-]wood shelters. It was specially for the ministers. There was a seat in front under the projection of the cover for them to sit on, and standing room to preach from. Within were bundles of rye-straw upon the bare ground for them to spread and sleep on. Fortunate, indeed, was the man of the cloth who had a quilt to cover him, and an extra sheaf of straw for a pillow. These were the luxurious provisions for the clergy.

In front of the stand they built a series of rough board benches without backs for the congregation. A wide aisle went down the center, separating the men and women. To provide for preaching day and night, ministers from the mainland were invited. Only a few came, Vincent recalled years later, in 1858:

> The number of preachers in attendance was of course small; the exact number is not now known. Nor are the names of those who preached, except two or three. . . . The waving trees, the whispering breeze, the pathetic appeals, the earnest prayers, and the songs of praise, as well as the trembling of sinners . . . and the shining countenances of Christians lighted up with holy joy, all conspired to say "Surely the Lord is in this place."

Most of Vincent's "shining countenances" belonged to Island Methodists, who lived in sailcloth tents for four days: "Nine tents, many of them small and rudely constructed, some of vessels' sails drawn over poles, graced the little circle, being furnished within with chests and trunks, possibly with a few benches and straw upon the bare ground for beds at night. At bed-time, a high cloth curtain was extended across the tent, about in the middle, to separate the space into lodging apartments for the two sexes. (At first, we had no family tents.)"

Food was brought picnic-style from home, dishes that needed little additional cooking. Without refrigeration, not even any ice, it was a challenge during the hot days of August. A few women did cook over open fires: "Tables for meals were set under the shade of the trees, in rear of the tents. These tables were spread for the ministry as well as for the brotherhood. For supplies of food such as could not well be carried from home ready prepared for the table, cooking arrangements were improvised out back of the tables, where camp fires were safely made."

That first meeting lasted from Wednesday through Saturday. Those present were so pleased that before leaving they contributed nearly enough money "to cover the whole expense of the present meeting, and to purchase the lumber." They would be back next year. William Butler agreed to allow them to leave the structures standing over the winter. The following August the second meeting drew more from off-Island: "Brethren were present from New Bedford, Fairhaven, Falmouth, Nantucket, So. Yarmouth, Sandwich, Fall River, Bristol, and several other places. Our meeting was more fully attended than it was last year." Word of the beauty of the place was spreading: "The preachers present . . . even the aged and more experienced of them, were unanimous in pronouncing this the best place for a camp meeting of any they had ever seen."

Maintenance of the grounds was done by Edgartown Methodists, but control of the meetings was quickly taken over by mainland ministers. Within a few years they and the congregations who came with them far outnumbered Vineyarders on the campground. Pease's dream of a simple retreat for Islanders had vanished. Local Methodists had become unimportant—except as custodians.

Getting to the campground from the mainland was not easy, but once congregants got there, its placid beauty was overwhelming, as the Reverend Franklin Fisk of Yarmouth Port discovered in 1838: "The Camp Meeting broke up at 12 o'clock on Tuesday night. . . . At midnight, under the exhilarating influence of the full moon . . . beaming down among the trees . . . we left the ground. O lovely spot! Shall I ever visit it again? There is something peculiarly dear to me about the Vineyard. There is not another place on earth which ever seemed to me so much like paradise." As they walked at midnight under a full moon to the Eastville beach to board a waiting boat for the sail to Yarmouth across moonlit Nantucket Sound, they surely were filled to overflowing with a love of God and His creation.

Word of the grove's loveliness kept spreading. Attendance increased. It seemed that it would go on forever, but after nine years the mainland ministers who controlled such things decided it was time to move on. Hebron Vincent, the camp meeting secretary, explained: "Having been held here for nine successive years, it had become 'an old story,' and that to remove it to some other place, where such meetings have never been held, would . . . accomplish a greater amount of good."

So there was no camp meeting on the Vineyard in 1845. The preachers'

Vineyard camp meetings, which began in 1835, were moved in 1844 by the Providence Methodist District to Westport, Massachusetts. After one year the meetings returned to find the new preachers' stand and benches shown in this lithograph from Hebron Vincent's *A History of the Wesleyan Grove, Martha's Vineyard, Camp Meeting.* (MVHS Collections)

stand and the benches were torn down, the lumber sold. The grove, so cherished by worshippers, was returned to Farmer Butler's sheep. Jeremiah Pease's dream had ended.

The 1845 meeting was held at Westport Point, Massachusetts, near the Rhode Island border, much more convenient to the Providence office of the Methodist District. The new location was described as "tolerably good, yet the ground was quite rough. . . . An excellent boiling spring of water nearby conduced greatly to the comfort of the encampment."

Some of the faithful Vineyard Methodists attended, among them Jeremiah Pease and Hebron Vincent. Pease wrote in his diary: "1845, August 16. Went to Camp Meeting in Sloop *Vineyard*, arrived at Westport about 2 PM, stayed there until the meeting closed on Tuesday Morning, returned in Steam Boat *Massachusetts* via N. Bedford. . . . There were not so many

The Congregational church in Edgartown, built in 1845, is still in use today.
This photograph was taken more than forty years after it was built on South
Summer Street, which was then a sandy lane. (MVHS Collections)

people present as generally attended the Camp Meetings at the Vineyard,
except Sunday . . . a greater number attended on that day."

Vineyard meetings had not been held on Sunday, having ended on Saturday. The Sunday meeting was new and popular. Hebron Vincent
described it: "A vast concourse gathered on the Sabbath, estimated at
between five and six thousand. . . . It was considered very safe to put down
the number of conversions at twenty."

Although Westport was on the mainland, it was easier to get there by
boat than by wagon. New Bedford Methodists chartered the steamboat
Massachusetts for the trip. The Vineyard Methodists joined them for their
voyage home. As Vincent wrote, God was also on board: "On our way
[back] to New Bedford, on board the fine steamer, *Massachusetts*, Capt.
Lot Phinney, Master, Dr. Pitman, by the request of the company, preached
a most able and soul-stirring sermon. . . . Tears moistened the eyes of
many present, not excepting those of our excellent and noble-hearted
commander."

Not all Vineyarders were unhappy when the camp meeting left the
Island, certainly not the Baptists, who were envious of the greater popularity of the Methodists. (They soon built their own campground on East

Chop.) Congregationalists, too, must have been pleased, as they had suffered from the loss of members to the Methodists and the Baptists. These losses had so injured their pride that in 1828, even before camp meetings began, a group of Congregationalists decided to build a larger church in Edgartown. Not that it was needed: with the congregation shrinking, the old church was large enough. But they needed a spiritual lift. The new church provided that. Its towering spire and simple, graceful interior made the plain Methodist church seem dowdy. Methodists may have been gaining members, but the Congregationalists were still standing proud.

Edgartown Baptists also built themselves a new sanctuary. They, too, needed to lift their spirits. They had been the first evangelicals on the Island, but the Methodists had soon overtaken them. That success, it seems, was due more to the persuasive power of charismatic Methodist evangelists than to deep doctrinal differences, although there were objections to the Baptists' insistence on adult baptism by total immersion.

While all this religious fervor was happening, non-Methodists showed little interest. Those "crazy sects" were not something to concern the establishment. A journal kept by Dr. Leroy M. Yale of Holmes Hole from 1829 to 1849, the years surrounding those first camp meetings, does not even mention them. Dr. Yale was a keen observer of mankind. His thoughtful observations of the public mood in 1833 do not flatter the Islanders:

> There is a marked enmity towards any one who has prospered in business and apparently [is] rising above the State of mediocrity in point of wealth.
>
> In relation to such as come to this place from abroad, there exists apparently much jealousy lest they should take some interest in the affairs of a public nature, or in some way exert an influence for their individual benefit, as though they [the natives] possessed some reserved or inherent rights which a Stranger (as they term those who gained a residence here) has not the right to interfere with. . . . [It] is for the most part merely envy.

The doctor lived and practiced in Holmes Hole within sight of Eastville, where thousands of Methodists went ashore each August as they headed for the camp meeting. He makes no mention of them or of the meetings. It is not that he is nonreligious. In 1833 he wrote of his concern when the Sabbath passed without a local church service:

It is Sabbath and we have no preaching in the village today. The only organized Societies in this place are the Methodists and Baptists and there is but one meeting house in which both Societies worship alternately, the Methodists . . . half of the time & the Baptists, at present, only one-third of the time. Consequently, we have no preaching a part of the time. . . . The Methodists are now about building a meeting house for their own use. They have also opened a Singing School for . . . a choir of singers for the new house.

Dr. Yale was a Congregationalist. After more than ten years without a church in his town, he decided to do something about it. Along with a teacher, Nathan Mayhew, and the merchant James L. Barrows, both of Holmes Hole, he raised money (much of it his own) to build the first Congregational church in the village. A minister was brought over from the mainland. Yale's work so upset the other denominations that they tried to persuade an off-Island doctor to come over to compete with him: "This step, *viz.*, the organization of the [Congregational] church & building of the meeting house, has called out the most violent opposition by the Baptists & Methodists. So much so that they . . . have advanced money to the amount of 2 or 4 hundred dollars to set up a physician in opposition to me."

Religion was not all that occupied the minds of residents during those years. In Edgartown, David Davis, an educated man who had run a private academy in town for years, organized a lyceum in 1836, the year after the campground opened. Meetings were held in the main hall of his discontinued Davis Academy.

The lyceum movement had become very popular in Massachusetts. It gave men a chance to debate civic issues, both local and national. Although lyceums were exclusively male, some, including the one in Edgartown, allowed women to attend on occasion, but they were not permitted to enter into the discussions. You're welcome if you can keep quiet—that was the invitation.

The record book of the Edgartown Lyceum from 1836 to 1854 shows more than seventy members. The debate topics provide a sampling of what was on Islanders' minds during those years. Listed are 122 debates over nearly twenty years. Not one was about camp meetings or religious revivals. A few were about religious matters. One in the lyceum's early years was "Ought an Atheist be allowed his Oath in a Court of Justice?" After the debate the audience voted overwhelmingly in support of the atheist's rights. Another topic was "Have differences of opinion in politics caused more bloodshed than differences of opinion in religion?" This vote too was one-sided, in the negative: religion had caused more bloodshed than politics, they voted. Together these two votes show a surprising open-mindedness by the public in religious matters, at a time when religion was much more a part of public life than it is today.

Not debated was a petition to the state by some Edgartown residents to be allowed to secede and form a separate town. In March 1836 a group of thirty-six men, led by Ichabod Norton of Farm Neck, asked Massachusetts to create a new town that would include the northern and western parts of Edgartown. The signers, the petition said, were "all incommodiously and very unhappily" living in remote sections of the shire town and had to travel long distances to attend town meetings. The new town would be named Farmington (they were mostly farmers). In Boston the petition was turned over to legislative committees for study. Two years later it was withdrawn without action and also without having been debated in the lyceum. Equally surprising is that no debates were held on the morality of slavery, a question much on the nation's mind. Frederick Douglass twice visited the Island and delivered abolitionist speeches, but the lyceum did not follow up with a debate. In Nantucket, which was where Douglass was heading, the Quakers strongly supported abolition, but Vineyarders seem to have been almost indifferent. Several debates were held on slavery-related issues, but all were on technical questions, none on its morality. Argued was whether additional slave states should be admitted into the Union; also debated was whether coastal vessels should be prohibited from carrying slaves between the states. But there were no debates on whether slaves should be freed or whether humans could "own" another person.

A similar debating club, not called a lyceum, was founded in Holmes Hole five years after the Edgartown Lyceum. Dr. Yale mentions it, along with other news:

> February 9, 1841: Some time last week there was a debating club organized in the village & last evening they held their first meeting. . . . The subject for discussion was: "Ought this Island to be exempt from military duty?" It was decided by a tie vote.
>
> There was also a meeting of the Baptist Society in which they voted to appropriate their surplus funds, about 400 dollars, to the object of building a parsonage & Vestry. . . .

There appears to be quite a spirit of enterprise in getting out small vessels for [whaling in] the Atlantic Ocean. Some 2 or 3 having been bought to be fitted at Edgartown.

During 1841 and 1842 five whalers were financed with Edgartown money to find and kill Atlantic whales. These were smaller vessels, usually schooners, and investors hoped that the shorter Atlantic voyages would make them more profitable than the whalers that went on three- and four-year voyages to the north Pacific.

Whaling had become the principal occupation of Island males. Starting as young as thirteen or fourteen, they signed on as crew on whaleships, mostly owned in New Bedford or Nantucket. In the decade of 1810–19 twenty Islanders went whaling on New Bedford ships, and nearly half of them (nine) were men of color, meaning Indian or black. During the next ten years, 1820–29, there were seventy-two males who signed on, a nearly fourfold increase (fourteen were of color). In the 1830s the number dropped to forty-one (ten were of color).

As mentioned earlier, the Vineyard was not a major owner of whaleships. However, because so many of its men served on vessels owned elsewhere, the Island became involved in many whaling legends, famous and infamous.

In 1824 probably the most bloody whaling mutiny of all time involved the whaleship *Globe*. The ship was owned in New Bedford, but all its officers, including the master, were from the Vineyard. All were killed in the mutiny: Captain Thomas Worth, William Beetle, John Lumbert, and Nathaniel Fisher. Fomenting the mutiny was a boatsteerer, Samuel Comstock from Nantucket, who had a grandiose plan to set up his kingdom on a South Sea island and build his castle with lumber from the *Globe*. He, too, was killed, not by fellow mutineers, but by loyal crewmen fearful for their own lives All together, thirteen men were murdered, seven of them Vineyarders.

Another Vineyard involvement in whaling violence was in 1842 aboard the *Sharon*. The master, Captain Howes Norris of Holmes Hole, was brutally murdered and his body dismembered by three crewmen, all South Sea islanders. The captain had for months been physically abusing his black steward and had finally beat him to death. Three black South Sea islanders, believing that they would be next, killed Captain Norris while the rest of the crew and officers were off capturing harpooned whales.

Oil portrait of Captain Thomas Worth, who was killed with all his officers aboard
the whaleship *Globe* in 1824. It was the bloodiest mutiny in whaling history.
All the officers were Vineyarders. (MVHS Collections)

When the whaleboats returned, the heroic Third Mate Benjamin Clough (not a Vineyarder) managed to climb aboard the *Sharon* during the night and kill two of the murderers. (This story is told in Joan Druett's *In the Wake of Madness* [2003].)

Less violent is a third example of the Vineyard's connection to whaling lore. It involves Herman Melville, whose *Moby-Dick* is considered by many to be literature's finest whaling story. Melville shipped aboard the whaleship *Acushnet* of New Bedford, whose master was Valentine Pease Jr. of Edgartown. Melville's fictional Captain Ahab, some claim, was modeled after Pease. That is unlikely, said those who knew Pease on land, but others point out that whaling masters often became changed individuals once at sea.

Many Vineyarders were aboard the whaling fleet, taking part in its rise and fall. They were on ships destroyed by Confederate raiders during the Civil War; and on vessels crushed by Arctic ice in the late 1890s. One Island mariner in the Arctic disaster was Captain George Fred Tilton of Chilmark, who, with two Eskimos and dog teams, left the ice-trapped fleet to walk thousands of miles across the ice to bring help. He told the story in his book, *"Cap'n George Fred" Himself*, published in 1969. The loss of so many whaleships to the Arctic ice pack brought an end to the dying whaling industry. Men who had spent much of their lives at sea came home seeking other ways to make a living.

They found many changes in the simple Vineyard lifestyle they had left years earlier, changes that must have troubled many of them. Many of the changes during the second half of the 1800s involved religion. The Congregationalists, dominant for so long, suddenly were losing in the competition with the Methodists and Baptists. In August 1841 the Methodists, having outgrown the large meetinghouse they had built only a few years before (now Edgartown's Town Hall), bought some land on the opposite side of Main Street for seven hundred dollars and in two years built a new church. It was and remains Edgartown's grandest structure, now known as the Old Whaling Church. Hebron Vincent explained:

> The [old] church building, although of medium size for the community, was quite too small. Every pew in it was occupied and twenty more were wanted. . . . The whaling business, the chief interest of the place, was then good, our people were doing well, we had a large number of mechanics [he had written "carpenters," but crossed it out, replacing it

By 1843 the Methodists had become the largest congregation in Edgartown and had outgrown two earlier churches. This grand structure, still in use, was built that year on Main Street to accommodate the growing membership. (Shute Collection, MVHS)

with "mechanics"] in our [Methodist] Society . . . and the demand was . . . for a more commodious church building. . . . Land was secured, a draft was made by Bro. Frederick Baylies, a Master builder. . . .

Among the many noble-hearted men who were foremost in this work was Josiah Gorham, a comparative Stranger [newcomer], formerly of Nantucket, but now for quite a series of years a resident here. He was an Oil Manufacturer, a man of some wealth, yet he was not eaten up with the world. . . . He was public spirited . . . in the cause of education. Although he had no children to educate, and was a large taxpayer, he always favored the appropriating of liberal sums for this object. He shared largely, as did some others, the responsibilities of this new church enterprise. . . .

The new church edifice—the present church—was completed in the autumn of 1843. The enterprise had been conducted by a building committee of which the venerable Thomas M. Coffin was the first named, and the company of work men was headed by Mr. Ellis Lewis.

Hebron Vincent, who was personally involved, has provided some revealing facts: (1) he credits Frederick Baylies Jr., today called the architect and builder of the church, with offering only a draft of the proposed building, perhaps a sketch based on an architectural pattern book, such as Asher Benjamin's; (2) he says that Josiah Gorham, an oil manufacturer who had moved to Edgartown from Nantucket, "shared largely" in the cost; and (3) he states that the church was built by a "company of work men . . . headed by Mr. Ellis Lewis." Today neither Gorham nor Lewis is given credit. Instead, we are told that the church was paid for by Edgartown whaling masters and was designed and built by Frederick Baylies Jr., architect and builder.

Grafton Norton of Edgartown was among the "some others" who helped with the financing. His contribution was a loan of five hundred dollars, at 6 percent interest. Signing the note along with the generous Josiah Gorham were Jeremiah Pease, John Osborn, Thomas M. Coffin, Charles Worth, Hiram Jernegan, and Frederick Baylies. The loan and all accrued interest were paid off in 1849, mostly by the sale of pews to members. Very little of it, apparently, came from whaling masters.

Josiah Gorham is listed in the 1850 census as an Edgartown "oil manufacturer," fifty-seven years old, married, with $3,200 worth of real estate—an impressive amount, although only a fraction of what Dr. Daniel Fisher owned after his recent purchase of his partner Gorham's half of the oil business. Gorham was born in Barnstable, his wife in Nantucket. They had no children. An Irish maid lived with them in their Water Street home. Apparently they rented rooms in their large house to John Linton, a laborer, his wife, and their two children, as the census shows them living there. Perhaps Linton worked in the oil manufactory.

Gorham came to Edgartown in the 1830s to start an oil and candle manufacturing business. He sold half interest in it in 1836 to Dr. Daniel Fisher. They were partners for several years, until Fisher bought him out. Gorham's role in creating that enterprise has been forgotten, eclipsed by the better-known Dr. Fisher. Incidentally, neither was a native Islander.

The 1843 Methodist church that Gorham had helped finance was the most impressive structure in the village (even today it overwhelms other buildings on Main Street). Handsome as it was, it didn't please all. Choir members complained that the loft from which they sang was poorly built. They petitioned the building committee in September 1843, while construction was going on, asking that more consideration be given to them, who received little financial help from the congregation: "The Choir have at considerable expense, furnished their own music, &c., one of our members having paid some thirty dollars for the use of the double bass viol, an instrument which has been of signal service to the singing. . . . We also respectfully request that the carpet now in the [old] church be assigned for the gallery of the new house. . . . It is much needed as the floor is made of the very poorest materials."

Edgartown was not the only Island village where Methodism was flourishing. Societies in Chilmark, Holmes Hole, (West) Tisbury, and North Tisbury were all growing. Their nightly meetings, laughed at by traditionalists because of the shouting and wailing that went on until late each night, were first held in private homes. But soon the societies were able to build houses of worship. The first up-Island church was moved there from Edgartown. When that town's Methodists built their new church on Main Street in 1821, their old building was sold to the Chilmark Methodists, who took it apart, hauled it up-Island, and reassembled it. The transplanting weakened it so much that it had to be replaced about twenty years later, as Hebron Vincent explained:

> The plain, wood-colored building brought hither from Edgartown had answered as a place of worship for quite a number of years, but taking it apart for the sake of greater convenience of transportation, had operated injuriously upon it as to its durability; and now . . . the brethren there had seen that a new House must supersede it. . . . In January 1843, occurred the dedication. . . . Among the many who had helped in this church enterprise . . . was Capt. Charles Weeks . . . a successful commander of a whale ship. . . . Retiring from the sea, he purchased a good farm in Chilmark . . . in 1837. . . . He was usually the leader of religious meetings in the absence of the minister.

At Holmes Hole the Methodists were also doing well, especially after the arrival of the Reverend Edward T. Taylor, a former mariner who later became famous as the "Sailor's Preacher." Although assigned to the Edgartown Methodists in the 1820s, he often preached in Holmes Hole. It was during those years that the Holmes Hole society built its first meeting-house, today's Capawock Hall.

Taylor is credited with being the first preacher to hold prayer meetings aboard whaleships before they left on a voyage, calling on God to bring good luck to the ship. Such meetings were first held by him, it is said, in Edgartown. Methodists boarded the ready-to-sail vessel at the wharf to hear Taylor call for God's help in killing his largest mammals. Again, Vincent informs us: "The sermon was in Mr. Taylor's characteristic pungent style, and his prayer almost assumed the dramatic. Sending up his fervent petition for the Divine protection of his brother sailors, and a prosperous voyage, he would enter in imagination into the affrays with the big fish and ask God to direct the harpoons into the 'leviathans of the deep.'"

Pity the whales. Nobody prayed for them.

Except for Gay Head, where the Indians were mostly Baptists, the Island had become predominantly Methodist during those years. Methodist success began in Eastville, even before the nearby campground was created. The lay leader Jeremiah Pease had conducted services there twice a week for years, traveling from Edgartown village by horse and buggy. Methodist societies also prospered on the north shore and at Pohoganut (sometimes spelled Pohoganot) on the south shore. The Reverend Joseph B. Brown, who was assigned to the western end of the Island in 1837, included Pohoganut in his parish. It had been a "wild" place before he arrived. Vincent describes the situation: "He preached at a place called 'Pohogonot,' a part of Edgartown about five or six miles from town. Quite a number were converted there. . . . The violin and the dance, for which that section had been noted, gave place to prayer and praise to God."

In the winter of 1852 the Edgartown Methodists were so eager for salvation that they held the longest revival ever conducted on the Island. Prayer meetings, intense and emotional, were held in the vestry of the new church for one hundred consecutive nights—more than three months of continuous exhorting. Vincent described the extent to which the village was emotionally involved:

> A sea captain who was keeping a bowling alley was so powerfully convicted that he declared to some of the young men—his customers—he should quit the business and that he was going that evening to the Methodist Vestry and . . . ask the Christians to pray for him. . . . The

young men, quite incredulous, went to the meeting to see if the Captain would keep his promise, which he did, and he said to them, "No more bowling alley!"

A few evenings later, while a dance in the Hall nearby was progressing, several of the young men . . . left the dance, went to the meeting and came forward for prayers. And the dance, which was intended to extend far into the night, as usual, was broken up at ten o'clock.

But the most marked case of all was a gentleman of high respect and ability who had been a skeptic. He was Principal of the Dukes County Academy in West Tisbury. . . . He was induced to attend the Methodist prayer meeting to be held in the Vestry. . . . He went voluntarily to the "anxious seat" where he soon kneeled. Immediately, he was overpowered with mental agony, insomuch that he felt sensations of suffocation, which led him for relief to tear off his cravat. For some half hour, he writhed in the greatest distress . . . "prayer ardent" being offered up in his behalf. He then became calm and soon arose as though into a new world. . . . He has since held various business relations in different parts of the country, and a responsible position to which he was appointed by the President of the United States, [but] he cherishes a fresh and grateful remembrance of the . . . wonderful change which [took place] in that vestry. . . . The gentleman was Freeman N. Blake Esq.

Blake was principal of the academy for only two years, 1852 to 1854. It was during his first winter on the Island that he became "born again." After becoming a distinguished lawyer, he served for a time as a U.S. consul to Canada.

Readers will recall that it was during this prolonged revival that Jeremiah Pease's wife became very ill, perhaps being emotionally upset by her husband's total commitment during those hundred nights. (He was chorister and exhorter.) Pease never mentioned whether his wife, from a steadfast Congregationalist family, ever became a Methodist.

While all this religious activity was going on, important changes of other kinds were occurring. During the 1830s the first steamboat began regular ferry service, replacing the sailing packets. It was not a Vineyard enterprise. The Nantucket steamboat *Telegraph* began making regular runs, three times a week, between that island and New Bedford, with stops at Holmes Hole and Woods Hole. In 1842 the Nantucket company built a larger and faster steamboat, the *Massachusetts*, for the New Bedford run. Edgartown residents had long petitioned the Nantucket company to include a stop at their village, and in 1843 one was added. The stop extended the running time so much that Nantucket residents complained and it was soon eliminated.

The steamboat enabled a traveler to leave Boston by train at 8:30 A.M., catch the ferry at New Bedford, and arrive at Holmes Hole shortly after noon. (Today it takes just about as long.) The steamboat then continued to Nantucket, where it spent the night, and returned to New Bedford the next day. On the alternate days, if you wanted to get to the Island from the mainland, a sailing packet filled in, as we learn from the journal of Dr. Albert C. Koch, a German paleontologist who went to Gay Head in 1844 searching for fossils:

> Monday, July 22. At eight o'clock in the morning, I departed from Boston by train to go via New Bedford to Martha's Vineyard. . . . I arrived [at New Bedford] at 10:30 and right away had my things brought . . . to a small, dainty, four-masted ship which connects this place and the town of Holmes Hole. . . . A steamboat also travels the same route, [but] it runs only three times a week. . . . At eleven o'clock, our boat set sail; the crew was very small . . . two very deft men, of whom the older was introduced to me as the captain and the younger as the mate. . . . We covered the 28 English miles to Holmes Hole in four hours, landing at three o'clock. I had fun watching the captain and the mate alternate at the helm, and when both were needed to change the sails, how they fastened the rudder with a rope and left it alone.

Residents of Edgartown, proud of their shire town, did not like having to travel by horse and buggy to Holmes Hole to get the steamboat. A group of them put up money to build the Island's first locally owned steamboat. On August 25, 1845, the *Naushon* arrived to begin service between Edgartown and New Bedford, with a stop at Woods Hole. Jeremiah Pease recorded the town's reaction:

> August 26, [1845]. Steam Boat *Naushon*, Capt. H. W. Smith, arrives from N. York having been built there for this place. She being the first Steam Boat ever owned here, quite a rejoicing with many on the acc't.
>
> August 27. S. B. *Naushon* sails for N. Bedford with 320 passengers, principally from this Town. P.M. the wind changes to N.E. suddenly with rain, a Gale for a few hours. The Steamboat proves very satisfactory on acc't. of her speed and moddle [model, meaning design] in a heavy sea.

Steamboat service between Edgartown and New Bedford was not profitable and after three years it ended. The *Naushon* was sold to a group in New York and renamed *News Boy* because it met incoming vessels off Sandy Hook and sped in with the latest newspapers from Europe.

Edgartown swallowed its pride and again begged the Nantucket steamboat owners to include a stop there. It was turned down. Soon Nantucket steamers gave up the run to New Bedford, going instead to the closer Hyannis to connect with the railroad to Boston.

When a branch line was laid to Fairhaven by the Boston-Hyannis Railroad, some businessmen there thought it would be good for business to run a ferry to Edgartown. They financed a steamboat, the *Metacomet*, to begin service in the fall of 1854. Suddenly the Nantucket company decided it would add an Edgartown stop to its Hyannis run. This abrupt change caused the *Vineyard Gazette's* editor, Edgar Marchant, to explode:

NOBLE STEAMBOAT ENTERPRISE!!!

This is about as cool a piece of impudence as it ever was our fortune to record. During the past five years we have been without direct steamboat communication with New Bedford and all of our efforts to induce the Nantucket Steamboat Company to cause their boat to stop here have been treated with the most marked contempt. . . . Some enterprising capitalists abroad [in Fairhaven] determined to build a fast sailing, commodious steamer expressly to accommodate the whole Vineyard people . . . [and the boat] will soon commence her trips between this place and Fair Haven, touching at Holmes Hole and Woods Hole.

The [Nantucket] boat is not wanted here and will not be patronized. . . . We should be surprised, indeed, to know that a single Edgartonian would take passage on the Nantucket boat. . . . Our people know that the object . . . [is to] cause the withdrawal of the boat built expressly for our accommodation, and then leave us to whistle over deserted hopes.

When the *Metacomet* began its run to Fairhaven in October 1854, the *Gazette* puffed with pride, exclaiming that three days a week you could now leave Edgartown at 7:45 A.M., connect with the Boston train in Fairhaven at 11:20 A.M., and be in Boston early in the afternoon. That first month, more than twelve hundred persons took the *Metacomet* to Fairhaven. It was, the *Gazette* said, "a good beginning." In December the cheerleading editor said that business "had far exceeded the anticipations of the parties interested."

But despite the *Gazette*'s cheering, the *Metacomet*, like the earlier *Naushon*, was not profitable. To attract more patrons, fares were reduced to one dollar from Edgartown to Fairhaven and seventy-five cents from Holmes Hole. That was still not cheap; one dollar was what a schoolteacher made in a day. If it took a schoolteacher's daily wage to get to the mainland, few Vineyarders could afford to go. The *Metacomet* continued to lose money and in 1857, three years after it began, the service was abandoned.

Again Edgartown had no ferry. The *Eagle's Wing*, a discarded Nantucket steamer, was purchased to make the run to New Bedford. Edgartown swallowed its pride and put Nantucket's castoff into service.

That pride had gotten a much-needed boost ten years before, in 1846, when Edgar Marchant began publishing *The Vineyard Gazette*, the Island's first newspaper. Marchant, born in Edgartown in 1814, had left the Island as a young man to learn the newspaper business. We know little about him, but he may have started his career at the *Gloucester Telegraph,* at least so the *Gazette* files suggest. He also seems to have worked in New York City, and it may have been while there that he met and married Janet Turner, a Scottish immigrant. Their first child was born in New York City in 1844. Two years later he returned to Edgartown, a thirty-two-year-old native, eager to own his own newspaper.

Janet's brother, a printer, was the paper's first typesetter. It seems likely that he and Edgar had worked for the same newspaper in New York. *The Vineyard Gazette* began publishing each Friday in 1846. (Its name then included *The*. The weekly, now simply *Vineyard Gazette*, still comes out every Friday—also on Tuesdays in summer—and it is the oldest continuously run business in the village.) Marchant quickly saw where the Island was headed. In October 1847, long before many summer visitors began arriving, he predicted that the Vineyard would soon become the East Coast's "Watering Place."

At about the time the first *Gazette* was published, there was another boost for Edgartown's pride: the Methodist camp meeting returned to East Chop after a one-year absence. It had taken only one meeting at Westport Point to convince mainland Methodists that the "old, old story" was still worth telling, as the hymn says.

With the return of the camp meeting in August 1846, the Methodists were so sure it would stay that they signed a ten-year lease on the campground. A roomier preachers' stand was built, as were more benches for

The *Vineyard Gazette* was started by Edgar Marchant in 1846 above a meat market at Four Corners in Edgartown. It moved twice, ending up on South Summer Street, where it is today. (Shute Collection, MVHS)

the congregation. (The new benches had backrests.) Improved transportation, with steamboats and steam trains on the mainland, helped increase attendance. Day-trippers began pouring in on camp-meeting Sundays, enjoying both the voyage and the preaching.

Not every ship that arrived was ferrying happy passengers. Some were filled with the sick and the dying. In early 1849 one such vessel, carrying Irish immigrants to Boston, anchored in Holmes Hole. The passengers were seriously ill with ship fever (typhus), brought on by unsanitary conditions during the long voyage. The captain called for help. Dr. Yale was taken out to the disease-laden vessel. He could do little to help the suffering passengers, but the visit did much to him. He told his wife soon after the ship left and he began to weaken with fever, "I believe, Mother, that something is due that ship."

Within a month he was dead of ship fever. He was only forty-seven years old. So beloved was the village doctor that as his coffin was being carried to the cemetery on the shoulders of pallbearers, a group of townspeople stopped the procession and asked for one last look at him. The coffin was opened to allow the grieving citizens to pay their final respects to their doctor and friend.

Dr. Yale had moved to Holmes Hole immediately after finishing Harvard Medical School. He had not intended for the Island to be the site of his lifelong practice, but it was. When Dr. Daniel Fisher, who had preceded Yale as the village doctor, married Grace C. Coffin in 1829, she persuaded her new husband to move to Edgartown, where she lived. The village fathers of Holmes Hole wrote to Harvard College, seeking a replacement. Dr. Yale, a new graduate, accepted their offer and arrived in Holmes Hole aboard the packet from Boston in July 1829. Taking care of the residents of Holmes Hole became his life's work. He married a much younger woman, the daughter of the widowed village innkeeper. (Their son, Leroy Jr., became a distinguished children's doctor in New York and a highly regarded artist whose etchings still receive acclaim.) As we have already seen, the elder Yale was one of the founders of the Congregational Church in Holmes Hole.

The two doctors, Yale and Fisher, became friends. It was Fisher who took care of Yale during his final illness. By this time Fisher had become the Island's wealthiest man, not from his fees as a doctor, but from his entrepreneurial skills. As noted earlier, in 1836 he purchased the Edgartown whale oil manufactory and candle factory from Josiah Gorham. He also owned a bakery that made hardtack for whalers; to provide flour he built a gristmill in North Tisbury, where he dammed a stream to provide waterpower. When Island farms couldn't provide enough grain to meet his needs, he imported it from the mainland.

Fisher's financial success was helped by his marriage to Grace Coffin. Her well-to-do father gave the couple some land on Main Street in Edgartown, and on it in 1842 Doctor Fisher built an impressive home. The house today is one of Edgartown's treasures, along with Memorial Wharf on Dock Street, also owned by the doctor. He certainly couldn't have accomplished so much with doctor's fees.

By 1850 there were eleven physicians on the Island, five of them in Edgartown. The other four besides Fisher were J. Hovey Lucas, John Pierce, Clement F. Shiverick, who died in 1857, and a surgeon and dentist, Joseph R. Dillingham. Six years later another arrived. He was Dr. Edwin Mayberry, who was the Island's first specialist, a surgeon. The *Gazette* reported a major procedure he performed in 1856 on Chappaquiddick

Island. The patient, Margaret Peters, underwent an operation that, the *Gazette* wrote, "was probably one of the most critical ever undertaken in this vicinity." Her breast was removed, along with "a six-pound cancerous tumor." Dillingham administered the anesthesia, the paper stated. This was ten years after the first demonstration of the use of ether for that purpose at Massachusetts General Hospital in Boston, and now it apparently had arrived on the Vineyard. The operation took place in the patient's home, as did most medical care at that time. (The Island's first hospital opened in Holmes Hole in 1879, when the United States Marine Hospital Service took over the abandoned lighthouse at the head of Holmes Hole harbor and converted it into a small hospital for mariners.)

Margaret Peters is listed in the 1849 census of Massachusetts Indians as a Chappaquiddick Indian, fifty-nine years old, which would make her sixty-six when she was operated on. Only one other Peters is listed: Aurilla, twenty-six, perhaps her daughter. In March 1857 the state authorized payment for medical care for Margaret. The 1861 census of Vineyard Wampanoags lists no Margaret Peters. No doubt she had died.

So many Irish were now coming into the country and to the Vineyard that hysteria began to develop over their religion, Roman Catholicism. A new political party, its members drawn mostly from the Whigs, was formed. Officially the Native American Party, it was better known as the Know-Nothing party. When its members, unwilling to admit to being anti-Catholic, were asked about the party's position on the subject, they replied, "I know nothing about it."

On the Vineyard the Whigs, who for years had dominated Island politics, were soon absorbed by the Know-Nothings. In 1854 the *Gazette* seemed to come out in favor of the new party when it warned of a dangerous worldwide conspiracy that was already spreading its sinister net over the Vineyard: "A Catholic priest arrived in town on Tuesday and took lodging at the Edgartown Hotel. He came here to look after a 'TWIGG' of 'Know Nothings' and it is said, obtained the names of every member . . . soon [to] be published to the world, under Catholic auspices."

A month later Edgar Marchant, the *Gazette's* editor, bluntly tabulated how much it cost the poor Irish working girls to be Catholic:

> It may interest some of our people to know that the Catholics are trying to acquire an influence in Dukes County. A Catholic priest has commenced his regular visits to our Island. Last week, he visited Holmes'

Hole and Edgartown, pardoning the sins of all the Irish population, granting indulgences, and praying souls through purgatory—for a consideration. There are about fifty Catholic girls in the places named, nearly all of whom, it is believed, paid tribute to him while he was here. One girl said to a Protestant friend that she should give five dollars to have her sins pardoned, and seven dollars to have her mother relieved from purgatory.

We are informed that, at a moderate estimate, the priest received not less than 200 dollars during his visit here. We are sorry that these girls live and labor under such an infatuation . . . [that] a man . . . [would] impose upon poor, ignorant and deluded girls.

The priest while here also performed the Catholic marriage ceremony for a couple who were married some thirteen months since by a Protestant clergyman. Mr. Jose Silva was remarried to his wife, Mary. . . .

It becomes the Protestant churches to awaken to the dangers that surround them, so that they may be unitedly prepared to stand firm against the foe.

The anti-Catholic movement quickly gained adherents on the Island. The Know-Nothings dominated the 1854 election. Henry J. Gardner, their candidate for governor, received more than twice as many votes as the Whig and Democratic candidates combined. Only in Chilmark were the Know-Nothings denied a majority, but they did receive twenty votes, the same as the Democrats. (The Whigs got only a handful.) In the next election the Know-Nothings easily carried Chilmark.

Marchant's warnings about the papal threat turned out to have been idle. It was another twenty-five years before a Roman Catholic service was held on the Vineyard. That was in 1880 and it was conducted by a visiting "mission priest" who came to Cottage City (now Oak Bluffs) from New Bedford. The Catholic mission from off-Island continued for another twenty years, until Cottage City Catholics built the Sacred Heart Church. Their first full-time resident priest, the Reverend Patrick E. McGee, moved to the Island in 1903. Soon after arriving, he wrote to George A. Hough, editor of the *New Bedford Standard Times*, to thank him for the letters of introduction he had written to Island residents. Hough, the father of Henry Beetle Hough, who later took over as editor of the *Gazette*, was a regular summer resident at his camp, called Fish Hook, on Indian Hill.

Father McGee described his visit in 1903 with Charles H. Marchant, who was then editor of the *Gazette*. His welcome was warm, a far cry from what he would have been given by the elder Marchant, Edgar, fifty years earlier: "I went to Edgartown yesterday and saw Mr. Merchant. . . . I am receiving a cordial reception from every one and marks of esteem. The Catholics here are delighted to have a resident priest. The old folks were praying to have a priest near at their death. . . . The folks here are all used to nautical terms. I see a lurking smile at times when I ask, 'What do you mean by that?'"

Twenty years later two more Catholic churches had been organized: St. Augustine's in Vineyard Haven and St. Elizabeth's in Edgartown. By this time the Island's worry about a papal conquest had subsided. But in 1854 it had been real. Catholics paid the price of religious prejudice, as had a small band of Quakers 150 years before, when they came to the Vineyard from Nantucket. The early Irish female domestics, as well as the handful of Portuguese mariners who lived on the Island in the 1850s, would have been thrilled to know that finally in 1903 there was a resident priest, something they had only dreamed of.

We don't know the name of the first Portuguese to settle on the Island, but we can make a guess. The 1850 census lists seven men who had been born in the Azores, all mariners: three lived in Edgartown, two in Tisbury, and two in Chilmark. They were between twenty and forty years old, except for one patriarch, who was living in Tisbury in 1850. Emanuel Joseph, seventy-six years old, a mariner, born in the Azores and married to Mehitable (widow Luce), seventy-nine years old, who was born in Tisbury. The *Tisbury Vital Records* lists the marriage of Emanuel Joseph and Mrs. Mehitable Luce on April 7, 1796. Surely Emanuel must have been the first Portuguese to settle here.

John J. Mendance, another mariner from Fayal in the Azores, married an Irish house servant, Ann, in Edgartown in 1846. They had a child, William. Ann died of consumption when baby William was only six months old. Little William died at the age of three years.

Forty years later, Edgartown's favorite candy store was owned by William J. Mendence, who lived in a big house on North Water Street. We have been unable to find a relationship between the men, but it could be that John remarried and that William J. was his child by that wife. The name William and initial J would suggest some family connection.

Also listed in the 1850 census is Francis J. Silvia, forty, born in Pico, the Azores. He was a mariner living on Nantucket; in 1838 he married Jane S. Dunham of Edgartown. They lived with her father, Joseph Dunham, a widower and a boatbuilder. When the father died in 1849, Jane's brother, Joseph Dunham Jr., took over the business.

Soon after Francis and Jane were married, they moved to his birthplace in Pico, where their daughter Mary Jane was born in 1842. We know that the family was living there because of an advertisement Francis placed in a newspaper there in 1841:

NOTICE TO WHALEMEN

The subscriber having lately removed with his family from Edgartown, Mass., to Magdalen, of Pico, opposite Fayal, (Western Islands) hereby gives notice to all Vessels touching at the Islands, that he is prepared and will furnish on short notice, such Fruit and Vegetables as the Islands afford and at the lowest possible prices. Francis J. Silvia, Western Islands

They didn't stay in Pico long. Their second child, Susannah, was born in Edgartown in 1843. In 1849 another daughter, Emma Retina, was born, also in Edgartown. The 1850 census lists the entire family as living in the house of the boatbuilder Joseph Dunham, Jane's brother, in Edgartown. Their firstborn, Mary Jane, eight, is listed as Mary C. Nunes, which probably was her father's family name when she was born in Pico. Why the middle name Jane was dropped and her middle initial changed to "C" we cannot explain, but the evidence seems to indicate the two are the same person.

Francis J. Silvia (often spelled "Silva") again went whaling. No ordinary seaman, he was first officer of the whaleship *Governor Troup* and took command in Honolulu in May 1845 when the master died at sea. When Emma Retina was born in 1849, he was listed in the *Vital Records* as "master mariner." In 1859 he was master of the whaler *Atlantic* of New Bedford, so he continued to go whaling even after his wife, Jane, died in 1856.

Theirs was not a happy marriage, it seems. When Jane died, she left all her property, including their residence on North Water Street, to her daughters Susannah and Emma. (The house had been paid for by her father and was in her name.) She named her brother, Joseph Dunham Jr., as the guardian of her daughters. Her husband, Francis, was not mentioned in the will. Nor was her daughter Mary Jane, now fourteen years old, who was living with the family of Charles W. Pease, a prosperous Edgartown farmer.

Susannah appears ten years later in the 1860 census as owning fourteen hundred dollars in real estate and three hundred dollars in personal property, a large amount for anyone, especially a seventeen-year-old girl.

Francis seems to have left the family and returned to the Azores. We don't know when but do know he was there in 1869, living with his second wife, when his daughter Emma went to visit him. He died in 1892.

Was it still true, as Dr. Yale had written in 1833, that "in relation to such as come to this place from abroad, there exists apparently much jealousy"? Certainly, Francis J. Silvia, born in the Azores, had proved that the Portuguese could succeed, not only at raising fruit and vegetables, but in the world dominated by the "whites."

The 1850 census shows that almost all the Island's residents were white, Protestant, and of English ancestry, much as they had been for centuries. It couldn't have been easy to be an immigrant, speaking another language. Of the more than 380 heads of families in Edgartown (which then included Oak Bluffs), 295, more than 75 percent, had been born on the Vineyard, and another 75 were Americans born off-Island. Only 14 had been born in a foreign country. Seven of the 14 were from the Azores. The other seven were from Canada, England, Scotland, Norway, New Zealand, and the West Indies. Among the 75 born off-Island but in the United States were many who had moved to the Island to be its ministers, teachers, and physicians. Others were skilled workers such as coopers, coastal pilots, and shoemakers; there were even a blacksmith, a barber, a baker, and a musician who played the organ for a church.

In addition to the foreigners who were heads of families, there was a small number of foreign-born residents, unmarried and living with local families. Most were from Ireland: eight single women working as domestic servants (their average age was twenty-four) and two unmarried Irishmen, twenty-eight and twenty-six, both laborers.

The Island was hardly a diversely populated place in 1850, a time when the nation was becoming so. There was much more diversity on whaleships. Legend has it that they were the nation's first racially integrated workplaces, and certainly fo'c'sles (forecastles) did house a variety of nationalities. As whaling voyages lengthened and crews made less money, masters were forced to recruit crews in distant places. There was another factor, as Elmo P. Hohman explains in *The American Whaleman:* Yankee males had lost interest in whaling. What he writes makes those "who go down to the sea in ships" seem less than our best:

More and more [in the mid-1800s] the intelligent and ambitious young American refused to go to sea, even in New England, and least of all on a whaler. This drift away from the sea began as early as the thirties, was greatly accelerated during the fifties by the lure of California gold. . . . As the better types of Americans forsook the forecastles, their bunks were filled by criminal or lascivious adventurers, by a motley collection of South Sea Islanders known as Kanakas, by cross-breed negroes and Portuguese from the Azores and the Cape Verdes, and by the outcasts and renegades from . . . the Old World and the New. . . .

By 1880 the dregs of American-born men comprised only one-third of the 3,896 hands who manned the New Bedford whaling fleet. Another third was made up of Portuguese; and the remainder included negroes, Kanakas and scattered individuals from most of the great ports of Europe and of Asia.

Like those changing forecastles, the Vineyard, so long homogeneous, was starting to change. Longtime Island families were becoming separated as young men left in search of a better future. Farming families, their numbers expanding, saw a bleak future on an Island with limited farmland. Many went to Maine, so many that they named their town New Vineyard. Others settled in Ohio, and some went as far west as Iowa.

In most cases those who left were descendants of the early settlers. Rarely did persons of color leave. They didn't have the money. Owning land was something they could only dream of. Most Indians, now virtually all intermarried with blacks and Portuguese, were living on Indian Lands, where they were denied the vote and public services were primitive, if they existed at all. They had become wards of the state, isolated in rural ghettos. The only English on Gay Head were the families of the lighthouse keepers. (It was not until 1920 that the government finally named a Gay Head Indian, Charles W. Vanderhoop, to be the keeper.)

Gay Head in 1844 remained a remote, desolate place, according to Dr. Albert Koch, the German paleontologist who had gone there seeking fossils in the clay:

> July 23rd. After ten o'clock, I started my journey to Gay Head [from Holmes Hole] . . . a distance of 18 English miles; the first 11 miles of the way can be traveled without risk by carriage and I rode the stretch with a man who twice a week, carries the mail in a one-horse carriage. . . . The part of the Island I had to traverse on foot was very barren . . . no wonder

that our white fellow citizens left this desolate region as the last refuge to the poor Indians. . . . I left the carriage at the last house [it was probably at one of the Mayhew farmhouses in today's Squibnocket Beach area of Chilmark] which was surrounded by a few trees. . . . From here . . . only bare hills . . . frequently broken by ocean inlets and small sand steppes . . . separated into irregular fields by man-made walls of field stones. Here and there rose a house, which . . . looked lonely and melancholy indeed without a garden or the shadow of a tree. . . . After a very arduous march I arrived at the house of the old Indian who, I had been told, would, for pay, give lodging to strangers. . . . [I was provided] a very decent room in which a large, genuine American double bed played the leading role. . . . I ate and drank better than I could have expected.

The German's journal provides an eloquent description of Gay Head's colorful cliffs 160 years ago:

On the shores of Gay Head, all colors of the rainbow show themselves in such a brilliance and such a beautiful fusion as only the richest fantasy of a painter could imagine. . . . The landscape takes on an almost unearthly and magical appearance which probably has no equal in the whole world. . . . The red color plays a leading role . . . from a large mass of the best red ochre, which is found here in such quantity that in stormy weather the waves wash it off so that the ocean is dyed blood red for one English mile. . . . The white comes first from an alabaster-white special sand . . . which in appearance has much similarity to kitchen salt, secondly, from a very beautiful white pipe clay, which is found in abundance and sold by the Indians to the whites for clay pipes.

Koch was at Gay Head for more than a week, hiring Indians to dig for fossils. They found fifteen sharks' teeth and a few vertebrae he thought to be from "saurians" (dinosaurs). During the week

a boat arrived to take on a load of white clay, which is used in great quantities by alum factories as well as for [clay pipes]. . . . This clay is regarded as public property, and every inhabitant of Gay Head who is willing to dig and help load the ship receives a part of the profit, which for these people is not small. A ton . . . of this clay is sold for three dollars, and a man can, without much exertion, produce a ton a day. The ship which is now here loads approximately 90 tons.

The whaleship *Splendid* at wharf at the end of Main Street, Edgartown.
During the Gold Rush the ship was bought by the Dukes County Mining Company to
carry its gold-seeking members to California. (Shute Collection, MVHS)

Not long after Koch left the Island with his sacks of fossils, many thousands of men began digging in another place. They were not digging for fossils, but for gold. It was the California Gold Rush of '49, which began soon after a mechanic building a sawmill for Johann Sutter on the Sacramento River in early 1848 spotted gold nuggets tumbling along the raceway to the mill.

The country quickly became infected by the gold bug. The Vineyard was no exception. The first of the Island's gold seekers, sixteen men, sailed from Holmes Hole on February 7, 1849, aboard the schooner *Rialto*. They were followed by many more. Vineyarders, joined by off-Islanders, organized mining companies and bought or chartered vessels to take them to California. In all, six Vineyard ships made the long trip around South America. Two others, from Nantucket and Mattapoisett, also carried Island argonauts to the goldfields. More than two hundred Vineyard men left in the first nine months of 1849, surely the Island's fastest exodus. More than ever, the Vineyard suffered from a shortage of men.

It was not only adventurous single men who left. Among those departing were heads of families who were eager to strike it rich in California and saw little chance of doing so at home. Aboard the *Splendid* (owned by the Dukes County Mining Company) and the *Walter Scott* (Edgartown Mining Company) the average age of officers and directors was forty-one years; seven of ten were heads of families. The average age of the ordinary members was younger, thirty-four years, and half of them were heads of households.

These mining companies were serious. They had strict rules: no drinking, no swearing. All the gold discovered would be shared equally. Decisions would be made by majority vote, even as to who would run the ship. There would be a strict observance of the Sabbath; no work would be done on that day. A letter in the *Gazette* on May 10, 1850, written aboard the ship *Splendid* en route to California, describes the religious dedication of those heading for gold: "At the ringing of the bell on a pleasant Sabbath morning, about all the crew are to be found assembled on the quarter deck, attending meeting; and it is truly a scene of deep interest, and well worthy of recording, that on the deck of one lonely bark, upon the deep, 60 to 70 men, neatly attired in their sailor suits, listen to the instructions from God's word."

Things changed quickly once they got to the goldfields. Most companies soon disbanded and rules were forgotten, including the observance of the Sabbath. The Dukes County Mining Company was broken up as soon as the *Splendid* arrived in San Francisco, each member paying the captain one hundred dollars for his passage. (Some who signed notes to pay later failed to do so, which resulted in a number of lawsuits.) Freed of the communal commitments, members took off for the mines as individuals; any gold they found would be entirely theirs.

Cyrus Pease, a son of Jeremiah and the twin brother of William, who had been so critical of the behavior of Methodists, was secretary of the Edgartown Mining Company. He sailed on the *Walter Scott* on May 7, 1850. A talented artist, Cyrus made a number of sketches during the voyage and in California. One sketch of the *Walter Scott* he titled "Shippe of fooles," emphasizing his disillusionment. When the *Walter Scott* arrived in San Francisco, Captain Henry Pease 2nd agreed to let certain members buy their way out of the company. Cyrus did so. He headed for the hills, as he wrote to Lucy Crane of Vermont, whom he hoped to marry when he returned, his pockets filled with gold:

This painting, entitled *A Mining Camp on the Calavaras River, California, 1850,* is believed to have been done by Frederick Pease of Edgartown, who sailed with the Edgartown Mining Company in September 1849 to California on the bark *Sarah,* bought by members to take them to the goldfields. (MVHS Collections)

I left for the mines with all the materials for comfort, *viz.,* a coffee pot, frying pan and some lucifer matches. . . . Some nights, while on the journey it was so pleasant that I did not even pitch my tent, but wrapping my blanket about me, I threw myself upon the ground and slept like an Indian. Upon our arrival at the mines, we commenced building a stone house . . . which looked like something between a bear's den and the cell of St. Anthony. After digging some gold, I returned again to our ship after my brother [John A. Pease], according to promise. There, learned that the Edgartown Mining (or undermining) Company had disbanded. . . . The rainy season . . . rendered a return to the mines impracticable and I determined to remain . . . in San Francisco.

John has not succeeded very well at the mines and, from the experience of both of us, I fear that even the reasonable expectations which we entertained at starting from home will not be realized. The accounts which [we] then had of the mines were much exaggerated. . . . A few were successful and their good fortune was trumpeted the length and breadth of the country by those interested in the influx of population.

Benton, Fremont & Co., have much to answer for. [Missouri's Senator Thomas Hart Benton was the great-uncle of the Vineyard artist the late Tom Benton and an early booster of California, as was his son-in-law, Captain John C. Frémont, its appointed governor in 1846–47].

Soon Cyrus returned to Edgartown, only to learn that his intended, Lucy, whom he had fallen in love with while painting her portrait a few years earlier, had not waited for him, but had married a St. Louis doctor. Years later Lucy said of Cyrus: "The poor fellow went to California in '49 and was swallowed up in the crowds of those who failed to draw a prize."

Disappointed in love, he joined the U.S. Revenue Marine Service, rose to captain, and retired in 1877. He continued his occasional painting, never married, and was considered somewhat eccentric, a characteristic considerably aggravated by his fondness for alcohol. He died in 1887.

The *Walter Scott* was the second mining company ship to sail from the Vineyard. A short time earlier, the brig *Vesta* had left, taking the Winnegahee Trading and Mining Company with twenty-two Vineyard men, all from Tisbury and Chilmark, except one from Edgartown. Soon after, the *Walter Scott* sailed with thirty-five Edgartown men and nine from other Island towns. It was followed by the *Sarah* and the *Splendid*, carrying mostly Edgartown men. Other Islanders went to California in the schooner *Two Brothers* of Nantucket, the bark *Oscar* from Mattapoisett, and the schooner *L. M. Yale* of Holmes Hole, named for Dr. Yale, who died before the schooner, which he helped finance, was launched.

Most Vineyard men did not stay in California long. They soon discovered that gold was not easy to get, but sickness was. At least twelve died while in California or while going or returning. Many returned sick, with little financial gain. On January 2, 1851, Frederick Baylies Jr., in Edgartown, wrote to his son, Henry, then in Alabama, about some of the returning forty-niners: "S. Stewart, John A., Frederick and I. D. Pease Jr., have arrived at last. They left San Francisco about the middle of Sept. [1850] in a sailing vessel. . . . John A. Pease is quite sick, complaint Fever & Ague, Frederick [Pease] has been quite sick, but is better. . . . What they have made I know not, but think they have had enough of California."

One Islander who surely must have had enough of California was Clement Vincent of Edgartown. He had accumulated four thousand dollars in the goldfields, but all of it had been stolen.

Some Islanders did make money. One who claimed to have struck it rich without lifting a shovel was Timothy C. Osborn, twenty-two, who had left on the *Splendid* as a passenger, not a member of the mining company. In California he started a store, selling essential goods to the miners, and soon became rich, or so the *Gazette* reported. Rich or not, he was back in Edgartown in December 1850, working at his old job as a clerk.

As early as July 1850, the *Gazette* reported that five Gold Rushers had already returned. Among them were Charles Vincent with fifteen hundred dollars in gold and Ichabod Luce, who brought home three thousand dollars, as well as another five thousand, the paper said, that he had brought home for men still in the diggings. If true, and there is no reason for doubt, these are large sums to have earned in so short a time. Schoolteachers worked ten years to make three thousand dollars.

Most, however, came home disappointed and broke; some did not come back at all. Henry Baylies, who did not go, had commented on those deaths in his diary months before: "February 15, 1850. Letters from California are very discouraging. Disappointments, disease & terrific suffering & death heads the list. Thus the love of Gold hath allured, ensnared & destroyed those souls who by economical industry might have lived very happily with their families for years."

An article in the *Gazette*, signed "Caution," was printed shortly after the ship *Walter Scott* sailed. The writer prophesized (correctly, it turned out) that the men would be lucky to come home with enough to repay what they were spending to get there and back. Another letter writer responded critically, giving a dismal account of the Island's economy in 1850:

> The writer ["Caution"] supposes the *Walter Scott*'s company will obtain enough "to pay their debts" and have a little left to start upon. . . . Permit us to ask if that is more than some of them would have done if they had remained at home? . . . Even the carpenters [in Edgartown] have little to do. . . . Coopers [complain] that casks are obtained elsewhere and boat builders are idle, while the packets tow boats [over] from New Bedford. The baker, too, has complaints. . . .
>
> What inducement have you to remain here on this island? We can see none for any man who has not enough of "this world's goods.". . . What encouragement any one can find to remain here we cannot perceive. Is the whaling interest alarmed, lest others should obtain something?

The 1850 census gives us a skewed view of how many men were working at the time on the Island. Many men who were in California, or on the way to California, when the census was taken are listed as mariners, their previous occupation, and not as gold seekers. Of 1,463 men in the census, 686 are listed as mariners, nearly half; another 342 call themselves farmers; 117, laborers. These three occupations account for more than three-quarters of the adult male population.

We don't know exactly how many of the 1,463 men were in California in 1850, but certainly it was more than 200, most of them shown in the census as "mariners." Also listed as though they were still on the Island are 71 carpenters and cabinetmakers, 14 tailors, 14 coopers, 10 boatbuilders, 19 blacksmiths, and 10 physicians. We know that many of them were in California, not working on the Island.

Census data do tell us how few "industries" the Island had in which men and women could find work. The largest, employing fourteen men, was the candle works and oil manufactory in Edgartown owned by Dr. Daniel Fisher. (Fisher at this point was the richest man on the Island; his real estate was valued at $18,700.) The brick works in Chilmark, owned by Smith and Barrows, had eleven men on the payroll. In (West) Tisbury, Thomas Bradley's woolen mill on Mill Pond employed four men and three women and produced seven thousand yards of satinet and nine thousand yards of kersey a year. Charles Cottle's tannery in Holmes Hole had three male employees. A boot- and shoemaker in Holmes Hole and the paint mill in Chilmark each had one worker. Also listed in the census as industries were four whaleships owned in Holmes Hole and one in Edgartown, as well as six mackerel vessels, two out of Holmes Hole and four out of Edgartown. A company at the herring run on Mattakesett Creek hired eight men in season to catch and ship 1,250 pounds of herring.

Inhabitants on the Indian Lands were not included in the census. Four Gay Head Indians were included, however. They had sailed for California as crew on the Edgartown ship *Splendid* with the Dukes County Mining Company and therefore were listed as Edgartown residents. They were William Jeffers, Paul Cuff, Levi Cuff, and Hebron Wansley.

Whalers, already having trouble filling their casks with oil, were further hurt as the Gold Rush tempted men to jump ship and head for the diggings. It is not surprising that whalemen went. They were gamblers at heart. Nobody would go chasing whales for four years with no guarantee of pay if he was not a gambler. It was inevitable that when the odds of winning suddenly looked better in the goldfields, they would switch tables in the casino of life. Richard Ellis wrote in *Men and Whales:* "When gold was discovered at Sutter's Mill in California in 1848, whaleships saw a whole-sale defection of their crews—and sometimes their captains as well—as soon as they docked in San Francisco."

Gold wasn't the sole cause of the decline of whaling: overkilling had made the business a money loser. According to the whaling historian Alexander Starbuck, of the sixty-eight whalers scheduled to return to New Bedford and Fairhaven in 1858, well over half, forty-four of them, lost money. The whale fishery's total loss that year was "at least $1,000,000," he wrote. In their years of high profit, whalemen had so depleted the whale population that ships had to go farther and stay out longer. Yet they often came home with less oil.

The sperm oil catch dropped 50 percent in each of the two decades between 1846 and 1866. Between 1846 and 1855 it fell from 160,000 barrels to 81,000. In the next decade it fell to 37,000 barrels. The second decade, of course, was a time of war, and the catch was affected by the destruction of many whaleships by the Confederate raiders *Alabama* and *Shenandoah*. But the decline had started in the 1840s, before the war.

The approaching Civil War had another impact as the northeastern states became hotbeds of abolitionism. The first antislavery society was formed in Philadelphia in 1833. In a few years, the abolitionist movement had reached the Vineyard. Jeremiah Pease wrote about an Eastville meeting: "March 4, 1838. Went to East Side, Holmes Hole. . . . Slavery preaching at evening." Although Pease doesn't give any details, it would seem likely that the preacher was an abolitionist seeking followers. As was so often the case through its history, the Island wasn't eager for a drastic change. Whites were comfortable in their relationships with persons of color. Slavery seemed far away for most. Occasionally a black preacher would be allowed to speak at camp meeting, seeking contributions to help some black mother buy her child out of slavery, but that was about the extent of the Island's enthusiasm for abolition. Black singing groups sometimes performed in the villages to raise money, but such happenings were few. Island blacks, who never went to camp meetings, rarely attended public gatherings and did not demand access in the unlikely event it was denied. Both sides thought that being comfortable was easier than being defiant.

But there were exceptions. One Island resident flaunted his support of slavery. He was John Presbury Norton of Lambert's Cove, a man important enough politically to have been collector of customs in Edgartown from 1830 to 1842. He brazenly petitioned the Massachusetts General Court in

1849 to pass a law permitting him to own slaves: "February 10. Petition to the Massachusetts Senate and House by John P. Norton of Tisbury requesting that a law be passed 'permitting him to import from the slave-holding States one or more slaves, and hold them in perpetual servitude, for the purpose of cultivating his farm.'" State legislators were shocked. Who was this Vineyard antediluvian with the nerve to ask them to allow him to buy slaves in a state where slavery had been illegal since 1783? They were insulted: "A motion to commit this petition to the Committee on the Judiciary 'excited some debate, several members contending that it was an insult to the House and that the petitioner should have leave to withdraw.'"

We have no evidence that Islanders recoiled at the insensitivity of Norton's petition, which suggests that on the Island there was no strong opposition to slavery in the mid-1800s. Members of minorities, Indians and blacks, were opposed, as one would expect, but they were neither vocal nor influential.

In New Bedford and on Nantucket abolitionists were more active. There was an Underground Railroad station in New Bedford where fugitive slaves, having arrived as stowaways on coastal vessels, were helped to Canada and freedom. Such incidents occurred very rarely on the Vineyard. But in September 1854 at Holmes Hole a black man, said to be a fugitive slave, escaped during the night from the vessel on which he had stowed away in Florida. The captain, when the stowaway revealed himself during the voyage, stopped at Holmes Hole to turn him over to the customs officer. Unfamiliar with the procedure, the Holmes Hole officer wrote to the Boston collector for advice. One night, before a response from Boston had been received, the slave escaped. The *Gazette* reported on September 22: "A RUNAWAY SLAVE—The bark *Franklin* which arrived at Holmes Hole from Jacksonville, Florida, had a slave on board who secreted himself in the hold while the vessel was loading. During the night, while the vessel was lying at anchor, he took a boat and made good his escape to the shore; since which his whereabouts have been known to only a select few. He was from 25 to 30 years of age."

In its next issue, on September 29, the *Gazette* ran a follow-up story:

After the escape of the slave from the *Franklin*, he landed on West Chop and proceeded to Gay Head, where he entered a swamp and remain[ed] concealed for several days. On the 16th inst., a warrant was placed in the hands of Deputy Sheriff Lambert of Chilmark for his arrest on a charge of larceny, the offense alleged being the stealing of a boat from the *Franklin.* . . . Just previous . . . two women from the lovely village of Holmes Hole . . . heard of the slave and were determined to save him from capture. . . . They drove with all speed to the swamp at Gay Head . . . boldly entered the swamp . . . after a short search, they found the slave, who endeavored to escape, but after being furnished with food and learning that the heroic women were his friends . . . a woman's dress and bonnet were soon placed on him and they all emerged from the swamp and jumping into the wagon drove directly to Manainshe [Menemsha] Bite and entered a boat . . . which the same women had engaged to meet them at the place before leaving Holmes Hole. . . . The warp was unfastened and the already hoisted sails filled to the breeze!

After arrival . . . at New Bedford, the women took the slave to the residence of an abolitionist and arrangements were made . . . [to forward] the slave to Canada.

The following week the *Gazette* concluded the story: "The slave who made his escape from a vessel in Holmes Hole is reported as having arrived in Canada."

The account of the slave's rescue was published in many New England newspapers. The Boston Vigilance Committee interviewed those involved, including the slave himself. In the book *Slave Testimony,* edited by John W. Blassingame (1977), the slave's own story is reprinted as it first appeared in a Boston newspaper in 1858. The interview with the slave, Edinbur Randall, seems to have taken place in New Bedford. The article is summarized here as his version of the story.

Randall said he was born in Alabama of an Indian mother and a Negro father. They were not slaves. Only four years old when his parents died, he was taken into the home of a farmer, Gabriel Smith, where he was well treated and grew up to become a farmhand. Smith died when Randall was eighteen. He continued living on the farm, which Smith's daughter, Martha, had taken over. When she married an Irish immigrant, Randall's life changed drastically. The Irishman badly mistreated him. Frequently beaten and fearing for his life, he escaped from the farm and lived for several months on berries and other wild things in the forest. Making his way to the port of Jacksonville, he watched the *Franklin* being loaded at the wharf with pine lumber. The night before it was to sail, he sneaked aboard and hid in the forward hold.

After a few days at sea, he sought help. Sympathetic sailors gave him clothing and food. The captain and officers, however, showed no sympathy, saying they would send him back to the south at their first opportunity. As we have seen, the first stop was Holmes Hole, where the captain reported him to authorities. Randall protested that he was not a slave and not subject to the Fugitive Slave Act, but no one believed him. The sailors told him his best chance at freedom would be in Gay Head, and so he made his way there after his escape. He described what happened next:

> Made towards Gay Head, where I found the Indians, who readily took me in, and kindly ministered to my necessities.
>
> The next day a young Indian, William Francis, came to the house where I was, and said that the deputy Sheriff, Thomas H. Lambert, was up on Gay Head, with a warrant to arrest a colored sailor, who stole the boat from the ship *Franklin*, and offered a large reward to the Indians to find him. . . . The Indians told me to go into a swamp near by. I took their advice, and went into the thickest bushes about one hundred yards, and remained there some time; at length Beulah Vanderhoop, the Indian woman who took me into her house, came to the swamp, called me out, and put a gown, shawl, and bonnet upon me, and took me some distance to the house of her grandmother, Mrs. Peters, hid me in the garret, and then went to engage a boat to take me from the island. . . . [She] engaged two Indian boatmen, Samuel Peters and Zaccheus Cooper . . . and I was accompanied to their boat by a number of Indians, whose kind efforts for my escape I can never forget. The boat left the Island with a favorable wind, and I was soon put ashore upon the main land, among other friends of the slave.

Years later, in February 1921, the *Vineyard Gazette* published a somewhat different account by Netta Vanderhoop, who, the paper said, had written it in 1867, when she was fifteen. She repeated what she had been told by her family about the fugitive. (She was only two when the escape took place in 1854.) Like Randall, she does not mention any Holmes Hole women playing a role in the rescue. Nor is there any mention of the rescued man ending up in Canada. Netta says he settled in New Bedford and often returned to Gay Head to visit his benefactor, Beulah Vanderhoop, whom he called Mother.

The *Gazette* reported some fugitive slaves being rescued in Edgartown the following spring, May 1855, but gives no details: "SLAVES:—We learn that two or three slaves, fresh from the South, were in town last week. They were conveyed to New Bedford by one of the colored residents of Chapaquidic."

There may have been other slaves who escaped from ships in Island harbors, but we have found no mention of them. The published accounts indicate that white Vineyarders were not involved in their rescue. That seems to have been left to other people of color.

Island whites, like most northerners, were opposed to the spread of slavery. They didn't want it to be extended by the admission into the Union of proslavery states. But they were not abolitionists, who demanded that the existing slaves be freed. Public meetings opposing the admission of slave states were held occasionally, sponsored usually by the Know-Nothing party, which had added the issue of slavery to its anti-Catholicism.

One such meeting was held in Edgartown in 1855. Edgar Marchant of the *Gazette* was elected chairman. Speakers included David Davis, Charles J. Barney, Samuel Osborn Jr., and Ichabod Luce, all of whom later became Republicans and strong Lincoln supporters. These men, strongly opposed as they were to admitting proslavery states, probably had never taken any interest in the lives of two black women born on the Island, one as a slave.

The women were Nancy Michael and her daughter, Rebecca Francis. The daughter, forty-four, had just died. When she died, her son, William, a cooper and boatsteerer on the *Waverly* of New Bedford, was on his way home from a whaling voyage in the Pacific. Nancy and her family lived in a rented house (probably more shack than house) on Pease's Point Way, then the edge of the village. She died at eighty-four, two years after Rebecca.

This family of three generations (Nancy, Rebecca, and William) was descended from African slaves owned in Chilmark in the 1700s. Nancy's mother (also named Rebecca) was a slave owned by Colonel Cornelius Bassett of Chilmark. Her father was probably Sharper Michael, son of Rose, another African slave, owned by Zaccheus Mayhew, a Chilmark justice of the peace. Born before Massachusetts outlawed slavery, Nancy was considered a slave; an 1852 court ruled that with the passage of the law prohibiting slavery in 1783, she became "born free," despite having been born a slave. When Colonel Bassett died in 1779, Nancy was sold, at seven years of age, to Joseph Allen of Tisbury, who "held and used her as a slave for a series of years." She and her brother, Pero, along with another female slave, Cloe, were inventoried in Bassett's estate:

1 Negro boy called pero aged 18 years—£300
1 Negro woman called cloe, aged 27 years—£150
1 Gall Dto. [ditto] called nancy, aged 7 years—£180

Sometime before 1812 Nancy, now a free person, moved to Edgartown, where she "fell into distress" and became a town pauper, a condition that continued throughout the rest of her life. As late as 1854 the town was spending eighty dollars a year for her support. In that year the town bought from her for ten dollars a house she had inherited in 1819 from her brother James. The money presumably was used to help pay for her support.

From that start in slavery and poverty, these three generations of black women, seemingly without any support from males, produced the Island's only black whaling master, Captain William A. Martin of Chappaquiddick. It is a Vineyard saga.

When William's mother, Rebecca, died, little notice was taken of it. We know of it only from Jeremiah Pease's diary: "October 29, 1854: Attended meetings at E'ville [Eastville]. Rebecca, a coloured woman, dies, she was the Daut. of Nancy Michael, aged about 50 years. She died about 8 o'clock A.M. October 30, 1854. A little rain. Funeral of the above coloured Woman, Rebecca. Service by Rev'd. Mr. Keller [Methodist]." Pease gives no details, but he seems to have known Rebecca, who perhaps attended his Methodist prayer meetings. He may have gone to her funeral, along with other white Methodists from Eastville, although he doesn't say that. Two years later, in December 1856, when Nancy died, Pease did not mention it in his diary. The *Gazette* did publish her obituary. It is a most unusual article, sometimes warm and sympathetic, sometimes disparaging and mocking:

AN OLD LANDMARK GONE. Mrs. Nancy Michael, known to most of our readers by the familiar cognomen of "Black Nance" is no more. She departed this life on Saturday last, at a very advanced age. Probably she was not far from 100 years old. She had changed but little in her appearance for 40 years past; and those who knew her 50 years ago looked upon her as an old woman. She was a very remarkable character in her day. Naturally possessed of kind feelings, she was very fond of children, and usually attentive to their wants; and there are but few among us who have not at some time been indebted to her.

Possessed of a strong natural mind, she acquired great influence over some of our people, by many of whom she was looked upon as a witch. She professed to have the power of giving good or bad luck to those bound on long voyages; and it was no unusual thing for those about to leave on whaling voyages to resort to her, to propitiate her favor by presents, etc., before leaving home. Special woes were denounced by her upon those who were too independent to acknowledge her influence. In case of bad news from any vessel commanded by one who had defied her power, she was in ecstasies, and her fiendish spirit would at once take full control of her.

At such times she might be seen in our streets, shaking her long, bony fingers at all unbelievers in her magical power; and pouring forth the most bitter invectives upon those whom she looked upon as her enemies. Her strange power and influence over many continued till the day of her death, though for two or three years past she was mostly confined to her room.

Taking her all in all, she was a most singular character, and it will doubtless be a long time before we shall look upon her like again. She was a professor of religion, and we believe at one time adorned the profession. "May her good deeds long live in our remembrance, and her evil be interred with her bones."

Graciously, the *Gazette* did not recite the many times Nancy's daughter, Rebecca (who was not mentioned, nor was her grandson, William A. Martin), had been in trouble with the law, sometimes on the complaint of Nancy herself. Rebecca was a regular at the county jail, usually overnight on a charge of "breaking the peace" (drunkenness). She was once charged with theft, another time with "lude" behavior. Her missteps seem to have been triggered by alcohol, and an understanding sheriff took that into account, holding her only until she was sober.

Jail records show her first as Rebecca Ann Michael (sometimes Michaels); later she is Rebecca Ann Martin. Then, after marrying John Francis in 1831, she becomes Rebecca Ann Francis. The Martin name was adopted, it would seem, when a man named Martin fathered her only known child, William, in 1827.

His mother's behavior being what it was, young William must have been raised by his grandmother. Although we know nothing of his early years, William most likely went to sea as a boy. He was a cooper and boat-steerer on the *Waverly* in the North Pacific from 1851 to 1854. He had signed on with a 1/37th lay, better than those of the second and third mates, a tribute to his skills. (A lay was a share in the profits.) Only the captain and first mate had better lays. Others of Martin's known voyages

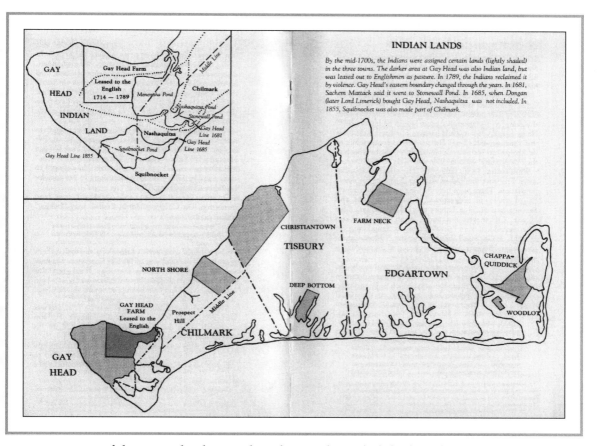

A map of the Vineyard Indian Lands. Indian Lands are shaded. The Indians living on them could not buy or sell land, nor could they vote. Most were on Gay Head and Chappaquiddick. In the mid-1800s the lands were divided up among the families living there, and Guardians were appointed to "supervise" them. (MVHS Collections)

were on the *Almira* and *Europa*. On the *Europa*, in 1857, he was first officer and log keeper. (The log exists.) Before sailing on that voyage, he married Sarah G. Brown of Chappaquiddick, who was one-quarter Indian.

He was first officer on the *Clarice* in the 1870s. He was promoted to master and commanded the *Golden City, Emma Jane,* and *Eunice H. Adams,* all owned by Samuel Osborn Jr. of Edgartown. The promotion made Martin the Island's only black whaling master. While commanding the *Eunice H. Adams* (1887–90), he left in mid-voyage, probably because of illness, and he seems not to have gone to sea after that.

Captain Martin died in his "captain's house" on Chappaquiddick on September 5, 1907, after being a paralytic for seven years. The house had been inherited by his wife, Sarah, from her parents. It was hardly a "captain's house"—it was certainly no match for those on William Street or Water Street. But William Martin, a black man, didn't need a trophy house to prove his success.

Sarah's parents were Abraham, a black, and Lucy Brown, half Indian. In the 1849 report on Indians that went to Governor George N. Briggs, both are listed as Indians on Chappaquiddick. When their daughter, Sarah, also listed as Indian, married William A. Martin in 1857, she was twenty-five and he was twenty-eight.

The Walling map, published in 1857, shows a house belonging to A. Brown on the Chappaquiddick Indian Lands near Tom's Neck Point. About 1907 Hope J. Heath wrote in the *Gazette* of spending her summers in that Chappaquiddick house. Her family, she wrote, rented it from Mrs. Sarah Martin. It was "a little gray shingled house overlooking Pogue Pond." She did not mention (and she probably didn't know) that it was a captain's house, home of the Vineyard's only black whaling master.

That house also was probably one of the "neat and comfortable" houses on Chappaquiddick that John Milton Earle of Worcester visited between 1859 and 1861 while making his sympathetic study of the Indians of Massachusetts. Earle's report followed the Briggs report mentioned earlier. It was one of a series of studies the state funded as it tried to ease its conscience over the fate of its Indians.

Earle stated that seventeen families, totaling seventy-four persons, were living in the Indian Lands on Chappaquiddick. Also living there were seven "foreigners" (persons not born there). Earle's remarks about the Chappaquiddick Indians sound familiar, having been written often:

> In the division of the island between the Indians and the whites, the latter, as usual, obtained much the better portion. That belonging to the Indians is bleak and exposed, the soil light, sandy, gravelly and barren, and without wood for either fuel or fencing, yielding, as was well said by the commissioners in 1849, "a precarious subsistence to the most untiring industry." . . .
>
> Most of the residents have framed houses and things in and about them have a neat and comfortable appearance, as much so as among their white neighbors. . . .
>
> Under the law of 1828, the territory of this tribe has been divided . . . among the inhabitants. . . . A certain quantity was assigned to each indi-

In the 1850s the original Gay Head Light was replaced by a brick tower equipped
with the largest of the new French Fresnel lenses, a scientific wonder that brought
attention to that remote end of the Island for the first time. Magazine and newspaper
writers who came to see the lens left overwhelmed by the beauty of the cliffs,
and they made Gay Head famous. (MVHS Collections)

vidual, including those of every age. . . . The whole amount assigned to
any one family was set off in one lot. . . . The father held and occupied
the same . . . usually during his lifetime. . . .

Like all the other Indians of the State . . . those of Chappaquiddick
are disfranchised, with the exception of two families who reside on the
other side of the line, in Edgartown, and own property there for which
they are taxed.

In Christiantown, another of the Island's Indian Lands, Earle counted
53 Indians, all native to the Island. Gay Head, with the largest Indian population, had 46 families totaling 204 persons, of whom 10 were "foreigners." Gay Head differed from the other Indian Lands in that its residents
had refused to allow the land to be divided among families, preferring to
keep it owned in common, each Indian being allowed to use as much land
as he needed, in line with Indian heritage.

A few years earlier, a description of Gay Head was published in a letter to the *Namasket* (Middleboro) *Gazette*. The writer went there in 1856 to see the exciting new Fresnel lens in the brand-new brick lighthouse tower. The lens was one of the scientific wonders of the age, having been exhibited in an exposition in Paris before being installed at Gay Head. The letter gives excellent details:

> Here [in Gay Head] a good Christian family, by name, How-was-wee, received us and provided the bodily needful for several days. The natives here number about 200 and live very comfortably—their condition is better than those at Marshpee. They appear temperate, moral and industrious. Unlike their brethren in Marshpee, they prefer their land to remain undivided, each one cultivating as much as he chooses, the revenue of the remainder going for general purposes. They have a little church of about 50 members, preaching for the most part being provided by a fund at Harvard College. There is also a school of between 40 and 50 scholars, that would compare favorably with the schools in this town [Middleboro]. We never before had the pleasure of looking into 80 or 90 black eyes at once, each beaming with true native intelligence.
>
> This part of the island seems for the most part to be a bed of valuable white and red clay. It is worth $3.50 per ton on the spot and is carried off in cart loads to Providence, Taunton and other places. Sometimes in calm weather, large ships anchor near the cliffs and load; at such times they all turn out, the women as well as the men; the men cut out the clay in lumps; while the women stand in rows down to the vessel and pass it along in their hands after the manner of passing pails of water sometimes at fires; they afterwards divide the money, one man having as much as two women. As another source of profit to them, I will mention their cranberries, of which some years they pick nearly 300 bushels.

With the arrival of the wondrous Fresnel lens from France, Gay Head suddenly became a place of great interest to writers. However, life changed little for the Indians. Their refusal to accept private ownership of land was a sticking point with the state. As the historian George Ellis warned many years later, in 1882, there could be no peaceful coexistence with Massachusetts until the Gay Head Indians gave up their "communism."

Although Gay Head residents continued to resist change, there were many taking place on the rest of the Island.

The first wooden "cottage" was built in the campground early in the

1850s by the Reverend Frederick Upham. It was hardly a cottage, being a simple wooden box the same size, seven by ten feet, as the tent it replaced. But it had attributes no canvas shelter had. It was dry. Upham, who had been the Methodist minister in Edgartown from 1848 until 1850, was a longtime camp-meeting participant. After a heavy rain drenched the campground and its tent dwellers one night in 1869, *Zion's Herald,* the Methodist weekly, described Upham's delight: "Out of his box, he walked serene in the morning and, rubbing his hands in his humorous and devout style, dryly remarked, 'Bless God for shingles.'"

A Wareham man named Dykes had bought the campground's thirty acres in 1856 for one thousand dollars. He offered to sell it to the Methodists for sixteen hundred dollars; or, if they preferred, he would lease it to them for one hundred dollars a year. (They were paying only fifteen dollars under the existing lease.) The Methodists immediately began looking for another site, which caused the speculator to cancel his purchase, and the lease was unchanged.

In 1850 the U.S. Congress appropriated four thousand dollars to complete the wooden causeway from the shore to Edgartown Harbor Light. The light, mounted atop the keeper's house, which had been built on a man-made island in shoal water, could be reached only by boat. The causeway, when finished, became famous in Vineyard legend as the "Bridge of Sighs." Young lovers walked out on it nightly, enchanted by the beauty of the moonlit harbor and each other.

A major breakthrough in 1856 gave the Island telegraphic communication with the mainland when a submarine cable was laid from West Chop to Woods Hole. A giant celebration marked the event. A few weeks later the cable was cut by a ship's anchor. No telegrams were received for a while.

The brand-new keeper's house at Gay Head leaked so much that extensive repairs had to be made when the keeper's family became sick with an illness caused, it was said, by the moisture.

Edgartown got the Island's first high school after the state began enforcing the law requiring towns to provide free education through twelve grades. The town advertised that it would sell schoolbooks to high school pupils at no profit (as the law required).

The Dukes County Shoe and Boot Company began business on Dock Street in Edgartown. Nathaniel Jernegan was president. It never made a profit and lasted only six years.

Edgartown Harbor Light, which was on a man-made island for a number of years, was connected to land about 1850 by a long wooden bridge that became a popular strolling place for young lovers and was called the "Bridge of Sighs." (MVHS Collections)

In Pennsylvania in 1859 a man drilling for water struck oil. It was the country's first oil well. Whaling would never be the same.

In 1850 Captain Ira Darrow, who ran a packet between Edgartown and the mainland, took the first step toward making Marchant's prediction of three years before a reality. The *Gazette* reported: "We are glad to know that a commodious bathing house has just been erected and opened for the accommodation of the public by Ira Darrow Esq. It is situated below the residence of Mr. Darrow [on North Water Street in Edgartown].

In April 1861 the federal Fort Sumter in South Carolina was fired on by Confederate forces and forced to surrender. The Civil War had begun.

Marchant's prediction that the Island would become famous as the East Coast's "Watering Place" would have to be set aside for a while.

7

The Civil War: Its Bounties, Its Substitutes, the Draft, and the Dead

There never was a period of political upheaval on the Vineyard to match that in the months before the 1860 presidential election. An island that had always been somewhat indifferent to national politics suddenly found itself fully involved. It was a confusing time for the whole nation, threatened as it was with revolt by southern states over the issue of slavery. Northern abolitionists, far noisier than their numbers warranted, were demanding freedom for the slaves. Southerners were ready to secede from the Union.

Four political groups had been formed on the Island. They held meetings, "conventions" as they were grandly called, to decide what course to take. The largest of the four groups favored the new Republican party and its candidate, Abraham Lincoln. They were members of the Lincoln Club, made up mostly of former Whigs and Know-Nothings. In Edgartown many were the same men who for years had controlled the town's politics, including Charles J. Barney (who had left the Whigs to head the Know-Nothings), Richard L. Pease, John Vinson, Jeremiah Pease Jr., Samuel Osborn Jr., and Nathaniel M. Jernegan, all former Whigs. So committed were Lincoln supporters that when the Republicans held a convention in Boston in October 1860, 175 of them chartered the steamer *Eagle's Wing* and went to it by water.

A second group of Republicans supported John Bell of Tennessee, whose running mate was Edward Everett of Massachusetts, a former governor and now Harvard's president. Its members also were former Whigs and Know-Nothings, besides some dissident Democrats. They differed from the Lincoln men in their strong opposition to the Personal Liberty Act, a recent Massachusetts law that was passed to obstruct enforcement of the Fugitive Slave Acts of 1793 and 1850. These men opposed secession, but they felt slavery was a southern problem and northerners should not get involved. Slaves were property, and any slaves who managed to run away should be returned to their owners. That explained their opposition to the Personal Liberty Act, which required that a jury trial be held at which the runaway could testify on his own behalf before he could be returned. Meeting in the counting room of Daniel Fisher and Company, the Bell supporters included, in addition to Dr. Fisher, Abraham Osborn, Benjamin Worth, and John A. Baylies, leading citizens all.

The third group was made up of most of the Island's regular Democrats. They supported Stephen Douglas for president. Like the Bell group, they opposed the Personal Liberty Act, but they were Democrats and Douglas was their nominee. He believed people (meaning white males, of course) who lived in new territories had a right to decide whether to allow slavery. It was nobody else's business. Members included Henry Pease 2nd, Rodolphus Pease, Seth Cleveland, Samuel W. Lewis, and the *Vineyard Gazette* editor, Edgar Marchant.

Democrats had long been a minority party on the Island. Chilmark was the only town where they had had any amount of success. In 1856 that town had voted for the Democrat James Buchanan, who won nationally and was now president.

On the Island, as in the nation, Democrats were divided over slavery. Not all Island Democrats supported Douglas, whose position on the issue was ambiguous. Those who did not go along with Douglas made up the fourth group. So eager were they to placate the South that they supported the proslavery candidate, John C. Breckinridge of Kentucky, the incumbent vice president. This small group held its "conventions" in the office of a longtime Democrat, Captain Ira Darrow. Constant Norton of Edgartown was president and James Norton of Tisbury was secretary. Eager above everything else to preserve the Union, they were for the status quo: keep things the way they are; don't rock the boat.

Abraham Lincoln won the election and the four Island groups disbanded. He carried the Vineyard with 59 percent of the vote, a far higher percentage than the 39 percent he received nationally. By winning the heavily populated northern states, he had won a majority in the electoral college, in spite of his low popular vote.

Vinegard Gazette.

EDGARTOWN:

FRIDAY, NOV. 9, 1860.

PRICE OF THE GAZETTE:
Only One Dollar Per Year, in Advance.

BY EDGAR MARCHANT.

THE ELECTION RETURNS.

EDGARTOWN.

Electors—
Bell and Everett,	27
Douglas and Johnson,	42
Breckinridge and Lane,	33
Lincoln and Hamlin,	171

Governor—
Amos A. Lawrence,	21
Benjamin F. Butler,	27
E. D. Beach,	48
John A. Andrew,	173

Lieutenant Governor—
George Marston,	21
David N. Carpenter,	26
Charles Thompson,	49
John Z. Goodrich,	171

For Representative to General Court—
Daniel Flanders, (Breck. D.)	16
Allen Tilton, (Rep.)	120
Edgar Marchant, (Doug. D.)	148

County Commissioner—
Herman Vincent,	41
James N. Tilton,	86
Thomas H. Lambert,	149

Senator—
Thomas B. Field,	3
David Smith,	16
Silvester Bourne,	16
Elijah Swift,	66
Charles Dillingham,	163

Representative to Congress—
Frederick C. Sanford,	24
Daniel Fisher,	88
Thomas D. Elliot,	158

Edgartown, as shown in this clipping from the *Gazette* of November 9, 1860, voted by more than 62 percent for Abraham Lincoln. His Island total was 59 percent. Nationally he received only 39 percent, but he won the electoral vote. The other Republican candidate, Bell, received the fewest votes in Edgartown. Democrats were split between Douglas and Breckinridge; the latter, the only proslavery candidate, got 12 percent. (MVHS Collections)

Lincoln's election with a minority of the votes cast caused the *Gazette*'s Marchant, a Douglas Democrat, to worry about whether the new president would be able to keep the nation together. The editor feared disaster lay ahead and quoted Wendell Phillips, the noted Massachusetts abolitionist: "[For] the first time in history a slave has chosen a President. . . . What but the slave question was the turning point? The South cannot look without some anxiety upon political triumph effected by the free states combined against the slave states. South Carolina has already taken the initiative in the matter of a southern secession." The likelihood of a breakup of the Union troubled Marchant and other Vineyarders. Although their man Lincoln had won, they could not feel "merry" about it. Marchant wrote: "People feel sorrow because the late election has created serious fears for the safety of the Union."

Southerners had fears of their own. They were afraid that the new president, despite his campaign promises to the contrary, would give in to the northern abolitionists and free their slaves. That would bring disaster, economically and socially. Vineyarders shared that southern worry. To ease their concerns, Marchant printed a collection of quotations from Lincoln's speeches to show that he would not abolish slavery:

> There is no right and ought to be no inclination in the people of the Free States to enter into the Slave States and interfere with the question of Slavery at all. . . .
>
> I would not be the man to introduce [the Fugitive Slave Act] as a new subject of agitation upon the general question of slavery.
>
> If the people [in a territory] shall . . . do such an extraordinary thing as to adopt a Slave constitution . . . I see no alternative . . . but to admit them into the Union.
>
> I am not, nor ever have been, in favor of bringing about in any way the social and political equality of the white and black races. I am not, nor ever have been, in favor of making voters or jurors of negroes, nor of qualifying them to hold office or to intermarry with white people. . . . I do not understand that because I do not want a negro woman as a slave I must necessarily want her for a wife. . . . I will, to the very last, stand by the law of this state [Illinois] which forbids the marrying of white people with negroes.

Although he had not supported Lincoln, Marchant favored the president's conciliatory position: "The question whether slavery is right or wrong is not the question we have now to discuss. . . . Will we be brethren, and live peaceably together, and respect each others' right and promote each others' welfare; these are the real questions."

The outgoing president, Buchanan, felt the same way: nothing should be done to interfere with slavery where it already existed: the Fugitive Slave Act should be enforced; Personal Liberty Laws and secession were unconstitutional. All parties, it seemed, were opposed to anything that might break up the Union. All, that is, except the southerners.

On December 20, 1860, even before Lincoln was inaugurated, South Carolina seceded. Within forty days, six more states had done the same thing and joined the Confederacy. Eight other states were expected to join. The Confederates began taking over federal property in their states, especially the forts and arsenals.

Early in January 1861 the federal government tried to send supplies to Fort Sumter, the only fort it still held in South Carolina. Sumter was still under construction, standing on a man-made island outside Charleston. The unarmed supply ship *The Star of the West* was fired upon by Confederates in nearby forts and forced to turn back. Major Robert Anderson, commanding the small, beleaguered force in Fort Sumter, sent a message under a white flag to the South Carolina governor, stating that if he did not disclaim the firing, he (Anderson) would consider it to be an act of war (a bold threat with nothing to back it up).

On the Vineyard, hopes of conciliation continued, despite the confrontation at Fort Sumter. Marchant pursued that course: "The Republican party are about to enter upon office and power. . . . Let the party remember that conciliation and reasonable compromise can alone save the country . . . and a refusal to listen to the zealots of their own party, can alone . . . preserve our beloved Union."

Henry L. Whiting, a leading (West) Tisbury resident, wrote to the *Gazette* calling for a county convention to urge repeal of the Personal Liberty Act. Henry Bradley of Tisbury presented a petition to the General Court signed by seventy-five citizens urging its repeal. It was clear: Islanders were for conciliation.

When Lincoln was inaugurated in March 1861, what he had to say about the slavery issue pleased Vineyarders: "I declare that I have no purpose, either directly or indirectly, to interfere with the institution of slavery in the states where it exists. I believe I have no lawful right to do so."

Perhaps the nation could be spared the war that many feared was coming. Perhaps Lincoln could save the Union. In Edgartown, Marchant was doing his part: "[Let us] persuade our people to let slavery alone. . . . Our meddling . . . has done no good to the slave—none to the master—none to the church—none to the country—but evil, evil only, and evil continually. . . . Had we not better let the subject alone (the everlasting Nigger question)? Six months or even three months of silence, would restore peace to the country."

While the vigorous editor was exhausting himself pleading the cause, most Islanders had lost interest. There were no abolitionist meetings, no protests against secession. The divisions that had separated the four groups before the election had been forgotten. Marchant realized that his readers were tired of his arguments. They wanted to get on with their lives. He went along and in a lighter tone revisited his goal of making the Island a famous watering hole: "As all the world has come or is coming to the Vineyard this summer for recreation and fishing, we wish to give some advice. But first let us thank the editor of the *Boston Courier* for helping this matter along by giving a first-rate notice of Sword-fishing and saying, 'that the best place to enjoy this sport is probably at Edgartown, on the Vineyard.'"

Then, in jest we must believe, Marchant invited all the nation's leading editors and politicians to visit the Vineyard and forget their political antagonism: "If they are terribly pugnacious and excited, let them go out and harpoon sharks and bang them on the head with a good-sized club, and also to turn their attention to Sword-fishing. . . . Or, if you please, present the eye with a picture of harmony, wherein Douglas and Lincoln, Bell and Breckinridge are all seen rowing a four-oared red boat in a Regatta in our harbor, contending with other boats for a prize."

Despite the country's problems, or perhaps because of them, the 1861 Methodist camp meeting was bigger than ever. At least five hundred tents circled the preachers' stand, now rebuilt and greatly enlarged. A telegraph office was set up in the campground. A daily campground newspaper began in 1862. Visitors, many of them influential citizens, poured in: "The meetings are made up, mostly of people from New Bedford, Providence and other large places embraced within that Conference. Among its attendants are to be found people from the higher walks of social and civil life, who take their families with them."

Word of the Island's recreational appeal had spread. But there were some less appealing disclosures. A visitor from Hallowell, Maine, wrote in his hometown paper:

Tisbury, more familiarly known to the seafaring class as "Holmes Hole," is becoming quite a favorable resort for those who have in years past chosen the more exciting scenes of Newport and Saratoga, but now find a quiet and cheerful "home" at the Mansion House, kept by a hospitable and gentlemanly retired "son of the Ocean," Capt. [Leander] West. . . . There is not a drinking saloon in town . . . and there has not a lawyer resided here for twelve years, the last one had to leave town or starve, for want of employment.

The citizens have obtained most of their wealth in the whaling business, which has been carried on extensively through the agency of Hon. T. Bradley. . . .

A sad feature among the citizens of Tisbury is a predisposition to insanity. Within a very few years, twelve persons have been carried to the "Insane Asylum." . . . The upper part of the Island contains an almost incredible number of deaf and dumb persons and many blind from birth. These calamities can only be accounted for . . . by the intermarriage of relatives.

When the article was reprinted in the *Gazette*, there was a quick and angry response from a Chilmark reader: "Within 50 years there have been

This lithograph by William H. Sturtevant provides an excellent view of Holmes Hole harbor and the prosperous village of Tisbury in 1858. Steamers were just beginning to replace sailboats. One is barely visible at lower right, behind Bradley's shipyard, its stack emitting black smoke. (MVHS Collections)

eight families into which deaf and dumb children were born. In four cases, the parents were related, in the other four, they were not. We know of no child ever being born blind in this part of the Vineyard."

It was not until twenty years later that Alexander Graham Bell began his study of the unexplained incidence of deaf-mutism on the Vineyard. This Maine visitor may have been the first to make this phenomenon known off-Island, greatly exaggerated though the account was. No wonder it troubled the Chilmark letter writer. Another letter, this one from Edgartown, asked why the visitor from Maine had not visited his town, where much more was happening, thanks in part to Dr. Fisher:

> If the Hon. T. Bradley has done much for Tisbury, Hon. Daniel Fisher . . . has done far more for our town. . . . A bank has been chartered in the past few years and is doing business in a neat brick building. . . . Doctor Fisher is president. His oil manufactory and candle works, located here, are the largest in the country, and he is now building mills a few miles from the village, which will be of great advantage to the people of the Island.
>
> A new brick Court House has been recently erected; an extensive factory for making shoes; another for the manufacture of soap, &c., &c.
>
> As a place of resort in summer, for fishing and gaming, I am not aware that any spot can be found equal to it. We have two hotels . . . every variety of fish abound . . . blue, sword and codfish, halibut, scuphaugs, blackfish, boneta, tautaugs, etc. The fowl are equally numerous. . . . Larks, plovers, dippers, red-heads, brant, wild geese, canvas-back and black ducks.

He didn't mention the impressive captains' houses (the Island's first trophy houses) that had recently been built on Water Street by the town's affluent whaling masters.

The new soap manufactory he mentioned had been started by Sands and Smith; it produced "Yellow and White Erasive Soap, and Toilet Soap, together with common varieties of Hard and Soft Soap. . . . Grease and tallow taken in exchange for soap," their advertisement stated. We don't know where it was located, but probably on the waterfront.

The Dukes County Boot and Shoe Company, headed by Nathaniel Jernegan, was another new manufactory in Edgartown. It produced 16,200 pairs of shoes and paid out four thousand dollars in wages in its first year, seven hundred of that to females. Such jobs were scarce for Island women. Shares in the company were being offered to the public. It needed the money, the offering said, to buy more machinery for its Dock Street factory.

Edgartown wasn't the only place where things were happening. In Chilmark the brick works at Roaring Brook had shipped 700,000 bricks from its wharf on the north shore in 1859 and expected to ship more in 1860. Also on the north shore, about two miles east of the brickyard, there was a large paint mill that had recently started production. It was not the first such mill on the Island. In the late 1700s one had been operating in or near Gay Head, but we can find no details other than that it did exist. There also was a smaller paint mill on Roaring Brook behind the brickyard, which was owned by brothers Francis and Hiram Nye from Falmouth.

The new paint mill east of the brickyard was also owned off-Island. It milled six to eight tons of paint a day. The paint was not a fluid, ready to apply, but a dry pigment made of clay of various colors, red, yellow and white, ground into a fine powder by the steam- and water-powered mill and shipped off-Island. In 1866 the mill was destroyed by fire, but it was soon rebuilt and was back in operation within a year. Its paint seems to have been used principally to color oilcloth, a floor covering then coming into vogue.

The paint mill and the brickyard were the first two up-Island exporting industries we know of, both shipping quantities of their products to the mainland from wharves on Vineyard Sound. Years before, as mentioned previously, tons of clay, unprocessed, had been exported from Gay Head.

Predating all this was what may have been the first up-Island industry, Chilmark's fulling mill. It dates back to the 1700s, but we have little information on it. A fulling mill converted coarse, loosely woven woolen cloth into a softer and tighter fabric by scrubbing it with clay ("fuller's earth" it was called) and then beating it with water-driven wooden paddles. When the fabric dried, it shrank into a tighter, more usable material. The mill was a noisy place while the heavy pounding was going on.

Henry Cleveland had a mill, powered by water flowing from Mill Pond in the center of West Tisbury, that produced satinet, kersey, and flannel fabrics with local wool. Satinet and kersey were woven with a combination of cotton and wool yarns and, being very durable, were popular with mariners and for use in army and navy uniforms. The mill's indigo blue yarn was also in great demand by Vineyard knitters.

Captain John R. Sands, a partner and sales manager in the new soap factory, was eager to sell Vineyard products, especially his soap, in the

South. He loaded the schooner *John Oliver* with shoes, whale oil, spermaceti candles, and plenty of soap, as well as potatoes, turnips, onions, cranberries, and quince, and sailed for South Carolina. He hoped to start a profitable export business with Charleston merchants. His timing was poor. Shortly after the *John Oliver* arrived there, South Carolina seceded from the Union and ended its business ties with the North.

Edgartown's Dr. Daniel Fisher, expanding his empire, invited visitors to see his new gristmill in North Tisbury, where flour was ground from winter wheat imported from Kentucky. The flour sold for six dollars a barrel. He had dammed Mill River to provide waterpower and built a road to the mill from Tisbury. A Chilmark resident, Mrs. Mary G. Tilton, accepted his invitation. While she watched the grinding, her clothing was caught in the machinery, and before the mill could be stopped her left leg was crushed. It had to be amputated at the knee.

Hers was not a happy life. Five years earlier, her husband, Captain Otis Tilton, had been killed, along with two other officers, by mutineers aboard the whaler *John* of New Bedford, and she was left with two daughters, ages three and six.

Bad news was not infrequent in those days. The schooner *Mogul*, sailing to New Bedford with a load of up-Island apples and bricks from the Roaring Brook brickyard, was swamped and sank in Vineyard Sound. Captain William A. Luce and his brother were lost. The schooner *Dorcas Ireland* was blown ashore on Nomans Land while sailing to Boston with a load of southern cotton for the mills of Lowell—perhaps the last such shipment before the war.

An enterprising citizen planned to open a billiard hall in Edgartown where men could spend their evenings. It would keep them out of trouble, he claimed. There was a strong outcry from church members. Billiards would bring in gambling and that was a sin. But one *Gazette* reader thought otherwise: "Edgartown is certainly not overstocked with places of amusement. . . . [Playing billiards] would take up a portion of the hours spent in sitting in the stores hugging the stoves."

One of the Island's legends was beginning. Nancy Luce, living alone with her animals in (West) Tisbury, was starting her career as an eccentric poet. Two of her pet hens had died, one in 1858, the other in 1859, deeply grieving her. In 1860 she somehow managed to have published in New Bedford, with the help of her physician, Dr. William Luce, her first booklet, *Poor Little Hearts*—a memorial to her pets. It was the start of her amazing rise to Island celebrity, as she became the first Vineyard woman to support herself by the pen. She was just starting her rise to fame in 1861 when she wrote to the *Gazette*, offering advice to other hen owners:

MR. EDITOR: I send you a piece to put in your paper, if you please, without charging me.

My pullets commenced laying [at] 4 months of age. My bantie sort lay as well in the winter as they do in the summer. They must have good fine meal scalded with milk, and warm bread made of milk and good southern corn, and warm milk to drink in winter, and a warm clean house. . . . Be good to your hens and not cruel. Consider how you would feel if you could not help yourselves and folks was cruel to you and let you suffer. I have kept about 8 hens which layed rising 1500 eggs a year.

NANCY LUCE

Most Vineyarders, unlike Nancy Luce, had other worries than keeping their hens laying. One such was from Chilmark, who signed his letter to the *Gazette* only "Democrat." His letter was prophetic: "As for Mr. Lincoln, we like him well enough, although we don't want to let him know it at present. He is good at splitting rails, and if things are to go on so, it will soon be seen that he can not only split rails, but also these United States."

That splitting soon began. Fort Sumter was fired on and burned by Confederate forces on April 12, 1861. Major Anderson and his small force, almost out of supplies, abandoned the fort. Despite heavy cannonading and much damage to the fort's buildings, there were no casualties (although one man was killed when a cannon exploded while firing a "celebratory" forty-eight-gun salute just before the evacuation).

The Civil War had started.

The next day President Lincoln called for seventy-five thousand volunteers to serve in the army for three months. Their task, Lincoln said, would be to retake the federal property, especially the forts, that the Confederates had confiscated. An optimistic *Gazette* editor thought it wouldn't take long: "Thousands have already responded to the call. In a week or two the government will show its strong arm and traitors will feel its power. Treason must be put down at once or all is lost."

In the next issue Marchant placed an engraving of Old Glory atop the editorial column. It stayed there throughout the war. His editorial was bloodthirsty:

We fling today the Glorious banner of the Stars and Stripes to the breeze.
. . . Down with the traitors. Let them swing from the yard arms and from
the gibbets. . . . Let Jefferson Davis, and Wigfall and Toombs and Rhett,
and a host of others like them, receive the reward due to enemies of the
freest and fairest government on earth.

But let not their carcasses be interred in American soil to contaminate
the earth and the air of heaven with their foul pollution. No. Let them be
cast into the sea and become food for sharks and other voracious mon-
sters of the deep. . . .

A company or two of veteran whalemen, armed with the harpoon or
with lance and spade, would . . . send terror into the hearts of Southern
traitors.

If President Lincoln would call upon the whalemen of Nantucket,
New Bedford and the Vineyard, he could raise a regiment before [which]
no human could stand for a day. . . . This same martial spirit pervades the
people of the whole Vineyard. . . . Let every man be ready to shoulder his
arms!

Despite Marchant's jingoism, Vineyard whalemen didn't line up to
shoulder their arms. Not one man on the Island volunteered in response
to Lincoln's call, but a former Vineyarder, H. Vincent Butler, who had
been living in Providence for three years, did join the Rhode Island Volunteers, a marine artillery unit. Much later, when each town was given a
quota to be filled by volunteers, Edgartown claimed Butler as one of its
volunteers, because he had been born there—a meritless claim.

Within weeks four more states seceded. North and South readied
themselves for the bloodiest war in American history. The Island became
caught up in the hysteria, if not in the volunteering. Tisbury voted to raise
two thousand dollars to join in with New Bedford and hire an armed
steamer to patrol Buzzard's Bay and Vineyard Sound. It asked the state to
supply three rifled cannon and one hundred stand of small arms to repel
any invasion. Edgartown mounted a "Liberty Pole" atop the Town Hall and
ordered a large flag from New Bedford. Charles H. Shute hung an American flag outside his store, along with a banner proclaiming, "Down with
Home Traitors." War was on everybody's mind: "A great Union demonstration was held in Edgartown on Tuesday last. . . . A vigilance committee of
13 appointed. At Holmes Hole, a similar meeting was held Wednesday.
The people there are awake and ready for action."

The women of Holmes Hole began collecting clothing and blankets for the Massachusetts volunteers. Edgartown men formed a "Home Guard" of seventy-five volunteers, led by Cyrus Pease. The town borrowed twelve hundred dollars to buy them uniforms. Chilmark and (West) Tisbury joined forces to form an up-Island Home Guard, headquartered in Agricultural Hall. When Tisbury tried to raise a company to man the three cannon it had requested from the state, only five men signed up. The Island's war hysteria didn't include manpower, it seemed. Lieutenant George M. Macy of Nantucket had signed up thirty young men on that island in August 1861 and he hoped to enlist "many more from our Island," the *Gazette* wrote. When he came to seek volunteers, only three men joined: Barzilla Crowell, Elisha M. Smith, and Peleg Davenport. When the three men left, they were given a royal sendoff: "The Volunteers from Holmes Hole started today on the *Canonicus*, under the command of Lieut. Macy of Nantucket. The citizens contributed some 20 dollars towards a purse, which was handed them on the pier. They left in good spirits. . . . Any in Edgartown who wish to assist their country in her time of need . . . can join the Nantucket and Vineyard boys."

That sarcastic remark about Edgartown was not fair. One of the three, Elisha M. Smith, was from Edgartown and was later given that town's bounty, although he had signed up in Tisbury. Two more Tisbury men soon joined that first group of three Islanders at Camp Meigs, the state's mustering-in camp at Readville (in today's Hyde Park, south of Boston). They were James Wilbur and Benjamin N. Luce. These five were the first Vineyarders to enlist in the Civil War.

They were an unlucky five. Three died in the service, two of them in battle, Peleg Davenport at Fredericksburg and Elisha M. Smith at Gettysburg. The third, James Wilbur, died of typhoid fever. The other two were wounded and disabled, but they survived. Barzilla Crowell had his left leg amputated after being wounded in Virginia, and Benjamin Luce lost the use of his left hand from wounds at Fredericksburg.

As an unnamed Edgartown sailor wrote in the *Gazette*, there was a less dangerous way to serve : "The Navy is the best place in the world. Very little work and plenty to eat. . . . We want some of those spunky Edgartown boys here."

Unfortunately, those who enlisted in the navy were not counted toward the town's quota of volunteers. The navy didn't need men; the army did—more and more every day. There still was no enthusiasm on the Vineyard to enlist. Part of the reason may have been a lack of conviction about the rightness of the war. In June 1861 one Menemsha resident, who signed his letter to the *Gazette* "Spindle Shanks Jr.," openly opposed the war:

> We are not traitors here at Menamsha [*sic*] but we want our government to remember that in making war upon the Southern states we are pursuing a suicidal course and that it will eventually bring ruin and destruction upon the whole of this great and glorious country.
>
> In regard to the slavery question, some of us think there is no great harm in it if thereby we can enlighten their dark and benighted minds and improve their moral condition. Indeed, we think it would be no great trouble for us to find several texts of Scripture to support this view.

This brought an irate response from a reader who signed his letter "Union." He advised the Menemsha man to be careful what he said or he might find himself "being accommodated with a coat that will be hard to get off."

By the end of the summer of 1861 even Marchant had lost his enthusiasm. The war must not totally occupy us, he wrote. There are many other things to do:

> We have not yet got to paradise and we must snatch our pleasures as we can on our way. . . . Farming is carried on with profit and soon . . . even the shoe business, which has proved so disastrous here, may, in other hands, become profitable. Many think that the whaling business must soon be given up altogether, but we believe that money can still be made in that direction. . . . Genuine whale oil was hardly known in the great towns and cities. . . that hurt us. . . . [To] bring back the people to whale oil [we must] send only the pure article into the market, the use of which will be cheaper, safer, and more pleasant and healthful than any other oils.

Others agreed. New Bedford businessmen were offering a prize of three thousand dollars for the most improved whale-oil lamp in an effort to fight off the competition of petroleum. The *Gazette* was in favor: "Kerosene, Camphene and fluid are dangerous and smelly and all that is needed is an improved whale-oil lamp to bring back the whaling business."

Whaling was not the only Island industry that needed help. The Dukes County Boot and Shoe Company, despite Marchant's optimism, was still having a hard time. Hoping to make the company profitable, shareholders had elected two new men to run it: Samuel Osborn Jr., president, and Captain S. W. Crosby, assistant president. But within a few weeks both resigned, and a month later the company closed. Shareholders were assessed $165 per share to pay off the debt. Marchant's hopes for a profitable shoe company were dashed.

Not all was dark. Thomas Bradley's shipyard in Holmes Hole had just launched the brig *Island Queen,* the largest vessel ever built on the Island. And the swordfishing was good, as the *Gazette* reported:

> Sword fish have this season been taken in unusually large numbers. . . . There are now some thirty vessels out on the favorite fishing ground for them, which is about 15 or 20 miles south and east of Noman's. . . . The season for them is from the middle of June to September. The usual size of the sword fish taken there is from 10 to 12 feet long, weighing from 400 to 500 pounds.
>
> Their flesh is esteemed a great delicacy and commands a ready sale in New York and most of the cities and towns south. It comes nearer the consistency and qualities of meat than any other fish that swims in our waters.
>
> The sport of taking them is usually of the most exciting character. After the fish is harpooned, it [swims] away with the rope playing out and sometimes an hour is used up before it is brought on board.

Dr. Daniel Fisher's son had the record catch. A mighty fish it was: "Largest Swordfish ever taken in these waters. By Daniel Fisher II, the fish was 13 feet long, weighed 700 pounds. Very fat."

Swordfishing may have been more sporting, but most fishermen went after the fish that ordinary people preferred. The swordfish had not yet become family fare on the Island. "MACKEREL FLEET: Seventy sail of schooners belonging to the mackerel fleet were anchored in Menemsha Bight, rocking to and fro like the boughs of some lofty pine trees. About 7 o'clock the sailors raised the sails . . . presenting a scene truly magnificent as they sailed out to sea. A few codfish and halibut have been taken, enabling the most active and successful to make fair wages."

Not all fish ended up on the kitchen table. Fishermen could still make money filling oil lamps: "About 15 boats and 20 men are occupied dog-fishing off Menemsha. The oil obtained from dogfish is said to be nearly equal to sperm for burning."

One industrious fisherman tried to bring back the oyster harvest by

More available and cheaper to produce than whale oil, petroleum took over after the
Civil War. Whaling ships sat rotting at wharves around New England, like this one
at Morse's wharf in Edgartown. That wharf, totally rebuilt, is now owned
by the Edgartown Yacht Club.

stocking one of Edgartown's ponds. The *Gazette* saw another reason to be
optimistic:

> The Selectmen of this town have granted a license to Mr. Peter West to
> plant, grow and dig oysters in a certain part of Squash Meadow Pond for
> 20 years. The oysters grown on this Island are of a very superior quality
> . . . and hundreds upon hundreds of bushels of the finest of bivalves were
> [once] taken from its waters. . . . It is again becoming stocked and we
> shall hail with delight the day which once more brings to our village, as
> of old, cart load after cart load of these fine shellfish.

Not all residents were as enterprising. With few jobs available and time
heavy on their hands, many men, both young and old, were turning to alcohol. Stores were not permitted to sell alcohol in any Island town. Each
town had a liquor agent who could sell alcohol for "medicinal" purposes.
Business was good: "We learn from the Finance Committee of Edgartown
that the sales of liquor for the past two years amount to upwards of 1200
gallons—more than half being rum. A large amount of *medicine* for a town
of 2000 inhabitants, say the committee in their report."

Edgartown residents complained that many young "rowdies" from Holmes Hole were invading their town, where, they believed, illegal liquor purchases were more easily made. After taking their "medicine," they roamed downtown streets at night, creating disorder and bothering young ladies who were out strolling. The *Gazette* advised parents to keep their daughters at home.

One reason Holmes Hole men came to Edgartown was because the Sons of Temperance chapter in their own village had chased them out. The Holmes Hole chapter had been formed only five months before, and already 140 men and women were members. It was a powerful force, and it wasn't long before a similar chapter was formed in Edgartown.

Churches in Edgartown joined in the fight for temperance. The Baptist Society made a major change in its building to make room for its evening meetings, no doubt aimed at keeping their young people from the temptations of alcohol: "The old vestry building will be dispensed with. The ground under the house has been removed and a fine large room finished off for a vestry, where the Sabbath school and evening meetings hereafter will be held. The old vestry has been sold to Mr. Thomas Dunham who is now engaged in removing the same, preparatory for finishing it for a dwelling house."

Except for "medicinal" liquor sales, the Island's business was in a slump. The steamer *Eagle's Wing* cut back its winter service to two round trips a week to New Bedford. The public responded with disapproval. Without frequent, dependable service, one letter writer said, there could be no hope of prosperity. Business would not come to the Island if ferries ran only twice a week. There had to be one trip every day for six months of the year and one every other day in the winter. He complained that the existing service was uncertain, schedules were ignored, sailings were canceled or left port early at the whim of the captain. Up-Islanders made the long trip to Holmes Hole only to learn that the trip had been canceled or that the steamer had left early because it had to make a side trip to tow a boat to Falmouth.

When the new *Monohansett* went into service in June 1862, things looked promising. The *Gazette* said: "Vineyard people have suffered much from the lack of regular communication with the mainland. . . . Now that we have a steamboat, let us all take courage once more."

The new service didn't last long. In the fall of 1862 the New Bedford owners chartered the *Monohansett* to the Union army for a profitable five

Built in 1862 to replace the unpopular *Eagle's Wing*, the paddle wheeler *Monohansett* carried passengers between New Bedford and the Vineyard until 1864, when it was chartered by the Union and taken to Virginia to be one of General Grant's dispatch ships. It is believed that Grant came aboard on occasion. (MVHS Collections)

hundred dollars a day. It sailed to Alexandria, Virginia, where for more than a month the steamboat was a troop transport. Vineyarders went back to sails, hiring the schooner *L. Snow* for their ferry. There was much criticism of the New Bedford owners who had taken the new steamer away for a month to make more money. In 1863 the *Monohansett* again went into army service, this time staying almost two years. There was a war on, Vineyarders were reminded.

The *Monohansett*'s proudest moments came in August 1864, when it was assigned to General Ulysses S. Grant's headquarters as a dispatch ship. He sometimes came on board. On the boat's return to civilian life, the main saloon was labeled "General Grant's Stateroom," in honor of its Civil War service. A table from the stateroom is now at the Martha's Vineyard Historical Society in Edgartown.

Charlie Macreading Vincent, one of Edgartown's early volunteers, was a witness to the paddle wheeler's military service in South Carolina. He wrote in his journal: "November 6, 1863: Much to my joy, found the good steamer *Monohansett* lying in the stream. I lined [?] her from the wharf and soon hove in sight of the big Captain Crowell, who loomed up 'like a herring in a strap tub.'. . . He invited me to come aboard and . . . I had the pleasure of seeing Charlie Smith, Capt. Wm. B. Fisher and several others from the Vineyard, among them the good natured 'Fred Cook.'"

In February Charlie's unit was transferred to Jacksonville, Florida, and once again the *Monohansett* was in the harbor. Also in Jacksonville was a former Edgartown schoolteacher, Lieutenant George B. Mussey, a white officer with the 55th Massachusetts Volunteer Infantry (Colored). It was a pleasant interlude for Charlie: "February 28, 1864 . . . met Lieut. Mussey and Lieut. Thomas M. Sweet of the 24th Mass. and they were very kind to me. Through the kindness of Lieut. Mussey I got a feed for my horse and a breakfast for myself. . . . Spent the evening on the *Monohansett* and had a very pleasant time. Charlie Smith was very kind to me. Truly I am among friends and I am very thankful it is so."

Charlie was so envious of Lieutenant Mussey's lifestyle that he wrote to his father to ask if his uncle Richard L. Pease could get him commissioned as a lieutenant and assigned to one of the black units, all of which had only white officers. It didn't work out. Charlie did become a lieutenant when discharged at the end of the war, a pro forma promotion given to longtime sergeants.

It was during this decade, the 1860s, that croquet was introduced into the country from England. It was a very "proper" game, one of the few that men and women could play together. It soon became the principal recreation at Vineyard camp meetings. Courts were set up in and out of the campground, and between prayer meetings the pilgrims played (except, of course, on the Sabbath). The game never caught on with year-round residents. It was played by campgrounders, summer people. Genuine Vineyarders had little time for such things. James M. Cooms Jr., a Vineyard native who had a brief stretch as editor of the *Gazette* while in his twenties, seemed not to think highly of the game of croquet; he wrote: "[It is] a game that tends, we are told, to the softening of the brain, but which, at least, we shall pronounce absurd. The radical difference between this game and billiards—which the prejudice of the people tend to denounce as demoralizing—is that one is played upon the ground and the other upon a well-finished and convenient table."

Cooms, who upset so many Vineyarders while editor that he had to resign after four years, rarely found anything happy to comment on. Despite his sour attitude, he went on to have a successful career in newspapers, becoming a longtime owner and editor of a paper in Middleboro, Massachusetts, where he died in the early 1900s.

Methodists became so proficient at the game that they wanted something more challenging, and so a more sophisticated form, called roque, was introduced in about 1880. It was played on smooth clay courts framed by planks, which allowed the ball to be banked, as in billiards. The name "roque" was created by dropping the first and last letters from croquet.

Some believe that roque was invented by James W. Tufts, a wealthy soda fountain manufacturer who owned a cottage on Waban Park in Cottage City (now Oak Bluffs). It is known that he built the first two roque courts on Waban Park.

In 1903 the *Martha's Vineyard Herald* defined the game: "Roque means the modern, refined, boiled down, purified, superfine, short handled, narrow wicketed, fenced in, back breaking, anti-profanity producing style of croquet."

By 1906 there were eight courts, with a paid caretaker, on Waban Park, and others scattered around Cottage City. A national association of roque clubs was formed, and it held at least one tournament in Oak Bluffs. We don't know when the game began to lose popularity with Vineyard summer people, but it probably wasn't until World War I.

Camp meetings and croquet playing were welcome distractions from the mounting casualties in the Civil War. Edgar Marchant strongly argued that the war should be viewed not as a crusade to end slavery, but as a war to save the Union, to bring an end to secession: "We talk not now of emancipation. We are not bathing ourselves in blood . . . to compel them to free their slaves. . . . That would be madness. . . . We are moving on to suppress a rebellion."

In July 1862 President Lincoln called for more volunteers. Massachusetts was asked to provide fifteen thousand. New quotas were assigned throughout the state: Edgartown, twenty men; Tisbury, fifteen; and Chilmark, four. To stimulate recruiting on the Island, Frederick Manter of (West) Tisbury announced: "I will give $50 each to the first two men on the Vineyard who will volunteer to join our army. . . . The money will be paid on the day of enlistment."

Manter may have been the first individual to offer money as a recruiting tool, but the towns quickly followed. Edgartown voted a bounty of $100 to each unmarried volunteer, $125 to those with dependents; Tisbury voted $125, plus $1 a month for each dependent. Chilmark went along, even bringing up the unwelcome thought that a draft might be coming: *"Voted:* To pay the sum of one hundred dollars to each of the first four volunteers, or, in case of no volunteers . . . to each of the first four persons hereafter drafted, provided such persons shall pass the necessary examination before the authorized officer." Chilmark was the first town to mention the possibility of its men being drafted, something abhorrent to all. There never had been a draft in the nation, and it was certainly not something anyone wanted. Bounties were the alternative: pay men to sign up and no draft would be needed.

Other towns began paying bounties. But despite the incentives, only two thousand Massachusetts men volunteered, far short of the fifteen thousand that President Lincoln had called for; none was from the Vineyard. The Island was in no mood to send its men to war. It had just had its first war death. Sergeant Frederick M. Vincent of (West) Tisbury had died of disease on Ship Island, Mississippi, after only a few months in the army. His unit, the 3rd Massachusetts Regiment (Cavalry), had arrived on Ship Island a month before, and his sudden death shocked the village.

When Sergeant George B. Mussey of Edgartown went home on a thirty-day leave from the 1st Regiment of Massachusetts Volunteer Cavalry at Hilton Head in May 1862, he brought news of a concern that was troubling many soldiers. The sergeant, along with others in his unit, held strongly negative opinions of blacks. Their commander, General David Hunter, commander of the Department of the South, had just announced that "all persons of color . . . in Fort Pulaski and on Cockspur island, Georgia [which his units had just captured], are hereby confiscated and declared free." If they were needed, they would be accepted as volunteers. He soon freed all persons "heretofore held as slaves" in the states of Georgia, Florida, and South Carolina. This was a bold step, contrary to President Lincoln's thinking.

Ten days later President Lincoln annulled the general's orders. Freeing the slaves, Lincoln said, was a power "I reserve for myself."

Hunter's statements were in the news when Mussey arrived on the Island on his furlough. The *Gazette* interviewed him and asked him what the soldiers thought about the issue. He responded:

> The effect of Hunter's proclamation upon the soldiers of the division was very marked, as all, with the fewest exceptions, looked upon it with feelings of disgust. . . . Our army is not yet at all disposed to fight to free such

a class of lawless beings without a plan for immediate colonization [to Africa]. . . . The attempt to educate them by . . . the band of female teachers has been a sad failure as will Gen. Hunter's attempt to raise a negro brigade and fit them . . . for combat, unless the war goes on for several generations.

Mussey was later promoted to lieutenant and assigned to the 55th Massachusetts Volunteer Infantry (Colored), providing an interesting insight into the thinking of the white officers who were chosen to lead the "colored" units.

Governor Andrew of Massachusetts agreed with General Hunter. He made that clear when he came to the Vineyard to address the closing ceremony of the 1862 camp meeting, the first nonpreacher to do so. The governor told the huge congregation of ten thousand that God also agreed with General Hunter: "I believe that from the day our Government turned its back upon the proclamation of General Hunter, the blessing of God has been withdrawn from our arms. We were marching on, conquering and to conquer, but since that day I have seen no victories." Governor Andrew may have been motivated by the great shortage he faced in volunteers needed to fill his state's quota. By opening enlistment to men of color, he might solve his problem. General Hunter, known as "Black Dave," did not give up his crusade and organized the North's first black fighting unit, the 1st Carolina Regiment. Many in it were freed slaves.

Lincoln was not pleased with Hunter's action and soon had him transferred to administrative duties in Washington, D.C. It wasn't until May 1864 that he was again assigned a field command, and this time it was in West Virginia, not in the South. By then Lincoln had come around to Hunter's position and was eager to send blacks into combat, as he wrote to Andrew Johnson, then the military governor of Tennessee: "The bare sight of fifty thousand armed, and drilled black soldiers on the banks of the Mississippi, would end the rebellion at once." This change in Lincoln's position had an effect on the lives of at least two Vineyard men of color. Both joined the 5th Massachusetts Cavalry (Colored), the army's first black cavalry unit.

One of the men, James W. Curtis, was married to Frances E. Prince, a Chappaquiddick Indian. He volunteered in January 1864. The other was James Diamond, who had also married an Indian, Abiah Manning of Gay Head. His induction into the 5th Cavalry was less voluntary than Curtis's.

Years before, in 1858, he had been sentenced to ten months in Dukes County Jail for breaking into the Chilmark Store. He escaped from the poorly guarded jail and, when he was recaptured in May 1863, he was sentenced to one year of hard labor. But he was offered an alternative: join the army and you will be pardoned. He joined.

Although the nation's most deadly war was going on in the South, it didn't interfere with camp meetings. In 1862 the *Gazette* found space on a page filled with war news for a light-hearted article on the camp meeting:

> Nothing is more amusing than the scene that is presented on the arrival of a steamer at this place [Eastville], which contains a small cluster of houses. The shore is alive with ox carts and innumerable vehicles of every description, attached to which are jaded skeletons of horses who seem actually bewildered by the amazing transmigration of bodies.
>
> Such an everlasting hurry-skurry of business you never saw! Such a pleasant conglomeration of beds and boxes, bundles, and rocking chairs and babies you never dreamed of! The distance to the Camp is a trifle over a mile and a half, which does not preclude pedestrianism, the most preferable, especially if one knows how to cut off a portion of the distance by a ramble through the woods.

Whether attendance at the camp meeting had encouraged their action, we don't know, but a week after the meeting three Edgartown men told Cornelius Marchant, the town's enlistment agent, that they were ready to enlist. They were Samuel Pent, Benjamin Dowling, and William Harrington. Charles Macreading Vincent, an apprentice printer at the *Gazette,* joined them soon after. But they were only four, and a total of twenty was needed to fill the town's quota. A draft seemed to be getting closer. Governor Andrew had been certain that Massachusetts would never need a draft when he spoke at the 1862 camp meeting: "I cannot believe that this glorious old Bay State of ours shall ever see a conscript son marching to the defense of the liberties of his country. No conscripts in the old Bay State! All are volunteers in the army of the Lord."

The governor may have believed a draft would never be needed in the "old Bay State," but the "volunteers in the army of the Lord" failed to respond to his call. Something had to be done. The three Island towns decided more money was the answer. Edgartown raised its bounty from $100 to $500 for three-year men, and to $300 for nine-month volunteers, plus $25 for their dependents. Tisbury raised its payment from $125 to

The journal kept by Charles Macreading Vincent of Edgartown during his Civil War service describes the day in 1862 when he and seven others left the Island to join the Union army with the Massachusetts Volunteers. The Historical Society has his journal, metal identification tag, and photograph. After the war he was a successful newspaper editor on the Island and in Boston. (MVHS Collections)

$500. Chilmark was even more generous, raising its bonus of $100 to $600 for three-year volunteers and $300 for nine-month men.

The higher payments worked. All three towns filled their quotas immediately. Because the bounties were much larger than those paid by mainland towns, off-Islanders offered to enlist as Vineyarders. Edgartown heard from forty men willing to volunteer as local residents if paid the bounty. The town said it didn't need them—not yet. The *Gazette* exuded pride: "OUR QUOTAS: Both quotas for Edgartown may now be considered full. Twenty men have enlisted under the three years' call and twenty-seven for nine months. If more are needed, they can be obtained. So we are all right at last."

On August 29, 1862, eight of the Edgartown recruits left to go to war. Charlie Macreading Vincent, who was one of them, described their departure in his journal:

> Today we, the volunteers from Edgartown, to the number of eight: John R. Ellis, Benj. Smith, Richard G. Shute, Alonzo Ripley, Elihu M. Bunker, Francis Pease, Jr., W. H. Harrington and Chas. M. Vincent, started from the goodly town of our abode, on our way to the defence of the glorious Union and the cause of civil and religious liberty. There was a large concourse of friends and relatives at the wharf from which we embarked in the schooner *L. Snow*, Captain A. L. Cleaveland, for New Bedford.

The *Gazette*'s confidence was premature. Things were not all right at last. The war was going badly for the Union. Its capital city, Washington, was being threatened. More men were needed. A draft seemed imminent. The *Gazette* cautioned: "There is no time to wait for the draft. The men are wanted now and must go forward at once, to the aid of our friends battling for the capital."

With expectations of the draft, men on the Vineyard were taking no chances. They began applying for exemptions. Of nearly eight hundred men in Dukes County eligible to be drafted, two-thirds were given exemptions. About a hundred of them were excused for physical reasons. The others were excused for such reasons as having an essential occupation or being the sole support of children or elderly parents. The *Gazette,* with a wink, professed shock at the number of exemptions for health reasons: "The amount of sickness among our men, just at this time, is certainly alarming." Poor health was spreading, it seemed. The number of exemptions given in Boston for health deficiencies was so "alarming" that the federal government sent inspectors there to determine the reason.

As the Union losses kept mounting, President Lincoln called for more men. Island towns were given new quotas: Chilmark, twelve; Edgartown, thirty-seven; and Tisbury, thirty-seven.

There was no way to get that many volunteers on the Island. By the end of October 1862 only eleven Edgartown men had signed up. They were quickly mustered into the 3rd Regiment of Massachusetts Volunteers and shipped to New Bern, North Carolina. The Edgartown volunteers were James M. Tilton, James Smith, Jethro Worth, Edward E. Beetle, John

P. Fisher, Joseph A. Ripley, Joseph H. Wilbur, Francis P. Vincent, Charles W. Cleaveland, Henry Wilbur, and Francis Norton.

The Island was still far short of meeting its quota. Then a month later, the state, still trying to straighten out its records, announced, without explanation, that the Vineyard did not need to send any more men; its quota had been met. The pressure was off, but the war's toll continued. The Island learned that two more of its men, one in the army and the other in the navy, had died, both of sickness.

The soldier was William H. Harrington, thirty-three, of Edgartown, who died of typhoid fever at Minor's Hill, Virginia. He was one of the eight men who had left three months before to the townspeople's cheers. He and the seven others had been mustered into the 40th Massachusetts Volunteers and immediately sent to Virginia to stop the Confederate drive on Washington. Early in October he had optimistically written home: "We are now encamped at the foot of Munson's Hill. . . . We expect to be home very soon, for we all think the war will soon end."

Less than three months later, the war did end for him, tragically. When his body arrived in Edgartown, the whole village turned out in his honor. The war was beginning to get much closer to Vineyarders.

Master's Mate Francis Adlington Jr., of Edgartown, was the first Island sailor to die. The cause was "remittent fever" aboard the Union naval ship *Vermont*. He was twenty-nine and had been a whaleman before being commissioned a master's mate, a highly desirable rank. But it didn't protect him from the fever.

After the battle of Gettysburg in July 1863, where 23,000 Union men were killed, wounded, or declared missing, the state finally initiated the draft. A drawing was held in New Bedford and 124 Vineyard names were picked, which created a draft pool from which men would be called up to meet the coming quotas. The ceremony was described in the *Gazette* by its New Bedford correspondent, "Catchelot": "I was on the platform Monday last when the *dreaded wheel* was set in motion and saw nothing to lead me to believe the thing was not done fair. Your townsman, Richard L. Pease, was stationed at the crank and if there are any secrets he knows them. I was sorry you [the editor, Cooms] got *elected,* and knowing your pluck . . . I feel you will either *march* or pay the price of your ticket."

As Catchelot wrote, one of the names drawn was that of James M. Cooms Jr., the new editor of the *Gazette*. He had taken over the paper from its founding editor, Edgar Marchant, four months before. Cooms, an

Edgartown native and a printer on the *Gazette,* was twenty-three and single, a prime prospect for army service. He never did go into the service. Two years later, in August 1865, after the war was over, he married Charlotte Marchant, Edgar's niece.

The *Gazette* listed the names drawn and explained the rules of the draft and the reasons for exemptions, which were many. Exemption wasn't the only way to avoid service. By paying the government three hundred dollars, a man received a "commutation" and his name was not even placed in the "dreaded wheel." If he hadn't done that and his name was drawn, he could hire a substitute to take his place, or the town could replace him with a hired substitute. Catchelot referred to these options as "the price of your ticket" in his letter to Cooms.

Cooms was satisfied with the system and praised its "fairness," which, it seemed, meant that every able-bodied man could be drafted into the service unless, like him, he had three hundred dollars. His editorial made it sound like pure democracy: "Not a postmaster or a clergyman, who is able to shoulder a musket, is exempt, any more than the most obscure laborer. Congregations may raise the three hundred dollars to furnish a substitute for their pastor, if they cannot spare him. . . . As for editors and reporters, nothing short of $300 will clear their skirts from the draft."

Despite the editor's praise for the draft, there were so many opportunities to be declared exempt that of the 124 Vineyard men whose names were drawn in New Bedford, we can find only 4 who served in the army. There may have been 5 others, but as their names differ slightly (usually middle initials) from those in the service records, we cannot be certain. Even if we include them, of the 124 men whose names were drawn, only 9 put on a uniform. Six others whose names were drawn served in the navy and 5 others might have done so (again, their names were slightly different from those in the official records). So at the very most, of the 124 men whose names were drawn, only 20 (16 percent) ever went to war.

For Vineyard mariners, the navy was an attractive alternative. The more experienced among those who joined were certified as master's mates, a much more desirable post than being cannon fodder in the army. The Edgartown sailor quoted earlier had made the point: the navy was "the best place in the world," if you had to go to war.

The draft had many inadequacies. Names were placed in the wheel for the drawing with the assumption that the men would be available to serve if called up. On the Island, and in many other coastal towns, one-third of

225

those whose names were drawn were away at sea and unavailable. (Some had gone to sea with that in mind.) Many whose names were in the lottery wheel were already in the navy and unavailable for the army. They, although in the navy, were not credited toward the town quota.

These subtractions made the pool of Vineyard men available to serve so small that the towns decided they must find another way to meet their quotas. At town meetings, each voted to borrow enough money to hire off-Island substitutes, as permitted by law. Men were sent to Boston to do the buying through enlistment brokers, an occupation that had quickly developed when it became obvious that money could be made by selling men as recruits—not too much different from selling them as slaves.

To pay for their substitutes, the towns took out loans. Edgartown was soon thirty thousand dollars in debt, paying twenty-five hundred dollars in interest annually, twice as much as it was paying for its schools. The war had become expensive for Island villages.

Of the fifty-eight men to whom Edgartown paid bounties, nearly half are names unknown on the Island. Many had Irish names and had been signed up in places such as Lowell and Boston, where unemployment was high and men were available. The substitute system opened the door to corrupt practices. Recruiting agents would get the men to sign up, collect the bounties, and share them with the recruits. While still in the Massachusetts mustering-in camp, many men would desert and report back to the agent, who would give them a new name and sell them to another town. It became a scam.

A spot-check of the men credited to Island towns who were mustered into the 42nd Infantry Regiment, Massachusetts Volunteers, shows that of the eight men in it to whom Vineyard towns paid bounties, seven had deserted within a month. All had been signed up by brokers. None was an Islander.

But desertions were not what troubled Vineyarders. Their complaint was that many of the men they had paid bounties to were not credited toward the town quota. Edgartown claimed that it had paid $10,350 to men for whom it never received credit. The procedure was so flawed that Richard L. Pease of Edgartown (Charles M. Vincent's uncle) in June 1864 began a statewide campaign to change it. With Henry L. Whiting and the Reverend William H. Sturtevant, both of (West) Tisbury, Pease published a "Circular" that detailed the system's failings. It was sent to towns around the state. Besides demanding accurate crediting of recruits the towns had paid for, it also asked that they be credited for men who enlisted in the navy. The circular concluded with a call for united action: "Will your town join with us, and other towns, in a convention to be holden at the Marlboro Hotel in Boston, the twenty-second day of June, instant, at 11-1/2 o'clock A.M., to take such action as may be deemed most certain to result in securing for each town in the State the full credit to which it is entitled, for men heretofore furnished for the army and navy of the United States?"

It was a bold move: three men from a little-known island calling for a revolt against the state of Massachusetts. They were not alone for long. So many delegates arrived at the Marlboro Hotel for the convention in answer to the call that it had to be moved to the larger Parker House.

After two days, the complaints were summarized in a petition that was taken to the State House and presented to Governor Andrew. He quickly ordered a major overhaul, promising that "any number of clerks required to make the revision would be promptly furnished . . . [and he would] do all in his power . . . to secure to every city and town . . . its just and equitable rights."

He asked his adjutant general to look into the problem. That official, William Schouler, blamed it on the bounty system and payments by the towns to the recruiting brokers: "These bounties warmed into life a certain class of men known as recruiting or substitute brokers, who agree to furnish men to fill the quotas of towns for a specified sum. I have not a high opinion of this class; and I have no doubt that many of the selectmen and town agents have been grossly swindled by them. . . . I have no doubt that in many cases, the recruits and the broker were fellow-partners in the swindle."

There was truth in Schouler's charge. He offered a solution to the swindle: "The cause has been the free use of money by trading with brokers and swindlers. And the remedy is not to pay a cent of bounty or premium until the recruit is mustered in; and then to pay it to the recruits and not to the brokers."

His advice did not sit well with the Reverend William Sturtevant of (West) Tisbury, who had been one of the two Islanders to call for the reform. Under the heading "Who Is to Blame?" he wrote in the *Gazette* that the problem was the failure of the state to credit the towns for the men they provided. Desertions and multiple enlistments were not the towns' concerns. They were problems for the army. All he wanted was credit to the town for the men it had hired.

In September 1864 the federal government, perhaps reacting to the Pease-Sturtevant convention, agreed to give the towns credit for men serving in the navy. Edgartown had forty-five of them and now, instead of needing more volunteers, it had a surplus.

While all this controversy was going on at home, other Islanders not in uniform were facing enemy guns. They were the officers and men aboard the whaleships that were being captured and burned by the two Confederate raiders *Alabama* and *Shenandoah*. These mariners were ordered at gunpoint to abandon their ships, becoming prisoners, although only briefly, aboard the Confederate raiders before being dropped off ashore or put aboard another whaleship that had been spared for that purpose.

In October 1862 the *Alabama,* commanded by Captain Raphael Semmes, began its destructive career by capturing and burning the Edgartown whaler *Ocmulgee* just off the Azores. The crew had just killed a large sperm whale and was busy "cutting in," or peeling the oil-laden blubber from its carcass prior to boiling out the oil, when the *Alabama* sailed up and captured and burned the ship as its first trophy. The raider had just been built in England. The master of the *Ocmulgee* was Abraham Osborn Jr. of Edgartown, the son of the principal owner. They had left Edgartown on July 2 on a whaling voyage into the Pacific and, as was customary, had gone to the Western Islands (the Azores) to fill out the crew. Soon after leaving for the Pacific, a sperm whale was spotted and killed. That turned out to be an unlucky catch. Had they not stopped to kill and cut in the whale, they would have been far distant when the *Alabama* arrived.

The *Ocmulgee* was the first of five whalers with Vineyard connections destroyed by the raiders. The bark *Virginia,* Captain Shadrack R. Tilton of Chilmark, was burned soon after the *Ocmulgee*. The third victim was the *Levi Starbuck,* Captain Thomas H. Mellen of Tisbury.

When the *Alabama* was sunk off the coast of France by a Union warship in June 1864, the *Shenandoah* quickly took its place The *Shenandoah* was a fast armed ship equipped with both sail and steam power, as the *Alabama* had been. It also was built and financed by the English, who provided many of the crew, being eager to buy bales of southern cotton to keep their textile mills operating.

The *Shenandoah* did its marauding in the Pacific. Two of its victims had Vineyard connections: the *William Thompson,* Captain Francis Cottle Smith, and the *Waverly,* Captain Richard Holley. Both masters were from Edgartown. The two whalers were sunk, along with a score more vessels, in the North Pacific some weeks after the end of the war. Captain Waddell of the *Shenandoah* claimed he had not received official word that the war was over, although some of the whaling masters knew it and told him so. He finally believed it when the master of a British ship confirmed it.

Ten years after the war, payments for damages were made by England to the owners of the whaleships. The Edgartown owners of the *Ocmulgee*, the Osborns, received $94,102, which included interest at 4 percent from the date the ship was destroyed. The Osborns had claimed they were owed $400,000. We don't know what the other owners received.

By early 1864 the tide of war had swung to the Union. Losses on both sides continued to be heavy. President Lincoln called for more men. Quotas continued to be so high that towns were unable to meet them, so once again they turned to the draft. More names were pulled from the wheel in New Bedford, with thirty-two names drawn for Edgartown (which needed twenty-one recruits), forty-three for Tisbury (twenty-eight needed), and twenty-one for Chilmark (fourteen needed). As was the case in earlier drawings, few of the men whose names were drawn went to war. Official records show that only three Vineyard men of the ninety-six whose names were drawn put on an army uniform.

Clearly, the Civil War draft was an inefficient and unfair way to recruit soldiers. In July 1863 fifty-four Vineyard men whose names were on the list that made them eligible to be drafted went to New Bedford to apply for exemptions, as men had a year before. The result was similar. Nearly all (fifty-one) were declared exempt. Of the three who were turned down, two paid three hundred dollars to buy commutation, leaving only one to face service.

Although the draft did add about 150,000 men to the Union army, three-quarters of them were not draftees but were paid substitutes for men who had been drafted. Only about 20 percent of all soldiers in the Union army were genuine draftees. The Vineyard numbers were similar. Few names drawn in New Bedford show up in the service records, most having been replaced by substitutes paid by their towns or by the men drafted.

In 1865, after the war had ended, a state analysis declared the 1863 draft to have been a failure. Among its findings:

Massachusetts drew 32,077 names as eligible to be drafted. Of them, 2,883 failed to report when called, 2,322 furnished substitutes, 3,702 paid commutation money to the state to be exempted. Only 807 of those whose names were drawn entered the service, while 22,363 were exempted for various reasons: 12,581 were physically disabled; 876 were the only sons of widows; 614 only sons of aged parents; 363 were fathers of motherless children under 12; 138 had two brothers already in the service; 35 had been convicted of felonies; and 3,367 pleaded alienage.

These numbers don't add up to the 22,363 exempted, but that is an indication of the sloppy way draft numbers were handled. Certainly, there was much opportunity for fraud.

As the war's toll kept rising, so did the calls for men. An agent from Holmes Hole was sent to the mainland looking for recruits and returned to report that he could get twelve men for $175 each, in addition to the bounty.

When the federal government in 1864 authorized the enlistment of blacks in the army, Tisbury saw this as a way to meet the town's quota. Twenty Tisbury men pledged nearly two thousand dollars of their own money to send agents into the South to recruit freed slaves as substitutes to meet the town's quota. They were easy to recruit, as the Massachusetts state bounty was larger than that of any other state. The *Gazette* ran an article signed by "J. M. Forbes and seventy-one others," in which people of the state were asked to contribute fifty thousand dollars to send agents into the South to sign up "50,000 acclimated [black] soldiers. . . . It seems to us that the prompt enlistment of colored men is all important to the Union cause."

With the army accepting black volunteers, recruiters came to Gay Head from the mainland looking for them. The *Gazette* reported that a New Bedford man had left with five men from Gay Head. The paper's concern was over which town would be given credit for them: New Bedford or Chilmark? (Gay Head was still part of Chilmark.)

One of the five volunteers from Gay Head may have been Alfred Rose, fifteen years old, who enlisted in May 1864. He is the only volunteer we have found in the records who is listed as from Gay Head. Private Rose served in Company K of the 23rd U.S. (Colored) Infantry and was killed in the failed mine assault at Petersburg, Virginia, in July 1864, only two months after he enlisted, which indicates how little training the troops, and especially the black troops, were given before being sent into battle. He is the only Vineyard Wampanoag we know of who was killed in combat and at fifteen certainly the youngest Vineyarder to die. The Petersburg

No.	Name.	Town	1st Pay.t	Limit of Bounty	Cost of Substitute
1	G. F. Baxter	Tisbury	$. 10.— $.	$. 1 $.	
2	Cyrus Manter	"	10.—		
3	Benj: Athern 2d	"	? 10.—		
4	John Look 2d	"	10.—		
5	Bartlett Pease	"	10.—		
6	Wm P. Bodfish	X	10.—		
7	Josiah H. Vincent	"	10.—		
8	Mayhew Look	X	10.—		
9	Allen Look		10.—		
10	Wm H. Sturtevant	X	10		
11	Leonard A. Luce		10.—		
12	Thomas Waldron		10.—		
13	H. L. Whiting	X	10.—		
14	Hariph M. Smith				
15	Charles Lambert		10.—		
16	Constant D. Luce	X	10.—		
17	Leavitt T. Norton				
18	G. T. Hough				
19	Leander W. Mayhew		10.—		
20	G. H. Gorham	X	10.—	1	

List of subscribers for Personal Substitutes In order of credit.

There were legal ways to avoid serving in the Union army during the Civil War.
One was to hire a substitute (often a freed black) to take one's place. Many Island men
paid a ten-dollar fee for this option. Most towns had such a list; this is a part of Tisbury's.
(MVHS Collections)

assault in which he was killed is famous for the Union's blundering. General Grant wrote: "The effort was a stupendous failure . . . due to inefficiency on the part of the corps commander and the incompetency of the division commander."

Another Vineyard soldier might have been a Wampanoag. In his three-volume work, *The History of Martha's Vineyard, Dukes County, Massachusetts,* Charles E. Banks lists a Peter Johnson "of Gay Head" as serving in the 44th Regiment. Official records show a Peter Johnson, "resident, Martha's Vineyard," who enlisted in December 1863 at age twenty-six. We cannot find him on the roster of the 44th Massachusetts Regiment, which was mustered nearly a year before he volunteered, so it is unlikely that he was in that unit. Official records do not give a unit for Peter Johnson nor do they give Gay Head as his residence; instead, he is listed as being from Martha's Vineyard. He remains a mystery.

Edgartown, still far from meeting its quota, called a town meeting to authorize the town to borrow money to buy more substitutes. The *Gazette* beat the drums: "Let us all take heed. . . . Money in plenty we have, but men we have not and consequently money must buy men. . . . Let noble thoughts arrest the stagnation of the mind and let the soul expand under the influence of generous action and soon the coffers will be filled with enlistment funds."

No decision was reached, so another town meeting was called soon after. The announcement of that second meeting made the task sound easy: "Come to Town Meeting Saturday to authorize our recruiting agent to obtain as many men as he can to fill our quota. They can be had for $50 over the bounty." At that meeting the voters authorized the town to borrow an additional three thousand dollars to buy substitutes from off-Island. The town had already borrowed about thirty thousand dollars for bounties and other payments to soldiers. But there seemed to be no other way. Within a month it was reported that the Island's recruiting agent, Thomas Bradley, had hired another twenty-five off-Island men to help fill the quota.

At least fifty Island men were in the navy and, despite the earlier federal ruling that they be counted, the Island still hadn't received credit for them. The *Gazette* took up the cause: "About fifty of our town's brave sons [are] as busily engaged in harpooning of Jeff Davis's privateers or sending bombs into the very vitals of inflexible forts as they had ever been in catching whales."

We have placed so much emphasis on the hiring of substitutes that readers may come away with the impression that the Island did not do its part in the war. That would be wrong. There were, according to one account, 185 men serving in the army and credited to the Vineyard. There is no definite figure on how many of them were resident Islanders and how many were paid substitutes from off-Island. Our estimate is that about 30 percent were substitutes. This is not much different from other places in Massachusetts. The hiring of substitutes was not shameful and certainly not illegal. When one considers that about one-third of the Island's men of eligible age for war duty were at sea and so unavailable, and that there were more than 100 Vineyarders who served in the navy, the total number of Vineyard men in service, at least 250, becomes an honorable figure. The Island never failed to meet its quotas, whether with residents or with substitutes.

The service records are so confused that it is impossible to state with certainty who was, and who was not, a Vineyard resident. As one Vineyarder (name unknown, but probably Beriah T. Hillman, writing around 1900) who served during the war wrote: "Complications in the muster rolls and town credits . . . show why it is impossible to establish a correct list of soldiers properly belonging to a given town."

We cannot even state with certainty how many Vineyard men were killed or wounded. We have mentioned some men who died in service, but not all. Here is a list of those whose deaths we have been able to confirm:

SOLDIERS

John Carr, Edgartown, killed in battle at Port Hudson, Louisiana. (Not listed in 1860 census in Edgartown; may be a substitute.)

Thomas D. Cleveland, Edgartown, in Fort Monroe, Virginia, of a disease contracted in a Confederate prison.

Peleg B. Davenport, Tisbury, of wounds at Fredericksburg, Virginia.

Cyrus B. Fisher, Edgartown, of disease in Andersonville prison, Georgia.

William H. Harrington, Edgartown, of disease at Minor's Hill, Virginia.

George W. Lewis, Tisbury, killed in battle at Spotsylvania Courthouse, Virginia. No war records found. (His name came from a cemetery gravestone.)

Lewis P. Luce, Tisbury, of disease at Baton Rouge, Louisiana.

Timothy Mayhew, Chilmark, of disease at Port Hudson, Louisiana.

Alfred P. Rose, Gay Head, killed in battle at Petersburg, Virginia.

Benjamin Smith, Edgartown, of disease at Alexandria, Virginia.

Chauncey C. Smith, Edgartown, of disease contracted at
  Gettysburg. Discharged, he returned home and died soon after.

Elisha M. Smith, Edgartown, killed at Gettysburg, Pennsylvania.

Frederick M. Vincent, Tisbury, of disease at Ship Island,
  Mississippi.

Thomas A. West, Tisbury, killed in battle at Winchester, Virginia.

James Wilbur, Edgartown, died of typhus.

SAILORS

Francis Adlington Jr., Edgartown, of disease, aboard the ship
  Vermont, place unknown.

Roland Smith, Edgartown, of disease at Chelsea, Massachusetts.

Henry Clay Wade, Edgartown, of disease at Pensacola, Florida.

There may have been others. If any reader can provide additional information, the author will be most grateful.

In January 1865 Congress passed a constitutional amendment ending slavery and sent it to the states to be ratified. In Edgartown a meeting of enthusiastic citizens urged approval. Both the public and the *Gazette* had changed their position on slavery. They had previously called it "the South's problem." It was now the nation's problem. The *Gazette*'s switch may have been due to the change in editor. Edgar Marchant, the founding editor, had turned the paper over to James Cooms Jr. Not one to mince words, he took his new "bully pulpit" seriously. His editorial strongly supporting the slavery amendment explained why some minds, including those at the *Gazette,* had been changed: the issue of secession had initiated a civil war, which in turn had brought slavery to an end: "We cannot, hereafter, be justly charged with inconsistency. . . . The future historian will point to the leaders of the rebellion as being the indirect cause of the abolition of slavery on this continent—showing how good is made to spring out of evil."

Despite his youth, Cooms had a Puritanical streak. He didn't like what was going on in his hometown. Vice and sin abounded: "Let it be decided now whether riot and vulgarity shall fill our streets evening after evening and streams of iniquity flow on until we have lost our moral character irretrievably."

One month later he was justified. Seven young women (he did not print their names) were found guilty of "street walking" and sentenced to the house of correction for sixty days. The seven women in their jail cells could hear the bells ringing in joyous celebration in April 1865 when General Robert E. Lee surrendered and the war ended. In every Island town church bells rang continuously all day. During the night some young men, eager to keep the party going, entered the Edgartown Methodist church and rang its bell so vigorously that the balance wheel broke and the bell could not be rung again for some weeks.

The joy was short-lived. President Lincoln was assassinated at Ford's Theatre two weeks later. The *Gazette* ran a thick black border around its pages. Memorial services were held on the Island on the day of his funeral. Cannon were fired by a revenue cutter in Edgartown harbor every half hour from sunrise to sunset. The Island was in shock.

Lincoln had just been reelected in a landslide. On the Vineyard he received even more votes than in his first election. In Tisbury there were 195 votes for Lincoln and only 50 for George McClellan. Edgartown was even more Republican, with 232 for Lincoln and 52 for McClellan. Chilmark was the only town with any strong voting against the president: 42 for Lincoln and 35 for McClellan. Gosnold, on the Elizabeth Islands (formerly part of Chilmark, now independent), cast 7 votes, 6 of them for the president and 1 for McClellan, prompting what may have been the first piece of humorous verse ever published by the *Gazette*:

> THE VOTE OF GOSNOLD
> *It seemeth queer, and all amiss,*
> *But I have it now, by Heavens!*
> *The returns show the voting lists,*
> *Were all at "sixes and sevens."*
>   *S. PIGRAM*

With the war over, Cooms devoted his editorials to more political issues. The young editor seemed to enjoy controversy. He was ahead of his time on how to treat the freed slaves. They should be allowed to vote, he argued: "As they helped with the bayonet so too . . . with the help of the ballot they will help to reconstruct, recuperate and help to carry out in those States the establishment of peace and equity where, even now, anarchy and misrule hold sway."

He even was so bold as to recommend an eight-hour workday. The twelve-hour day, six days a week, was standard at the time. Again Cooms was ahead of the times.

An undated photograph of one of the larger tents in the campground. The abundance of flags suggests that secular patriotism was displacing religious fervor, as camp-meeting pilgrimages were becoming more recreational and less spiritual.
(Shute Collection, MVHS)

But he was not the least bit diplomatic. He visited the campground and was unimpressed with so much croquet playing, as we have seen. But there were other reasons for his negative views about camp meetings. They had become too secular: "[It is] an irregular and tiresome life amid the haunts of poisonous mosquitoes and under the arbitrary rule of the select few. . . . [The leaders] must seek another spot where the incongruous elements of secularism will not too often intermingle and too often predominate over the religious fervour that should prevail."

The growth of the camp meeting was too much for the oak grove to take.
Its trees died and the shade disappeared. In 1870 this huge tent was erected for shelter.
Most pilgrims seem to be women, although many men are visible standing in the rear.
In 1879 the leaky tent was replaced by a larger steel structure. (MVHS Collections)

The religious fervor that had inspired Jeremiah Pease when he staked out the campground in 1835 had steadily declined. The physical pleasures of August on the Vineyard were more and more becoming the attraction.

That did not trouble most Islanders. They welcomed the influx of pleasure seekers and sought ways to encourage more to come. One way was to improve the still-undependable ferry. Henry L. Whiting and others began raising funds for the Martha's Vineyard Steamboat Company to buy a steamboat that would serve the Island exclusively. He urged the people of Edgartown to invest. It would make the Vineyard no longer dependent on the New Bedford steamboat owners. Those who had already bought shares, he wrote in the *Gazette,* were mostly from Tisbury and Chilmark. More Edgartown investors were needed. The investment would bring prosperity: "Let our capitalists and businessmen turn their attention to the development of our ample home resources. Then instead of our deserted streets and idle wharves our beautiful island may be full of life and enterprise and prosperity."

Those "deserted streets and idle wharves" were making the Island less attractive to its young men. There was little to do except to farm, and even that was declining. A man who signed himself "Rustic" wrote a two-part report that Cooms published in the *Gazette.* The value of goods produced on the Island, he wrote, "excepting manufactured oil and sperm candles," was $300,000. Two-thirds of that amount, $200,000, came from farming. But, he added unhappily, men were leaving the farms to seek better opportunities on the mainland: "In 1845 there were 12,000 sheep in this county. In 1855, there were but 9000 and I judge that to be about the present number [in 1865]. . . . Many of our farmers, dissatisfied with their condition, have sought prosperity in distant places; but . . . prosperity brings no peace while the home-yearning still lives in the heart. . . . Stick by the paternal acres, my young friends."

When that was written in 1865 the war was ending, but peace did not bring any improvement. Nearly thirty Island families left within a few months for the Midwest. Property values in both Dukes and Nantucket counties had fallen during the war. They, along with Plymouth County, were the only counties in the state to have such declines. It isn't clear why that had happened, but the prospects seemed bleak.

By the spring of 1865 the Martha's Vineyard Steamboat Company had raised enough capital to go into business. Thomas Bradley of Tisbury was elected president, and Ira Darrow of Edgartown, secretary. The new company purchased the steamer *Helen Augusta* in New York. It was a modern vessel, the first "propeller," as such non–paddle wheelers were called, to be put into Island service (the larger *Monohansett,* owned in New Bedford, was a paddle wheeler). The *Gazette* described the boat as "a neat little craft [with] excellent speed." The schedule called for departure from Edgartown at 7:30 A.M. three days a week, and departure from New Bedford on the following days for the return to Edgartown, after the arrival of the morning train from Boston.

As Oak Bluffs prospered in summer, Edgartown fell to a low point economically. Ferry service was infrequent. In the late 1800s the *Martha's Vineyard* would interrupt its Nantucket–New Bedford run to make a stop at Edgartown. Later, one steamer would tie up overnight in Edgartown, leaving at 6 A.M. for New Bedford. (MVHS Collections)

The Maine Steamboat Company in 1865 announced that its steamer *City of Bath* would stop at Holmes Hole twice a week during the summer, on Wednesday evenings en route from Boston to New York and Saturday evenings on the return to Boston. The Island for the first time had a direct connection to the two major cities of the Northeast.

Perhaps there was hope. Cooms thanked the *New Bedford Mercury* for pointing out that Edgar Marchant's dream of an East Coast watering place was beginning to come true: "The Martha's Vineyard campground is now called 'a poor man's Saratoga.'"

One Edgartown businessman was investing his money on the Island, if not in a new industry, at least in a new house. For two years not one house had been built in town. Now, a handsome home for Samuel Osborn Jr. was going up on South Summer Street. (It is today's Charlotte Inn.) It would cost six thousand dollars, the *Gazette* trumpeted. But one new house wasn't enough to satisfy young Cooms: "No town or city more than Edgartown requires a regeneracy in its business. . . . It needs but a small tithe of the money that is now dodging taxation or deposited for 6 percent . . . to regain its former prosperity. It is only selfishness that influences men to hide away in strong vaults their accumulated wealth."

He had more cause to continue being negative when in December 1865 Richard G. Shute and Charles M. Vincent, two Civil War veterans and Edgartown natives, left town to go to Connecticut to start a photographic business: "The same story, going to look for business. Can our citizens read the handwriting on the wall?"

There was plenty going on, but it was all offshore. Vineyarders watched it sail past, as the *Gazette* reported: "On June 26th [1866] from sunrise to 6 P.M. 290 vessels passed Falmouth on the way through Vineyard Sound. At one time, 127 were counted within a distance of three miles, having come out of Holmes Hole on a change in wind. . . . A gentleman of Tisbury, whose house is near a high hill commanding a view of the Sound for its entire length, one day counted 366 sail in sight at one time."

The war had ended; better times were coming back to the nation, but not, it seemed, to the Island.

8

Secession: Was It Worth It? Cottage City Wonders

The Civil War was over. The South had surrendered and once again the Union was whole. Secession was no longer dividing the nation. But in one of the strange coincidences of history, on the island of Martha's Vineyard another battle over secession was just beginning—a battle without bombs, only bombast.

The seeds of secession had been planted thirty years before with the creation of a campground on East Chop, the northern end of Edgartown, in an area uninhabited except by William Butler's sheep. There Methodists had found peace and God. In a shady oak grove they gathered every August to pray for salvation as scores of preachers warned them of Hell. Each night after soulful prayer, they went to their tents and slept fitfully on a layer of straw.

It became the favorite camp meeting among the many held in New England. At first, Methodists by the hundreds came from off-Island; soon they were coming by the thousands. All took home pleasant memories of a beautiful spot under the oaks, a spot they called Wesleyan Grove.

One of those who came in 1865, the year the Civil War ended, was Erastus P. Carpenter of Foxboro. He was not a typical pilgrim, not someone happy to give up his comfort to find his God. He was accustomed to the good life, to good food and a good bed. A wealthy straw hat manufacturer, he hadn't expected that to be saved he would have to sleep in a tent, eat poor food around a crowded table, and line up to use a smelly privy. But he had little choice.

There were no hotels. Outside the campground, one or two vacant farm buildings were used during camp meetings as boardinghouses. At night sleeping space was rented in them, complete with a bundle of straw tossed on the floor for a bed. The guests generally were not pilgrims: they were the service workers, the food handlers, the teamsters and porters who met the crowds as they came off the steamboats seeking transportation to the grove.

Crude accommodations like these were not Erastus Carpenter's style. He employed thousands in Foxboro and lived in a handsome mansion. His success had come from straw (his factory was the largest straw hat factory in the world, it was said), but he didn't enjoy sleeping on a bundle of it on a bare floor. Nevertheless, he loved Wesleyan Grove and its serenity. Surely, he thought, such a place should be enjoyed by more than those God-fearing Methodists who came for a few days of praying in August. His entrepreneurial mind saw an opportunity: he would make East Chop available to all. He talked his plan over with a friend, the Boston merchant William S. Hills, and the Oak Bluffs Land and Wharf Company was born.

Acres of land stood vacant east of the campground. Most was high ground, stretching along the bluffs, overlooking the ocean. It was owned by Captain Shubael L. Norton of Edgartown, whose father had bought it from the estate of William Butler years before. Shubael Norton was a retired mariner who had sailed square-riggers in the China trade. Carpenter and Hills invited him to join the company. Two other captains from Edgartown, Ira Darrow and Grafton Collins, were invited, as was William Bradley, a wealthy Tisbury merchant.

Under Erastus Carpenter's leadership, the new company bought the land from Captain Norton "for a song." Norton and Darrow were made trustees, authorized to sell building lots, thousands of them. Nobody realized it then, but these six men were the advance guard of the battle for secession.

The next year, 1866, the company built a wharf that extended into the Sound at the northern end of its property. It was the first such wharf ever built out into Vineyard Sound, where severe winter storms made the ocean tumultuous and wharves useless. Many Vineyarders thought it was folly; the wharf wouldn't last until spring.

When the wharf made it through the winter, a primitive hotel was built at its head. It was a multipurpose building that housed a hotel of sorts, a store, a restaurant, and a sales office for the Oak Bluffs Land and Wharf Company.

Seeing all this activity going on next door, the camp-meeting folks became worried and built a seven-foot-high picket fence around their thirty-five acres of campground to keep out the heathen. The editor of the *Vineyard Gazette* saw trouble brewing: "It is reported that when the high fence around the Grove, now in process of erection, is completed, direct communication with the East side, owned by the [Oak Bluffs Land and Wharf] Company is to be cut off. . . . The idea of constructing it without convenient gates and any opening on that side is an indication . . . [of] the spirit of opposition . . . [by] those who control the campground." Campground folks were so concerned that they bought three hundred acres on the west side of Lake Anthony, opposite the Oak Bluffs Company's land. It would be a retreat for them should that company's secularism become overpowering.

It wasn't long before the campground directors realized that the fence was unnecessary. The company was not so heathenish after all. Its owners were all good Christian men who agreed to adopt the restrictions proposed by their Methodist neighbors. Within a few years the fence had fallen into such disrepair that residents living near it asked to be allowed to maintain it themselves or else to tear it down.

Carpenter was not a typical get-rich-quick land speculator. He intended to build a house there himself, and he wanted his development to be a jewel of which he would be proud. He hired the Boston landscape architect Robert Morris Copeland to draw up a plan. It may have been among the first planned residential communities in the United States. Copeland and his men visited the Island, surveyed the land, and laid out one thousand small lots along curving roadways. Each lot was marked with four stakes; a fifth stake was driven in its center with the lot number on it.

After studying Copeland's proposal, Carpenter went to the Island to see how it looked on the ground. He didn't like what he saw. There were too many stakes. More open spaces and more parkland were needed. "We must give the people more breathing space," he was later quoted as having said.

Walking across the spaces that would become Ocean Park and Waban Park, he ordered the men to pull up the stakes. There would be no buildings there. At his insistence more parks were added in the revised plan, a total of ten. The largest would be Ocean Park, at the head of the new wharf. An arriving tourist's first view would be of an expanse of open parkland. Carpenter knew what would sell.

On the Fourth of July 1867 the revised plan was ready. Hundreds of copies were posted in train depots and hotel lobbies around New England. A bold advertisement ran in the *Vineyard Gazette* on July 5, 1867:

Home by the Seaside:
"Oak Bluffs"
A new summer resort.
One thousand lots for sale
laid out by Robert Morris Copeland, Esq., of Boston,
the well-known landscape gardener. Cheap and quiet homes
by the sea shore during the summer months. Plans available
for beautiful cottages, costing from $300 to $1000.
Ira Darrow, William Bradley,
Shubael L. Norton, Erastus Carpenter,
Grafton N. Collins, William S. Hills.

It was the first time the name Oak Bluffs had appeared in print. The *Gazette* liked it: "The Land and Wharf Company have given their grounds the unique and taking name of 'Oak Bluffs,' upon which they offer a thousand lots for sale. They have now completed the most substantial and convenient wharf that could have been erected in this vicinity, within 40 rods of the Campground proper."

The *Gazette* saw the wharf as a convenience to the campground, since it replaced the more distant one at Eastville. But that wasn't what Carpenter had in mind. He hadn't built the wharf to serve the campground; he had built it for Oak Bluffs. Sales of lots were brisk. In the first three years, Shubael L. Norton sold more than five hundred lots from his office at the head of the wharf. In the following two years, three hundred more were sold.

But Norton didn't sell the choicest lots. They were sold personally by Erastus Carpenter to a select group of men—men he knew would build impressive "cottages" that would make him proud. He offered them the best water-view lots, which bordered on the park at the head of the wharf. He wanted that large expanse of open land, the first view the tourist had, to be a park framed by expensive summer homes with spires and piazzas. He built the first one for himself.

Among those he solicited was Dr. Harrison A. Tucker of Brooklyn, New York, who had been visiting the Island since 1858, renting cottages in the campground. He wanted a summer home on the Island, but not one of those tentlike cottages in the campground. Made wealthy by sales of his

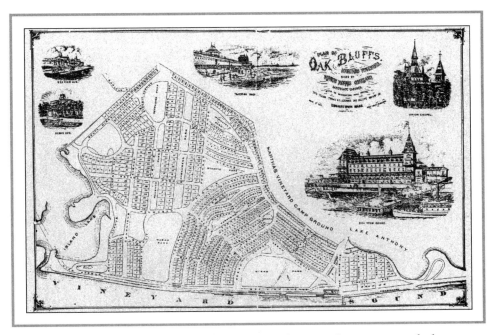

The developer Erastus Carpenter of Foxboro was the man who came up with the name
Oak Bluffs in 1867. He hired Robert Morris Copeland, a prominent Boston landscape
architect, to lay out the building lots, insisting that many acres of land be left open
as parks. After several rejections, Copeland submitted this plan, which is close
to how the village has turned out. (MVHS Collections)

patent medicines, each "tailor made" for a precise illness, he could afford
to build whatever he wanted.

Carpenter met with the doctor in 1868. Tucker described their meeting
some years later: "I lived at that time on the campground. [Carpenter] said:
'I would like to take you outside and show you what we have here.' We
walked on to the bluffs. He said they had formed a company for the purpose of organizing a summer resort and, 'I would like you to have a selec-
tion of some of the best lots as there is only two now sold, one [is] where
my cottage is.'" Tucker quickly signed on, buying a house that had already
been built near Carpenter's. But he wasn't happy with the view and soon
decided to build his own "cottage," as summer homes were called then, on
a better spot. He bought several lots and combined them to have space for
a larger cottage, the one known today as Dr. Tucker's house.

Carpenter sold lots to other wealthy men from Connecticut and Massachusetts, entrepreneurs made rich by the postwar boom. Among them
were Philip Corbin, the lock manufacturer, and Timothy Stanley, the tool-

In 1868 Erastus Carpenter proposed an "Illumination" by the cottage owners
to attract prospective buyers from the mainland to Oak Bluffs. Excursion boats
were run on that night in August. The event became so popular that by 1900 cottage
owners were going to great efforts to outdo their neighbors. Each paper Japanese
lantern had a candle that had to be lit by hand—no easy task.
(Shute Collection, MVHS)

maker. As word spread, other new entrepreneurs, too nouveau riche to be
acceptable at places like Newport, bought land and built impressive houses.
By selecting such buyers, Carpenter created the Oak Bluffs he wanted,
with Ocean Park as its centerpiece.

Erastus Carpenter began the annual "Illumination." On the weekend
before the 1868 camp meeting, to promote his development, he brought
the Town Band from Foxboro to Oak Bluffs to parade and give a concert
in the park. He asked the owners of the few cottages already built to hang
Japanese lanterns on their piazzas. His house had the largest display. Later

he added fireworks. Soon the event spread to Clinton Avenue, on the edge of the campground, and finally, some years later, into the campground itself. The Illumination did not start as a campground event. In fact, in its early years, the Methodists considered it ungodly. The huge crowds that came from the mainland to admire the lighted fairyland stayed for the weekend and were so disrespectful of the Sabbath that the campground directors passed a resolution requesting that steamers not run on camp-meeting Sundays. Furthermore: "We respectfully request all persons to refrain from visiting the Camp Ground on the Sabbath." The resolution didn't work; the steamers kept running, the crowds kept coming, and word of the Illumination spread. Carpenter had been right. Ocean Park, where the fireworks and the Illumination took place, was the drawing card. His insistence on open space was paying off.

During the winter of 1870 he wrote to Captain Norton, the sales agent for the company, urging him to fertilize the park's grass in a way that would be frowned on today:

> Would also [ask you to] finish up the 2 parks [Ocean and Waban parks] where you have been grading, by carting on a sufficient quantity of soil . . . for grass to grow. . . . Why not clear out all the privies and cesspools and make a compost heap on [the] Parks with what stable and hog manure you may find on the premises and have it in readiness to spread in the spring. Taking all the privies, stables, etc., with some loam, it would make quite a large quantity of most desirable compost to spread for the growth of grass.

By 1871 everybody, it seemed, was going to the Vineyard. At least so the *Whaleman's Shipping List,* a marine newspaper published in New Bedford, thought:

HO FOR THE VINEYARD!

A large stream of travel is now rushing through this city [New Bedford] to the Vineyard. Every conceivable kind of vehicle groans with its freight of humanity; men and women of all nations and all natures, of all sections and complexions—the Portuguese, the Englishman, the Frenchman, the Southerner, the Easterner—all going to the Eden-like city by the sea. What a wonderful transformation! Forty years ago, it was a barren waste, and now it is one of the most fashionable watering places on the Atlantic coast.

These years were perhaps the most frenzied in Vineyard history, unequaled before or since. More than a thousand buildings were erected in the small area bounded on the east by Vineyard Sound, on the west by the campground, and on the south by Farm Pond. These were not the tent-sized cottages of the campground. Many of them were large and expensive. Among them was the Sea View House at the head of the steamboat wharf. Henry Beetle Hough described the hotel in *Martha's Vineyard: Summer Resort* (1936).

> It is a legend. . . . One saw it from the steamboat, dominating the waterfront; one walked past it on the plank walk, or sat on the broad verandas which completely encircled it; if one was lucky, one stopped there, and was conscious of enjoying the finest accommodations and the finest society that the resort afforded. . . . It was a colossus, a marvel not only in itself, but because it transformed the whole aspect, the whole character of the community. Its towers were an imaginative flight, its whole effect was that of a fantasy, a wish-fulfillment, of the time. Like some chateau of dreams it stood, magnificent.

It was a nineteenth-century Disneyland. Its magnificence exuded confidence, the feeling of success. Soon ten more hotels had been built, each less majestic than the Sea View, but large and impressive nonetheless, with scores of guest rooms, broad piazzas, and spacious ballrooms.

Eager land developers moved in, buying up all the empty spaces they could find. Virtually the entire peninsula of East Chop, which only a few years earlier had been pasture, was divided into thousands of tiny lots, with each subdivision carefully plotted and promoted by Island real estate agents. One new developer, the largest, was the campground, which had long opposed such speculation. When the association realized it would not need its retreat, it decided to sell the three hundred acres as a development called Vineyard Highlands. Some in the campground objected, but the development went ahead despite them. The new company, called the Vineyard Grove Company, built a wharf and put up the Highland House at its head, following the pattern set by the Oak Bluffs Land and Wharf Company.

There were now two large wharves only a few hundred yards apart, both extending into the Sound. Steamboats from the mainland stopped first at Highland wharf to unload the "religious" passengers and then proceeded to the Oak Bluffs wharf to let off the "seculars."

The Vineyard Grove Company built a long, wooden walkway above the muddy shore of Lake Anthony so arriving pilgrims could walk directly into the campground. Later a horse-drawn railway was put in service, running into Wesleyan Grove.

A former Methodist minister was hired to sell the lots on the Highlands to make certain they went only to the right people. He described the somewhat strained relationship between the secular Oak Bluffs Company and the religiously inclined Vineyard Grove Company: "There was considerable competition, pretty sharp competition, between the two companies at the time. . . . We fought rather shy of each other, but we had civil acquaintance."

In 1873 there were eighteen subdivisions advertising in the *Seaside Gazette*, a short-lived newspaper of the day. In addition to Vineyard Highlands, there were Bellevue Heights, Lagoon Heights, Oklahoma, Prospect Heights, and smaller developments such as Forest Hill, Englewood, Oak Grove, and Oakland. On the Holmes Hole side of the Lagoon, C. C. Hines bought an entire peninsula and divided it into ninety-eight lots, three-quarters of them with water frontage, to form Cedar Neck.

The mood was so buoyant that nothing seemed impossible. Tarleton C. Luce, who had sold much of his family land to the Vineyard Grove Company, announced that he would build a large opera house on his new development at Bellevue Heights in time for the 1873 season. Construction was delayed only by a shortage of lumber. A steady stream of schooners from Maine couldn't keep up with the demand. On the Highlands a steam-driven planing mill was busy dressing the rough boards as soon as they were unloaded.

The boom was even spreading toward Edgartown. A new development, Ocean Heights, was laid out overlooking Sengekontacket Pond, soon followed by another on Trapp's Pond. The *Gazette*, ecstatic to see activity moving in its direction, asked: "Who comes next in the line of new enterprises? Welcome all!" Edgartown needed the new enterprise. The oil manufactory of Daniel Fisher had closed down; only his candle factory continued in operation. "The Fort," as the land on upper Main Street where Fisher had stored his whale oil was called, had been bought by Dukes County. Oil-stained and odiferous, it would be the site of a jail, the only new construction in town.

A fire in 1872 had crippled the old village and it was slow recovering. Starting in Richard Shute's photographic studio on lower Main Street below Four Corners, it had quickly spread to adjoining buildings. The

Shute building, the Munroe store, and the office of Dr. John Pierce were completely destroyed; badly damaged were four other buildings. It was Edgartown's worst fire since 1807.

Suddenly, there were too many developments, a surplus of land for sale. None was doing well. Sales on the Highlands were so slow that the campground association gave the Baptist association enough land to set up a campground, hoping more Baptists would follow. Lots were given to Baptist ministers who agreed to build cottages on them. By 1880 both denominations were holding camp meetings in August. There was no conflict with schedules. The Baptists always held theirs first, leaving free for the Methodists the traditional week at the end of August.

The Sea View House was the crown jewel of Carpenter's summer resort, the largest and most elegant hotel on the Island. It opened in July 1872 with a grand celebration attended by Boston dignitaries. Twenty years later, in September 1892, shortly after closing for the season, it was destroyed by fire. The nearby skating rink was also destroyed.
(Shute Collection, MVHS)

More than two thousand acres on East Chop had been subdivided. Edgartown businessmen, hopeful about the prospects of the Ocean Heights and Trapp's Pond developments, wondered how they could keep the movement coming south. There was plenty of open space around Old Town. In decline for years as whaling moved from New England to California, it now had little more than a courthouse and county jail to provide jobs. Attempts had been made to start new businesses, but none had lasted.

What was needed, the businessmen proposed, was a direct road from Oak Bluffs to Edgartown. Instead of making a long circle around Senge-kontacket Pond, it would run along the beach and thus cut travel time. The road wouldn't be cheap. A bridge had to be built across the opening into the pond from Vineyard Sound. At town meeting, Edgartown busi-nessmen praised the plan, and they persuaded residents to invest forty thousand dollars of the town's tax money in the project. It would be money well spent, bringing jobs and prosperity, they argued.

In the summer of 1872 the road was finished, just in time for the ded-ication of the majestic Sea View House. A gala was held in its ballroom. An Edgartown native, Joseph Thaxter Pease, the son of Jeremiah Pease, who had started everything when he laid out the campground in 1835, gave the welcoming address to the dignitaries from the mainland, calling himself "someone who is native here, and to the manor born." He was the treas-urer of the Oak Bluffs Company, which owned the hotel and much more in Cottage City. He may have been the only Edgartown resident who rode along the brand-new Beach Road to the party. He predicted that the Sea View House would bring prosperity to the whole Island, creating a new business of recreation and recuperation. When the honored guest, Judge Thomas Russell, the customs collector of Boston, spoke, he praised the company and Joseph Pease's role in it, closing with "May Pease be with you always."

The next morning the dignitaries boarded a chartered steamboat for Katama. As the vessel steamed into Edgartown harbor, a cannon was fired from the steamboat wharf, hoping no doubt to attract the illustrious group to stop there. But the visitors never got any closer than that. Katama was their destination, the site of Erastus Carpenter's latest grand plan. With East Chop now taken over by competitors, he had discovered a new opportunity at South Beach.

With other investors, Carpenter formed the Katama Land Company, buying six hundred acres on the western shore of Katama Bay, about three miles south of Edgartown village. Again he hired Robert Morris Copeland of Boston to design the subdivision. Dominating the plan was a huge hotel to be called Mattakessett Lodge, even larger than the Sea View. An imposing gatehouse would stand at the head of a wharf to impress arriving visitors with the grandeur of Katama. The gatehouse was quickly built and began taking guests in August. Carpenter promised that the much larger hotel would be built the next year. It never was, and the fifty-room gatehouse, slightly modified, became Mattakessett Lodge.

The directors voted to give Carpenter a waterfront lot for his cottage to get things started. It was quickly built, followed by a large clambake pavilion and a bowling alley. Katama's remoteness was its handicap. Land sales were slow. Only one other cottage was built after Carpenter built his. Despite the loveliness of the setting, the pounding surf at nearby South Beach, and the calm bay for swimming and fishing, Katama was just too far away. The company bought a small steamboat to carry potential buyers from Oak Bluffs to the new wharf and gatehouse. It was a pleasant boat ride, but it took too long. There had to be a faster way.

Carpenter, who was president of a railroad in Framingham, decided what was needed was a railroad. It was the era of railroads. Tracks were being laid everywhere. Trains now ran from New York to California. Why not from Oak Bluffs to Katama? He convinced several Edgartown businessmen to join him. Samuel Osborn Jr., Edgartown's leading businessman and politician, agreed to participate. They were a most unlikely combination. Carpenter's Oak Bluffs was the boom town that Osborn despised, as it had pushed Edgartown into the shadows.

In March 1874 the two men met with potential investors. Among them were Captains Nathaniel Jernegan, Jared Jernegan, Richard Holley, William S. Lewis, and John O. Norton, all former whaling masters from Edgartown, along with William Wing of New Bedford. The *Vineyard Gazette* was enthusiastic:

> If the railroad is built, $20,000 will go into the pockets of our laboring men. . . . Every spare horse will be employed, and all will feel the magical influence of new, prosperous and vigorous undertakings. . . . Go to the Town Meeting on Saturday and give your vote for the railroad. You will never regret it. . . . When we have a railroad, we shall see improvements made in our village never before thought of. The "snort of the iron horse" will arouse men from their lethargy and infuse new life into their veins.

At the special town meeting, Osborn proposed that the town put up $15,000, provided that another $25,000 was raised privately. Bonds would then be issued for another $35,000, so the total capital would be $75,000. Nine miles of narrow-gauge railroad could be built for that, Osborn said.

It was a poor time to be investing in a railroad. Nine months before, in September 1873, Jay Cooke and Company, which had financed the Northern Pacific Railroad, had failed, which triggered the Panic of 1873. More than five thousand businesses had gone broke. Such national financial cycles rarely affected the Island, and so Carpenter and Osborn pushed ahead. A railroad, they were sure, would bring prosperity to Edgartown.

At the town meeting, the residents, saddled with debt for the construction of the Beach Road, were hesitant. They had been told that the Beach Road would bring prosperity, but it had not. Why should they believe this new promise? Ichabod Norton Luce, the Gay Head lighthouse keeper from 1862 to 1866 who was now living in Edgartown, was critical: "It is as absurd to ask the town to develop Katama as to ask it to keep Mr. Osborn's ship in repair and find her in spars and rigging. The Katama Land Company is abundantly able to develop their property, and if they want a railroad let them build one." Captain Nathaniel M. Jernegan had a different view. Hardly a disinterested observer, he was the sales agent for the Katama Land Company. He was sure the railroad would be a success. It would, he said, bring "a handsome profit," and the town would make money on its investment. Osborn joined in Jernegan's optimism: "I expect a net return of ten percent."

A two-thirds majority was necessary to pass the proposal. The vote was close: 149 for, only 2 more than the 147 required, 72 against. Ichabod Norton Luce was not pleased. It was not the town's business, he wrote in a letter to the *Gazette*: "Take care of your poor, your schools, your roads: these are the legitimate functions of a town government. Let private projects take care of themselves. . . . The work will be done with imported Irishmen. . . . When you take into the account the number of men and horses employed [now] in carrying passengers to the South Beach . . . [with] all to be done by the iron horse fed with fire, it is to the laboring man a very serious matter."

Edgartown borrowed the fifteen thousand dollars from two off-Island banks, and the railroad company began spending it. No time was wasted. By the first week in August all but one mile of the nine-mile track had been completed along the shorter route the builders had chosen. The

Railroad tracks ran along the beach, shown here in 1892, from Oak Bluffs
to Trapp's Pond in Edgartown, and then across firmer ground to Katama. Storms often
washed out the tracks, which required expensive repairs. Always in financial trouble,
the railroad closed down in 1900 and the locomotive was taken to Boston by boat.
(Shute Collection, MVHS)

track ran along the beach from Oak Bluffs to Edgartown, turned south
across the fields to upper Main Street, where a depot was built, and then
to Katama, skirting the cemetery.

The first run was made in late August, which was a remarkable
accomplishment in such a short time. The locomotive proved to be inadequate. It was a so-called dummy engine, a passenger car with a steam
engine in it, the kind used at the time in cities for rapid transit. A standard locomotive was ordered. When it arrived in Woods Hole an accident
occurred. The flat car carrying the new locomotive was waiting at the pier
to be taken to the Island when it was hit by a rolling freight car and the
engine was knocked off the end of the wharf; it sank in an unplanned
saltwater christening. Pulled up the next day, it was taken back to Boston
for repairs. It finally arrived at Katama on August 27, 1874, and was put
into service at once.

Its arrival coincided with that of President Ulysses S. Grant, the first
president ever to visit the Island. Though he slept three nights in the
campground cottage of Methodist Bishop Haven, Grant showed little

interest in the Vineyard or its residents. He went to Nantucket and Hyannis the first day and on the next to Naushon, where he met with the Boston financier and political supporter James Forbes. He arrived back in Oak Bluffs late Saturday afternoon, in time to rest briefly before attending a gala in his honor at the Sea View House.

It was the most elegant function the Island had ever seen. Several hundred men and women, mostly summer people, attended, many in for-

President Grant (right) and his party on the porch of the Bishop Haven cottage on Clinton Avenue, Wesleyan Grove, 1874. Mrs. Grant is directly behind the president. The man at the far left is Orville Babcock, Grant's personal secretary, who was widely believed to be at the center of the scandals that plagued the Grant administration. (Photograph by Charles Shute; MVHS Collections)

mal dress. Thousands of curious folks lined the hotel piazza, peering in windows, eager for a glimpse of the president. For more than an hour, he and Mrs. Grant stood in a receiving line, shaking hands with Islanders and off-Islanders. When the weary president and his Methodist hosts left for bed at midnight, those remaining picked up the tempo and danced until dawn. Newspapers in Boston, New York, and Washington spread the news: the president had found a new national "watering place." The Vineyard's future looked bright.

The next morning, Grant and his wife attended a service under the camp meeting tent, but he never saw any more of the Island than Oak Bluffs and the campground. His visit had brought a few problems. A New York woman staying in the Highland House in Oak Bluffs at the time had jewelry valued at one thousand dollars taken from her room. Constable James Pent was stabbed as he tried to break up "a party of roughs" who were fighting outside the Sea View House while the gala was taking place. In Edgartown two men were arrested for breaking into the home of Mrs. Eunice Coffin. The "real" world had come to the Vineyard, along with the president and the railroad. It was a more complicated world. The Island was changing.

These were minor crimes compared with another that occurred that summer. When an Oak Bluffs mariner, Almar F. Dickson, returned from a seven-week coastal voyage, he discovered his cottage empty. His wife had taken most of the furniture and moved in with Deputy Sheriff John N. Vinson, to live in what was called "criminal intimacy." Mrs. Dickson's sister, Mrs. Phoebe Dexter, was also living in the house with Samuel K. Elliott of Worcester. Mrs. Dexter had been separated from her husband for several years. The two women said they were there only as housekeepers.

The abandoned Dickson tried to convince his wife to return home. She refused. On a Saturday night a few weeks later, he and his brother-in-law, Caleb C. Smith (the brother of the two women), with four other men arrived at the cottage of "criminal intimacy" at 89 Tuckernuck Avenue in a wagon. With them in the wagon were a bucket of tar, a feather pillow, and some rope. Smith knocked on the door. When Elliott opened it, Smith ordered him to get into the wagon. Elliott, apparently expecting as much might happen, drew a gun and pulled the trigger. The gun misfired. Smith's friends waiting in the wagon saw what was happening and joined the struggle. They dragged Elliott out of the house. During the fracas Elliott again pulled the trigger. This time the gun fired and the bullet hit

Smith in the chest. It did not stop him. He helped load Elliott into the wagon. They drove into the darkness, apparently to tar and feather Elliott.

Weakened by loss of blood from the wound, Smith fell off the wagon. The others went to help him, but he soon died. In the confusion, Elliott escaped. Sheriff Howes Norris was notified, and he arrested Elliott as well as Dickson and his accomplices. A grand jury was convened and it indicted Elliott. The next day he was acquitted in a jury trial. The shooting had been in self-defense, the jury ruled.

The man who had "stolen" Almar Dickson's wife, Deputy Sheriff John Vinson, missed all the excitement. He had hurriedly left the Island when he learned his "housekeeper's" husband was home from the sea. Later, when he returned to the Island, he resigned as deputy sheriff, to nobody's surprise.

The threat of a lynching, the sex scandal, and the flight of the deputy sheriff all sent shock waves through the community. For the first time the Vineyard was getting publicity of a kind it didn't want, and some felt didn't deserve. Metropolitan newspapers, including those in Boston and New York, had reporters at the trial. Bold headlines proclaimed the lurid story of a religious campground mired in sin. The editor of the *Seaside Gazette* pointed out that the violence had nothing to do with the campground or with the camp meeting: "The parties all resided off the campground; the fracas occurred in another part of the city, on land in no way connected with the campground. The fair fame of our camp meeting is in no way imperiled."

That same year, 1874, Professor Nathaniel S. Shaler, who later created Seven Gates Farm in North Tisbury, brought more unwanted publicity when he wrote about Edgartown in the *Atlantic Monthly*:

> The pretty village of Edgartown . . . in a commercial sense is a place far advanced in decay: of all its whaleships, which got from the sea the hard-earned fortunes of its people, there is but one left. This lies upon the ways, stripped of its rigging, looking like a mere effigy of a living craft. . . . As soon as a mariner comes to fortune, his first effort is to get a comfortable home, a big, square, roomy house, which shall always be ship-shape and well painted. . . . These comfortable homes, like those of New Bedford, mark a period of prosperity which has passed, never to return. Little by little, the population is drifting away; some houses stand empty, and the quick agents of decay which make havoc with our frail New England houses will soon be at work at them.

Shaler was a geologist who found little to interest him in Edgartown and the sandy, rock-free eastern half of the Island. He was a snob and an elitist who had little respect for the summer visitors in Oak Bluffs:

> So far, the newcomers [to the Island] have displayed the admirable lack of discrimination so characteristic of those who haunt the shore in summer; there are two or three great resorts for summer visitors growing up on the low shore of the eastern end of the island, whose interminable sand—its barrenness scarcely veiled by a thin copse of scrubby oaks—is engaged in a give-and-take struggle with the sea. Oak Bluffs, where oaks and bluffs are both on average less than ten feet high, has grown to be a pasteboard summer town capable of giving bad food and uneasy rest to 20,000 people.

To Professor Shaler Oak Bluffs may have been a "pasteboard summer town," but it was not to the thousands who loved it. They were happy with the "bad food and uneasy rest." On "Big Sunday," the final weekend of the 1875 camp meeting, ten steamboats were busy carrying those "tasteless" multitudes to Oak Bluffs from the mainland. The editor of the *Seaside Gazette* described the crowds that Shaler so disliked:

> "Camp meeting is playing out," was a phrase that became quite the fashion a few years since. . . . No clearer refutation of such an egregious falsehood could be derived than was manifest in the immense crowds that poured into the city yesterday, transported hither by every conceivable naval conveyance from the palatial steamer *Plymouth Rock* to the more democratic sloop or fishing smack. . . . They came from all conditions of life. The wealthy millionaire and family . . . the rustic Romeo with his verdant Juliet from off-Island . . . the mechanic, the storekeeper and the clerk all unite in making the pilgrimage.

The diverse crowd was orderly. Sixty special policemen were on duty in the village that day, but only one arrest, that of a boisterous drunk, had to be made.

There was no denying that Erastus Carpenter and his Oak Bluffs Land and Wharf Company had created a success, so much so that East Chop property owners had taken over the top rankings among all Edgartown taxpayers. In 1872 the Oak Bluffs Land and Wharf Company paid $1,242 in taxes, the Vineyard Grove Company paid $1,351, and Tarleton C. Luce, who had created Bellevue Heights west of the campground, paid $522. All this was paid on pasture land that not long before had owed little or no taxes. These new taxpayers displaced from the top of the list such men as Dr. Daniel Fisher, who owned an elegant house on Edgartown's upper Main Street and a candle manufactory on the waterfront. His tax bill was $619, half what the new Oak Bluffs Land and Wharf Company paid.

Providing as they were more than half the town's revenues, East Chop taxpayers began demanding more benefits, most of all better fire protection. With so many buildings so close together, Oak Bluffs had a great risk of disaster. The huge hotels were potential firetraps. Edgartown's leaders ignored the pleas. They were weary of the demands coming from Oak Bluffs. It was getting too big for its britches. It wasn't a year-round community; it was just a summer colony. Yet it was getting all the press attention. To off-Islanders Oak Bluffs had become Martha's Vineyard. When *Porter's American Monthly* sent a writer to describe what it called "America's newest watering place" in 1877, his report barely mentioned Edgartown. Instead, it was filled with praise for Oak Bluffs:

> Oak Bluffs exceeded our anticipation . . . the walks along its borders next to the ocean having no equal, within our knowledge, except that of The Cliffs at Newport. The cottages are numerous, large and attractive . . . spacious, tasty and expensive mansions. Here too most of the large and well-appointed hotels are located, including the "Sea View," the "Pawnee House," "Island House," "Grover House" and others too numerous to mention. The "Highland House," a large . . . hotel, . . . is situated upon the Vineyard Grove bluffs, adjacent to the Baptist camp grounds. . . . But the hotel of Oak Bluffs and of this great watering-place is the Sea View House . . . nearly three hundred feet in length, four stories high, has some two hundred rooms . . . directly upon the ocean shore. . . .
>
> Some eight or nine miles below Oak Bluffs is . . . "Katama" [where] the hotel, whose special name is "Mattakeset Lodge," was erected two years ago. . . . A fine narrow gauge railroad connects this place with Edgartown and Oak Bluffs.

That was his only mention of Edgartown. The once-proud shire town had become merely a place the train went through on its way to Katama. Where was the prosperity that the railroad was supposed to bring? The railroad hadn't made Edgartown prosperous. Nor had it made a profit. Every year when it looked as though it might make a profit, a winter storm would come along and wash away the track that ran along the beach, which would require expensive repairs. Sam Osborn's 10 percent dividend forecast never materialized. Edgartown taxpayers ran out of patience. At a town meeting in January 1877 they voted to sell the town's stock in the railroad for whatever it would bring. It brought little. Antone L. Silvia of New Bedford bought all the town's shares for $315—shares for which the town had paid fifteen thousand dollars only a few years earlier.

Despite its losses, the railroad kept puffing along without Edgartown's support. It managed to settle with some of its major creditors and got rid of much of its debt by bankruptcy. Somehow it kept its track in repair. It even bought a new passenger car and extended its track from Mattakessett Lodge to the sand dunes of South Beach. Erastus Carpenter's railroad might not make money, but it could spend it. (Sam Osborn sued the company later for money he had lent it to buy track for the South Beach extension.)

The railroad had been built to provide faster transportation from the steamboat wharf in Oak Bluffs to Katama's Mattakessett Lodge (visible in the background), but it didn't save the hotel from going out of business in 1879. The railroad continued to run to Katama, carrying customers to the very popular clambakes held there.
(MVHS Collections)

With its new spur running to within a short walk of the ocean at South Beach, the railroad began promoting moonlight excursions on those balmy summer nights when the surf was high and the moon was full. In 1878 the *Island Review,* another short-lived summer newspaper, described their romantic appeal: "On Wednesday evening, many took the late train from the Bluffs to Katama, sat on the sand and watched the moonbeams sparkling over the restless bosom of the far-spreading Atlantic and silvering the surf as it broke and foamed upon the beach." Other special trains carried hundreds to dances and clambakes at Katama. There, far from hectic Cottage City, visitors found themselves in a dream world of natural wonder. These excursions boosted passenger business so much that in the same year Edgartown sold its stock, the railroad made its first profit.

There may have been romance on moonlit South Beach, but the taxpayers of Cottage City felt none. Politically, they were helpless. The place was a collection of buildings empty all winter. A nonvoting population had no influence on how its tax money was spent. In summer fifteen thousand persons lived in Cottage City; in winter the population was about five hundred. Control of town meetings was securely in the hands of old Edgartown, which guaranteed that most of the tax money was spent there.

Cottage City residents pointed to the unfairness of the two recent expenditures that had been approved over their objections. One was to build the Beach Road between Cottage City and Edgartown at a cost of seventy thousand dollars; the other was investing fifteen thousand dollars in the railroad from Cottage City to Katama. These two expenditures had put Edgartown deep in debt with no advantage to Cottage City. In fact, both were attempts to drain business from Cottage City to Edgartown. The *Island Review,* itself struggling to survive, proposed a solution in 1878:

> This [Beach] road cost $40,000 more than it ought and the non-resident taxpayer is called upon to pay one-half of the expense of this great tap (we were about to write swindle). Edgartown next, in direct opposition to the voters of this section, added to the town debt by sinking, in hot haste, in less than three years, the sum of $15,000 in the Railroad, or "Tap No. 2," and at the same time utterly destroyed [the value of] the Beach Road, just then completed, as for nearly the entire length they are side by side.
>
> Our citizens and corporations light and clean our streets, build our sidewalks, make all new roads needed except through or "trunk" roads,

and . . . pay the greater part of the Police expenses of the district. . . . Our conclusion is inevitable. [We must] have separation. . . . Let us depart in peace.

The battle for secession had begun. It wasn't the first time it had been proposed. Cottage City had been trying for years to get the state legislature to make it a separate town, but the state had done nothing. The Island's representative, Beriah T. Hillman, although from Chilmark, was safely in the pocket of the Edgartown establishment, having been elected with its support. There was a long-standing Island protocol in which the three towns, Edgartown, Tisbury, and Chilmark, rotated the state representative's office. Nominations were controlled by the county leaders in Edgartown. Whenever a Cottage City petition to secede was brought up in the State House, Representative Hillman opposed it and so no vote was taken. After three such failures, Cottage City had had enough. A meeting was called by those "Non-Resident and Resident Tax-Payers in favor of a division . . . and an incorporation of the Town of Cottage City [made up of] Oak Bluffs, Vineyard Grove, Vineyard Highlands, Eastville, Lagoon Heights and vicinity." Twenty-five major taxpayers signed the advertisement, mostly off-Islanders. Only three were year-round residents: Howes Norris of Eastville, Joseph Dias of Vineyard Grove, and Ichabod N. Luce of Eastville. At the meeting the crowd learned what was happening: "One thousand dollars had been raised to defray expenses of the [secession] movement. Several prominent gentlemen addressed the meeting, giving urgent reasons for the division of the town. The attendance was large and the spirit . . . hopeful and determined. . . . The opposition are already weakening."

With the one thousand dollars the secessionists bought the print shop of the failing *Island Review* and soon began publishing a weekly called the *Cottage City Star*. The name was more hope than reality, there being, as yet, no town of Cottage City. A former Methodist minister was hired as its editor, the Reverend Edward W. Hatfield. In the first issue Hatfield wrote: "The *Cottage City Star* has its local abiding place at Vineyard Grove (the place aspiring to the name of 'Cottage City'). . . . It is owned by an Association of persons more interested in having such an organ existing among us than [in] pecuniary advantage."

What he didn't say was that the real purpose of the newspaper was to make Cottage City a separate town, no longer just part of Edgartown. Hatfield, with the help of Howes Norris, created a newspaper that soon was superior to Edgartown's *Vineyard Gazette*. The secessionists knew that they would need the support of the whole Island, so they published news from everywhere: Lambert's Cove, Gay Head, Squibnocket, and even Nomans Land had regular news columns. Only Edgartown was missing. For a year the *Star* was unable to find anyone living there who was willing to be its correspondent. The political pressure would be too great. Soon the *Star* was outselling the *Gazette* everywhere except in Edgartown.

The Edgartown "clique," controlled by Samuel Osborn Jr., knew it must do something. It may have been only coincidence, but when Edgartown's first board of health was appointed in the summer of 1879, its first action seemed to be a punishment aimed at "that part of Edgartown known as the Camp Ground, Oak Bluffs and Vineyard Highlands." It warned those property owners there "of the importance of maintaining strict sanitary regulations during the heated season now upon us, and in a locality so densely populated in the months of July and August." The board of health had a point. So many thousands crowded into that small area around the campground during the summer that there was indeed great danger of contamination of wells by human waste. In addition to residents, there were more than ten thousand day-trippers arriving almost daily.

Human waste had long been a campground concern. There just wasn't enough space for every tent or cottage to have its own privy, so communal toilets were built under the preachers' stand. In a regulation aimed more at modesty than at sanitation, the protocol for using the privies before curfew each evening was officially spelled out, rather bewilderingly:

> The Walks for Retirement are, for the Ladies, in the direction in the FRONT OF THE STAND (being a South Easterly direction therefrom, and including the space between the Road leading from the Ground to the East, or nearest Landing, and that leading to the Pond, directly in the rear of the New Bedford County Street Tent), and for the Gentlemen, in the direction in the REAR OF THE STAND, being a North Westerly direction therefrom, and including all the space on this side of the encampment between the two roads above named.

But simply directing the traffic wasn't enough. Larger crowds required more toilets. The need became so apparent that when the Oak Bluffs Company gave the campground a half acre of land near Lake Anthony to straighten out a disputed boundary, the land was used for more privies, something that did not please the company: "On it, [the Campground Association] built or placed their public privies. It was and is a nuisance and injury to the Oak Bluffs Company, but there was no redress. Expensive stables and sheds were built to cover this nuisance from public view."

The privies were built along the shore of Meadow Lake (now Sunset Lake), a lowland used for years as a dump for swill and human waste. On Siloam Avenue near the lake on land leased from the campground, Captain Joseph Dias, a leader in the secession drive, ran the Vineyard Grove House. The Edgartown Board of Health decided his well should be one of the first to be tested. The test was done in a most casual manner. A water sample was pumped into a jug with no tight seal on it and taken to Edgartown, where it was held overnight before being sent to Boston for testing. There a Professor Nichols tested the sample and declared the water contaminated, unfit for human consumption. Notices were printed and handed out to passengers on arriving steamboats to warn of contaminated water in the campground, where most were planning to visit.

The *Cottage City Star*'s editor was furious. There had been no complaints about the hotel's water. Nobody who had stayed there and drunk its water had become ill. The whole thing was, the *Star* charged, an act of retaliation against Captain Dias for his support of secession. The worried hotel keeper took two samples of water from the well himself and sent them to Boston to be tested. No contamination was found. Convinced that this was an unwarranted attack on Captain Dias and the secession demand, Cottage City decided that there had to be a major change. Somehow, a representative must be elected who would support its petition to secede.

It was Chilmark's turn to hold the representative's office, under the agreed-to rotation. The secessionists put Stephen Flanders of Chilmark on the primary ballot, opposing Beriah T. Hillman, the "machine" candidate, also of Chilmark. They ran candidates for county treasurer and county commissioner. None won the primary, so all three were named candidates of a new entity, "The People's Ticket," and placed on the election ballot under its name.

The *Cottage City Star* gave up on Edgartown but asked the rest of the Island to support its candidate, Flanders: "The people of Edgartown . . . believe that Edgartown is the world, and they are the inhabitants thereof, and that all outsiders are from the moon or some unknown corner of space and are not entitled to any consideration at their hands either by right or by courtesy. . . . Voters, break the yoke placed about your neck by this grasping old town. . . . Vote the People's Ticket." The election was close—a victory for the secessionists. Two of their candidates, the state representative and the county commissioner, were elected. Their candidate for county treasurer lost by only 20 of the 840 votes cast. It was a great victory. A proud *Cottage City Star* proclaimed: "Sound the Hogag!! The People Victorious!! Glorious News!!"

For the first time the power of the Edgartown establishment had been broken. The *Star* gloated: "Mr. Samuel Osborn is said to look as if a heavy white frost had struck him."

The election was notable for another reason. It was the first time the Indians in Gay Head had been allowed to vote. All but one of their twenty-four votes went to Stephen Flanders, the prosecession candidate, providing more than half his winning margin of forty votes. The Gay Head vote was even more decisive to the election of County Commissioner Lorenzo Smith, another prosecession candidate. His victory margin was only four votes. It was one of the closest elections in Island history, and the Gay Head Indians, voting for the first time, had played an important role.

The election of 1879 was memorable for another reason, as the *Star* pointed out: "It was the first time the citizens of Edgartown ever witnessed the sight of ladies publicly electioneering [for] votes. . . . It showed how desperate the leaders had become."

To celebrate their victory, the secession forces held a gala dinner at Captain Joseph Dias's Vineyard Grove House, where the drinking water had been declared unfit for humans.

The Edgartown machine didn't take the results without protest. It demanded that the election of Representative Flanders be revoked and asked the state to investigate several improprieties it said had occurred. The claim was made that the required notices of the election had not been posted in Gay Head. There were, it was said, irregularities on Gosnold (the Elizabeth Islands) and in Tisbury, where some voters had not paid their poll taxes until after the election.

After many weeks the state ruled that there had been a few minor errors in procedures, but they had not been deliberate and did not warrant overriding the clear intent of the people. Flanders was confirmed as the winner.

Trying to close the Island's widening split, the *Star* editorialized after the decision: "Every[body] knows that to build up Cottage City is the salvation of Martha's Vineyard. . . . All sensible people know there is no hope of turning the tide from Cottage City to Edgartown or Gay Head. . . . Already this place [Cottage City] furnishes a market for our farmers. . . . Diabolical newspaper men [at the *Gazette*] and people . . . are engaged in constant endeavors to create strife. . . . Show by your acts that you disapprove."

With a friend now in the State House, the secessionists quickly sent their fourth petition to the legislature. With the active support of Representative Flanders, it passed both houses quickly. At 4:00 P.M. on February 17, 1880, the governor signed it. Cottage City was no longer merely a hopeful name on a newspaper masthead; it was now the official name of a town. The *Star* reported: "The quill with which the bill was signed was presented to the local committee and will be preserved."

Lobbying in vain against the bill had been several of Edgartown's leading citizens, as the *Star* reported, sarcastically: "A touching sight—the trio from Edgartown, Messrs. Osborn, Clough and Dunham, with arms interlocked, passing up Washington Street on Saturday afternoon, apparently seeking a little harmless diversion from the trials at the State House amid the gay frivolities of an afternoon on Boston's great thoroughfare, or, possibly they were off for the children's matinee at the Globe [theater]."

A month later, in March 1880, many members of the state legislature, all supporters of secession, went to Cottage City to celebrate. The Old Colony Railroad added a private car to the train carrying them to Woods Hole. It was a joyful occasion. After a splendid meal in the Vineyard Grove House, no doubt with much banter about the contaminated water being served, the group moved to the chapel on the campground, where many local residents had gathered. It was a big crowd, eager to celebrate, but as one off-Island speaker pointed out, there were noticeable absences: "I'm happy to see old friends and acquaintances and happy to see your union of feeling; but I should have been more happy to see some of my old friends from Edgartown here, too."

Not present for a different reason was Erastus P. Carpenter, the man most responsible for the victory. He probably was on a trip to Europe to study the latest styles in straw bonnets. Surely, had he been in Foxboro, he would have been honored to attend this victory gala. He and his associates had opened up acres of pastureland, creating a lively village that now had 1,106 taxable buildings valued at $1,212,527, among them 18 hotels and 44 stores, shops, and restaurants. The village had been paying 60 percent of all the tax money collected by the town of Edgartown. Now as a separate town, Cottage City was ranked in the top half of the 306 towns in Massachusetts in real estate valuation—that's how much it had grown in only a dozen years.

The victory celebration lasted well into the night. Many lighthearted speeches were given. One, more serious, was by a Melrose lawyer who advised the assembled residents that the time for discord was over: "Let there be no divisions among you. Treat Eastville well—it is all Cottage City now, no Eastville. . . . Let a general broad-handed liberality rule this town. Let divisions go. Let Eastville, the Highlands, the Grove, Oak Bluffs, all go . . . they are all Cottage City now." The new town, consisting as it did of many disconnected and competitive land companies, would have to join forces and come together. It wouldn't be easy.

There was another problem ahead, one that none of those celebrating could have imagined: Erastus Carpenter was getting ready to cash in his Martha's Vineyard chips. Perhaps that was why he wasn't present at the celebration.

The first hint was an advertisement in the *Boston Journal*: the Katama Land Company was offering its property for sale:

MARTHA'S VINEYARD
For Sale for One-half of the Cost or,
Lease for a Term of Years
At a Low Price.
Seaside hotel of 60 rooms . . . two cottages, *clam-bake pavilion, billiard room, bowling alley, servants' quarters.* Also, 450 acres good farming land, farmhouse, farm buildings and wharf.

Erastus P. Carpenter, it seemed, was admitting that Katama had been a mistake. The railroad, the clambakes, the moonlight excursions, and the beautiful surf could not overcome the handicap of remoteness. He was getting out, beginning his total withdrawal from the Vineyard.

For most Vineyarders his withdrawal would matter little. They were living just as they had before Erastus arrived with his dream. Life was still a struggle for them. It wasn't easy before he came and it wasn't easy now. They had to work hard to get by. There were few steady jobs. The Island's largest employer was the R. W. Crocker harness factory on Main Street in Vineyard Haven. About twenty-five persons worked there in 1880 (at its peak, a few years later, there were sixty), producing more than one thousand sets of harness a year, almost all exported to the mainland. Another Vineyard Haven enterprise, only a year old, was the factory making overalls, which employed sixteen women. It was innovative. The sewing machines were powered by a steam engine, and Eugene L. Chadwick was in charge. There was another, very busy factory in town: "S. T. Meara, the celebrated Boot and Shoe Manufacturer, is receiving large orders. His factory is running on full time."

Sherman T. Meara was a young Irish immigrant who somehow ended up on the Vineyard. He enlisted in the Union army as a volunteer from Tisbury early in the Civil War. In April 1864, during his second tour of duty, he was captured and held in the infamous Andersonville Prison, from which he escaped in February 1865. When he was mustered out at the end of the war, he returned to the Island, where he married the daughter of Bayes Norton of Tisbury. He owned two shoe and cobbler shops and now had started the boot and shoe factory in Vineyard Haven.

For most Island men, however, the sea was their "factory." They were mariners, either in whaling or in commercial shipping. At least twenty-five were pilots, guiding vessels through the treacherous Vineyard and Nantucket Sounds. They lived aboard vessels anchored at the entrances to the Sounds, waiting for a call from a passing ship.

Up-Island, where there was waterpower, a number of gristmills provided employment for a few. A paint mill on the north shore used waterpower (later steam power) to grind clay of various colors into very fine powder that was shipped off-Island to be turned into paint. A seasonal operation, it employed five or six men. Nearby was the brick works, also seasonal, which with the help of a steam engine produced eight hundred thousand bricks a year, almost all exported.

Cranberry bogs along the north shore shipped more than a thousand barrels of those berries to the mainland annually. In West Tisbury the textile mill on Mill Pond made various felt fabrics from Island wool and employed half a dozen.

In Edgartown the largest employer was Dr. Daniel Fisher's candle works. (His oil refinery had closed.) For a short time a woodworking shop on North Water Street had produced trim for the gingerbread cottages in the campground.

In all three villages a few men worked at herring runs seasonally, loading thousands of the tiny fish into barrels for shipment to New York. Other fishermen tended fish traps along the north shore and went scalloping,

Charles Earle, Albert Vincent, and Edwin T. Smith haul in the annual catch of herring at Mattakessett, in Edgartown, a two-hundred-year-old Vineyard industry. Most of the harvest was shipped to New York City. (MVHS Collections)

quahauging, and eeling. A number of men from Lambert's Cove went to Naushon every year at sheepshearing time, and a surprising number from the cove spent their summers codfishing on Nomans Land.

Cutting and harvesting ice during the cold months was another source of employment. Ice was essential on fishing boats as well as in stores and homes as the newfangled iceboxes became popular. After mild winters Island ice soon ran out and shiploads were imported from Maine.

There were only a few jobs that would be considered steady today. House painting was perhaps the most common for men. For women the steady jobs were teaching school and clerking in retail stores. Few teachers were needed, but Edgartown and Vineyard Haven each had more than twenty stores open all year. But these were small, owner-operated shops that rarely hired clerks. Struggling as they did to make a living all year, Islanders must have wondered how so many off-Islanders could afford to vacation in Cottage City. Vacations were something Vineyarders had little experience with.

But those vacationing off-Islanders were what the Island was increasingly becoming dependent upon. It had become a "Pleasure Island" for those who came to indulge themselves in the gaiety of Cottage City in summer, gaiety at a level that even now is hard to believe. Central to it was the

The huge roller-skating rink at Oak Bluffs near the Sea View House was built in 1879 by Samuel Winslow of Worcester, a designer and manufacturer of early roller skates. He named one model the "Vineyard Skate." The building also was used for musicales and dramas. Seriously burned in the Sea View House fire in 1892, it had to be torn down.
(Shute Collection, MVHS)

skating rink built on the bluff next to the Sea View House by Samuel Winslow of Worcester. He was the inventor and manufacturer of the "Vineyard Skate." Roller skating was becoming popular and, unlike today, it had to be done indoors. Streets and sidewalks were not hard or smooth enough to skate on. Winslow's huge indoor rink was ugly on the outside but a wonderfully spacious building inside, with a smooth hardwood floor lighted by hundreds of lanterns hanging from the rafters. The rink itself was octagonal and surrounded by rows of seats for as many as one thousand spectators. Skates were rented for ten cents (fifteen cents in the evening). Admission was twenty-five cents (thirty-five cents in the evening). There were three sessions a day, morning, afternoon, and evening. In the evenings Winslow scheduled special events to boost attendance: bonbon parties, calico parties, costume balls, hockey and polo matches, fancy roller skating, and bicycle riding. His rink was the center of entertainment at Cottage City.

Excursions to the rink were run from Edgartown and Vineyard Haven. Tickets included a round-trip on the train from Edgartown, admission to the rink, and rental of skates, all for sixty-five cents. Excursions from Vine-yard Haven cost seventy cents, including a carriage ride both ways.

With no recorded music available, the rink hired musicians, many musicians, from off-Island. During the busiest periods Winslow had three bands taking turns on the stage, each with a dozen or more musicians. They were playing for more than the skaters; they were giving concerts for hundreds seated on benches around the rink, watching and listening. The repertoires of the bands were light, semiclassical works, usually by Euro-pean composers.

Music was everywhere. The large hotels provided their own bands for dancing. They regularly played from hotel piazzas to entertain the crowds of strollers. Guesthouses put on productions with singing, recitations, and skits, many of the performers being vacationing guests. The village was alive. There never was a time when so much music, played by live musi-cians, filled the Island air.

Ocean bathing was, of course, part of summer, but a relatively minor part. Only a few hardy souls went into the water. Sunbathing was unknown. A tan was something a fisherman or a farmer had on his face and forearms. Bathing costumes covered the female body. Women did not get tans. One letter writer demanded that short sleeves be forbidden, as they were too shocking. Another insisted that men wear shirts, not merely long pants to go into the water. An occasional young boy would be seen wearing only shorts, and other beachgoers were horrified.

Most vacationers went to the beach to watch rather than to bathe. (The word *swimming* was not yet in their vocabulary.) The *Cottage City Star* described the daily routine:

> The bathing-houses at Oak Bluffs and adjacent beaches are a scene of liveliness and frolic every day, especially between the hours of 10 and 12 A.M. Hundreds of people, old and young, fat and lean, avail themselves of this delightful and profitable pleasure daily and it is hard sometimes to tell who enjoys it most, the bathers in their varied and unique cos-tumes, or the throng of spectators who assemble each day on the bal-conies of the main buildings of the bathing houses.

Bathers changed into their costumes inside one of the hundreds of bathhouses. It was indelicate to be seen wearing a bathing costume any-where except on the beach. Women "bathed," very few knowing how to swim. Most males had learned to swim at an early age, but girls had not.

271

The young boys demonstrated their manliness by jumping or diving from the wharves and rafts to impress the females.

Gradually, women began to take up swimming. Late in the summer of 1883 one of them wrote to the *Star* requesting a second diving raft be anchored off Highland Beach just for women: "Many women would like to dive from the raft, but do not like to have to fight for space on the present raft overloaded with men."

Bicycle races were popular. Thousands lined the streets to watch the wheelmen pedal around Ocean Park and through nearby streets at high speed. The racers were mostly from off-Island cycling clubs, although a

Vacationers loved the Oak Bluffs waterfront, with its sandy bathing beach and observation tower. The large boulder visible in the center was called "Lover's Rock." This undated photograph must have been taken before the Sea View House burned down in 1892, as it is visible at the far right. (Stuart photo, MVHS Collections)

few Island summer people (men only, of course) took part. Even walking races were held: "On Saturday next there will be a walking match—go-as-you-please—at the Base Ball Grounds. These matches are interesting and usually attract quite a number of spectators."

The principal sport around the campground was croquet. During camp meeting visiting ministers and their Methodist brethren would play between the many services (except on the Sabbath). There were complaints that preachers shortened their sermons during camp meetings so they could have more time to play. So enthusiastic were the preachers about the game that in 1875 they formed the Five-C Club, which stood for Cottage City Clerical Croquet Club. They became so skilled at the original game that some began taking up the new and more sophisticated version, roque. A Martha's Vineyard Roque Club was established in 1890 by thirteen men, all summer residents of Cottage City (only one was a minister). The first roque courts had been built in Waban Park ten years earlier by James W. Tufts, a soda fountain manufacturer from Boston, who was one of the thirteen founders of the club. Roque was played with short-handled, heavy mallets and smaller balls. The court was of clay, extremely smooth and level, and framed by a border of wooden planks (later faced with rubber) so the balls could be caromed, as in billiards.

The Martha's Vineyard Historical Society has a copy of an agreement between Alfred E. Cox, president of the Roque Club, and a George someone (his last name illegible). The agreement hired George to maintain eight roque courts from May 21 to September 8, 1906, for twelve dollars a week. The courts were all in Waban Park, a public park, under an agreement with the Board of Park Commissioners of Cottage City. Gazebos were placed at the courts so that spectators could sit in the shade and watch the matches. Tournaments were held each summer and attracted many players from off-Island.

Year-round Vineyarders didn't become involved in roque. It was a sport for vacationers. More to their liking was horse racing. In 1873 a racetrack for trotters was built near the location of today's regional high school. The track was a half-mile circle, complete with a judges' stand. Most racing was with two-wheel sulkies, but there was a separate division for lightweight wagons. The track, owned by a Smith and a Pease, both of Edgartown, was never profitable and was sold at auction in 1875. In June 1873, just before the trotting park opened, the *Gazette* reported, in mock shock, that during "horse racing on Beach Road, . . . some money changed hands."

After the track was sold, Islanders went back to racing their sulkies on public roads until the early 1900s, especially State Road in Vineyard Haven and Beach Road in Edgartown. To celebrate Thanksgiving in 1900, a special day of racing was organized with seven sulkies taking part. Between the horse races, a bicycle race was run; Orrin Norton, Frank Norton, and Peter Lynch finished in that order. Sulky racing was beginning to lose enthusiastic followers.

Baseball games at Waban Park drew big crowds each summer. But there, too, they were mostly summer people. The teams were semiprofessional, being made up of college players who had been hired as waiters by the hotels, more for their athletic skills than for their serving skills. Aware of the promotional value of the sport, the hotels formed a Cape and Islands league of teams bearing their names.

One of the best players was Walter C. Camp of Yale, the captain of the Cottage City team who later became famous as "the father of American football." He turned down an offer of two hundred dollars a month to umpire league games, preferring to play for the Cottage City team. An athlete of many skills, he was also hired by Samuel Winslow to captain one of the two roller-skating hockey teams he maintained. Their weekly matches drew hundreds of spectators to Winslow's skating rink.

In 1884 a new form of less athletic entertainment arrived when F. O. Gordon of New York built a carousel on the bluff behind the skating rink: "The pavilion will contain not only the revolving horses, but will be fitted up as a first-class place for affording light entertainment." In a month it was ready to operate, seemingly powered by a steam engine, with "Free Rides for All" on opening day. This is the same carousel, "The Flying Horses," operating today on Circuit Avenue, a site it was moved to years later. Soon after that, a toboggan slide was built beside the carousel. The area along the bluffs, the serenity of which had so charmed Erastus Carpenter, was becoming a carnival ground.

There was another innovation in the summer of 1884: electricity came to Cottage City when two generators went into operation. A dozen or so electric arc lights were mounted on poles to illuminate a few important outside areas. It is not clear how many were installed inside the buildings—probably very few, as arc lights were smoky and dangerous. The skating rink may have had a couple. Some Methodists thought the Tabernacle, the new iron enclosure inside the campground that had replaced the huge canvas tent in 1879, should have signed up for electricity, but it preferred its traditional oil lamps.

A water line to supply several fire hydrants in the campground and along Circuit Avenue was being installed, but it would not go into service until the pumping station at Meadow Lake started up a year later, in 1885.

While these advances were taking place in Cottage City, year-round Vineyarders in the other towns were showing little interest. Especially uninterested must have been two Indian women who, from 1881 to 1884, spent a lot of time in court. Their problems were unrelated and not criminal. What they had in common was that both were Indians and both were women.

The first case involved riparian rights to Tisbury Great Pond. Riparian rights were a valuable source of income, as they were leased by their owners to fishermen. Those for Tisbury Great Pond were especially valuable. Priscilla Freeman was an elderly Indian widow whose ancestors had owned land on the pond for generations. She had gradually sold portions of it to support herself and her family, but she retained a house on Deep Bottom Cove. More recently, she had moved to Cottage City, but she still owned the Tisbury property.

Eighteen other owners of riparian rights on the pond had formed an association to lease fishing rights. They refused to admit Priscilla Freeman into their group despite her frequent pleadings. In 1871, acting on her complaint, the state awarded her two hundred dollars in damages, far less than her share of the rights would have brought. When the ten-year leases came up for renewal in 1881, she again asked for her share. Again she was denied.

Finally, after much pleading, her case came before the state legislature. The *Cottage City Star* took her side:

> "Bulldozing" is always reprehensible, but when a poor, lone Indian woman in Massachusetts is seeking to obtain her rights, which an oppressive monopoly of white folks are defrauding her of, it is particularly alarming. . . . Mrs. Priscilla Freeman has rights in the fishing of Deep Bottom Cove. . . . She has many sympathizers and friends in the neighborhood . . . yet when she solicits their aid they say they dare not go and testify; threats have been made against all who do. . . . Is it possible that this state of things exists in West Tisbury—a highly intelligent community where there is an academy and organized churches?

In 1879 the Tabernacle was erected to replace the leaky tent. Its frame is structural steel,
its roof corrugated iron, bold innovations at the time. Although the roof has been
repaired occasionally, the open-sided building remains in good condition more
than 125 years later. Unexpected were its fine acoustics, which make it an
excellent hall for recitals and concerts in addition to religious services
in the summer. (MVHS Collections)

One year later Priscilla was awarded five hundred dollars more in damages, but nothing was done about her riparian rights. She was then seventy-two years old and her case seems to have been dropped without any judgment.

The second Indian woman who was often in court was Eunice Rocker, also a widow. She was born on Chappaquiddick. Now, in 1881, like Priscilla, she was living in Cottage City. Her grandmother was Love (Madison) Prince. Eunice and her late husband, Antone, had nine children. He had died some years before of a heart attack while working on a bulkhead at Lake Anthony, leaving her without any means of support. She became a town pauper in Edgartown. After it separated from Edgartown, Cottage City claimed that, even though she lived in the new town, supporting her family as paupers was still Edgartown's responsibility. After long dispute, the case went to the state board, which avoided a judgment and ruled that because they were "chronic paupers," the family would be moved to the off-Island almshouse in Tewksbury.

When the constable and deputies went to the Rocker house to inform them of the order, a violent confrontation occurred. Eunice, her daughter Lena, her mother, her sister, and a friend all took part, allegedly attacking the officers with an ax and throwing boiling water on them. The police eventually subdued the belligerent women, and Eunice and her children were taken to Tewksbury.

The *Star,* which for months had been very critical of the Rocker family, sounded relieved: "Cottage City sent nine of her population to Tewksbury and three to jail on Friday." The three who had gone to jail were Eunice's mother, her sister, and the woman friend who had joined in the fracas.

The *Gazette* took the side of the Rockers. The *Star's* editor, always eager for an argument with the competition in Edgartown, took issue:

> Does any intelligent person (except the editor of the *Gazette*—admitting that a graduate of Tufts College and a full-fledged lawyer *must* be intelligent) for an instant presume that a family of pauper squatters can go into a town where they have no settlement and sit down on the taxpayers? It does seem as if some folks' wits were dimmed by a blind desire to foist upon Cottage City this family of Rocker paupers in order that they may have a chance to crow over one victory won over us.

Eunice and her daughter Lena sued Cottage City for injuries sustained during their removal. They claimed they were not paupers, as both were earning their living at the time. A long trial was held in New Bedford, at which twenty-six Vineyard witnesses testified. The jury awarded the Rockers twenty-five dollars and thus brought to a strange conclusion a most confusing case. Were the Rockers (and Priscilla Freeman) victims of discrimination because they were Indians and women who had married blacks? There is no way to know, but it is clear that they were treated shabbily.

In 1882 Erastus Carpenter's Oak Bluffs Land and Wharf Company was in financial trouble, which was not a surprise. Four years earlier, in 1878, the *Boston Herald* had hinted at trouble:

> The Oak Bluffs Land & Wharf Company has expended several hundred thousand dollars in improvements, or considerably more than has ever been received from the sale of lots. . . . The general shrinkage in value throughout the country has not left the Oak Bluffs Company unaffected

. . . though the Vineyard has been exceptional in its prosperity during these hard times. . . . The Cottage City of America is yet of the earth and liable to be stagnated like other things earthly.

In September 1882 the directors voted to take the losses and leave the Island. The company had already sold its pride, the Sea View House, to a pair of New Bedford hotel keepers, Bullock and Brownell, but it had other properties it wanted to sell.

But selling wasn't easy. After the boom years of the 1870s, investors had been pulling back, and property values had been falling. These declining values hit the new town of Cottage City hard. It had so many needs and so little money. High on its list of urgent needs was a solution to its longtime sanitation problem. When it became a separate town in early 1880, the village had appointed its own board of health, but the board was still organizing and nothing had been decided. The *Cottage City Star* emphasized the urgency: "The outdoor New England privy, located near the back kitchen door or window of one's neighbor, is a nuisance at best, and if they are to be tolerated they should be under wholesome regulations. . . . Our Board of Health must begin operations soon if they would satisfy . . . the non-resident who pays our taxes."

Inertia did seem to have taken over. Then, suddenly, in December 1880, the Massachusetts Board of Health issued a thirty-page report that declared the Cottage City water unsafe to drink. Professor Homer B. Sprague of Boston, a summer resident and president of Martha's Vineyard Summer Institute in Cottage City, wrote to the *Star* urging fast action. He worried that the public's fear of disease would cut his school's enrollment: "Now I am not an alarmist, but I feel that Cottage City will this very next season lose hundreds and perhaps thousands of visitors whom it would of [*sic*] had—visitors of the most desirable class—by reason of the failure to take prompt and wise measures for drainage and sewerage."

In March 1881 the board of health published ten rules for the disposal of waste of all kinds. None could be dumped into Lake Anthony or Meadow (Sunset) Lake. All privy vaults had to be sealed and watertight; no longer could they be just holes in the ground. Times for cleaning out privy vaults were strictly regulated:

> No privy vaults or cesspools shall be opened, or privies cleaned or their
> contents removed between the first day of June and the first day of

November . . . [except] between the hours of ten in the evening and five in the morning.

All privies and cesspools must be emptied and cleaned between the first day of November and the last day of December; and those used during the winter months must also be cleaned before the first day of June.

Sanitation was only one of the young town's problems. With a growing population, it needed a new school. Where would the money come from? Tax revenues were not increasing. Those new residents were not wealthy summer people who left their cottages in the fall, taking their children with them. Most were the Portuguese who had moved from New Bedford when jobs in the mills became scarce. They worked in the Island's hotels and at other seasonal jobs all summer, but when summer was over and their jobs ended, they didn't leave. The *Star* was understanding: "Of the scholars admitted and belonging to the primary school, nearly 25 percent are children of paupers or foreigners who pay no tax . . . [living in] shanties that are springing up with mushroom growth in the outskirts [of the village]. . . . We must not deny school rights to paupers and foreigners, even though they pay no tax and can scarcely understand our language."

There was also the town's continuing worry about fire. In one of its first expenditures it had bought two fire engines, selling the ancient hand pumper it had received from Edgartown years before. That engine had been much ridiculed as "the Elephant" because of its huge size and weight. It had proved to be totally inadequate and fortunately was never called upon to put out a major fire. The town sold it for six hundred dollars to help pay for the new engines. These were "chemical engines," so called because their chemicals, when mixed with water in the sealed tanks, built up gas pressure and forced the water through the hose, thus eliminating hand pumping.

Adequate for small fires, the two engines would be of little use in a conflagration. Work was continuing on the ten-inch water main from Meadow Lake through the campground and along Circuit Avenue, to supply a number of hydrants. The steam engine at Meadow Lake that would pump water into the main under pressure wasn't yet in operation.

The town had a new problem, larger even than the others. It involved land ownership, land that residents had always assumed was for public use. In March 1881 the Oak Bluffs Company, still disposing of its property, offered the town, at no cost, the four parks, Ocean, Waban, Hartford, and

Pennacock, in addition to nine avenues. Residents were caught by surprise. In a special town meeting, the offer was discussed and a committee of three was appointed to meet with company officials and to recommend what action Cottage City should take. Two weeks later the *Star* reported that a committee meeting had been held, "the result of which, we are led to believe, was not anything decisive."

Learning that the parks and avenues were not theirs had come as a shock to residents. From the start it had been understood that they were for the public. Erastus Carpenter had made that clear when he sold the choice lots, those bordering the parks, to his carefully selected buyers. He had promised that their cottages would always face open land. But the company had never given up its title to that land. Legally, it owned the land and could do whatever it wished with it. If the town didn't want it for free, the company would sell it to the highest bidder.

For three years no agreement could be reached. Voters seemed wary of the offer; there must be some hidden catch to it. Finally, the company's stockholders demanded to be paid for their parks and streets. They had lost enough money in the company. Carpenter withdrew the free offer and put a price of seventy-five hundred dollars on the land, giving the town first option to buy. Again the town did not respond. Late in 1884 another committee was formed, this one to meet with a lawyer to decide if the land could be legally sold. The *Star* explained: "The general feeling, or at least the predominant one, in the meeting was in favor of purchasing, if the company had something of real value to sell. If it had parted with its right to do as it pleased with the parks and avenues by its layout, and the later sale of lots . . . then the price was thought to be too high."

Erastus Carpenter was sure the property could be sold legally and that seventy-five hundred dollars was a fair price. He cited a Cottage City real estate man who said the land was worth much more: "I was aware that some of the stockholders [of my company] were dissatisfied that the management should offer the property at the low price of $7500 when they had been told by a prominent real estate agent of Cottage City 'that if the parks could be sold for building lots they would bring from $50,000 to $60,000.'" He urged the town to move quickly. Another party was eager to buy. But the committee still did nothing, believing that the land was already public and could not be sold.

Carpenter offered to let the town pay the seventy-five hundred dollars over twenty-five years, interest free, at three hundred dollars a year. Again, no action. Impatient, he set a deadline: decide by December 1, 1884, or the land would be sold to the other party. A week before the deadline the Cottage City selectmen asked for an extension. They wanted to "investigate the legal questions involved," as though the legality was a new subject. The extension was denied. Writing to the selectmen, Erastus Carpenter described his disappointment: "After spending so much time and thought on this matter, I need not add that I am more than disappointed at the failure of a plan so much in the town's interest and one which, as far as I know, received the full and unqualified endorsement of a large number of the citizens and the non-residents."

The deadline passed. The town still did nothing. In March 1885 two men from Boston, George C. Abbott, a lawyer, and his financial backer, Alvin Neal, gave the Oak Bluffs Land and Wharf Company a check for seventy-five hundred dollars. The parks of Cottage City now belonged to them. They would divide them into building lots and put them up for sale.

Cottage City went into shock. Its parks sold? Carpenter's "jewels," his open spaces, to be subdivided, filled with buildings? Residents must have wondered if secession from Edgartown had been such a good idea.

9

Fires, Water, Electricity, Telephones, and Another New Town

Despairing as residents of Cottage City were over the purchase of their parklands by George C. Abbott of Boston, those worries must have seemed trivial to their neighbors in Vineyard Haven. One year before, they had lost their entire business district in the most destructive fire in Island history. They were still trying to recover.

The fire happened on Saturday night, August 11, 1883. Vineyard Haven, compared with Cottage City, was a quiet town, even on Saturday nights in summer. The August day had been cool and raw, with a strong northeasterly wind and an unpleasant drizzle. Going to bed early was an easy choice—tomorrow would be better.

At 9:00 P.M. flames were seen coming from the rear of Crocker's harness factory on Main Street. The men who spotted the fire ran to nearby churches and rang the bells, arousing the neighbors, who could do little except get out of their houses, taking the few possessions they could hastily gather. The village had no fire apparatus and no alarm system, only its church bells.

Neighboring Cottage City, newly separated from Edgartown, did have fire engines. At its very first town meeting as a separate town in 1880, its citizens had voted to buy two chemical fire engines. Much of the pressure to secede from Edgartown had come from worries about fire in the congested campground. Edgartown refused to provide an adequate engine, turning over only an obsolete machine it no longer wanted. Fire protection was a high priority in the new village.

As the wind-driven flames spread down Main Street from the harness factory, a call for help went out to Cottage City over the telephone line installed only a few months before. Cottage City volunteers responded with one of the town's two new engines, Champion No. 1, and an older hook and ladder. But the response took more than an hour; Cottage City was three miles away and the heavy equipment had to be pulled by firemen on foot.

The clanging church bells brought out scores of Vineyard Haven residents, many carrying the leather fire pails that were required to be kept in every home. Bucket brigades were formed down to the harbor: the men passed the filled pails up the line while women and children passed back the empties. Buckets of water were no match for the flames, nor was the Cottage City apparatus. The fire roared down both sides of Main Street, turning everything into ashes.

The *Cottage City Star* described the scene: "It now swept unchecked, and unchallenged even, along both sides of Main Street, taking all buildings, including the Baptist church, until it reached the end of Main street, beyond the Mansion House." For six frightening hours, until three o'clock in the morning, the flames lit the sky for miles, bringing spectators and volunteers from West Tisbury and Edgartown. When the last building on Main Street, the Mansion House, collapsed into a heap of glowing ash, the bucket brigades and the chemical engine were able to stem the fire's advance. Helping them was the fact that as dawn approached the wind died down and swung to the south, sending the flying sparks back onto smoldering ruins.

During those six hours, more than sixty buildings were totally destroyed, half of them dwellings. Scores of residents were homeless. Destroyed, too, were the harness factory, the Baptist church, the Mansion House, four stables filled with hay, twenty stores, several doctors' offices, the post office, and the Masonic Hall. Remarkably, no one was killed, although one elderly woman, Mrs. James Davis, was so traumatized as she watched her home go up in flames that she died from a heart attack.

It was the most destructive fire in Island history.

Its heroes were the Cottage City firemen, who, after pulling their fire apparatus for three miles, had desperately tried to stem the inferno. Their own village had been obsessed with fear of such a conflagration for years. Now it was happening to their neighbors in a town that had no such fears, at least not enough to have voted to buy its own fire engine.

The Island's most destructive fire was in August 1883, when sixty buildings along
Vineyard Haven's Main Street burned for six hours. The village had no fire department.
The Cottage City firemen dragged their equipment to the fire to do what little they could.
A wind shift at dawn stopped the spreading blaze after it had destroyed the Mansion
House, far right. (Chamberlain photo, MVHS Collections)

At an emergency citizens' meeting the day after the fire, Vineyard
Haven residents passed a resolution: "RESOLVED that the thanks of the citizens of Vineyard Haven are hereby tendered to the officers and members
of the Cottage City fire department, the police, and to the citizens of that
town generally who so promptly came to the aid of our village during the
fire." One Vineyard Haven homeowner and businessman, away during the
blaze, added his thanks: "The undersigned takes this method of expressing
his grateful thanks to those—and more especially to the Cottage City fire
department—whose energetic efforts in the late fire in Vineyard Haven
were the means of saving his dwelling house and shop, during his absence
from home. S. G. BRADLEY."

All together, more than seventy persons were made homeless. Every
Island village came to their relief, along with Nantucket, New Bedford,
and several other mainland cities, including New York and Boston. It was
estimated that seventeen thousand dollars would be needed. Nearly that
amount was contributed.

The enormous destruction renewed the old demands for an adequate supply of water in Cottage City. A letter writer from Brooklyn, no doubt a cottage owner, wrote to the *Star*:

> Now that we have had such a terrible warning, that, together with the fact that our present fire apparatus is insufficient, will furnish a subject worthy of agitation. Take for instance the camp-ground with its numerous dwellings—should a fire gain headway, the consequences would be something awful.
>
> Now let the Selectman take notice of the advantages that Lake Anthony offers, the water of which could be brought to the center of the camp-ground, then a few fire plugs judiciously distributed in the crowded portions would prove efficient in time of need.

A hastily called meeting of Cottage City taxpayers named a committee to advise what should be done. When the committee submitted its report in March 1884, Cottage City citizens were asked, in town meeting, to appropriate fifteen thousand dollars for "the cost of introducing water for fire service and for fire apparatus." Captain Shubael L. Norton made a strong case for approval. There was so much at risk, he said: "[Our] present apparatus is valuable but inadequate to guard from the danger of fire the $1,300,000 worth of property owned in Cottage City—the destruction of which would probably be the ruin of the town."

The fifteen thousand dollars would be spent to lay a ten-inch water main from Meadow (now Sunset) Lake through the campground and along Circuit Avenue, with hydrants at several appropriate places. A pump house would be built at the lake to house a Herreshoff coil boiler of forty horsepower that, in four minutes after firing, would produce steam to drive the pump. A water tower would store water to use until the pump began operating. Another fire engine would be bought, this one with its own steam-driven water pump.

If approved, the money would give Cottage City a fire protection system that would make "our safety from fire as complete as it can be in a place of this size," the *Martha's Vineyard Herald* reassured its readers. The voters approved. The Vineyard Haven fire had taught them a lesson.

Cottage City was the most prosperous village on the Island. Edgartown, the shire town at the eastern end of the Island, was in deep decline. Its major business, whaling, had moved to the Pacific. The town's leading businessman, Sam Osborn Jr., was still sending out small whalers, mostly schooners, into the Atlantic to provide his refinery and candle works with oil. But it was a small operation.

Before the devastating fire Vineyard Haven had more year-round business than Cottage City. But it was small and brought in little money—nothing like the amounts that poured into Cottage City each summer. William Rotch had started a steam-driven gristmill near the steamboat wharf, the first such mill on the Island to use steam. In 1882 the *Star* reported that he was running it "wide open" because business was so good.

Crocker's Harness Works was also busy. It advertised for fifteen women to do light sewing, which would double the number it already employed. Women were just entering the job market. There were concerns about what might happen. Crocker reassured parents and husbands, promising that "they will work in a separate room from the male workers and will be in the company of several of our most respected women."

There was little industry up-Island. Work was mostly agricultural; sheep raising was especially prevalent. In Chilmark and Gay Head the clay deposits provided employment for a few men, but it was seasonal. The Chilmark brick factory employed a handful and it, too, did not operate in winter. By the end of the 1800s it was struggling to survive.

The paint mill, also using clay, had been destroyed by fire in 1866, but it was rebuilt quickly. Its peak years came in the 1870s. One day in November 1872 it shipped more than one thousand barrels of paint, each barrel weighing approximately three hundred pounds. (The schooner was so heavy that it ran aground after leaving the wharf, but it got off at high tide.) Those barrels were filled with a dry pigment of finely ground clay. The mill made from six to eight tons of such paint a day. Clay, separated by color, was placed in large outdoor vats to dry, protected from rain by movable covers similar to those used in salt mills. When completely dry, the clay was taken into the mill and ground between steam-driven grindstones, where it became a fine powder called paint.

Shipped off-Island, the paint's principal use was to color a floor covering then becoming popular, oilcloth, made by coating a loosely woven cloth with the Chilmark pigment liquefied in linseed oil. There were several oilcloth factories on the mainland that bought Chilmark paint. When the more durable linoleum went into production late in the 1800s, the market for oilcloth declined, as did sales of Chilmark paint.

Near the end of the century investors made a final effort to turn up-Island clay into profit. The *Martha's Vineyard Herald* on November 22, 1894, published this item:

> The Menemsha Clay Company of Gay Head, under the management of G. A. Duncan, is making a big stride towards getting out clay at Menemsha Creek, and thus far is establishing the best plant that has as yet been placed on the western part of the Island.
>
> The clay will be carried to a wharf, which will soon be commenced there, on cars weighing two tons, and large quantities are expected to be shipped after the plant is in good working order. Mr. Duncan states that the clay which they are about to mine is superior to any on Gay Head, and compares advantageously with Jersey clay. It will be shipped to Boston and New York principally for the manufacture of fancy fire brick and tiling. This is the company in which confectioner Huyler is extensively interested. At present a gang of eight men and teams are engaged in making a roadbed and other improvements.

What happened after that seems to have been lost to history. We are not sure exactly where the Menemsha clay was to be dug or where the new wharf was built, if it ever was.

We do know that for years clay digging had provided income to the Gay Head Indians, who struggled to survive on small gardens, sheep, and fish. During summer months there was an infusion of money for a few who carried the tourists arriving on excursion steamers to the top of the cliffs in oxcarts. Other Gay Headers, mostly women, began selling their handmade souvenirs in tiny shops atop the cliffs. Nearby there was a restaurant operated by a down-Island woman with Indian help.

Although some excursion boats landing at Gay Head came directly from the mainland, most brought day-trippers from Cottage City. That town, the Island's newest, was where things were happening. Not only was it the first to have adequate fire apparatus, it was also the first with gaslights in its cottages. The gas was supplied by the Cottage City Gas Works from a generating plant in Hiawatha Park. To lay the gas lines from the plant to the town, off-Islanders were brought in, many of them different-looking foreigners: "Our streets present quite a cosmopolitan appearance with gangs of men at work with pick and shovel laying the wrought iron pipe mains that are to carry gas to our cottages." Supervising the project was another off-Islander, a man from Pennsylvania, according to the *Herald*: "The foreman of the Cottage City Gas Works and his wife, from Phoenixville, Penn., are here for the winter."

Vineyard Haven was too much occupied with rebuilding its Main Street after the fire to think about gas lamps. Nor was it yet ready to spend money for water and fire protection. That would have to wait for a private investor. The Vineyard Haven Water Company was formed three years later, in 1887. It was headed by O. G. Stanley of Colorado, who had been visiting Vineyard Haven and saw a moneymaking opportunity on undeveloped West Chop. He convinced some wealthy friends in Boston to invest with him. Among them were blue-blooded Bostonians with such historic names as Peabody, Weld, and Forbes. Together they put up seventy-five thousand dollars and the company was formed. It bought thirty acres of land surrounding two spring-fed ponds at the head of Chappaquonset Pond (now Lake Tashmoo). From there it planned to pump pure, clear Tashmoo springwater into a standpipe, fifty feet high, on high ground west of the village.

The plan involved much more than water. The company had bought a square mile of land on West Chop, where it would create a summer resort unequaled on the East Coast, Stanley said. His vision was boundless. On a tour of the property, he told the editor of the *Herald* that the Island would soon be "one vast resort from Edgartown to Gay Head." There was water enough in Tashmoo to supply fifty thousand residents, and he planned to bring that many to the Island and to sell them water and land. Success was certain. A new day was dawning. Convinced by Stanley, the editor wrote:

> The land fronts mostly on the Sound. . . . [It] rises gradually from the shore, in places with an occasional bluff. . . . From the height the view is magnificent. The other shore, only four miles away, shows clearly, while to the east there is nothing between the eye and the Old World. The lighthouse standing on a small government tract occupies a prominent position. The territory is covered principally with an oak and pine growth and heavy undergrowth. It will be this winter's work to clear out all this and otherwise beautify the place. . . . The territory will undoubtedly be settled by Western people, as they better appreciate ocean resorts than do the people on or near the coast. An effort will be made to bring the people in colonies.

And it would all start with the pure water that poured freely from an Island spring, as it had been doing for thousands of years: "Water from Tashmoo Springs, which an eminent chemist has said is 'good for all uses,' will soon come flowing into the village of Vineyard Haven. This important event marks a new era for the Haven which some of the Vineyard's fondest admirers never dreamed of."

The *Vineyard Gazette* joined in the chorus, pointing out how much more than pure water was involved:

> The syndicate of Boston capitalists who are putting in the water works is made up of the same gentlemen who compose the West Chop Land Company. . . . An enterprise of [this] magnitude would not have been undertaken did not its promoters intend, in their capacity as a land company, to take active measures for extending the demand for water by building up the territory which they hold. . . . The future of Vineyard Haven may be said to look more promising than ever before in its history.

The *Herald*'s editor, no doubt prompted by Stanley, urged the town to wait until spring for any celebration. In the spring, thousands of mainlanders would be planning their summer vacations. That was the time for the headlines to appear. In Oak Bluffs the Reverend C. P. Sheldon, a retired minister who was editing the *Herald* (while the owner, Charles Strahan, was ill), sounded all the bugles:

> Our near neighbors of Vineyard Haven have an opportunity at their command of advertising their place as a summer resort that should not be neglected. The proposed celebration of the introduction of water instead of being local in its character should be made general, and instead of this fall, it should occur next spring, about the time the public are looking about for their summer resting place.
>
> A grand barbecue and clambake at Tashmoo Grove should tempt the inner man. Music by the Fitchburg band and a chorus of 100 voices should intone the universal gladness. Orators with worldwide reputation should voice the beauties and merits of Martha's Vineyard as a watering resort, and the entire affair be gotten up on a scale that would attract the attention of the press.
>
> It might be made a three days' jubilee. . . . The West Chop Land Company would cheerfully join the transportation companies in meeting the expenses and the entire Island would add its mite to help make the celebration a success.

Everyone knows, and everyone says, that all Martha's Vineyard needs is to let the traveling world know of its advantages and they will flock here in crowds. Here is an opportunity that should not be lost. It needs but the will to accomplish it. Will Vineyard Haveners do it?

Vineyard Haven residents ignored the editor's advice, and the grand celebration was held on December 15, 1887. Houses and businesses were decorated with flags and bunting. A demonstration was made of the new water system by firemen spraying two columns of water on the roof of the new harness factory, where the disastrous fire had started a few years before. Residents filled Association Hall to celebrate. Before the program began, the master of ceremonies, Stephen C. Luce, presented a gold watch to O. G. Stanley as a symbol of the village's gratitude.

And there was music: "The musical selections were charmingly rendered, the voices in the trio blending in wonderful harmony, and the solo (to which there was an encore) displaying the rare sweetness of Mrs. Strahan's voice and her command of the upper register." Mrs. Strahan was the wife of the owner of the *Martha's Vineyard Herald,* which praised her sweet

A Colorado summer visitor and real estate developer, O. G. Stanley, built the Lake Tashmoo pumping station in 1887 to provide safe water to home buyers on his West Chop development. Other Vineyard Haven residents benefited as water was piped into their houses and fire hydrants were installed along Main Street. The fire of 1883 had taught them a lesson.

voice. She and her husband, who was unable to attend the celebration because of his illness, frequently sang as a duet at public gatherings.

Lieutenant Governor John Quincy Adams Brackett was the main speaker, preceded by many others. After all the speeches ended, 250 especially chosen guests walked over to Capawock Hall, where a dinner of boned turkey, scalloped oysters, and lobster salad was enjoyed, garnished by more speeches, toasts, and songs. One of the songs, "Tashmoo Spring Water," had been written for the occasion (by whom wasn't said). There was a toast to the "Land Company" and another to the "Water Company," which brought "a lengthy recognition from Alex Porter (one of the stockholders) filled with mirth-producing points." By the time the celebrating had ended, it was past midnight, as Stanley learned "by consulting his new watch." It was, he said, "the end of the most successful celebration ever known on the Vineyard."

The next morning a group of tired but grateful residents went down to the wharf to send the investors off in style: "The Boston capitalists who came to attend the celebration returned on Friday morning, much pleased with their visit to the Island. Lieut. Gov. Brackett shook hands with those who went to the steamer to see the party off."

The waterworks deserved a celebration. Those "Boston capitalists" had spent seventy-five thousand dollars to provide the village with good drinking water and fire protection. Of course, this wasn't simply a gift. Water bills were high and rules were strict. A local joke was that on one hot day a woman offered a passerby a glass of water, but he refused it, saying that he was afraid she would be charged extra for providing water to others. When the town took the company over in 1905, it was a somewhat unfriendly action.

As essential as a water system is to quelling fires, it didn't help save two major hotels in Cottage City when they went up in flames. The system turned out to be of no use. The fires were too far away from any hydrant. The first hotel destroyed by fire was the Sea View House, which burned to the ground in September 1892. Flames were spotted about midnight on a Saturday night. Fortunately, the wind was blowing out to sea, sending a shower of sparks harmlessly into the Sound and saving many nearby buildings. Also destroyed was the footbridge from the Sea View to the wharf, along with an express office and the railroad ticket office at the head of the wharf. Destroyed too were the railroad tracks that ran onto the wharf and the "wye" track on which the locomotive was turned around for its return trip to Katama. The nearby skating rink (now renamed the Casino) could not be saved. The heat from the enormous fire was so intense that the firemen were forced to stand behind improvised wooden shields to get close enough to douse the rink in their vain effort to save it.

The Sea View had been the crown jewel of Cottage City, its most imposing structure. Only twenty years old, it had been built by the Oak Bluffs Land and Wharf Company under its president, Erastus P. Carpenter. By a strange coincidence, he had come to Cottage City that same afternoon and watched his proudest investment go up in flames. His company no longer owned the hotel, having sold it to its manager, Holder M. Brownell of New Bedford, in 1882. Despite Brownell's experience in running hotels on the mainland, it did not prosper. A few years later, in a foreclosure sale, it was bought by the Sea View Hotel and Wharf Company, created for that purpose. In 1889 Colonel Frederick J. Hart, operator of the Cochran Hotel in Washington, D.C., bought the hotel from the Sea View Company, which held the mortgage. The hotel was insured for $39,500, but most of that would go to the mortgage holder. The cause of the fire was never determined, although it was reported that the gas jets in all the rooms were open when the fire started, certainly a suspicious fact in an unoccupied building.

One year after that fire, in 1893, the Highland House, only a few hundred yards from the still-standing ruins of the Sea View, burned to the ground. Like the Sea View's, the blaze was discovered shortly after midnight on a Saturday. Two men returning from a dance in Vineyard Haven spotted flames and sounded the alarm. By the time the fire apparatus arrived, the building was totally engulfed.

Again Cottage City's fire protection system proved of no use. The nearest hydrant was fifteen hundred feet away. The chemical engines were ineffective against the conflagration. Constantly running out of water, they were refilled from nearby Lake Anthony, but no amount of water could have saved the hotel. The fire had gained too much headway. In fact, the firemen didn't even try to save the hotel, directing their hoses instead at the nearby Agassiz Hall, home of the Martha's Vineyard Summer Institute, and saving it.

Like the Sea View, the Highland House had been sold a few years before to new owners, one of whom was Augustus G. Wesley, who owned the Wesley House, which overlooked Lake Anthony. The new owners had renovated the Highland House and, it was said, carried only six thousand

In 1893, one year after the Sea View House fire, the nearby Highland House, on the beach at Oak Bluffs, burned down. It was too far from the nearest hydrant to be saved. Like the Sea View, it had closed for the season. The police started an investigation into possible arson. (MVHS Collections)

dollars in insurance. As the building had been unoccupied for weeks, authorities believed the fire could not have been an accident; it must have been set. The *Vineyard Gazette* agreed: "It is expected that the Selectmen will offer a reward for the conviction of the person or persons who set the fire, for it is the opinion of most of the people that the fire is of incendiary origin, and a thorough investigation will be made. Sheriff Jason L. Dexter left Edgartown for the scene of the fire [in Cottage City] at 3:30 o'clock this morning. . . . An investigation is being made, quietly but vigorously."

The incendiary theory was widely accepted. The *Martha's Vineyard Herald* urged vigilance: "Every man, woman and child in this town should become a private detective to ferret out the incendiary of the recent fires. Numerous summer residents have written urging a reward for the detection of the criminal who set fire to the Highland House."

Pressure to find the "fire bug" intensified two weeks later when John E. Francis, twenty-six, a fireman in the Steamer Company, died from "overexertion" that he'd experienced while fighting the Highland fire. Frightened Cottage City residents hired an all-night lookout to watch for fires from the tower of the Island House on Circuit Avenue. He had a direct electrical connection to the brand-new fire alarm, so there would be no delay in calling out the firemen.

In the months that followed the lookout was busy. With shocking frequency he spotted fires in unoccupied cottages. All were put out by the firemen before major destruction had occurred, but the fear intensified that there was a fire bug in town. Where would he strike next? The suspicion of arson caused the state of Massachusetts to send an investigating team to try to find the culprit. It accomplished nothing, the *Herald's* editor claimed: "It may be imprudent and even unjust of our citizens to condemn, as they do, the detective department connected with the State Fire Marshall for not discovering the perpetrator of the recent fires here, but our people feel perfectly helpless. . . . The fires continue as a regular weekly matter and our people are naturally indignant."

In that same issue, November 15, 1894, under the headline "Another Fire," the *Herald* described a suspicious wagon that was seen driving around Cottage City very late on the night of November 13. Teams weren't usually on the streets at that hour. The village night watchman and two other men followed the team until it crossed the Lagoon bridge and headed for Vineyard Haven.

On the way back to Circuit Avenue, the men smelled smoke and discovered that it was coming from the Wesley House on the edge of the campground. They sounded the alarm, and the firemen quickly put out the fire before much damage could be done. The smoke was so thick that they were forced to lie on the floor as they directed the water from their hoses. Some firemen inhaled so much smoke that they had to be helped from the building. Among them was Manuel Francis, twenty-nine, of the Steamer Company, the older brother of John E. Francis, who had died after the Highland House fire a year before.

It was the third Cottage City hotel to catch fire, each doing so while empty at the end of the season. All three fires began around midnight. All seemed suspicious. The Wesley House fire was so clearly the work of the fire bug that Sheriff Dexter again called for the state to investigate. Something had to be done, as the *Herald* made clear: "For weeks the people of Cottage City have been wild with suppressed excitement at the presence of a fire bug in their midst. Scores of men were secretly tramping the town as detectives, and professional detectives were supposed to be here, and the fact that the fires continued to occur added dread to the mystery, and many families did not undress at all, but slept as if the next moment their place would be on fire."

State Fire Marshal Whitcomb began questioning witnesses, a leading one being Augustus G. Wesley, owner of the hotel. Discrepancies in his testimony about his insurance were uncovered, so Whitcomb called him

Arson was suspected when fire broke out at the Wesley House in Oak Bluffs not long after the Highland House fire. This time the fire department was able to put it out with little damage. Police questioned the owner, Augustus G. Wesley, who soon admitted he had tried to burn his hotel down for the insurance. (MVHS Collections)

back for more questioning. His suspicions confirmed, Marshal Whitcomb told the hotel owner that he would arrest him. Wesley replied: "I am a good Christian, and like many another who has been wrongly accused, I can go to prison."

The popular French Canadian had come to Cottage City as a restaurant cook in 1874, saved his money, and built the hotel on land he leased from the campground. His was a remarkable accomplishment. "Born again" on the campground soon after coming to the Vineyard, he changed his last name from Goupée to Wesley, in memory of Methodism's founder, John Wesley, and the hotel's name was probably more in honor of John Wesley than of himself.

When confronted with his own conflicting statements and other testimony, Augustus Wesley fell apart: "He broke down and wept like a child, saying, 'This has gone far enough, I will confess.'"

He signed this confession:

I, Augustus G. Wesley . . . on November 13, 1894, . . . went from prayer meeting at the Methodist church in Cottage City to the Wesley Hotel, owned by me. I entered the hotel about half-past eight. I saturated some burlap in the closet under the stairs on the second floor with kerosene and wrapped it around a cigar box in which I placed a lighted candle. I did this for the purpose of setting fire to the building and contents in order to collect the insurance on them.

His arrest brought a sigh of relief. The *Herald* said: "Everyone, while lamenting the fall of such a man, involuntarily exclaimed, 'Now we will have no more fires.'"

That week, Manuel Francis, one of the firemen overcome by smoke in the Wesley House fire, died. He and his brother, John, two Portuguese men, were the first Island firemen to die in the line of duty. After Manuel died, the *Herald* said that "the Portuguese were so enraged that it is well that Wesley was secure behind Edgartown jail bars."

Augustus Wesley was guilty of setting fire to his own property, but he was not the town's fire bug. He was securely in prison when a cottage on the Highlands owned by Mrs. Muhlback Duffy caught fire. The blaze began in a closet on the second floor of the unoccupied house. It burned slowly and the firemen put it out after only slight damage was done. It was a botched job, clearly the work of a clumsy arsonist.

Within a few days two sisters, Julia and Lulu Demsell of Cottage City, along with Daniel Lewis of Tisbury, Julia's boyfriend, were arrested. The sisters were "colored," Daniel was white. On Daniel's testimony, he and Julia were indicted and tried for arson in Superior Court. They were found not guilty and released in May 1895. The fire bug was still at large.

Other Vineyard towns had fires, but not with the frequency of Cottage City. The Island's deadliest fire had occurred in Gay Head in March 1882. Mrs. Julia Johnson had left her three children in the house while she visited a neighbor. Somehow a fire broke out and all three children were burned to death, the oldest being only five. The following year, 1883, a Chilmark store owned by Mrs. M. Adams was destroyed by fire on a Saturday night in July. In Eastville a store burned to the ground in March 1884. It was owned by Howes Norris, the editor of the *Cottage City Star.* By the time the fire department from Cottage City got there, it was too late.

Cottage City's worst fire before the Sea View had been in October 1886. It almost brought disaster to the village. An empty stable on the shore of Lake Anthony started to burn, and before fire engines could get there the fire had destroyed several other sheds along the lake and was threatening to spread up Circuit Avenue. Fortunately, the firemen arrived just in time to prevent the flames from spreading to the Oak Bluffs Hotel and the Town Hall at the foot of Circuit Avenue. It was the first time water from the new hydrants was used to prevent greater disaster.

No doubt bad times were a factor in the hotel fires. The country was in a depression. There were strikes and riots by unemployed workers. Coxey's Army, a band of a hundred angry men from Ohio, marched to the Capitol in Washington in 1894. Arriving there, now four hundred strong, they were arrested for trespassing on the Capitol grounds. Their long march had been in vain. It was a time filled with frustration.

The Cottage City fires had made insurance companies suspicious, but their investigators were unable to find evidence to arrest anyone. The only convicted arsonist was Augustus Wesley, who was already in jail and couldn't have been responsible for the recent fires. Hotel fires didn't end with the Wesley House. In June 1898, on the Oak Bluffs side of the Lagoon, the Prospect House burned to the ground. Then in July 1906 the Innisfail Hotel (variously called Oklahoma Hall and Villa Bristhall) was destroyed by a raging brush fire. It was empty at the time, as were all the other hotels that were destroyed.

Edgartown had no major fires. It was also spared any serious effects from the 1893 economic downturn, probably because it had benefited very little from the boom that had preceded it. For years the town had been struggling, kept alive mostly by "old" money. Its fancy houses had been built before the Civil War with whaling money, not by newly rich entrepreneurs, as was the case in Cottage City.

Then in 1891 sleepy Edgartown seemed to be awakening. Three investors, headed by Edgartown's physician-druggist Dr. Thomas J. Walker, an immigrant from Canada, saw an opportunity at the end of North Water Street, then the outskirts of the village. Joining Dr. Walker were a minister named Townsend, from off-Island, and one of the Edgartown Mayhews. They bought some pastureland at the end of North Water Street and built the Harbor View Hotel. It was the town's first serious attempt to join in the resort business. A hotel had been built at Katama earlier, but it was so far from the village that neither it nor the railroad that was built to connect it to Cottage City had done much for Edgartown.

The building of the Harbor View was the most encouraging event the town had seen in years, but it was a gamble. Its major attraction was the spectacular view of the outer harbor and Cape Poge on the tip of Chappaquiddick. Directly in front of the hotel was the new harbor lighthouse on its man-made island. Beyond the view, the hotel offered little: no nearby parks with daily band concerts, no bathhouses one could walk to, no skating rink or casino with day and night entertainment. There wasn't even the excitement of the steamboat arriving four times a day. Edgartown was a quiet place, unlike Cottage City, where something was going on all the time.

The hotel's first manager was J. W. Drew, who ran it during its first year. Patronage at the new hotel soon declined, and the three owners were worried. Drew was replaced by William D. Carpenter, the son of Erastus Carpenter of Oak Bluffs and Katama fame. The young man had been a manager of his father's Sea Cliff Inn on Nantucket. From there he moved to the Vineyard to take over the failing Mattakessett Lodge at Katama, also started by his father. He was out of a job when the lodge was sold at auction to the Old Colony Railroad for seventy-two hundred dollars. Included in the sale was the run-down wharf in Katama Bay, several unoccupied cottages, a clambake house, and about five hundred acres of farmland. The Mattakessett Lodge alone had cost thirty thousand dollars to build twenty years earlier.

It was a poor time to open a new hotel. Businesses were failing in great numbers. By June 1894 two hundred of the nation's railroads had gone bankrupt. Times were so bad that the Island's only manufacturing plant, the Crocker Harness Works in Vineyard Haven, closed down for the first time. Still, there were investors who believed that the Vineyard, with its resort economy, was immune to such cycles.

One group of such investors built Makonikey Inn in 1893, the year the depression began. Located on a high bluff overlooking Vineyard Sound in an area known as Chickemoo, it was the Island's first hotel with its own electric-generating plant. Four or five cottages were built on the property to attract buyers for the two hundred lots that had been laid out. It had its own beach. The developers were all from the mainland, including the Reverend Elmer H. Capen, president of Tufts College.

The inn had twenty rooms, an electric light in each, and bathrooms on every floor (probably with water closets, although that was not advertised). There was a bathhouse in the rear of the hotel, which provided a choice of fresh- or saltwater bathing. (Two of its porcelain tubs have sur-

Edgartown's first major hotel, the Harbor View on North Water Street, was built in 1893 by a group of local investors headed by Dr. Joseph J. Walker. At first it was only the building at left, and it came close to shutting down during the depression of that time. In the early 1900s business improved and the addition at the right was built. Dr. Walker bought out the other investors. The hotel was owned by his family for many years. (MVHS Collections)

vived.) Designed for a discerning clientele, the inn had three private dining rooms in addition to the main salon. Steamboats from West Chop and the mainland carried guests directly to the new two-hundred-foot wharf in the Sound.

Great expectations: more than one hundred thousand dollars had been invested. But problems began soon after the Makonikey opened. According to Henry Beetle Hough in his *Summer Resort,* shortly after the hotel's opening, Italian workers who had not been paid stormed into the lobby to protest. Frightened, the guests hurriedly packed their bags and left. Hough wrote that the inn closed its doors on that day, August 24, 1893, and never reopened. But that is incorrect (as the story about the Italian workers may be also). Advertisements in the *Herald* show that the inn was still operating in 1895 and 1896.

The Makonikey never was solvent; it never was able to pay its bills. At the end of the 1896 season, bondholders took it over and sold it to a Maine lumber dealer (one of the creditors). He built more cottages on the property but was unable to sell them. The entire place then was vacant for a number of years. Early in the 1900s, George Mathews, a retired preacher, and his son, planning to make bricks from the clay on the property, built a kiln in one of the maintenance buildings. The plan was to fire the kiln with lignite from nearby bogs. But they soon discovered there wasn't enough heat in the peat to run the kiln and their plan was abandoned.

The clay again became of use when Andreas Andreassian—the "crazy Armenian potter," some called him—moved into one of the empty buildings and began turning artistic pottery. (It is said that some still exists.) But, like the others, he soon was forced by economics to shut down.

In 1913 the YWCA leased the property to open Camp Makonikey for Girls. It continued to be used as such until 1919. Today the structure that dominated the high bluff east of Lambert's Cove for years has disappeared, its site marked only by traces of stone foundations, a couple of porcelain bathtubs, and a few steel hoops and pipes from the old water tower. The building was demolished but not in an organized way. Its removal was the result of the gradual "borrowing" of wood by neighboring residents for their summer homes. Fine paneling and trim from the hotel's interior are said to adorn nearby homes today. The spirit of the Makonikey lives.

A common thread running through all these hotel investments is that the money came almost entirely from off-Island. Few were built with Vineyard money. The large hotels—the Sea View, the Highland House, the Prospect House, and others—were owned by off-Islanders, as were the water, gas, and electric companies. Vineyarders seemed little inclined to speculate. Vineyard money went into Edgartown's Harbor View Hotel, but some of its financing came from off-Island. Shares were sold to a few Edgartown residents at one hundred dollars each. The local money didn't seem to help. The Harbor View struggled to get through the depressed years of the 1890s. In 1895 Carpenter, the manager, was replaced by a retired school superintendent from Winthrop, F. A. Douglas, who put out a rather elegant brochure the next year, which opened with two stanzas from Longfellow's "The Secret of the Sea." The brochure then went on to describe the hotel from which guests would, in Longfellow's words, "gaze upon the sea [with] all the old romantic legends"; it had "bath and toilet rooms on each floor; pure spring water; gas, and electric bells, etc., etc. All are outside rooms, well ventilated. . . . A cottage of twelve rooms, beautifully furnished, with all modern conveniences is connected with the hotel for parties desiring the seclusion and quiet of cottage life. . . . Rates, $2.50 to $3.50 per day [apparently with meals]."

Douglas was helped as the national economic climate improved. Soon the Harbor View had doubled in size, even installing a tennis court on the front lawn for its vacationing guests. The Kelley House, closer to downtown, was the town's oldest hotel, having opened in 1748. It operated all year and was favored by businessmen.

Edgartown was eager to help promote its first resort hotel. In one fun-filled weekend celebrating the hotel's opening, the village put on footraces along Main Street, a high-jump competition, a baseball game in a field just past the county jail, rowing races, a tub race in the harbor, and a greased pig chase at some place not recorded. That evening the Harbor View Hop filled Starbuck Neck with music and gaiety. Edgartown was shedding its stuffy dignity. It was becoming a summer resort.

While Edgartown was boosting its new hotel, Cottage City residents demanded that something be done for their town, once the center of everything. It needed a new hotel, they said. A citizens' meeting asked the town to put up money to replace the destroyed Sea View and Highland Houses. If the town would put up some money, individual citizens would add more. A fine, new hotel could then be built and turned over, rent-free, to a competent manager.

Philip Corbin, a wealthy Cottage City summer resident from Connecticut, when asked to help finance the project, said that building a hotel is something the steamboat companies and the year-round residents should be doing—not summer people who have hometowns of their own to support.

Colonel Frederic J. Hart, the owner of the Sea View when it burned down, planned to replace it, or so he said, with a much larger and fancier hotel. A romantic, he published a booklet soon after the fire entitled "Lover's Rock, a Summer Idyl," containing a poem he had written of a romance that began when a lonely man staying at the old Sea View rescued a widow who had fallen off the pier. In rescuing her, he so overexerted himself that he collapsed and almost died on the beach near Lover's Rock. Fortunately, he revived and lived to marry the widow he had rescued. They live happily ever after in her cottage in Cottage City. At the end of his booklet Colonel Hart included a drawing of the new Sea View House to be built atop the bluff just north of the steamboat wharf. A magnificent structure it would be, or so he wrote:

> Three hundred feet long, facing the east and Vineyard Sound . . . every
> room looks directly out on the water. . . . Music room and parlors . . . with
> three great fire-places. . . . Reading rooms and card rooms, ladies' and

A huge glacial boulder, called an erratic, managed to find its way onto sandy Oak Bluffs beach. The name "Lover's Rock" was painted on it in bold letters, making it a popular subject for snapshots. This one was probably taken in the early 1900s.
(J. N. Chamberlain photo, MVHS Collections)

gents' billiard rooms flank the parlors. . . . The ball room, in the form of a half circle, opens into the lobby, utilizing [it] as a promenade for the dancers and the guests. The entire building will be lit by electric lights. Balconies at the end of each broad hall provide an easy descent to the ground below, forming perfect fire escapes.

After building up expectations of seeing a magnificent new Sea View that summer, he concluded: "I announce, with great regret, that this charming house, the best on the Atlantic coast, will not be ready for this season. The severe winter and many attendant delays have made it impossible. . . . Next year, friends, our house and grounds will be perfect."

It was never built. Hart seems to have disappeared back into his Washington hotel, leaving Cottage City to struggle with the job of clearing the still-visible ruins of his burned-down Sea View and the skating rink. (A second Sea View House was built some years later, but it was an economy version of the original, located on a different site, farther south, adjacent to Waban Park.)

When Cottage City residents got no response to their demand for a new hotel, they asked that at least something be done about the Sea View ruins. They were not an inviting sight for incoming tourists, the *Herald* said: "Picturesque ruins are well enough, in their way, in the Eternal City, but the ruins of the Sea View and the Rink will never strike the sober tourist as being that sort of remains. Let's bury them."

Some cleaning up had been done by the steamboat company when it rebuilt its fire-damaged wharf. The replacement looked cheap and dowdy, the *Herald* complained, but with age, it hoped it might become more picturesque.

Cottage City had more than ruins to worry about: George C. Abbott had come back. It had almost forgotten about him after its initial trauma over his purchase of the parks. The *Herald* was even joking about his plans. In November 1885 and in several later issues, it referred to him as "poor Abbott and his sheep-pasture speculators." To be sure, the parkland he had bought was once "sheep pasture," but he had plans to fill those acres with houses, large houses overlooking the ocean. It was nothing to joke about.

Abbott was the Boston lawyer who, with his partner and financial backer, Neal, had bought the parks and a number of avenues in Cottage City from the Oak Bluffs Land and Wharf Company for seventy-five hundred dollars in the spring of 1885, after the village would not take them as a gift. That fall Sea View Avenue was widened under a previous plan, which took land from the water side of Ocean Park—land then belonging to Abbott. He demanded reimbursement. The town offered him two hundred dollars, a nominal sum such as was customary in street-widening projects.

A ridiculous amount, Abbott responded. He sued the village for $7,000. In the trial the jury awarded him $2,545. The town appealed. The appeals judge, Oliver Wendell Holmes Jr., set aside the award. A second trial was held and a hung jury resulted. Things were looking better for Cottage City. Maybe Abbott wasn't a problem after all.

But George Abbott wouldn't go away. He still was determined to make a profit from his investment in the parks; he suggested to one local resident a simple solution: there were thirty-eight cottages bordering Ocean Park, all owned by well-to-do summer residents, and if each gave him $1,000, a total of $38,000, and the village added $7,500, he would return all the parks to the village. His profit: $38,000.

In another effort, he told those with cottages around Hartford Park, a

Ocean Park was (and still is) the crown jewel of Oak Bluffs. When George Abbott of Boston bought it and the other parks, there was a public outcry. A lawsuit settled the matter. Abbott had bought the parks, but he couldn't build on them or prevent the public from using them. (MVHS Collections)

tree-covered oasis south of Ocean Park, that he would sell them the park for $4,000. Nobody seemed willing to legalize the concept that Abbott, a private citizen, could "own" the parks. They belonged to the public and should forever remain that way. It was wrong for him to turn them into profit—some even considered it to be blackmail.

Abbott had two strong Vineyard allies in his struggle: Captain Grafton Collins and Captain Ira Darrow, both Edgartown residents. Collins did spend summers in a cottage he owned on Ocean Park, being one of only a few year-round Islanders who lived in the new town. (Fewer than 10 percent of Oak Bluffs lots were owned by year-round Islanders.) Both Collins and Darrow had opposed the secession of Cottage City in 1880. When Carpenter made them directors in his Oak Bluffs Land and Wharf Company, he was hoping they would bring supporters from Edgartown for his plans for Oak Bluffs. It hadn't worked out that way.

Captain Collins never liked Carpenter, the off-Islander who had bought land from Captain Shubael L. Norton and created that upstart Oak Bluffs. Because of him, Edgartown had lost tax revenues and had fallen into decline when the economy's engine shifted to Oak Bluffs. Captain Collins, whose house in Edgartown overlooked Collins Beach (named for his fam-

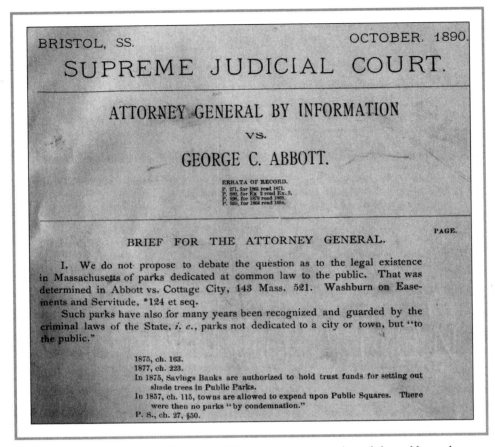

When Massachusetts sued George Abbott over his ownership of the public parks, the trial was a long one. Its transcript covered more than a thousand pages. Included in the testimony of scores of witnesses are many facts that are useful to historians.
(MVHS Collections)

ily), took Abbott's side. He was quoted as saying, "All [Carpenter] wants is to get a big name and make himself popular with the non-residents."

As one of the founders, Collins owned a large block of stock in the Martha's Vineyard Railroad. He sold them to Abbott, which, when added to those he already owned, allowed him to take control of the railroad away from Carpenter, its president. It was a clear victory for Abbott.

His power-grabbing moves so disturbed residents of Cottage City that fifty of them pledged one hundred dollars each to finance a legal battle against Abbott's claim to the parks. Two of the longest civil trials in Vineyard history were the result. The first, held in Edgartown in June 1887, ended when the jury, after deliberating all night, was unable to reach a verdict. A second trial was held in the summer of 1888 in the Bristol County Courthouse, in New Bedford, before a master of the court. There would be no jury to persuade this time. Transcripts of the trial fill more than one thousand pages.

The case against Abbott was headed by the state's attorney on behalf of the village of Cottage City. He set out to prove that from the start the parks had been dedicated to the public and therefore could not be controlled by a private individual. Legally, the land could be sold, but the buyer could not deny the public its use. That was the state's argument.

Abbott was his own principal witness. His testimony took two days and covered one hundred pages of the transcript. He insisted that the parklands had not been set aside for public use by the Oak Bluffs Company. Hiawatha Park, he argued, was used for the gasworks and the electric works, both privately owned, and there was even a piggery on Petaluma Park. That didn't sound like dedicated public land to him. He didn't point out that at the time those parks were at the outskirts of the village and of no interest to the public, unlike the centrally located Ocean and Waban parks. Abbott needed to prove that those two in-town parks had not been set aside for the public.

He called on James W. Tufts, the wealthy soda fountain manufacturer who owned a summer cottage on Waban Park and had built the first two roque courts there. Tufts couldn't remember ever asking for permission; he just built the courts on the park in front of his house. But, Abbott pressed, "Weren't they exclusively for you and your friends?" Tufts had to agree. He admitted that he locked up the sheds he had built to house the equipment when he left each fall. Abbott claimed that proved the parks were not for all, but only for the few.

Most of the witnesses Abbott called were Edgartown residents who had opposed the separation of Cottage City from the old town. They didn't like anything about the new village. The state's attorney, T. M. Stetson, pointed out that bias:

> In view of the fact that nearly every witness called by Abbott, who undertakes to testify anything in his favor (*viz.*, Collins, Donaldson, Ripley, Marchant, Dunham, R. L. Pease, John Pease, Dean, and Monroe) are life-long residents of Edgartown, seven miles off, it may be worthwhile to call attention to the hostility that has existed between Edgartown and

Cottage City ever since the new town was set off from the old in 1880 and Edgartown lost the revenue of its large tax list.

To dispute the testimony of those "life-long residents of Edgartown," Stetson called on summer residents who had bought land from Carpenter and built expensive cottages. All emphasized that they never would have done so had they not been assured that the parks were to be permanent. Testifying were such wealthy men as Philip Corbin, Timothy Stanley, Erastus P. Carpenter, George M. Landers, and Dr. Harrison Tucker, owners of large summer homes on Ocean Park. They testified that the public had unrestricted use of the parks. Abbott's case was weak. He testified that the public had at times been denied access to the parkland. But it was pointed out that in those few cases the ban had been temporary; it had been instituted only to protect the grass from damage.

On September 21, 1891, the judge ruled against Abbott: the parkland had been dedicated to the public from the beginning by the Oak Bluffs Land and Wharf Company. Abbott might "own" the parks, but he could not keep the public from using them and could not sell them as building lots.

Cottage City was jubilant; it celebrated with a bonfire in Ocean Park, followed by fireworks and a parade led by the Cottage City Drum Corps. But the village had not heard the last of George C. Abbott. He brought suit for damages of $225,000 against the Oak Bluffs Company. The suit was denied. His one remaining weapon was his control of the Martha's Vineyard Railroad. It wasn't a strong weapon, as the railroad was struggling to survive.

The railroad's reason for being, you will recall, was to carry tourists to the new resort at Katama, a favorite place of Erastus Carpenter's. Its hotel, Mattakessett Lodge, never had been profitable, but the clambake pavilion did make money and had just been rebuilt. On the new pavilion's opening day in 1892, the railroad sold excursions that included a round-trip from Cottage City to Katama and back and a genuine "Rhode Island clambake and shore dinner," with dancing to the six-piece Katama orchestra—all for one dollar!

It was the railroad's last gasp. While it still ran as far as Edgartown, the following year it dropped the trip to Katama, except for "special excursions when called for." In 1896 it shut down completely and put its tiny rolling stock of one locomotive, four passenger cars, and one baggage car up for sale. The locomotive was first named *Edgartown* and soon renamed *Active* (the name it is remembered by). It had just been rechristened *South Beach* in a futile effort to revive Katama. The little engine with the huge smoke-stack was sold off-Island and ended up as a switch engine in a freight yard.

When the locomotive left the Island, it steamed down Edgartown's Main Street on temporary tracks laid in short sections ahead of its journey to the steamboat wharf. There it was loaded on a schooner for the mainland. A few sad townspeople gathered to watch it leave. The end of the railroad marked the end of another of Erastus P. Carpenter's dreams. He had created it to carry the public to Katama, a place he loved for its remoteness and its quiet, punctuated only by the pounding surf. The quiet and the surf survived. The railroad did not.

Nearly as remote as the Mattakessett Lodge, the Prospect House on Lagoon Heights, west of Cottage City, found a novel way to stay in business. It was leased to a professor of music, Dr. Eben Tourjée of the New England Conservatory of Music in Boston, who used it in summer for his pupils, all girls. He rented a few extra rooms to carefully chosen guests; the girls had to be protected: "The Doctor has been most fortunate in obtaining such a charming home for the young ladies of the Conservatory. . . . The House is open to a select few in addition."

On the Tisbury side of the Lagoon, Oklahoma Hall, with its cottages, took a similar course in the summer of 1883. It was leased to a Canadian lady who ran a summer school of theater: "A woman from Montreal has taken the entire Oklahoma estate for the summer. She intends to set aside one cottage as a summer school of the arts, with recitals, etc. The hotel will be run by her in peace and quiet."

She hoped to fill the hotel with guests seeking "peace and quiet," whom she would entertain with recitals and theatricals performed by her students. Her venture didn't last long. Summer visitors were not looking for what she offered; they wanted more excitement. They found it in Cottage City, the Island's center of activity during the second half of the 1800s.

Probably the biggest excitement during these years came in March 1883, when Samuel W. Vincent dug up three human skeletons on the shore at Caleb's Pond on Chappaquiddick island. He was building a dike to form a herring run when he made the shocking discovery. The skeletons were clearly Indians. One was estimated to have been seven feet tall and was perfect in every detail, including, the news account said, a complete set of teeth. We do not know where the bones ended up. The report said only that Vincent had carefully removed them from their graves.

While Edgartown village was abuzz with talk about Vincent's discovery of ancient bones, Cottage City was looking to the future. This was ten years before the disastrous hotel fires that would set it back. There seemed to be no end to its summer prosperity. It may have been the first town in southeastern Massachusetts to have electricity. A small generating plant was built at Eastville near the store of Otis Foss, its two generators driven by a steam engine. The electricity was fed to arc lamps mounted on poles at a number of street intersections and in front of the largest hotels. During that first year interior electric lighting was rare. Only the ballroom of the Sea View and the huge floor of the skating rink had interior arc lights. Arc lights required red-hot carbon conductors, too dangerous and fume-producing for interior use. Soon the incandescent bulb would arrive and interior lighting would become commonplace.

Electricity brought the kinds of problems that today are labeled "not in my back yard." Residents of the Highlands, annoyed by the noise of the steam engine and the generators, demanded that the plant be moved. Such complaints and the company's shaky economic condition made its future doubtful. The *Cottage City Star* worried:

> What is to be done about the electric light this summer? It proved such an unqualified boon last season and was so universally indorsed that it seems a crying shame that we should forgo it now because of the lack of interest of those who should have the matter most at heart. . . . There should not be the slightest hesitancy in taking measures for its introduction here throughout every summer season. The company of last year failed to clear anything because the cost of running fifty electric lights amounted to enough to eat up all the profits; but the expense of maintaining a hundred lights would be very materially less in proportion. . . . The whole town should be pushing through to the consummation of the establishment here of a hundred or more electric lights. It would boom the place wonderfully.

The *Star*'s editor need not have worried. Fresh money arrived in 1884, along with an off-Island expert, William H. Leslie, to supervise an expansion. The plant was moved to Hiawatha Park, out of the village, safely away from complaining neighbors. Two new generators were ordered, but Leslie was so eager that he started operating before the second had arrived: "The electric light was started up Thursday night for the first time this season. As only one dynamo was operating only half the lights could be fed. Full operation expected next week."

By the following week there were forty-five arc lights burning in Cottage City, six of them in the campground. The resort was truly a fairyland, ablaze with light. When the skating rink opened for the season, its new tin roof freshly painted a deep red and the birch floor sanded to perfection, it had eight new electric lights inside. A minor glitch developed that first week: "The failure of the electric light for a short interval was quickly remedied by lighting the gas jets. . . . The rink is now open for the season, three sessions a day, with the new octagonal floor."

In 1884 the Cottage City Water Company laid eighteen hundred feet of cast-iron pipe from its Meadow Lake pump to supply two hydrants in the campground and five more on Circuit Avenue. A number of summer residents, including Dr. H. A. Tucker and Philip Corbin on Ocean Park, had the water line extended to their homes. The water was not safe to drink and was used for cooking and bathing, perhaps even for the water closets then coming into favor among the wealthy.

These wealthy summer residents were pushing toward a solution of the problem that had troubled Cottage City for years: what to do about its "sanitaries," as privies were called. The board of health had set up strict regulations that required leak-proof vaults, which could be cleaned only at specified times, their contents dumped in a town-controlled area by licensed haulers. The town bought a leakproof wagon to haul the fecal matter to a then-remote dump site near Farm Pond. It was most sensitive to the problems brought by its large summer population and knew that any outbreak of disease traceable to sanitation would be devastating to business.

There was growing objection to privies for another reason: they were an aesthetic disaster. They just didn't belong in such a lovely fairyland. If they couldn't be eliminated, they must be hidden. The *Star* editorialized: "Property owners should improve the rears of their cottages by enclosing outhouses with lattice work or fences and as far as possible hiding from public view everything offensible to the eye."

With the Island's increasing dependency on tourists, there came a greater sensitivity to public opinion. That became apparent when a subject that had been avoided for years came back into the news. In August 1884 the *Cottage City Star* briefly mentioned what would become a much bigger story: "Mr. F. Z. Maguire of Washington, D.C., is in town, searching various town records and county records, for the purpose of obtaining information and tracing causes of the cases of the deaf and dumb mutes."

Frank Z. Maguire was a private secretary to Professor Alexander Graham Bell, long a student of deafness and now the famous inventor of the telephone. He had sent Maguire to the Island to do some research. Maguire managed to fit some fun into his work schedule, the *Cottage City Chronicle* reported:

> Messrs. Frank Z. Maguire of Washington, D.C., Frank B. Skinner and Geo. N. Randall of Philadelphia, who have been guests at the Sea Side House in Edgartown, the past week, circumnavigated the Vineyard last Friday with Capt. John O. Norton as skipper, leaving the pier at 6 in the morning and arriving back at the point of departure at 6 the following morning—the quickest passage of the kind on record.
>
> The only stop was at Noman's Land at about 4 P.M. where the party remained a couple of hours while Mr. Maguire made some inquiries concerning deaf mutes there. Mr. Maguire who is investigating this subject generally, has today gone to Chilmark for more information.

Deaf-mutism on the Island was, of course, not news to residents, who treated it in a very matter-of-fact manner. Most deaf-mutes were in Chilmark, living normal lives as storekeepers and farmers. The hearing residents had a general knowledge of a simple sign language, adequate for basic communications. Deafness was a handicap, but not a major one, Islanders thought. Still, it was not something they were pleased to see in the headlines. It might scare away summer people worried about "catching" it.

The story had first made headlines in 1860 and surfaced again in 1869, when the *New Bedford Standard* made reference to deaf-mutes in an article about the Indians of the Vineyard; the remarks were totally unrelated to the theme: "On the west end of the Island, where there are more deaf mutes among the white population than anywhere else in the country, as far as we know, there have never been any deaf mutes among the Indians, living side by side with the white brethren of Chilmark and Tisbury."

Newspaper interest in the subject then died out, but now with the arrival of Bell's researcher, it was back. And with Bell's famous name connected to it, the news would soon become national. Maguire was seeking answers to one question: why were there more deaf-mutes on the Island than elsewhere? His employer, now comfortable with the income from his telephone company, had returned to his lifelong work in hearing and speech defects.

That interest went back to his youth. He was the son of a doctor in Scotland who had studied the anatomy of speech. Young Alec, as he was called, continued the work as a teacher of speech, helping those with speaking impairments. He saw that speaking and hearing were related. Because they couldn't hear sounds, deaf persons were unable to imitate the way words were spoken. Bell was teaching those who couldn't hear how to use their throat muscles and vocal cords to create intelligible sounds. He couldn't help them hear, but he could help them speak.

When he emigrated to Massachusetts from his birthplace in Scotland, he set up a school for speech therapy in Boston. He saw that deaf-mutism was inherited, but erratically. He wondered why that was. Were there other causes? This was before Gregor Mendel's genetic theories were well known in America, so Bell had no knowledge of dominant and recessive genes.

He and his several assistants pored over census records to discover where deaf-mutes lived so they could interview them. The records showed many more of them, as a percentage of population, on Martha's Vineyard than the average. Bell wondered why. He wanted to accept the idea of heredity, but it was flawed. There were too many cases of deaf-mutes marrying and having hearing children. He looked for other reasons, even speculating that, since most of the deaf-mutes were in Chilmark, clay might be a factor. It might be caused by the drinking water from wells driven near the clay beds.

When Maguire got back to Washington, he no doubt told Bell that he had met the man who knew the most about the genealogy and history of the Vineyard. He was Richard L. Pease, clerk of the county court and Island historian. In 1885 and again in 1887 Bell visited the Island to meet Pease. Together they went to Gay Head. They found there were no deaf-mutes among the Indians who lived atop the largest bed of clay on the Vineyard. The clay theory was dropped.

Bell and Pease came to a financial agreement: in exchange for Pease's help and for access to his notes, Bell agreed to finance (with up to twenty-five hundred dollars) the publication of Pease's history of the Island, a book he had been working on for years. Bell would also receive help from Pease's daughter, Harriet, the Island's most active genealogist. It was a friendly arrangement.

The next year, on September 9, 1888, Pease died of cancer after only a brief illness. When Bell learned of it, he returned to Edgartown to meet with the widowed Mrs. Pease. The financial arrangement was discussed. When he returned to Washington, Bell wrote to Mrs. Pease:

In return for all the information [your late husband] could give me concerning the Vineyard Ancestry of Deaf-Mutes, I was to pay the expenses of publishing his History of Martha's Vineyard—my liability being limited to $2500. Now, Mrs. Bell suggests that I simply pay you this amount . . . and you and your daughters [will] absolve me from all further responsibility. . . . You, of course, are to allow me full access to Mr. Pease's Manuscripts until my work upon the Deaf-Mutes of Martha's Vineyard is ready for the press. . . . The money would be raised by the sale of stock or bonds of the American Bell Telephone Company and perhaps you would prefer the investments themselves at the market price, instead of cash. You better consult some businessman.

We don't how Mrs. Pease chose to receive the funds, but it is likely that she took it in cash. Had she chosen stock in the new Bell telephone company and held it, her family would have become very rich. (Had she invested the cash in Vineyard land her heirs would have done well also.) Most likely, she used it for her living expenses, as she did not die wealthy.

The Martha's Vineyard Historical Society has copies of several pages of notes in Bell's handwriting, written before he visited the Island. They are headed "Martha's Vineyard, Gleanings from the Sixth Census [1840]." One page is headed: "Total Deaf & Dumb." It reads: "None in Edgartown; 5 in Tisbury; 11 in Chilmark. Total 16." Another page states there were 12 deaf-mutes on the Island in the 1830 census, all in Chilmark.

After his first Island visit, Bell presented a preliminary paper entitled "The Deaf-Mutes of Martha's Vineyard" at the National Academy of Sciences in 1886. An article was later published in the *American Annals of the Deaf and Dumb* that summarized the report (with a few new comments by Bell):

Nearly all the deaf-mutes of the Vineyard are natives of the little town of Chilmark, a scattered hamlet having in 1880 a population of nearly five hundred people, of whom twenty were deaf-mutes, which is in the proportion of one deaf-mute in twenty-five inhabitants. [Footnote signed A.G.B.: "Only two deaf-mutes were reported on the Island outside of Chilmark and West Tisbury, although the bulk of the population lies outside."]

Various causes have been suggested for this extraordinary phenomenon, such as heredity, consanguinity of parents, and the geological character of that portion of the Island, which is undulating—while the rest of the Island is flat—and which has a subsoil of clays of peculiar character. . . . But the cause of the prevalence of deafness in this locality has not yet been established beyond question. Dr. Bell showed by elaborate and ingenious genealogical charts the curious relationship by blood and marriage that exists among all these families, and the probability, though not yet absolute certainty, of their being descended from common ancestors belonging to the families containing deaf-mutes who resided in Chilmark and Tisbury over two hundred years ago; also their connection with the large deaf-mute families of Sandwich and Pittsfield, Mass., and Winthrop, New Sharon, Hartford, Fayette, and Sebec, in Maine.

Thomas Hart Benton, the famed artist, had a summer home on Menemsha Pond in Chilmark. Living nearby were a number of the deaf-mutes made famous earlier by Alexander Graham Bell. Among them was Josie West, whose portrait Benton painted in the 1920s. It is owned by the Martha's Vineyard Historical Society.

The article then quoted from a letter Bell had written to the editor of the journal while the article was in preparation: "My present investigation consists simply in the collection of a mass of genealogical material relating to the ancestry of the deaf. It has kept on widening to such an extent that I now perceive that the labor of tracing all the ramifications is too great to be undertaken by a single individual, unless he is prepared to devote his whole life to the subject—which I am not." With that admission of a weakening interest, Bell gave up his work on the deaf-mutes of Martha's Vineyard, taking up a new and more exciting interest: flying machines. It was the time of the Wright brothers and Bell was designing more efficient wing structures.

Six years after Bell's last visit to the Island, a sensational article appeared in the *Boston Sunday Herald* of January 20, 1895, datelined Squibnocket. Its headline read: "Deaf and Dumb in the Village of Squibnocket, Where One Person in Every Four Is Speechless." The reporter described a "peculiarly afflicted people," set apart from the rest of the Island: "In this isolated New England community of 146 persons, there are 36 men, women and children born deaf and dumb—almost exactly 25 percent of the population. In five families, out of 28 children, 15 are deaf."

The writer had been driven to Squibnocket from Vineyard Haven in a carriage whose driver was "a strapping big, blue-eyed fellow, uncommonly well developed physically, uncommonly bright mentally, but not able to tell me much about Chilmark which lives so much to itself and by itself that even the other Islanders have only the most general ideas of the state of affairs there existing."

The "uncommonly bright" driver might not have known much about Chilmark, but he knew enough to point out that the driver of the buggy passing them was from Chilmark. She was, he said, "one of the Adams sisters, those that used to travel with Tom Thumb and his wife." Knowingly or not, the driver had added another twist in the sensational story of a peculiar, isolated people in a small area of Chilmark called Squibnocket. Its publication brought a quick response from Florence Mayhew, who lived in Squibnocket. She corrected some of the writer's "facts":

> Chilmark has about 400 inhabitants, only 13 of them are deaf mutes. Three of the 13 are not natives of the place, but have married Chilmark men at a school [for the deaf] at Hartford. . . . Of the four families in which both father and mother are deaf mutes, there is but one deaf and dumb child or grandchild.

The dwarf strain in the Adams family does not come from the Chilmark branch, but from an entirely separate line.

Summer visitors can testify to finding Chilmark a panacea for nerves and tired brains, and the Chilmark people are hospitable even to unreliable reporters.

That same year the story continued to circulate when a scholarly journal published in Boston, the *Arena,* carried an article by S. Millington Miller entitled "The Ascent of Man." A bound volume of that year's issues is at the Martha's Vineyard Historical Society. "Chilmark's Tainted Stock" was written boldly on its spine by its previous owner. The first sentences in Miller's article emphasize that thought, hardly something the Vineyard wanted the country to read:

> There is a secluded hamlet on the Island of Martha's Vineyard called Chilmarth [*sic*]. One out of every twenty-five of its inhabitants is deaf. Many are blind and some are idiots. . . . Eleven years ago, Dr. Abraham [*sic*] Bell, the inventor of the Bell telephone, published a series of statistics showing that one-third (and he tells me that the ratio is actually much higher) of the children resulting from the intermarriage of deaf mutes are congenitally deaf; that such marriages are giving rise to a deaf and dumb species of the human race.

Miller, a medical doctor, argued in the article for abandoning sign language. Deaf persons must be taught to communicate orally, he wrote, so they will "mingle without disability in the general society." He came close to declaring that they should not be allowed to have children to stop the increase of the "deaf and dumb species of the human race." The Hartford school for the deaf that Florence Mayhew referred to, and where Miller's undesirable sign language was being taught, inadvertently helped in bringing an end to "Chilmark's Tainted Stock." A number of Vineyard men who attended the school met and married other deaf students, many of them deaf for reasons other than heredity, such as illness or accident. The mixing of their genes with those of Chilmark, as well as the immigration of Europeans to the Island, reduced its deaf population.

An interesting sidelight in Vineyard history is found in a letter Bell wrote to his wife from Edgartown on December 18, 1887. He was staying at the inn run by Captain Abraham Osborne Jr. (somehow the name picked up an "e" after the Civil War). In a previous letter, Bell had described the inn as "Captain Osborne's house—dignified by the name of

317

Ocean View Hotel. A queer place but I like it." The inventor of the telephone was comforted by its telegraph machine: "It is a comfort having a telegraph office right in the house where I am staying. I don't feel now so very far away. I can reach you in a moment. . . . The telegraph however takes all the spirit out of letter-writing—when I can telegraph you in a moment why should I spend time in writing a letter that will not reach you for days!"

It is ironic that Bell, who owned a telephone company, was relieved to have a telegraph machine in the house. There were telephones on the Island, of course, but not many in private homes. Five years earlier, in 1882, there had been a total of eighteen, but only two were in Edgartown: one at the railroad depot on upper Main Street, the other in Captain R. Holley's store downtown.

In 1883 a telephone connection to the mainland, using the underwater Western Union telegraph cable, had been established. Even with that, there apparently was no way to talk by telephone to Mrs. Bell in Washington. Had there been, surely the inventor of the telephone would have done so. Instead, he was pleased by the comfort of "having a telegraph office right in the house where I am staying."

Bell was much amused by Captain Osborne. He told his wife about the whaling master's tale of confronting Captain Raphael Semmes, the Confederate "pirate," during the Civil War. Osborne's whaleship, the *Ocmulgee*, was the first victim of Semmes's raider, the *Alabama*. Here is Bell's report of Osborne's account:

> I have spent the evening . . . listening to yarns from the mouth of Capt. Abraham Osborne. . . . I really shall have to try and put down . . . some of his stories, but they will lack the charm of sparkling eye and expressive gesture, and the quaint utterances of a seafaring man. If I could copy his language—"My stars!"—would be sprinkled through the whole story. . . .
>
> "Did you ever see the *Alabama,* Captain?"
>
> "My stars!—did I ever see the *Alabama?* I was took by her! My ship was the first prize she made."

Captain Osborne then described in detail how the *Alabama* had sent armed men aboard the *Ocmulgee,* killed his pet dog, ordered him and his crew to leave the ship, and then set it afire. Osborne, in irons aboard the *Alabama,* watched his ship burn. The men were unharmed and soon were set ashore on the Azores.

Bell's account of Osborne's tale makes no mention of any previous acquaintance with Semmes, as the traditional Vineyard version of the story has it. That tale, famous in Osborn family legend, states that before the war Captain Semmes had often been a guest in the Edgartown inn operated by Abraham's father, also Abraham, while Semmes was an inspector in the federal lighthouse service. On those visits, the story goes, he usually stayed with the Osborns. The late Joseph Chase Allen, a beloved raconteur, further embellished the story in his *Tales and Trails of Martha's Vineyard:* "By some strange freak of fate, the first ship that he [Semmes] captured and sank was commanded by the brother of the girl to whom he had been engaged and with whom he had often broken bread."

In recounting the *Alabama* story to Bell, Osborne made no mention of such acquaintance. Yet the tale has become as much a part of Vineyard history as the one about the three girls in Holmes Hole who, during the Revolution, blew up the town's Liberty Pole rather than have it taken by British sailors to replace a broken spar on their warship. Such tales survive because they are far more interesting than the truth.

Bell stayed in Edgartown and Vineyard Haven, going to Cottage City only to pick up telegrams brought there from the mainland by steamer when the telegraph line serving the Island (and his inn) was out of service, as it often was. Cottage City had little to interest him. It had no deaf-mutes or any historical records in its town hall. In fact, being newly separated from Edgartown, it didn't even have a town hall. So Bell probably wasn't aware of its continuing problem with "sanitaries." He never mentioned it in his letters.

But the problem hadn't gone away. The solution would require the village to prohibit the use of wells in congested areas, such as the campground, and provide safe running water to residents. Like anything likely to raise taxes, the proposal met opposition. Running water would soon bring those new-fangled flush toilets, and that meant sewers would be needed. The water company was privately financed, but sewers would require tax money. The *Herald* didn't seem concerned: "The saving of the labor at the pump handle; the comforts of a bath-room and water closet; the improved and ever verdant lawns and beautiful flower beds; the faculty for putting out incipient fires; the certainty of being able to check a conflagration; and the great reduction in insurance rates are among the advantages to be gained by the introduction of pure running water."

In the spring of 1890 the privately owned Cottage City Water Company was nearly finished building the pumping station on the small fresh-water pond at the head of the Lagoon. That water, safe to drink, would be pumped directly into a standpipe by a steam-driven pump and then piped into town.

The company had hired a gang of Portuguese laborers from off-Island to mix mortar for the masons finishing the pumping station. As the *Martha's Vineyard Herald* reported, a problem developed:

> On Thursday of last week [April 10, 1890] about twenty of our Portuguese laborers were put to work by Superintendent Parks at the pumping station. They worked until Saturday morning at 9 o'clock when Joe Smith, their interpreter, demanded an increase of pay from $1.35 to $1.50 a day.
>
> They were informed that their gang of 50 experienced workmen were paid $1.35 and if they chose to continue at that rate they would have steady work and more of their companions would be employed this week. They positively declined and the company at once cabled for 40 more laborers.
>
> The strikers were incensed and assembled at the Allen cottage, Lagoon Heights, to discuss the matter. Presently, they saw three Italians approaching, who had been sent as helpers to keep the masons at work until the new men telegraphed for could reach the Island. They were at once way-laid and threatened that if they went to work they would kill them.
>
> Mr. Parks, learning the state of affairs, called on the selectmen for a constable and Mr. Andrew Warren went to the spot and, explaining to the Portuguese the criminal character of their acts, soon persuaded them to quietly disperse.
>
> This week, numerous petty depredations have occurred at night. Coils of rope for derricks, truck wheels and other implements for the work have been carried off. . . . Arthur J. Barrett and John Walker were sworn in as special police officers.

The labor dispute was somehow resolved and two months later, in June 1890, the plant was ready. At exactly 8:33 A.M., on a lovely June day, pumping began. Outside the handsome castle-like building, a group of men and women gathered to celebrate. The *Boston Advertiser* took notice: "Beech Grove Spring Water [is] piped into every part of the community. The hydrant service for fire purposes is adequate to any possible demand. Rejoicing is universal over the improvement."

The town rejoiced and waited until the end of the summer to celebrate. Three days of parades, band concerts, fireworks, and a gala ball marked the memorable occasion. Over six hundred children, all dressed in white, attended Children's Day in the Casino (formerly the skating rink). At last Cottage City was rid of the threat of contaminated water.

There were other reasons for celebration. Cottage City was the place to be, the Island's fun spot. A wooden "toboggan slide" had been built near the skating rink in 1887. It was an immense structure, forty feet high at its start, one thousand feet long and eight feet wide. It cost one thousand dollars to build. We know nothing about who financed it or how the toboggans operated. There is one mention of "roller" sleds, so they must have had wheels. How they were steered or their fast descent controlled, we don't know. It seems mighty dangerous. In any case, the slide didn't last long. No doubt it went up in flames five years later, in 1892, along with the skating rink and the Sea View House.

There was a new steamer, the *Gay Head*. The Highlands wharf in Cottage City had been extended into deeper water to accommodate the steamer's greater draft. On Highland Beach (today the site of the East Chop Beach Club), one hundred bathhouses had been built, equipped with wringers and tubs for rinsing bathing costumes in freshwater. It had a new pavilion with a refreshment stand, the first such on Highland Beach. The Highlands company had also extended its street railway line from the campground down Lake Avenue, along Sea View Avenue to Waban Park, and added four cars to handle the expected increase in business.

Booming Cottage City needed more electricity, and to provide it a new company, the Electric Light and Power Company, was formed to replace the unreliable, inadequate power plant in Hiawatha Park. It promised electric power for both incandescent and arc lights in the whole town, in addition to power for a street railway it planned to build. The generating plant would be at Eastville and it would, the company hoped, sell power to Vineyard Haven as well as Cottage City. Electricity would flow all year, unlike the seasonal supply furnished by the original company.

The planned electric railway would run between Cottage City and Vineyard Haven. There would be no more horse-drawn cars. Horses were not only too slow but also too expensive, the company said. A horse that was bought in the spring for eighty-five dollars could be sold for only seventeen dollars at the end of the season. The company advertised for investors to buy sixty thousand dollars of its stock. The *Herald* was all for the plan, and it urged the company to extend its tracks to Edgartown.

But the electric cars never made it to Edgartown. There was trouble getting them even to Vineyard Haven. The problem was the drawbridge at the Lagoon opening. Not only was the bridge not sturdy enough to support the car, but there was trouble with the overhead trolley wire. The cars ran only as far as the bridge, where the riders got off and boarded a barge that carried them across the harbor into Vineyard Haven. The barge service operated for one season. (Trains ran only in summer.) It isn't clear if the bridge problem was ever solved. Even in the early 1900s passengers walked across the bridge and boarded a waiting trolley on the other side to finish their trip to Vineyard Haven.

The sudden move to "go electric" created confusion, especially around Eastville, where the power plant was located. Five different companies were stringing overhead wires, some even putting up their own poles along the same street. One company had put its poles in the middle of the road. Wires crossed and recrossed; short circuits were often the result. A hearing was called by the Cottage City selectmen in July 1895 to settle the matter. Attending were representatives from the street railroad (which had an overhead wire for its trolley), the electric company (whose wire carried electricity for lights), the federal government (whose telephone line connected the Island's lighthouses), the Bell Telephone Company (which had come to the Island in 1891), and a second telephone company (which was owned by Dr. C. F. Lane and was just starting up). During the long and argumentative hearing, little was resolved. All five organizations agreed to try to work out a solution. We don't know how the matter was finally resolved.

There were no such tangled wires in the other towns. Edgartown didn't get its first electric light until August 1894, when one light was installed in Shute's store on Main Street. It never did get an electric trolley. Its first telephones had come in 1882, when one public phone was installed in the railroad station on upper Main Street and another in a store downtown. Nor did Gay Head and Chilmark have problems with tangled wires. Most of Gay Head didn't get electricity until the end of World War II. It took even longer to get electricity to the lighthouse. That came only after Mrs. Frank Grieder, wife of the Gay Head lighthouse keeper, wrote to President Harry S. Truman when the nation exploded two atomic bombs ending World War II. In a conversation with me in 1980, she said: "I wrote to President Truman saying it was a disgrace that the lighthouse keeper on Gay

Head still didn't have electricity and running water in a country that could make an atomic bomb!" She received word that electricity would be coming, but it took another seven years before it arrived.

It no doubt would have come much sooner if the plans of the Martha's Vineyard Electric Railway had materialized. In December 1891 a group of investors thought an electric railway running from Cottage City to Gay Head through North Tisbury and Menemsha would be a profitable business. It offered twenty thousand dollars in stock to the public. The western towns were enthusiastic. Heading the company were five men: C. H. Emerson of South Framingham; G. M. Clough of Somerville; Charles Strahan of Cottage City, owner of the *Martha's Vineyard Herald;* and Henry L. Whiting and M. F. Cummings, both of Tisbury. The company's success seemed so certain that when G. W. Eldridge published his detailed map of the Vineyard in 1892, the railway was shown on it and labeled "Proposed Railway." When a second edition of the map came out twenty years later, the electric railway was still shown—and still labeled "Proposed."

It was, of course, never built.

The *Martha's Vineyard Herald* in 1903 discussed the long-promised railroad: "We will answer a question frequently asked: The electric railroad shown on Eldridge's map has never been built. It may be in the air like several large hotels and other Island schemes which have never struck the surface, but it's not to be found by tramping up-Island."

The quiet village of West Tisbury in the center of the Island had been spared all the confusion that progress was bringing. It enjoyed its lifestyle. Although not officially named West Tisbury, it began using that name some time between 1868 and 1880. The town was officially Tisbury, its eastern part being called Vineyard Haven. In public conversation there was no Tisbury, no East Tisbury, only a West Tisbury. That original village considered itself quite separate from Vineyard Haven, not only in geography but in character. The differences had become so marked that on the last day of 1884 a petition was presented to the Tisbury selectmen asking that the old village be allowed to separate from Vineyard Haven.

It was signed by ten leading citizens of West Tisbury. Their request was unlike the earlier Island secession movement in which a young Cottage City petitioned for separation from old Edgartown. In this case, the old village, West Tisbury, was asking to be separated from its offspring, Vineyard Haven.

A public meeting was held in mid-January 1890 to discuss what action to take. Those favoring division were led by Henry L. Whiting. Opposing were Rodolphus Crocker and several others from Vineyard Haven. West Tisbury's argument was a familiar one: its residents were paying higher taxes and getting little in return. And it would get worse, they said. Fast-growing Vineyard Haven would soon demand more fire equipment and schools, while the smaller West Tisbury would be hopelessly outvoted in town meetings.

The meeting became noisy and was getting nowhere. There was rancor on both sides. Exchanges were heated, often unpleasant. At a pause in the debate, one weary citizen from Vineyard Haven stood up: "Mr. [Willis] Howes moved to adjourn, which was carried, and everybody went home apparently satisfied that nothing was done."

But the debate did not stop with the meeting. Displeased with the lack of a decision, the West Tisbury citizens sent a petition to the state legislature calling for it to hold a hearing. In February 1892 several days of hearings took place in the State House. The *Martha's Vineyard Herald,* in favor of division, reported that the lawyer for West Tisbury, former New Bedford Mayor Walter Clifford, started off

> with consummate skill and cleverly wrested some of the best verbal weapons from the commander of the Vineyard Haven forces, Attorney Marcus B. B. Swift of Fall River. . . . [He argued] it is a case for a division of a town that fell outside the lines of those that had previously been considered. . . . It is not the case of a young offshoot of an old town, grown tired of the conservatism and old-fogyishness of its parent and seeking to control its own affairs; but it is an appeal on the part of a parent for protection . . . [from an] offspring . . . laying on her expenses for development and improvement . . . from which she derives no appreciable benefits. It is an appeal on behalf of a farming people to be set off from a people whose tendencies are "citified," and to be relieved from . . . the taxes which were perfectly proper for a seaport and summer resort, but were a heavy burden on farmers and fishers.

Clifford called as his first witness William J. Rotch, who pointed out that Vineyard Haven's larger population, 1,100, twice West Tisbury's 555, gave the old village little control over how its tax money was spent.

The main opposition witness was Rodolphus W. Crocker, owner of the Island's largest business, the harness factory, and Vineyard Haven's political "boss." He had been for the division at first, but when he learned that most people in town opposed it, he changed his mind. Asked what he thought was behind the petition, he said it was inspired by the politicians in Edgartown who saw Tisbury as threatening their control of Dukes County. As Vineyard Haven's population grew, he said, Edgartown "sought to retain its prestige by securing a division of Tisbury."

Witnesses on both sides mentioned politics so often that at one point the chairman, Senator John R. Thayer of Worcester, interjected: "Is there anything but politics on that Island?"

Allen Look of West Tisbury stated the case for the separation of the two settlements very clearly: "Formerly a man who owned 300 acres in West Tisbury was regarded as prosperous and influential. . . . Now, a man who owns 300 acres is to be pitied. He is burdened with the support of a watering place."

Captain William M. Randall of Vineyard Haven, a Democrat, said that except for the political ring's opposition to it, everybody in Vineyard Haven would be for division: "The Republican party are the ones who do not want division. . . . Since the division question has come up, the lines between the two old parties have been somewhat obliterated. . . . We Democrats have to vote for a Prohibitionist."

A more thoughtful witness for division was Professor Nathaniel Shaler of Harvard. A Kentuckian, he had known the Vineyard for more than thirty years, having visited it in his geological studies. He admitted to having "quickly acquired an affection for the Island and its people":

> A number of years ago I acquired considerable land in what is [now] known as the North Tisbury section to use as a playground for my second childhood. It consists of 24 or 26 abandoned farms. And they were really abandoned. . . . The houses were unoccupied and dilapidated. Of some two score houses only eight were worth saving. . . .
>
> In this case, the division is one by nature. . . . The people at the port [Vineyard Haven] are extremely prosperous, make money easily and can afford to pay large taxes. After you leave the town . . . you pass through waste and desolation until you get to . . . North Tisbury. This section is rendered hopelessly sterile by nature. I know that, for I bought a tract at $1 an acre . . . but found I could make no use of it whatever. . . .
>
> You cannot expect to reconcile a people divided by a diversity of inter-

ests and by nature and distance. On the one hand are a people who make money easily and spend generously, and on the other a people who can only live by the exercise of the greatest thrift. In view of these facts, I have come to the conclusion that a separation is essential.

The bill to divide the town of Tisbury passed the state legislature on April 28, 1892, and was signed by the governor the same day. Two days later the village of West Tisbury celebrated:

> A great demonstration was held and . . . nearly all the dwelling houses and the trading emporiums were brilliantly illuminated. Sky-rockets, Roman candles, &c., were in abundance on Wilton Terrace. . . .
>
> At about 8 P.M. a procession of over one hundred people formed near Geo. G. Gifford's store, and, headed by a fife and drum corps, R. G. Shute of Edgartown, leader, with torchlights and fish-horns, marched through the principal streets. At about 9 P.M., it proceeded to Agricultural Hall, where a bountiful repast had been prepared by the ladies, who had neatly and abundantly provided four large tables (three on the main floor and one on the platform) with delicious collation.

Taking part was a delegation from Gay Head: "It was most weird and spectral to see the descendants of the famous Pokanoket tribe of red men who had journeyed from Gay Head Saturday evening to West Tisbury, as they danced amid the flaming glare of torches and with enthusiastic whoops around the hanging effigy of Cape Cod's senator [Senator Simpkins, who had opposed division]."

The "new" village of West Tisbury could now officially use the name it had been using for years. Vineyard Haven was now officially Tisbury, beginning a confusing system of names that continues into the twenty-first century. Road signs point to a place called Vineyard Haven, but you never enter it. When you get there, a sign says you are entering Tisbury, although you had no desire to go there. You wanted to go to Vineyard Haven, but there is no town by that name, although that is where the ferryboat lands several times a day.

(Similar confusion now exists between Aquinnah and Gay Head. Visitors want to go to Gay Head, but when they get there they discover they are "Entering Aquinnah." Also, when you leave West Tisbury, heading up-Island—another mysterious term understood only by Islanders—you pass a sign saying you are "Entering Chilmark," just beyond the old Agricultural

Hall. If you are driving on the right-hand side of the road, as most of us do, you are not entering Chilmark but are still in West Tisbury for another mile. The town line runs down the center of the highway until Nab's Corner, where you finally enter Chilmark.)

During the 1880s a movement to get rid of the name Cottage City began. In the first place, proponents said, it was not a city, but only a town. Furthermore, residents did not like to be thought of as "cottagers," living in flimsy summer houses. It was the most modern town on the Island, leading all others in electric lights, telephones, and running water. The name Cottage City conjured up images of a campground. It had to be changed. The steamboat company didn't sell tickets to Cottage City. Porters had no luggage tags with Cottage City printed on them. Everybody called the place Oak Bluffs. That's what its name should be. So the argument went.

It was a long struggle. Demand for a change had started in 1884, but it didn't happen until twenty-three years later. By then, 1907, only the people sorting mail in the post office were still using the name Cottage City.

There were other changes going on in Cottage City. One was the population mix. There was a scent of discrimination in the Cottage City news column of the *Martha's Vineyard Herald* in June 1882: "The town is filling up with Portuguese, who are buying little tracts of land in the suburbs where they get up little homes and rear big families of children. They are crowding out all other laboring classes."

The village was becoming more colorful. The center of its summertime fun was the skating rink, managed by Frank E. Winslow. He was doing all he could to make it so, as the *Star* reported in the spring of 1882:

> The skating rink, Frank E. Winslow, manager, has been painted. On the exterior: sides are olive color with two shades of red trim. The front has more trim and looks gay. Inside walls are salmon color with blue trim. The arches are cobalt blue and the columns light and dark vermilion. The decorations are banners and 1500 new foreign lanterns. Hanging on the walls are huge portraits of Lincoln, Washington and Garfield done by J. O. Snell of Cottage City. It is the leading attraction all summer for doctors, lawyers, ministers, stately dames and pretty maidens.

Not to be outdone, the village's pride, the Sea View House, standing next to the skating rink, did the same. Olive, in various shades, was a popular color, it seems: "The huge Sea View House has been painted: The body of the house is a ripe olive shade, the trim is green olive, providing an interesting contrast. The roof is painted a Venetian red."

Uninterested in such faddish colors was the village of West Tisbury, where the Island's best known person, Nancy Luce, lived. She had become a celebrity, unwittingly. On their way to Gay Head, sightseeing carriages, their drivers eager for a break in the long trip, regularly stopped at her home on New Lane. Nancy Luce was an eccentric, but she was more than peculiar. She was the first person on the Island, male or female, to earn a living by writing and painting. Truly the Island's first artist, she was never thought of that way, either by visitors or by natives. To all she was "that crazy hen woman," an object of pity and sometimes of abuse and scorn. The Martha's Vineyard Historical Society has a few of her original works in its archives, and no one can examine them without admiring her artistry.

She was especially the subject of abuse during the week of the Agricultural Fair in West Tisbury each year. She lived only a mile or so from the fairground and so was an easy target for cruel young men and boys, and even a few sightseers. It is shocking that such behavior went unpunished by the authorities. Here are a few news items from the *Cottage City Star* during a few years late in her life. She was about seventy when this was taking place:

> Oct. 20, 1881. Miss Nancy Luce was visited by several parties during the fair. Report says she showed her bravery when persecuted by some of the parties by firing off a pistol, loaded with powder. One unlucky swain received the flash too near his face.
>
> Feb. 23, 1882. Miss Nancy Luce is fine. Those noisy visitors have other things to do, giving her poor, sick head a chance to rest.
>
> April 27, 1882. Nancy Luce has bought an old single-barreled pistol to drive off young men who annoy her at times in the summer. She will load it with much flash powder, but no shot.
>
> Oct. 26, 1882. Miss Nancy Luce, a maiden lady who lives alone, was visited recently by two unknown young men and she thought it best to defend herself by showing a pistol. They wrested it from her hands and her cries aroused a neighbor, who went to her assistance. She now has a new pistol and claims she has a right to defend herself. During the last day of the Agricultural Fair, twenty carriage loads of people visited her. Some of them carried their fun a little too far by shutting their hostess

In the 1800s, Nancy Luce of West Tisbury became famous as the "Hen Lady" because she
made pets of certain hens and even wrote poetry about them. When they died, she placed
carved marble tombstones on their graves. Capitalizing on her fame, she supported herself
by selling booklets of her poetry, and she was thus the Vineyard's first professional author.
(1880 photograph by Joseph Warren, MVHS Collections)

in a closet, but they made up with her by purchasing a large number of her books.

Feb. 8, 1883. Miss Nancy Luce is in her usual health and has not much been troubled by "her tormenters" of late; but she has been very much afflicted by the death of one of her neighbors, one she considered her best friend. Her grief has been so great that she thought it best to don the habiliments of mourning.

May 23, 1883. Miss Nancy Luce is enjoying better health. She has not been tormented of late by those wild, rattle-headed young people that at times have so afflicted her.

Nancy Luce died in April 1890 at seventy-nine years. She had suffered a small paralytic stroke in 1882 and had become so feeble that she no longer was able to keep her hens or her cow and depended upon a neighbor to deliver milk to her each day. Bread soaked in warm milk was her basic food. One day the neighbor found her lying on the floor of her small house, conscious but unable to get up. Dr. Luce, her doctor and friend (no relation), was summoned. Within a few hours she was unconscious and by morning she was dead. Her funeral was held in the Baptist church near her house on Wednesday, April 9, 1890. It would be interesting to know who attended and what was said about her life.

An obituary in the *Martha's Vineyard Herald* stressed her eccentric nature, describing the marble tombstones she had bought for her three favorite hens. (These stones are on display at the Historical Society.) Here are excerpts from the obituary:

At one time she was an object of very great interest, and in the summer the "foreigners from the Camp Ground," as Nancy called the summer visitors, came in large numbers to see her, hear her talk, and to buy her books and photographs. . . . Of late years her visitors have been very few, comparatively, and she sold such a small quantity of books she feared she should have to be supported by the town, but declared she would not go on the town, but would lie down and die if she could prevent it in no other way. . . . [Nancy Luce had written to William Rotch, another friend and adviser: "I will not be on the town. I will not be under no one, I will pitch down on the ground and die first."]

A small amount of money was found in the house, quite a lot of postage stamps, and some provisions. Two loaded pistols, cocked and capped, were also found. The neighbors were very kind to her, and vis-

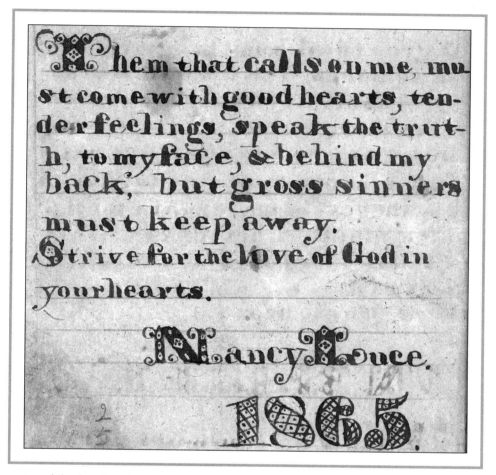

Them that calls on me, must come with good hearts, tender feelings, speak the truth, to my face, & behind my back, but gross sinners must keep away. Strive for the love of God in your hearts.

Nancy Luce.

1865.

One of the first booklets sold by Nancy Luce was entitled "Sickness" and was published in 1865. She hand-lettered the poems with her elaborate calligraphy and stitched the pages herself. Later, as sales increased, she had her booklets printed professionally in New Bedford. (MVHS Archives.)

ited her often to see that she did not suffer for anything. A two months' supply of milk had been paid for in advance.

With Nancy's death, the village of West Tisbury lost its tourist attraction. And the Island lost a remarkable woman who deserved a more sympathetic treatment from all.

Her memory soon faded, overwhelmed by events that crowded into the last decade of the nineteenth century. Most of them have been described in this chapter. When the decade ended, an event of enormous significance took place. It was in August 1900. The writer for the *Vineyard*

Gazette reported it as though it was merely another new fashion. Little could he know what was beginning: "Edgartown is in the swim with the other resorts. The horseless carriage is here. The first to appear is the loco-mobile of Mr. Elmer J. Bliss, president of the Regal Shoe Company, who brought this vehicle down from Boston Saturday night. Mr. Bliss had his locomobile out on Sunday and it worked very satisfactory on our streets."

Soon more such "locomobiles" arrived—and more—and more—through the years that have followed, bringing changes that nobody could have predicted. Nothing else ever had the impact of the horseless carriage.

The Island would never be the same.

10

Horseless Carriages, World War I, and Many Leather Jerkins

When Elmer J. Bliss drove his new Locomobile along Edgartown's North Water Street in 1900, he may have, as the *Gazette* declared, put the village "in the swim with the other resorts," but he did nothing to improve the town's popularity with the rest of the Island.

For years Edgartown's arrogance had been creating animosity among residents of the other villages. In 1880 it had tried to keep Gay Headers from voting in the critical election leading up to the separation of Cottage City. When that effort failed, the Gay Head vote swung the election and led to Cottage City's (today's Oak Bluffs) becoming a separate town.

Then in 1887 Edgartown again demonstrated its arrogance. Six years earlier, all Island towns, including Edgartown, had agreed to an alternating system when nominating a Republican candidate for representative to the Massachusetts General Court. (The Republican nomination was tantamount to election.) Under the agreement, an Edgartown resident would be nominated for two terms, a Tisbury man for two terms, followed by someone from Gay Head, Cottage City, and Chilmark, each town to get one term.

The system worked fine until Gay Head's turn came up. At the Republican convention, Edwin A. Vanderhoop of Gay Head was nominated, in keeping with the agreement. Edgartown Republicans opposed the move, claiming that Island voters would never elect a "colored" man. Encouraged by the *Vineyard Gazette*, Edgartown delegates held a rump convention and nominated a local resident, Captain Richard Holley. The Prohibition Party nominated the Reverend Edward W. Hatfield, which added to the confusion and brought on the most hateful political campaign in Island history.

So ugly was the campaign that on November 4, 1887, a few days before the general election, the *Martha's Vineyard Herald,* supporting Vanderhoop, distributed with that week's paper a blunt political broadside boldly entitled "The Truth," which urged voters to honor Gay Head's representational turn and elect Edwin Vanderhoop. Here are three quotations from it:

> Is Mr. Vanderhoop incompetent? Is Mr. Vanderhoop dishonest? Not a word against his ability or honesty has been heard. . . . The only objection is that he is a *"Nigger."*
>
> If you can't keep your pledge to the colored man you are blacker that he is.
>
> I deny emphatically and unequivocally the charges made by Hatfield at the Prohibitory Convention, that I sold rum. They are absolutely false.
>
> EDWIN D. VANDERHOOP

Vanderhoop easily won the election, 530 to 194. Edgartown's candidate, Captain Holley, carried only his home town, 138 to 74. Gay Head, as expected, voted unanimously for Vanderhoop, 24 to 0. After completing his term, Vanderhoop continued to be active in Republican party politics, but he was never again elected to state office. It was the only time a Gay Head resident ever represented the county, as the turn-taking system was soon abandoned.

Edgartown supported West Tisbury in its struggle to separate from Holmes Hole (later called Vineyard Haven) in 1892. When West Tisbury won its separation, Edgartown gained a few friends there, but it created enemies in Holmes Hole, whose residents said Edgartown's reason for wanting to divide Tisbury (the town's official name that included at the time both Holmes Hole and West Tisbury) was to keep it from taking over as county seat.

Both Holmes Hole and Cottage City were growing fast, and each wanted to take the courthouse away from Edgartown. It, along with the county jail, provided many jobs. They campaigned hard to get it, especially when, in 1896, the state ordered the county to add a large fireproof vault to the courthouse for safe storage of official records. If an addition had to be built for the vault, why not start over and build a new courthouse? the two towns argued. Edgartown voters, traditionally stingy with tax money, countered by offering to pay the entire cost of enlarging the courthouse, an unprecedented and perhaps illegal offer, since the courthouse belonged to the county, not to the town. The attorney for Vineyard Haven (officially

Tisbury, now separate from West Tisbury), in his argument to make that town the new county seat, scoffed at Edgartown's offer:

> Now they are praying to be allowed to pay for [the expansion] themselves. This is a step further in the bluffing game than [I] have ever known.
>
> [Vineyard Haven] is now the business center of the Island for twelve months in the year. It is not its people alone that petition [to move the county seat]. Three-quarters of the people on the Island want it moved.
>
> Cottage City is practically dead in the winter. There is nothing in Edgartown but a lot of nice people. Vineyard Haven is the metropolis of the Island.

He lost the argument. The state turned down the petition and a month later work began on an addition to the courthouse to include the fireproof vault. The county paid for it; Edgartown's self-serving offer had been rejected.

Although it held onto the courthouse, Edgartown's importance was weakened by the deaths of several of its leading citizens. Samuel Osborn Jr., the town's political and business leader, died in 1896. He had made most of his fortune in whaling (although he had never gone to sea himself), but by the time he died that enterprise had collapsed. His whaleship *Mattapoisett* was auctioned off for only $210, his schooner *Eunice H. Adams* went for $375, and thirty-seven varied lots of whaling equipment brought another $375. The only item that brought much money was the schooner *Hattie E. Smith*. Unlike the other vessels, it was still operating as a coastal freighter and sold for $1,180.

Another important Edgartown businessman who died in the 1890s was William H. Munroe. He had come to Edgartown as a tailor in 1839 and by wise investments in retailing (and in whaling during its prime) had become the town's largest taxpayer. His gravestone is the most impressive in the Edgartown cemetery. The *Gazette,* mourning the loss, added a note of hope:

> In the death of William Munroe another of those, who in bygone days, made Edgartown prosperous and influential among her sisters, has gone to his long home. The town has lost many such in the past decade. . . . The glory of the old whaling days has departed; the sound of the cooper's hammer and the caulker's iron is hushed; the creaking of the block and the flap of the sail, as the boys lay aloft, is no more heard; the last gallant

When the whaling business ended, Edgartown fell into an economic decline.
Instead of chasing whales, the ship *Mattapoisett* sat for years tied up at the town wharf,
waiting for a revival. These two men sat behind it, catching fish for their dinner.
(MVHS Collections)

ship, with her hardy crew, has sailed her last voyage from the old wharf.

But the sun is again rising, and in the sunshine of another day the town will awake, let us hope, to another era of prosperity.

There *was* hope. The town was gradually getting "in the swim" as it struggled to become a summer colony for the wealthy. By 1900 it had forty-seven families of summer residents, mostly well-to-do Massachusetts businessmen. Compared to Cottage City, it was a small colony, but there was a ray of hope.

The nation was suffering a financial downturn at the time, but the Island's increasing summer colony spared it from the worst, as the *Martha's Vineyard Herald* boasted in 1897: "Martha's Vineyard is fortunate in being out of reach of the maelstrom of financial disaster which now affects all sections of the country and all classes of people. . . . The wealthy, who are most affected by the downturn, are deserting the rich places like Newport and coming here."

As is often the case on the Island, spring that year was cold and wet. The wealthy folk who were "deserting the rich places like Newport" were slow to arrive. Had the Island's "magic" vanished already? The *Herald* saw no need to worry:

> Don't be discouraged by the backward season. . . . Warm summer weather set in yesterday. The people must have a seashore rest and they have found out that there is no better place than Martha's Vineyard, and no seashore where as much real enjoyment can be had for a moderate expenditure.
>
> We will have our usual summer contingent, and also a large class of patrons of more expensive resorts who are finding out they can obtain as much, if not more, pleasure on Martha's Vineyard at a less expense to their pocket-books.

There did always seem to be enough vacationers to come and keep the Island busy—at least during the summer months. Those summer people brought money, but they also brought problems, their automobiles among them. Elmer J. Bliss drove his steam-powered Locomobile into Edgartown in 1900. What Bliss started was becoming a flood within ten years. Streets, previously blissful (sorry!), had turned frightful for humans and animals as the smoky, noisy machines roared along them. Vineyarders were having trouble adjusting, Island newspapers wrote:

> If the automobile had a smokestack, a cowcatcher and a tender it would look less like a suspicious prowler.
>
> Why not make automobiles handsome and provide them with good-looking wheels? Up-to-date autos are mere ugly, crawling machines, not an ounce of the artistic or poetic about them. Pretty comfortable to ride on if they do lack beauty.
>
> The trolley car outclasses the railroad train as a killer of mankind, and the automobile is not far behind in the race as a cause of fatalities. Shank's mares are the only absolutely sure means of locomotion.
>
> If some one will invent a front attachment for automobiles in the form of a stuffed rocking horse on wheels, he will earn a place in the hall of fame. Something that will deceive comfortably is needed on the front

end of the present diabolical machines that scatter death and destruction in their wake.

Many valuable horses are owned on the Island. Bought at cheap prices, they were shipped here simply because they were afraid of electric cars and automobiles and for ten months in the year we are free from all such annoyances.

It is useless to cry out about these carriages. They are here and they have come to stay. . . . We can only hope that soon our Island horses will become educated up the point where they will not mind them.

In July 1902, noting that because "our most steady horses . . . are terribly frightened by a rapidly-moving automobile or motor bicycle," selectmen of Vineyard Haven voted that "no vehicle not propelled by a horse shall pass along any street in this town at speeds of more than six miles an hour."

The speed limit came too late to save Ariel Scott of West Tisbury. He was heading home from Vineyard Haven in his wagon when from the opposite direction an automobile came roaring down the hill near Lake Tashmoo. The car so frightened his horse that it bolted and ran off the road, overturning the wagon. Scott was thrown to the ground with multiple injuries. He died the next day, making July 19, 1902, the date on which the first Vineyarder died as the result of an accident involving an automobile.

The owner of the automobile, E. A. Mulliken of Quincy, a well-known Cottage City summer resident, was charged with manslaughter and speeding. His chauffeur, Frank Stanley, who Mulliken said was driving, told police he was not going more than nine miles an hour, although some claimed he had told them his speed had been fifteen miles an hour.

At the trial the judge heard testimony from Leavitt Norton of Vineyard Haven, who had come upon the accident and had taken the seriously injured man home. Also testifying were the two doctors who treated Scott, as well as his widow and others. The judge ruled that Mulliken was not guilty of manslaughter, but there was enough evidence of carelessness to hold him for the grand jury on the charge of involuntary manslaughter.

The grand jury found Mulliken to have been operating the vehicle in "a reckless, negligent and grossly careless manner" and to have caused it to go at "a high, unreasonable and unlawful rate of speed." Nothing was said about the chauffeur being the driver.

After failing to respond to the summons three times, Mulliken finally went on trial and pleaded nolo contendere. He was ordered to pay court costs of $175 and the case was put on file. Widow Scott then filed a civil case against Mulliken and was awarded $800 for the loss of her husband. The amount was not as small at it seems, being two years' pay for a teacher at the time.

That first fatal accident so worried Vineyard Haven residents that they banned one automobile, a public jitney, from using Main Street: "The passenger automobile running to the bridge, which this summer has taken the place of the electric cars, since the accident last week on the state road, is no longer allowed on Main Street but is kept to the old track on Beach Street."

The jitney had replaced the electric streetcar in which Vineyard Haven passengers bound for Cottage City had ridden as far as the Lagoon drawbridge. There they walked across the bridge and got into an electric trolley to ride into Cottage City. The drawbridge was not equipped with trolley tracks, apparently not being sturdy enough to carry the trolley's weight. Banning the car from Main Street didn't seem to hurt business, the *Herald* reported: "The automobile which makes regular trips to connect with the Cottage City trolley car is well patronized."

All this, of course, was happening only in summer. The electric cars shut down in September. No tears were shed. With a sigh of relief, Vineyarders took the Island back at the end of summer. At least, so the editor of the *Herald* thought: "Peaceful driving now. All the 'autos' have gone. Plenty of elbow room on the golf links and the croquet grounds."

The following spring, 1903, the Island got its first year-round automobile. Its reception was without fanfare: "A new automobile arrived on Wednesday's boat for George F. Armsby on the Neck." George F. Armsby was a newcomer. He had recently started a plumbing and heating business on Union Street in Vineyard Haven and lived on upper Main Street. The first resident to own an automobile, he and his automobile didn't stay long. He isn't listed in the 1907 Directory.

Not long after Armsby brought his motor car, Rodolphus Crocker Jr., owner of the harness factory started by his father, also got one, joining the parade that would soon put his factory out of business.

The parade was unstoppable. In July 1903 an entrepreneur from the mainland opened a "stable" for motor cars in Cottage City (the French word *garage* had not yet come into English usage): "Mr. W. B. de Wolf came from New Bedford last Saturday bringing with him a handsome

Among the motor vehicles on the Island was an open-sided bus owned by the Sibley brothers in Edgartown. It carried arriving vacationers from the ferries to the hotels. As the roads improved, it was also used for sightseeing trips up-Island.
(MVHS Collections)

automobile. He has opened an automobile stable on Sea View Avenue and will have some excellent machines for sale."

In that same issue of the *Herald,* de Wolf ran the Island's first automobile advertisement: "AUTOMOBILE STORAGE! I have leased the building next to the Cocassett stable on Sea View Avenue and I have room for automobile storage. I also have automobiles for sale. W. B. de Wolf, agent for the Knox Carriage."

He probably didn't sell many Knox Carriages to the natives. It would take a while before Vineyarders would view the horseless carriage as anything but a nuisance, even a hazard. The *Herald* made that clear: "Automobiles should barely crawl through the avenues of Oak Bluffs and the Camp ground. We are not sure that it would not be wise to have a flagman precede the machine."

Slowly that anti-automobile attitude began changing, but with little enthusiasm: "There is a semblance of beauty and a suggestion of grace about some of the latest arriving automobiles, but the average monster of this kind is as ugly and as ill-proportioned nondescript as can well be imagined and a few years from now will be found only among the scrap piles. Stylish automobiles now go humming through the avenues; ugly ones also and wheezy."

That was the opinion of the *Herald*. Three years later, in August 1906, the *Gazette's* unconvinced and still-annoyed editor reported: "There are 175 automobiles on the island at the present time. . . . Nearly all get to Edgartown every 24 hours, [it] seems on pleasant days." After six years of living with the motor car, the *Gazette* still saw it through the eyes of the horse: "The sensible, thinking horse must wonder what is the matter on the insides of the automobiles as he passes them on the road. The noises they make put heaves and all other horse complaints entirely in the shade."

Those other islanders on Nantucket were even less willing to accept the change. In 1906 they announced that automobiles were not welcome on their island. E. E. Landers, editor of the *Martha's Vineyard Herald,* quickly forgot his reservations; summer people, even with automobiles, were desirable. He invited them all to the Vineyard: "Our concrete streets and roads are great for automobiling. Come down here with your automobile. Nantucket doesn't want you, but we do." (Concrete was not the substance we know today, but a thin, hard coating on top of the gravel.)

Times were changing in other ways. One Vineyard Haven resident was doleful in his letter to the *Herald*:

> Times have changed since the days when we looked forward to camp meeting as the event of the year, and when the time arrived, "did up" in our best calico, packed a can-pail of eatables and were rowed over to the Eastside and then conveyed by carriages, driven by a local Jehu, to the scene of action. No one could have predicted then that a horseless carriage and a locomotive-less car would in future years convey us to a tentless camp meeting.

It was a familiar and never-ending lament over the loss of yesterday. But newcomers, unburdened with memories of "the good old days," continued to arrive, seeing the Island as a wonderful, unspoiled place they had just discovered. Many were celebrities, most of them in the theater. One was the leading Broadway comedian Sol Smith Russell, then starring in *April Weather* at Daly's Theatre, New York.

He bought land atop Tower Hill, overlooking Edgartown's inner harbor and with views across to Chappaquiddick. Most summer residents preferred houses along Water Street, close enough to town for walking, but the automobile was beginning to change that. More distant sections such as Tower Hill were being considered. Russell was among the first to recognize this. He built an elegant summer home, complete with a ninety-foot bowling alley. At the end of his long pier he put a pagoda-inspired boathouse, still a landmark today. Russell did not enjoy that lovely spot for long. Within a few years he suffered a stroke and died. In 1903 the property was bought by James W. Vose, head of the famed piano company Vose and Sons in Boston. The property is still in the Vose family in 2006.

Another entertainer who joined Russell in Edgartown in 1900 was Frank Keenan, then a Shakespearean actor and later a pioneering movie star and director. He regularly rented the William H. Pease house on North Water Street. His family, one of the best known in the entertainment world, summered on the Island for many years. Ed Wynn, the "Fire Chief" of television renown in the mid-1900s, was Frank Keenan's grandson; he enjoyed Edgartown for most of his long life and became another local celebrity.

Vineyard Haven also had its famous summer residents. Among them was Leland Powers, an actor and impersonator, who built a luxurious summer home on West Chop. Another Vineyard Haven summer resident, William Barry Owen, was from a different branch of the entertainment world. He had been the European sales agent of the Victor Talking Machine Company and had "created" the company's famous trademark, "His Master's Voice." Known around the world, it shows a dog (Nipper is his name) listening intently to sounds coming from the large horn of an early gramophone. Originally painted as fine art, the picture became the Victor trademark after its artist died and his brother was trying to sell it. Art collectors and museums in London couldn't see any "fine art" in it. So he turned to gramophone companies, just then coming into prominence. All turned it down. Only Owen showed any interest, stating that had the gramophone in the painting been one sold by Victor, he would have bought it. The artist's brother, also an artist, painted over the original gramophone, replacing it with a Victor machine. Owen bought the painting, which was renamed *His Master's Voice,* and the trademark was born.

When he retired, Owen settled in Vineyard Haven and began Owen's Farm, a poultry and florist business near Lambert's Cove. It became known as the Red Farm because its many buildings were all painted red. Eleven of them were barnlike structures that housed four thousand hens of many varieties. A few years later he and others formed a leather-stamping business, the Luxmoor Company, in Vineyard Haven. In the 1907 Directory it is listed as "leather decorators." Located in a large building below the present Martha's Vineyard National Bank building on Main Street, its leather products were used by furniture makers and upholsterers, as well as by tailors of women's clothing. The company had a short life on the Vineyard, as it moved to New Jersey before 1910.

Some years after Owen's death in 1914, his widow, Mae M. Owen, placed the land on which the leather factory had stood (as well as more land extending to the harbor) in a trust as a public park to be known as the William Barry Owen Park. It was later conveyed to the town, which now owns it.

Up-Island's summer "colonies" had started in 1888 when Professor Nathaniel Shaler of Harvard began buying up abandoned farms in North Tisbury, as mentioned earlier. He named his estate Seven Gates because he had to get off the wagon and open and close seven gates to get to his house. It was to be, he said, a "playground" for his elder years and he kept it that way, selling only a few carefully restricted lots to selected friends.

In Chilmark the first summer colony began when Henry Blackwell arrived during the Civil War. He was married to the pioneer feminist Lucy Stone, one of the first women to insist on keeping her maiden name after marriage. The family, famous for its bold, active women, among them the nation's first two female physicians and its first ordained female minister, still owns property in Chilmark.

The Blackwell colony began in 1864 when Henry and his friend Ainsworth Spofford, the Librarian of Congress, anchored off Squibnocket Landing, as it was then called, while cruising in a small boat. Blackwell wanted to mail a letter to his wife, and they went ashore to find a post office. They walked over Boston Hill to Beetlebung Corner, where Blackwell found a place to mail his letter. But he had found much more: he had found the place his family would enjoy for generations. He and other family members bought land for summer houses and for year-round living. Blackwell had eight brothers and sisters, and most of them lived in Chilmark year-round at some point in their lives, as have their descendants. Some married into Chilmark families. One was Florence Blackwell, daughter of Henry's brother Samuel, who married Postmaster E. Elliott Mayhew and became a founder of the Chilmark Public Library.

There are more than fifty Blackwells and their relatives buried in the

The first up-Island summer residents were the Blackwells, who came about the time of the Civil War. When Alice Stone Blackwell took this photograph of her family on Chilmark Pond in 1888, remote Chilmark was still little developed as a resort. It was a town you went through on your way to Gay Head. (MVHS Collections)

Chilmark cemetery on Abel's Hill, a testament to their devotion to the village. Among them is E. Gale Huntington, the founding editor of the *Dukes County Intelligencer,* the journal of the Martha's Vineyard Historical Society. Huntington's mother was Nan Blackwell, who had been adopted by Dr. Emily Blackwell, Henry's granddaughter. After she married Dr. Elon Obed Huntington, a navy surgeon, the couple bought the Asa Smith house at Squibnocket, where Gale and his three brothers grew up and attended Chilmark schools.

In Oak Bluffs a summer colony of Connecticut hardware people also began in the 1860s. Philip Corbin, the lock manufacturer from New Britain, was the first. He bought land facing Ocean Park from Erastus Carpenter's Oak Bluffs Land and Wharf Company in 1868. The hardware manufacturer William H. Hart, president of Stanley Tool Works, started vacationing in Oak Bluffs in 1871, renting various houses on Pequot Avenue. In 1915 he bought a large tract of what was considered useless marshland just south of Farm Pond on the outskirts of the town. He changed the flow of tidal water into the pond, creating a small harbor that his wife named Hart Haven. The mansion that he built across the road from the harbor was soon followed by other summer houses that family members built on the new private harbor.

The Harts, eager to preserve the natural beauty of the area, sold a mile of beach to the state for the northern end of the Joseph A. Sylvia State Beach. They also leased another large tract across the road for ninety-nine years to the Farm Neck Country Club. In both cases a restriction provided that there would be no buildings erected on them.

As the Hart family multiplied, some of them headed up-Island to Abel's Hill in Chilmark, where today they and others with Stanley Tool Works connections continue the Vineyard's "hardware" colony.

Far less visible was a much different summer colony in Oak Bluffs. It was never in the social news because its members came not to vacation but to work. And they were black. The colony began when Charles H. Shearer, a former professor at Hampton University, moved his family to Oak Bluffs to start a laundry serving white families summering on East Chop. Shearer had moved north after he married Henrietta, a Blackfoot Indian, and became the maître d' at Young's Hotel in Boston. The laundry did well and the Shearers prospered. Aware that there were few places where blacks could rent rooms, the Shearers decided to open a guesthouse for blacks and others of color. They renovated the laundry building into the Shearer Cottage, where through the years scores of famous blacks vacationed. Among them was the well-known composer and arranger Harry T. Burleigh, who is credited with such spirituals as "Deep River," "Nobody Knows the Trouble I've Seen," and "Were You There?" He introduced many black entertainers, including Paul Robeson and Ethel Waters, to the Vineyard and to the expanded Shearer Cottages. Another prominent black leader who stayed there was the Reverend Adam Clayton Powell, whose son, Adam Jr., later became a famous congressman with a summer home on the Highlands of East Chop, where other prominent blacks had bought property.

Among them was the West family, whose daughter Dorothy, a well-known writer, became a year-round resident. In 1971 she described that early black summer colony: "[There were] probably twelve cottages, all [filled with] Bostonians. . . . Neither arrogant nor obsequious, they neither overacted or played ostrich. . . . They were 'cool,' a common condition of black Bostonians."

For many years the Boston blacks kept coming, creating a well-regarded colony on the Highlands. They swam at High Beach, as Highland Beach was then called. When the East Chop Beach Club, which did not accept blacks, bought the beach, they had to move south to the beach on the other side of the opening into Lake Anthony. Later they drifted farther south to the beach opposite Waban Park. It was this beach that came to be called the Inkwell. Whether the name was the humorous invention of blacks or of deprecating whites is lost to history. Whoever the inventor, the name is now used by blacks and whites alike without prejudice.

As was true of both communities, black and white, there was little social interaction between the year-round residents and summer-home owners. White year-rounders were too busy earning money to go to the beach very often. Some who owned boats and used them for fishing most of the year would don handsome dark blue "uniforms," put on white shirts and neckties, and become charter-boat captains to the summer people. Those without boats just worked, trying to save enough to get through the winter.

A number of the year-round blacks ran their own businesses. Among them were John Pollard, who operated a dining room in the Highlands, George Wormley, owner of a gasoline station on New York Avenue, and George Frye, a cobbler and shoe store owner on Circuit Avenue. But most worked for others—as domestics if female, as laborers if male.

Year-round blacks in 1920 in Dukes County totaled only 175, most living in Oak Bluffs. Their leader, spiritual and civil, was the Reverend Oscar Denniston, a Jamaican who had been persuaded to come to the Island by the Reverend Madison Edwards, chaplain of the Seamen's Bethel in Vineyard Haven. Denniston served as the minister of the Bradley Memorial Chapel in Oak Bluffs until he died in the 1930s.

Long before blacks had to give it up, Highland Beach had been a favorite spot for a totally different group: students of a summer school for teachers, the Martha's Vineyard Summer Institute. Located in Agassiz Hall, on the bluff overlooking the beach, it brought thousands to Oak Bluffs during its nearly thirty-year existence. The institute began soon after Professor Louis Agassiz died in 1873 and the summer school he ran on Penikese Island, off Cuttyhunk, was closed. Agassiz, a distinguished geologist, spent his life unsuccessfully trying to disprove Darwin's theory of evolution. Colonel Homer B. Sprague, the headmaster of Girls' High School in Boston, who summered in Oak Bluffs, started the institute in 1878.

It had a tentative beginning. That first summer the student body and faculty totaled only fifty. With no buildings of its own, it held classes in such places as Union Chapel on Circuit Avenue, church vestries, and hotel rooms, as well as in the so-called Town Hall above the office of the *Cottage City Star.*

As the school's reputation spread, because of both its progressive curriculum and its resort setting, enrollment kept increasing. In a few years it was able to raise enough money to build classrooms on land donated by the Vineyard Grove Company. The new building was named Agassiz Hall, although as far as is known the Harvard naturalist had never been to Martha's Vineyard. We don't know what position the institute took on Darwin.

By 1884 the institute's faculty totaled thirty-five educators from all over the country. The students, mostly public school teachers eager to freshen their skills (while enjoying summer on the Vineyard), were taught the newest methods of instruction and were brought up to date on developments in their fields. Among its departments were history, mineralogy, didactics, music, philosophy, elocution, photography, and art. Heading the art faculty was Amelia M. Watson, some of whose watercolors of Island scenes are owned by the Martha's Vineyard Historical Society. The photographic pioneer Baldwin Coolidge, who like Amelia Watson later became well known, taught the new skill of dry-plate photography. There was also a course in kindergarten teaching, a new concept in public schools.

In 1890 the school had over seven hundred students, about half from Massachusetts, the rest from thirty-four states and countries. Included in the curriculum was a Berlitz School of Languages, one of the first branches of the now-famous language school that Maximilian Berlitz had opened in Providence, Rhode Island, twelve years earlier. By the late 1890s the institute enrollment peaked at nearly one thousand and a second building was erected.

Classes were held in the mornings. Afternoons and evenings were for bathing, excursions, and entertainments. Students put on programs of music and drama to which the public was invited.

Early in the 1900s state normal schools began offering free summer schools for teachers and the institute's enrollment declined. In 1906 it was closed and its buildings sold. We don't know what happened to them.

The institute was only one of a number of summer schools on the Island through the years. Another was the Harvard Summer School at Seven Gates Farm, started by Professor Shaler in the 1890s. The school was much smaller than the institute, and its faculty of Harvard professors taught courses in geology and mineralogy using the Island's ice-age heritage for a laboratory. The students lived in the old farmhouses that Shaler had bought when he began Seven Gates in 1888. Later summer schools offered courses in art, drama, and photography to provide "cultural" expansion for young summer residents, mostly female.

A more public opportunity for cultural expansion came in 1900, when Andrew Carnegie, the steel millionaire, began offering money to small towns for public libraries. Edgartown was one of those selected. It would receive $4,000 for a library if it provided the land and agreed to expend at least $400 a year for books and a librarian. Edgartown had been reluctant to spend any money on a public library. It was the only village on the Island not to have built one. Instead, it paid Chloe M. Pierce $150 a year to rent a room in her house. A similar amount was spent to hire a librarian. Now Carnegie was offering the town a chance to build a library of its own.

The townspeople were eager to accept the Carnegie offer. Two summer residents offered land; one of them was Mrs. Frederick Warren, who would make the lot next to her house on North Water Street available. She and other summer people gave money, including Elmer Bliss of first-automobile fame. In a town meeting voters approved unanimously. Construction began in October 1903 on the town's third brick building, the others being the courthouse and the bank. By 1904 the library opened, a gala event for Edgartown.

The new library was exciting, but for most summer visitors there were more exciting things to do than go to the library. One was to board the "new and elegant steel steamer" *Uncatena,* which offered "searchlight excursions" along the north shore. Passengers marveled as its 3,000-candlepower searchlight illuminated points of interest as the boat steamed to Gay Head with the band playing all the while.

The new library didn't stop Edgartown's decline. In March 1913 the town lost its customs house. For more than a century it, along with the courthouse, had been the village pride. But there were few ships coming in to pay duties now. For every dollar the office collected, it was spending six. And so the end came. The former suboffice in Vineyard Haven, which was somewhat busier, was made the customs house for the Island. Soon that, too, was closed.

It was a slow time, a time of quiet pleasures. Women spent their afternoons with friends, enjoying tea and petite sandwiches in lace-curtained

It took a while for bathing in the saltwater to become popular. When it did, bathers went to the beach fully clothed, changing into bathing costumes in bathhouses like these at Chadwick's Beach on Chappaquiddick. At first bathers had to come in their own boats, but soon Chadwick provided free steam-launch service. (MVHS Collections)

tearooms, while their daughters went to art classes and their sons hung around the docks. Daily routine called for going to the beach at 11:00 A.M. for a couple of hours. Nobody arrived wearing a bathing suit; all were fully clothed and changed into bathing costumes in a private bathhouse among the scores along the beach at Oak Bluffs or at James Chadwick's bathing beach on Chappaquiddick. Chadwick provided a free launch service from Edgartown for his bathhouse customers.

In their bathing costumes women were almost as fully clothed as in street clothes, with long sleeves, black stockings, and bathing shoes. Some men—and fewer of them went to the beach—were bold enough to go in the water topless, wearing shorts that when wet revealed, some said, more than should be allowed.

Swimming was for the young. Adults, mostly women, went bathing, a term that meant standing in chest-deep water and talking with friends. Many did not go into the water at all, preferring to stand on piazzas and balconies and watch.

With the new century came moving pictures. Summer resorts were good places to introduce the public to the miracle. In July 1900 a New York company with the unpronounceable name of Paley's Kalatecknoscope provided the Island with its first movies. The primitive films were shown in a darkened room under the Bathing Pavilion on the Oak Bluffs boardwalk. The next year the shows moved to Union Chapel, just outside the campground. The *Herald* reported improvement in the science, if not in the art:

> The flicker, which is one of the objections to the ordinary moving picture, is reduced to a minimum and it is possible to watch these for an hour at a time without ill effect to the eyes. The entertainment Mr. Paley is presenting at a few of the leading resorts, previous to the opening of the New York theatrical season, includes a long list of the best of films of varied and interesting subjects, interspersed with beautiful illustrated songs, rendered by the celebrated tenor, Signor Campagnl.

The movies of course had no sound, so it is not easy to imagine how Signor Campagnl "rendered" his songs. Perhaps they were played by a recording, but that seems unlikely. General admission was twenty-five cents, reserved seats thirty-five cents, children fifteen cents. There was little drama in the single-reel films with their subtitles. It was enough that the actors moved, jerkily to be sure, but they moved. A miracle it was.

In 1903 the American Vitagraph Company arrived and began showing its movies inside the Tabernacle. Crowds filled the auditorium and the *Herald* described their reaction: "The company's wonder work in this field never ceases to excite the amazement of the multitudes who always throng to these exhibitions." The Methodists apparently did not consider such use of their sacred space to be blasphemous. By now the campground and even the Tabernacle had taken on a secular character, except for the Sabbath and for two weeks in August when camp meeting was still held each year.

The Island's first movie theater was built in 1907 as a room on the ground floor of the new Cottage City Casino (later called the Tivoli), a large entertainment center owned by Herbert S. Peirce of New Bedford. An announcement, along with a drawing of the building, appeared in the *New Bedford Evening Standard* on December 15, 1906:

> The building will combine a number of features of which there has been a need, including stores and a moving picture hall on the first floor and a dance hall on the second floor. [It] is to be erected for Herbert S. Peirce of New Bedford. . . . Two towers, one at either end of the building, . . . will be open at the sides near the top, a fine view being obtained

from these vantage points. . . . The contract calls for completion of the building on June 10, 1907.

The moving picture hall, its name now the Tivoli Temple, was still in business in 1910, three years later. An advertisement in June of that year announced the opening of the Tivoli Temple for the season, showing "Moving Pictures and Illustrated Songs." It isn't clear how long it stayed in business after the "real" movie theaters began opening. At least four of them were operating in Oak Bluffs by the early 1920s.

Edgartown's first moving pictures were shown in the basement of the Town Hall starting in 1912. Carleton H. Dexter, a young man of twenty-three, was the proprietor. His family, among the Island's oldest, were descendants of the *Mayflower* pilgrims. Dexter had become a skilled operator of movie projectors while working in Boston after he graduated from Dean Academy. Returning to his hometown, he rented the basement of the Town Hall for a movie theater. He ran it until his death in 1916 at only twenty-seven years. When he died, the Town Hall movie theater seems to have closed. His son, Thomas Nevin Dexter, then far too young to take over, later became a local poet and genealogist and one of the founding members of the Martha's Vineyard Historical Society.

By 1915 the concept of movie "stars" had been created. Actors and actresses became household names as their latest films were shown in the Island theaters. In Edgartown that year, Carleton Dexter's Town Hall Theatre was showing such melodramas as *The Supreme Sacrifice,* starring Robert Warwick, during what may have been the theater's final year.

Oak Bluffs became the Island town with the first exclusive movie house in 1915, when the Eagle Theatre, "An Amusement House of Distinction," was built. Its name was adapted from that of its owner, the longtime Vineyard businessman A. P. Eagleston, who seemed to be involved in everything. (He owned clothing stores as well as the Eagleston Tea House and Gift Shop, probably run by his wife, at the Lagoon bridge in Vineyard Haven.) The Eagle ran a different movie daily, four days a week, with afternoon and evening shows. In a few years the plotless, single-reel movies had been succeeded by five-reel dramas. Top billing during one week in 1916 went to *Audrey,* in five reels, starring Pauline Frederick. On the same program was *Little Meena's Romance,* also in five reels, with Dorothy Gish. A two-reel Keystone comedy, *His Last Laugh,* filled out the bill. Business was booming, the *Herald* wrote, with two showings on many nights: "Crowds visit the Eagle Theatre every evening. . . . It has been found necessary to have the entrance and exits roped off to take care of the crowds. The 'Pastime' and 'Dreamland' and the 'Tivoli' make the town look like Broadway with their electric light displays."

Two summers later, in 1918, the Eagle opened the season with Mary Pickford in *The Little Princess*. The price of admission went up to twenty-five cents, because of "government regulations which require the collection of a war tax."

In the early 1900s the first movies were shown in a small room in the Tivoli building at Oak Bluffs. As they became popular, theaters were built, the first being the Eagle, named for its owner, A. P. Eagleston, standing here in front of his ticket office in the 1920s. (MVHS Collections)

Vineyard Haven didn't get its first movie theater, the Capawock, until 1919. It advertised that it would feature "Goldwyn Plays and Capitol Comedies." The first theater exclusively for movies to stay open all year, its slogan was "Learn the Capa-Walk!"

The Pastime Theatre in Oak Bluffs featured such cowboy films as Harry Carey in *Riders of Vengeance* and Tom Mix in *Treat 'Em Rough*. The Eagle Theatre showed more serious films, such as John Barrymore in *His Test of Honor* and Dorothy Gish in *Nobody Home*. Midweek it loosened up to show *A Desert Hero*, starring Fatty Arbuckle. The Oak Bluffs theaters had afternoon and evening shows, six days a week, but only in summer. The Capawock in Vineyard Haven and Dexter's Town Hall in Edgartown were open all year.

In 1920 Edgartown got its first real movie house when the Elm Theatre opened on Main Street. Its owner was Richard L. Colter, whose wife, Jessie, played the piano to accompany the silent films. In 1929 a group of investors headed by Alfred Hall of Edgartown bought it and changed its name to the Edgartown Playhouse. (The group, the Vineyard Theatre Trust, soon owned all Island movie theaters.) The Edgartown Playhouse was destroyed by fire in 1961 and was not rebuilt. The site has been landscaped and turned into a park by the Hall family and is open to the public.

The Tivoli Ballroom had opened in 1907, but it remained in the shadow of the movie theaters until 1916, when Will Hardy brought his Novelty Orchestra from Worcester. Hardy played the piano and with his six-piece orchestra he soon made the Tivoli Ballroom the entertainment center of the Island. It was a magnet, attracting not only summer people but year-round Islanders as well.

The second-floor ballroom opened onto a wide veranda. Dance music floated across the area through its open doors. In the 1930s some of the nation's best-known dance bands entertained in brief stands on weekends, but it was Will Hardy's sextet that created the magic of the Tivoli. He wrote a number of songs related to the Island, including "Tivoli Girl" in 1917, and "Here Comes the *Sankaty* with My Best Girl on Board" and "Vineyard Isle, That Wonderful Island of Mine" in 1928.

Between dances those in the ballroom stepped out onto the veranda to enjoy the cooling breeze from the Sound, the waters of which sparkled in the moonlight. You didn't have to dance to feel the Tivoli magic. Thousands were enthralled by the music as they strolled along Circuit Avenue, munching on a nickel bag of Darling's popcorn. Charles M. Bedell de-

At the head of the steamboat wharf in Oak Bluffs, the Tivoli building was more than a dance hall. Its ground floor held several shops, a shooting gallery, and a restaurant to attract arriving tourists. Across the street was the small skating rink that had replaced the huge rink destroyed in the 1892 Sea View hotel fire.
(MVHS Collections)

scribed that Tivoli magic when he was a boy in the 1920s in a letter to the *Gazette* in 1965:

> A boy heading home from the Pastime movie theatre could hear [the music]. As he passed the Wesley House, it would be overlaid by the sounds of laughter and conversation, gaining strength again during the walk across the causeway. But it was on the long diagonal path across the park in front of the Ocean View that the music might be recognized for what it really was—pure magic. Here, reflected by the waters of Lake Anthony, it seemed to merge with the rippled starlight, to swell and recede at the whim of the evening breeze.

Romantic? Indeed. Especially to a young boy walking home after a night strolling on Circuit Avenue.

On the ground floor of the Tivoli building, beneath the ballroom, was a series of shops: under the tower nearest to the water was Harry George's Waterfront Ice Cream Parlor; clustered in the center were Whiting's Milk Store, a baggage express counter and taxi stand, a souvenir shop, and a shooting gallery where patrons fired rifles at stationary and moving targets for impressive but useless prizes; at the other end, under the other tower, was a restaurant. It was a busy place.

The Tivoli was torn down in 1964 and replaced by the Oak Bluffs Town Hall, its magic having vanished years earlier. Hardy died in 1939 at his home in Oak Bluffs, but the ballroom's magic had started its decline before then. E. Allen White, who leased the building in 1946, closed down the dance hall, he said, "rather than have it go honky-tonk." In the 1950s Alfred E. Holmes, the Oak Bluffs postmaster, turned it into a roller-skating rink, bringing on a lawsuit by Frank Yan Ng of Fall River, who ran the restaurant below. The noise of the skaters on the floor above was driving his customers away, he claimed. When Ng won the suit, Holmes, unable to pay the damages, gave him the building, it was reported. In the 1960s, the fabled Tivoli reached its nadir, as it became an arena for female wrestlers (some of them Vineyarders) and boxing matches.

The Tivoli's success had begun at a most unlikely time. In 1916 Europe was being devastated by a great war then in its second year. America's involvement was becoming more and more likely, despite President Woodrow Wilson's promise of neutrality. The kaiser's U-boats kept prowling the Atlantic, sinking vessels of all kinds, including an Edgartown swordfishing schooner. The British liner *Lusitania* had been torpedoed off Ireland one year earlier, with the loss of 1,200 lives, including 114 Americans.

Yet the war didn't slow down the Tivoli or the Vineyard. The Island had been generally immune to economic slumps for years and seemed equally unaffected by the war in Europe. Business on the Island may actually have increased, since the Island offered a pleasant escape from such concerns. A store on Circuit Avenue in Oak Bluffs seemed to consider the war a merchandising tool when it advertised a shipment of yarn with an exciting new color:

YARN SHOP
Special Announcement
Submarine Blue
Dyed with colors that arrived from Germany on
the Submarine *Deutschland*, the first underwater craft
to cross the Atlantic with a cargo.

The advertisement ran in August 1916, one year after one of those German "underwater craft" sank the *Lusitania* and scores more still were seeking other targets for their torpedoes in the Atlantic!

Despite the threat of torpedoes during those war years, Oak Bluffs prospered. Its hotel porches each summer were crowded with guests, rocking their vacations away as they watched the ebb and flow of the happy crowds. In that ebb and flow were hundreds who strolled along Circuit Avenue—not on sidewalks, since the avenue had no curbs. Those happy strollers took over the avenue; occasionally, and reluctantly, they stepped aside to allow an annoyed automobile driver to ease his way through.

The war in Europe did not spoil those simple pleasures. One boy from Montclair, New Jersey, was traveling to the Island the week the war began to spend his first summer on East Chop. As young Robert M. Ferris III remembered it many years later, the war wasn't on his or anyone's mind:

> If you were in lower Manhattan . . . on a Friday afternoon in late June 1914, you'd be caught up in the bustle of people lugging bags and assorted objects, including children, through the traffic jammed under the elevated tracks. Many were rushing from the Hoboken ferry to the Fall River Line pier two blocks away to board the steamer *Priscilla,* the night boat, to start their trip to the Cape and the Islands.
>
> My mother, by some miracle, managed to get me, my brother John and all our luggage through the confusion and settled aboard the steamer . . . for our first summer in East Chop. I was almost 5.
>
> We made other trips on the *Priscilla* in following years, but that first one was the memorable one for me. The slightly musty smell of our stateroom, the deep sound of her horn signaling departure, the throb of her engine and the frightening creaking of her wooden structure as she rolled in the swells off Point Judith, even now in memory send a chill of excitement down my back.

Three years later, in 1917, Ferris did notice a difference brought on by the war, but it increased the fun: "After our entry into the war we were accompanied by a submarine-chaser escort. It added to the excitement." Once he was on the Island, the war became more distant, forgotten even. Then, one day while he was playing baseball, "word came that the tug *Perth Amboy* had been shelled by a German submarine right off the lightship and was just then [being] tied up at the dock in Vineyard Haven. . . . [We] piled into [a] station wagon (called a beach wagon in those days, a Model T Ford, I think) and [went] to see the suddenly famous tug, where we each got a piece of German shrapnel." The war was getting closer.

Circuit Avenue, Oak Bluffs, before 1920. When a photographer set up his tripod, shopkeepers came out to have their pictures taken. The automobile era was just beginning and curbstones were scarce. Even in the 1930s strollers walked down the center of the avenue, moving aside for the occasional motor car. (MVHS Collections)

In July 1915 the 5th Regiment of the Massachusetts Volunteer Infantry came to the Vineyard, landing at the Eastville pier aboard the steamer *New Hampshire* from New Bedford. The regiment was not in the U.S. Army; its 850 men, ninety horses, and six supply wagons pulled by mule teams were part of the state militia. The men pitched their tents near the beach at Eastville that first night and the next day broke camp and marched through Oak Bluffs to Farm Neck, where they set up camp on the Norton farm. To the *Gazette* it was glorious:

> The regiment made a splendid appearance as it swung along Circuit Avenue through Oak Bluffs, a long procession of baggage and supply wagons drawn by large mules. Some of the wagons were so heavily laden that it took four mules to draw one. . . . A person standing between Pena-cook and Tuckernuck avenues could see Circuit avenue from Narra-gansett avenue to the top of the hill filled with a solid moving mass of

men, as they went on their way. . . . The music of the band was inspiring and the various companies marched well and looked fine. They carried all their equipment on their backs, the rolled blanket, knapsack, canteen, etc., and their rifles over the right shoulder. . . . No such body of troops has disturbed the quiet of those hills since Grey's raiders in the Revolution, a century and a half ago. . . .

It went into permanent camp until Friday on the large tract of land on the State road, a little way above Memorial Park [in Edgartown]. . . . The camping ground extends from the State Road through to the West Tisbury road and is owned by George S. Norton. . . .

In the morning, the Fifth marched down Main Street, wheeled into South Water, and marched away for the day's work on the Katama Plains. Headed by the field [officers] and staff, the band playing inspiring music, and the full regiment following, it made a fine picture. . . . The machine gun company [declared] the Katama firing range the best they had seen. . . .

The Militia is the State's first line of defense and, while it is pretty to see the soldiers go marching by, we should remember that they would be called upon . . . should our country be threatened with trouble, either from foreign or domestic foes.

That worrisome threat came on April 2, 1917. The United States, more worried than threatened, declared war on Germany. By happenstance that evening a representative of the Naval Coast Defense Reserve was meeting with Edgartown boat owners in the Home Club. He had come to urge them to volunteer their boats to protect the coast should it become necessary. The men were eager to take part, although they asked for a little advance notice: "One of the boatmen, voicing the general feeling of all said: 'If we can be of use, we are ready. We would like to know if the Navy wants us within the next two weeks, before we begin the season's work. If they want us, we will sacrifice the season's work and go.'"

They didn't get any advance warning. The war had begun for America. The Selective Service Act, passed on May 18, 1917, made men between twenty-one and thirty subject to the draft. It took a while to get it under way, and at the end of August the *Gazette* assured those who would soon be called that it was not a disgrace to be drafted:

Very soon the young men who have been drafted from Dukes County will be called to the colors. . . . The fact that they will be taken without their desire or consent detracts nothing from the debt that the country will owe them. . . . They are performing a more arduous service than those who have volunteered, who had the opportunity to select the branch of service in which they are to serve, the one which seemed the most attractive to them. The Conscript, on the other hand, has no say in the matter. . . . These men will fight for us and it is our duty to see that their hardship is made no more severe than necessary. . . . Let a Committee of Dukes County people be formed to make these Dukes County boys their especial charge. If they have dependents let us see that they are not neglected. If they need anything that they cannot get, let us get it for them. . . . Every Dukes County man who goes into the service ought to be listed by such a committee and his whereabouts kept track of, in order that his necessities may be known and supplied.

If such a committee was formed, its records seem to have been lost. Surviving records show that 170 Islanders went into the service: Edgartown 40; Oak Bluffs 47; Vineyard Haven and West Tisbury 62; Chilmark 4; Gay Head 17 (11 of them in the coast guard). Two Vineyarders were killed in action, neither while serving with the Americans: Lieutenant Walter D. Rheno of Vineyard Haven, an aviator in the French army, and Neil McLaurin of Edgartown, in the Canadian army. (McLaurin's residency can't be established.) At least three other Vineyarders died in the war from disease.

When the war ended in 1918, the Barnstable district commander congratulated the Vineyard men who had served as registrars of the draft. It was, he wrote, "the first time in the history of these United States, [that] a thoroughly democratic army has been raised without . . . draft riots and local disturbances and it has been primarily due to the honest, conscientious efforts of the Registrars [of the draft] acting from a patriotic motive that is consistently American." Among those conscientious registrars were Judge Edmund G. Eldridge and William J. Rotch of West Tisbury.

Only a few months before the war ended, an unexpected event brought it much closer. On August 10, 1918, the schooner *Progress,* owned and captained by Bob Jackson of Edgartown, was swordfishing off Georges Bank, southeast of Nantucket, as it had done throughout the war. The *Progress* was among a large fleet of swordfishermen when a U.S. Navy destroyer came by to warn them that a German U-boat was in the vicinity. The skippers weren't worried. They had heard such warnings before and nothing had ever happened. Fishing was too good to worry about a suspected U-boat. The *Progress* had been out nearly two weeks and its hold was almost full. One more day would be enough, Jackson told the crew, most of them Vineyarders. When the wind came up and it became too rough to spot the fish, Jackson decided to stay out an extra day and hoisted a steadying sail while waiting for a wind change. He recalled what happened next:

> We were laying under riding sail. It was too rough to fish. About 10 in the morning the cook sung out for dinner. One minute later, we heard a heavy gun. We rushed up on the deck and saw a submarine. It was firing at the fishing boats in the vicinity. All three hoisted their sails and tried to escape.
>
> After the submarine fired a couple of shots at them, the fleeing boats hauled down their sails, but the U-boat kept on firing. She fired in all about 15 shots.

The U-boat commander ordered the crews of three New Bedford schooners to abandon their vessels and get into dories. German sailors went on board and took fresh provisions from the galleys. Explosive charges were attached to the sterns of the schooners and set off. They sank immediately. Their crews in dories headed for shore, 120 miles to the northwest. The U-boat then turned its attention to the rest of the fleet, including the *Progress*. Jackson and his crew were ordered to abandon ship; its galley was raided. A charge was detonated and the *Progress* sank quickly. The fleet of dories headed for land. (At least nine swordfishing schooners had been sunk, their crews filling twenty dories.)

A thick fog came in during the night and the fleet became separated. When it cleared in the morning, Jackson's dory was alone. After thirty hours of rowing and sailing with a spritsail, Jackson and his two crewmen were picked up by a fishing boat. All the other fishermen were soon picked up or made it to shore on their own. No lives were lost.

The attack was useless as far as the war effort was concerned. It was a desperate act by the U-boat, unable to return to its base, to get much-needed food.

Three months later, on November 11, 1918, the armistice was signed. The German government compensated the owners of the fishing vessels for their losses, including the value of the fish in the holds. Early the next summer, Jackson sailed into Edgartown aboard a new schooner, the *Liberty*, that he had bought with the compensation money. The *Liberty* had a long, productive life, sailing out of Edgartown until World War II—but not under Captain Bob Jackson; he had sold the *Liberty*.

It was a time of labor unrest. When the war ended workers learned that although companies had made millions during the war, they had received little of the profits. Strikes became frequent. Angry workers demanded the right to organize into unions. Even fishermen, previously proud of their independence, began trying to organize. In 1919 a number of them in New York and Boston went on strike. They sought a minimum wage based on the price paid for their catch; they demanded that all be paid in full within twenty-four hours after the catch was sold; and they said that no man would go on another trip until he had been paid for the previous one.

These demands seemed reasonable, but there was strong opposition to any strike by fishermen on the Cape and the Islands. Wages were not a big issue there, according to Captain Phil Norton of Edgartown. He also claimed that fishermen were always paid quickly:

> On our way home, or after we got home, the captain had the money and would divide it up. First, the boat got her share, a "clear fifth," of the gross. Then the expenses for gas and oil were taken out. What was left was divided into eight shares for the men, plus a half-share for wear and tear on the engine. Everybody got the same share, including the captain, except that the cook and engineer usually got an extra $25. Of course, if the captain owned the boat, he got that one-fifth in addition to his equal share.

Island captains decided to fish with nonunion crews. Captain Bob Jackson was a leader of the antistrikers. He was eager to go fishing in his new (and appropriately named) schooner, *Liberty*. Nobody was going to tell him whom he could hire or what and when he would pay his men. When told he wouldn't be able to sell any fish caught by a nonunion crew, he organized a group of captains to take the *Liberty* out. They became known as the "Crew of Captains." Because all were captains (management, in effect), they assumed they could fish without joining the union and sell their catch when they got back. When the *Liberty* reached Georges Bank, there were a dozen or more strikebreakers already fishing. The swordfishing was good. They had no problem harpooning; the problem would be in selling.

When the *Liberty* sailed into Boston to sell its catch, striking dockworkers refused to unload it and told Jackson it would be the same in New York. So he sailed to New Bedford, where the fish were unloaded and shipped by rail to New York to be delivered to the wholesalers. But fish handlers—"lumpers," as they were called—at New York's Fulton Fish Market would not unload them from the freight cars and they quickly rotted. Jackson was so disgusted that he sold his brand-new *Liberty* to Claude Wagner of Edgartown, who had been fishing with him for years, having been one of the crew when the *Progress* was sunk by the U-boat.

Jackson and the other captains on that famous "Crew of Captains" never sold their fish, but they did break the strike. They sued the Fishermen's Union for damages. In April 1920 a hearing was held in Edgartown by "fishermen seeking to have the unions restrained from interfering with their right to fish where they will and to market their fish where they will." Any legal process takes time, and while it was going on many more tons of fish rotted, some of them Vineyard owned. In May 1920 Captain Angus R. Lohnes of Edgartown sailed his vessel *Minerva* into Fulton Fish Market with seventeen thousand pounds of mackerel consigned to several wholesalers. His reception was not routine:

> On the morning of May 7th, as the fish handlers from the different concerns appeared on the dock . . . to unload the *Minerva's* fish, a United Sea Food Workers' Union representative appeared on the dock and waved the men back and ordered them not to handle the fish.
>
> The *Minerva's* fish laid in the hold of the vessel until the morning of Monday, May 10, when the fish handlers finally acted under orders from Wagner [the union representative] after the crew had finally told Wagner that they would join the Fishermen's Union of the Atlantic. On getting the promise, Wagner delivered to Capt. Lohnes a slip of paper to show to the union fish handlers: "May 10, '20. Take fish out of *Minerva*. OK. Wagner."

During that same week, on Wednesday, May 12, 1920, another Edgartown skipper, Captain Levi Jackson, arrived at Fulton Market in the *Priscilla II* with fifteen hundred pounds of mackerel consigned to New York wholesalers. Again a union representative stopped the unloading. For three days the crew refused to join the union and the *Priscilla* sat in the dock, the fish spoiling. Then,

> late in the afternoon of Saturday, May 16, after the market had closed until Monday, Captain [Levi] Jackson unloaded his fish (which were then bursted and spoiled) in two piles on the float in the rear of the place

of business of the dealers to whom his fish had been futilely consigned, he placed a small American flag on each pile of fish and also left on each pile a card on which was the following: "These fish were caught under the American flag and have rotted under the American flag."

In December 1920 the court handed down its ruling on the Edgartown captains' suit. It was a victory for Captain Bob Jackson and his crew. The *Gazette* applauded:

> The Fish Handlers' Union will have to pay Capt. Robert L. Jackson $365 as reimbursement for fish "lost or destroyed" in transit during the boycott declared against Capt. Jackson and other captains. . . . The fishermen charged that the Fishermen's Union of the Atlantic sought to "acquire domination and monopolistic control of the entire fishing industry of the Atlantic Coast," and the charges are upheld by Master [William H.] Hitchcock. . . . Bringing the suit against the Union were Chester H. Robinson, John S. Reynolds and Earl Wade of Tisbury, Charles H. Blount and Stillman C. Cash of Nantucket, Arthur F. Butler of New Bedford, and Robert L. Jackson, George R. Paul, Angus R. Lohnes, Samuel B. Norton and Antone Silvia of Edgartown.

Other newspapers, strongly antiunion, were jubilant. *The New Bedford Standard* editorialized:

> It is a victory for fair play and for the public interest. The sea is free to fish in; its food belongs to those who need it. What the union sought to accomplish . . . was to prevent this fish from reaching the market by combining with freight-handlers to that end. Such a conspiracy against the people's food supply was clearly evil.
>
> The Edgartown independents deserve the thanks of the public for fighting this issue out. Theirs is a spirit of independence and liberty that evokes admiration.

Captain Bob Jackson quickly built another schooner, the *Hazel M. Jackson,* and it, along with the *Liberty,* the *B. T. Hillman,* and the *Malvina B.,* became the pride of Edgartown's waterfront for years. Jackson was regarded as the top swordfisherman in Massachusetts. He had an unerring aim with the harpoon. His son Bob said: "The old man, you couldn't beat him. Out of a hundred fish, he'd probably miss only two." Some seasons he harpooned twelve hundred swordfish. He became a legend.

Jackson's son, "young Bob," was not listed among those who brought the strikebreaking suit, but he had been on that famous voyage, the only non-captain in the "Crew of Captains." He was still in high school and it was his first swordfishing trip. His father let him join the crew to help in the galley, but he didn't want him to become a fisherman. He wanted his son to finish high school and go to college, but young Bob was determined to become a fisherman. He never went to college. Most of his life was spent fishing. He did take a few years off to skipper yachts owned by wealthy men, including Vernon Stouffer, who owned the famous chain of restaurants. Bob had a pass at Stouffer's and could eat for free in any them.

Young Bob's fame never equaled his father's, but it came close. A number of years ago he talked with me about his life as a swordfisherman: "You'd have eight men in the crew, with usually five up in the rigging, spotting fish. But I've seen the time when you didn't need anyone up in the rigging. . . . The water was just alive with them. . . . Just pick which one you wanted. We'd fish from eight in the morning until five at night. We'd stay out two weeks, sometimes three. One trip we brought in close to two hundred swords. She was really full."

Another Edgartown captain, Phil Norton, described the life aboard a swordfishing schooner. The men ate well:

> Good food. They all had good cooks. George Thomas was our cook and George Paul was old man Bob's cook. Another Paul was Horace Hillman's cook. They were the best cooks.
>
> First, you had breakfast, about 4 or 5 in the morning because the cook was up at just the crack of day cutting up the side of a lamb or steaks or something. Plenty of good food. We had breakfast over by 5. Lunch was at 9:30 so we wouldn't be eating in the middle of the day when the fish were up, and then ate supper about 3 o'clock.
>
> After supper we had to dress the fish and clean everything up. . . . We'd cover them with canvas and let 'em lay on deck overnight so that the animal heat would be lost before we put them on ice. We would slide narrow bars of ice into the bellies of the fish to keep them cold. Buried in cracked ice they would stay fresh for weeks.

The food was good, but the accommodations were not. Everybody except the engineer slept in the tiny forecastle, a small triangular cabin far forward, which left most of the hull for icing the fish. In the "fo'c'sle," as it was pronounced, the bunks were wide but had little headroom, hardly enough for a big man to sleep comfortably on his side.

Captain Norton had his own theory about mercury, long before it became a news item:

> There were seven bunks in the fo'c'sle. I was engineer and I slept along-side the engine, in a little cabin. Let me tell you something . . . there's a lot of talk about mercury in swordfish, well, after you've been out about a week and the fish are iced down in the hold, the shiny stuff on their bellies would wash off and go down into the bilge water. . . . One morning I woke up and all the pennies in my pocket had turned bright silver— that's how bad the air was and that was mercury in the air. . . . I don't think mercury is in the meat, it is on the outside.

All but three of the eight-man crew would go up in the rigging to spot fish. When one was struck, the action began:

> Usually, you'd have eight men in a crew, five aloft, one of them sitting on a board, leaning on the masthead. . . . You have got to have three men down below: the striker, who was usually the captain; the engineer to keep the engine running; and the cook. When the striker hit one, the cook would toss a barrel with a hundred fathoms of line tied to the harpoon's iron to mark the fish. The lowest man on the crosstree would come down as fast as he could and jump in the dory and row over to the keg and start hauling for all he was worth.
>
> If he thought the iron was right through the fish he could pull like the devil. If he thought the iron might tear out, he had to be more careful. When the iron went right through the fish there was no way for it to come back, it would break the line before it did.
>
> If the boat is close enough she'd come over and hoist the fish in. . . . If the boat was too far away and if the fish wasn't too big, like a two hundred pounder, you'd float him in over the side of the dory. You'd haul up the tail and put your foot on the rail and flip it in. Sometimes you'd go underwater about six inches and you'd give the fish a yank and in he'd come, end over end, water and all on top of you sometimes. That's the way you got them in when the boat wasn't around. You had to get him inside the dory or the sharks would get him.

For schooners swordfishing was the big moneymaker. They would start in early June off the southern coast of New Jersey, following the swordfish as they headed north. In late summer they were on Georges Bank. Later the schooners would still be chasing the swordfish as far north as Nova Scotia.

In winter the schooner fishermen did other fishing, gill netting and mackerel fishing, and they also spent periods handlining (catching cod with a baited hook, one at a time) and trawling. These fishermen could earn up to three thousand dollars a year, which made them among the best-paid men in town. "You could build a house for three thousand dollars," young Bob Jackson recalled.

There was a month or more during the winter when the boats would stay in port, being painted and repaired by the crew without pay. Maintenance was part of their duty as crew.

On November 2, 1918, a little more than a week before the armistice ended the fighting in Europe, another war-related event shook up the Island, although no Vineyarder was directly involved. It happened right off Vineyard Haven harbor. The British steamship *Port Hunter,* loaded with matériel for the war, had left Boston the day before, intending to join a convoy off New York City for the Atlantic crossing. It was a clear, calm night, but very dark. The moon would not rise until six in the morning.

The *Port Hunter* was carrying two thousand tons of steel billets and another nine hundred tons of railway wheels and axles, all for the French, placed low in the hold as ballast. That heavy, compact cargo left plenty of space for forty thousand bulky boxes, most of them packed with winter clothing for the American troops, items badly needed as winter approached. Included in the two thousand tons of clothing were 205,797 warm leather jerkins lined with soft flannel, which would become familiar to Islanders later.

At 2:00 A.M., as the *Port Hunter* was steaming west past East Chop, heading for New York, the pilot saw the lights of a ship just rounding West Chop and heading toward him. It was a tug with two heavy barges in tow and it swung wide around West Chop, taking the north side of the channel between Hedge Shoal and the Vineyard. The *Port Hunter* was in the south side of the channel, closer to land.

In those days there was no radio communication between vessels, and pilots relied on the ship's lights to determine position and right of way. Generally, vessels approaching each other from opposite directions passed port to port, red light to red. But when conditions warranted and there was no time or space to make a port passing, as was the case here, passing starboard to starboard, green to green, is permissible.

The two pilots seemed comfortable with a green-to-green passing until, as they drew close, for some unexplained reason, the *Port Hunter* turned hard to starboard, apparently intending to pass port to port. The move came too late. As the *Port Hunter* crossed its bow, the tug *Covington*, its heavy tow making it impossible to change course quickly, rammed into the port side of the freighter near its bow. At 2:02 A.M., an SOS went out over the *Port Hunter's* telegraph. It was sinking fast. The *Covington* anchored its barges and went to the *Port Hunter's* aid. Whether it was able to help is unclear, but when daylight came the *Port Hunter* could be seen aground on Hedge Fence Shoal, filling with water, its decks already awash in the swells.

The crew was taken off while the heavily laden vessel was being pounded by the swells. The cargo, estimated to be worth nearly six million dollars, was at the mercy of the sea. Salvage crews sent by the navy were on the scene within a week, but their work soon stopped without explanation. By this time the war had ended. Nobody seemed to think it was urgent to salvage winter clothing for men in the trenches. They would soon be home.

There were many rumors and false reports about the war being circulated at the time. On November 7, 1918, the *Gazette* spread one with this brief, "stop-the-press" dispatch:

END OF WAR IN SIGHT

As the *Gazette* goes to press, the cheering news comes that today Germany has signed the Armistice terms and hostilities have been called off.

Here in Edgartown, the people are cheering, the church bells are ringing, the whistles are tooting, the dogs are barking, the autos are honking, and verily it looks as if the old town might turn inside out.

The whole country had been taken in. The erroneous November 7 bulletin had been filed by the United Press from Paris. It was soon retracted, but not before eager newspapers, like the *Gazette*, had printed it.

Then at 11:00 A.M., European time, on the eleventh day of the eleventh month of 1918, the Armistice did take effect. With three days to check its accuracy, this time the November 14 *Gazette* boldly and correctly announced:

The Hun
Is Dun!
Great War Ends.
Victory and Peace

The big news first came to Edgartown at 4 A.M. on Monday through a telephone call to Mr. Chester E. Pease from Mrs. George D. Flynn of Fall River, with a request to forward it to Mr. Flynn at Pohogonut, who was stopping at his place there with a party of friends. Mr. Pease quickly called up a few friends and gave them the glad tidings and when Steamer *Uncatena* went out at 5:30 A.M., Capt. Marshall ordered the whistle blown from the wharf to beyond Harbor Light.

But most of the people here were first made aware that the great world event had surely happened and that the war was about to end victoriously, when at 6:30 A.M. the Congregational church bell began to ring, quickly followed by the bells of the other churches.

Charles H. Johnson at the rope of the Congregational church; Jack Donnelly at the Baptist; Sylvester Luce at the Methodist. Of course, many others took a turn at the good work afterwards.

[One was] Miss Chloe Coffin, who came to the Baptist church early and requested to be allowed to ring the bell. . . . In July 1863, when news came that Vicksburg had surrendered, Miss Coffin's mother, the late Mrs. Charlotte Coffin, had rung the same Baptist bell to sound the glad tidings to the people . . . an interesting incident of the glorious day.

Soon with bells clanging, autos honking, horns tooting, and all the other noises that young America knows so well how to produce on short notice, the old town started in a varied program of celebration which did not end until after the light bearers of the evening had burned out their last torch and the rejoicers had wended their way home in the midnight hours.

The Torchlight Parade was a whopper. Messrs. Colter, Vose, Fernald, and their scores of helpers, pulled off a great stunt.

The celebrating resumed the next day with a huge gathering of citizens in Edgartown's Town Hall:

The Rally at the Town Hall on Tuesday evening . . . perhaps in a more conventional way testified to the interest of our people in the great conclusions which had been brought about. . . . The several speakers dwelt much on the great work which yet confronts the United States and allied nations in working out the problems which will follow peace, one of which will be to feed a world already short of food. . . .

Taking a review of all that was said and done in Edgartown from Monday morning until Tuesday night, it can be again stated that the old town fittingly and enthusiastically observed the virtual end of the Great World War.

When the celebrating died down, the Island's attention returned to the *Port Hunter*, the sunken British freighter whose mast was still visible on Hedge Fence Shoal off West Chop. The government had hired the Mercantile Wrecking Company of New Bedford, a family enterprise headed by Barney Zeitz, to recover the cargo. It wasn't until June 1919 that it ended its work. When that happened, the private scavengers moved in. Over the next few months, hundreds of boats hovered over the wreck, grappling for the spoils. Some were from the Vineyard, but most were from the mainland. All assumed that with the official salvaging ended, the abandoned wreck was open to them. The navy felt otherwise and sent a patrol vessel out to stop the salvaging, although under maritime law an abandoned wreck can be salvaged by anyone.

The bewilderment had been going on for more than a year, as conflicting newspaper stories make clear:

January 30, 1919: The *Port Hunter* is fast sinking deeper into the sand. Its cargo rots as the government lags.

February 13, 1919: The French government sends a lighter and divers to salvage its iron from the *Port Hunter*. The Mercantile Wrecking Company, hired by the navy, begins salvaging.

May 3, 1919: A Vineyard Haven tailor advertises that he will make a leather coat out of two *Port Hunter* vests for four dollars. Thefts of the salvaged goods from the Sanitary Laundry are reported.

May 22, 1919: A Boston newspaper account by a visitor just back from the Island: "A large ship carrying government supplies sank in the roadstead and in a few days leather jackets and other items of apparel abounded on the Vineyard. A lady of my acquaintance looked out her window and observed a clothesline hung heavily with shirts. The neighbor informed her, 'They have had grand catch of shirts this morning and are going fishing for drawers this afternoon.' It is said that many mortgages on the Vineyard have been paid off this year."

June 19, 1919: The salvaging of U.S. Army goods is nearly finished. The cost of the salvage work is one thousand dollars a day. It has already recovered about four million dollars' worth of army supplies.

June 28, 1919: The U.S. government salvagers, Barney Zeitz of New Bedford, have completed their work. A diver reports that the hull is broken in half. Salvaged bundles of wire are piling up on the dock. The French cargo includes three thousand tons of metal and seventeen hundred tons of soft coal. Expert salvagers from Merritt and Chapman will view the wreck to determine if the hull can be raised.

July 31, 1919: French salvaging is yet to begin.

August 7, 1919: Three robberies occur in Vineyard Haven. *Port Hunter* goods were stolen by off-Islanders who came over in small boats. One theft was at the Oak Bluffs Sanitary Laundry, where five hundred dollars' worth of *Port Hunter* clothing was taken. The clothing was there being washed to clear it of salt water.

August 14, 1919: Federal agents are on the Island to investigate the illegal salvaging of the wrecked *Port Hunter*. A total of 1,100 leather jerkins have been located in New Bedford, along with 95 olive-drab army shirts. On the Vineyard 30 dozen shirts were found at the laundry; agents found three bales of underwear and other clothing at a blacksmith shop. At a farmhouse they discovered 1,923 jerkins and 1,480 other garments still in bales. In Oak Bluffs a *Port Hunter* souvenir stand, next to the shooting gallery, was closed down and its goods seized. The government is not concerned with individual garments seen here and there. It isn't after "the chicken feed" and does not intend to pull a *Port Hunter* shirt off any man's back.

September 18, 1919: Work is to begin soon on the salvaging of the French cargo.

October 2, 1919: Those who turned in soap and candles taken from the *Port Hunter* to the navy earlier will be reimbursed if they send receipts to the headquarters in Boston.

October 9, 1919: A congressional probe into the *Port Hunter* salvage operation discloses that many items were taken by fishermen before the official salvaging began. Vineyard men testify in their defense, claiming that the cargo was rotting and would have soon been worthless if they had not "rescued" it.

November 6, 1919: French salvagers are on the job trying to recover the steel from the *Port Hunter*.

November 20, 1919: The French salvage operation is stopped. It is not worth the high cost, caused by strong currents and the fact that shifting sand is burying the hull.

December 4, 1919: A bold robbery of *Port Hunter* clothing occurs in Vineyard Haven. Taken are sixteen to twenty leather vests and eight olive drab shirts. In their flight the robbers drop a vest and two shirts in a neighboring yard.

December 11, 1919: A newborn child was left at the front door of a family in Edgartown the previous Monday night. The baby was wrapped in two *Port Hunter* shirts.

No swords had been beaten into plowshares, no spears into pruning hooks, but two olive drab shirts destined for soldiers in the trenches of Europe had been pulled from the ocean and turned into swaddling clothes for a newborn child abandoned on a cold night in Edgartown.

The Great War had finally ended.

11

Enclaves, the Lindberghs, Minorities, World War II, and the Change

Before 1900, the Vineyard, like much of New England, was fairly homogeneous. Its inhabitants were mostly white, Anglo-Saxon, and Protestant (the acronym WASP came later). Some Catholics, Portuguese mostly, had settled on the Island, but they were relatively few. By 1880 there were enough to build a Catholic church in Oak Bluffs. It was only a "mission church," with no priest in residence. One came over from New Bedford to conduct services two or three times a month. Not until 1903 was the congregation able to afford a full-time pastor.

Outside Oak Bluffs there was less diversity, if any at all. The late Howard Andrews of Edgartown, who was of Portuguese ancestry, recalled the 1920s:

> All the Azoreans or Cape Verdeans lived over by the old Catholic church, down by Lake Street in Oak Bluffs. . . . In Edgartown there were no colored. There were Indians over in Chappaquiddick, Marian Harding and some of those, and her mother and her relatives. . . . And only one Jew, "Buzzy" Hall's father [Alfred Hall]. If you were Jewish and wanted to rent a room at the Harborside, they wouldn't rent it to you. . . . I remember as plain as day when you couldn't rent a room in Edgartown if you were Jewish. Colored people just never tried. . . . There was only the Open Door Club for the colored servants.

But changes were on the way. With the arrival of the twentieth century, the nation began taking on a new complexion. Twenty million immigrants, most of them Europeans, arrived during the early years of the century, an average of one million a year. Few, if any, had Martha's Vineyard as their destination. Certainly not one young man, a Lithuanian Jew, who landed in New York City in 1904. He was Samuel Krangle and he had never heard of Martha's Vineyard.

Two different stories are told by family members about his migration. The first was told by his son David to Nancy Hamilton in 1991, during an interview she had with him for a film. The second is from his daughter, Anne, in a 1995 interview with Linsey Lee, the Martha's Vineyard Historical Society's Oral History director. Both were asked if they knew why their father had left Lithuania, then part of czarist Russia. David said it was probably to avoid military service. The Russo-Japanese War was going on and no doubt he expected to be called up.

Anne, David's younger sister, recalls it differently:

> He was brought up [in Lithuania]—at that time it was Russia. There were bad times and the czar had to have a scapegoat, so who do they usually pick on? . . . the Jewish people. . . . They made a curfew for Jews; they couldn't be on the streets after dark. [My father] was the oldest in the family. . . . He used to get up very early and walk in the dark to work in a bakery. . . . Cossacks on horseback were on the streets at night and if any [Jew] was on the street in the dark they stopped him. . . . This Cossack took a whip to my father, who was fifteen years old. He made up his mind right then "to leave this country just as soon as I can."
>
> He dropped out of school to work full-time. It took him two years to save the two hundred dollars to come steerage to America.

Take your pick of the stories. Both agree that soon after arriving in New York, the young emigrant, unhappy with his job in a screwdriver factory, left the city and moved in with a cousin in New Bedford. One day his cousin spotted an advertisement seeking a young man to work on a farm for the summer on Martha's Vineyard. Applicants could pick up a free ticket at the New Bedford steamboat wharf. The young man liked the offer, so his cousin took him down to the wharf and put him on the steamer. The ticket had been paid for by Captain Hiram Daggett, a retired sea captain who owned a farm in Eastville, about where the hospital is now.

After arriving in New York, the young man had changed his name to Samuel Cronig. His daughter, Anne, couldn't explain why he chose that name. She told Linsey Lee: "I don't know how he ever took the name

Cronig. . . . He was going to be an American . . . so he came up with the name Samuel Cronig . . . and all his brothers took it when he brought them over later."

Samuel liked the Vineyard. At the end of his summer job on the farm in 1905, he went to work for Bodfish and Call, grocers, living in a room over the store. (Bodfish and Call later merged with two other stores to become Smith, Bodfish and Swift, the ancestor of today's SBS.) He started out working in the back of the store, bagging potatoes and performing other similar tasks. As his English improved, he got out of the back room and soon was delivering orders in a horse and wagon. By 1909 he had saved enough money to send for his brother Edward.

There is confusion about the arrival dates of the Jewish families. They spoke little English and no Islander spoke Yiddish or Russian, so it is not surprising that the details of their arrival were not accurately recorded. Both Samuel and Edward Cronig are listed in the 1910 federal census as living in Vineyard Haven. Samuel is described as a salesman in a grocery store, "working on own account," and Edward as an apprentice carpenter, also "working on own account," meaning not in the employ of another. The statements are confusing, as there is no record of Samuel owning a store in 1910.

By 1911 Samuel had saved enough money to send for Lizzy Levany (Levine), who lived in Minsk, Russia. He had met her while working there after he dropped out of school. Soon after she arrived they married, and the following year their son David was born. A second son, Carlyle, was born in 1914, followed by a daughter, Anne, in 1917.

That year, 1917, the four brothers, Samuel, Edward, Theodore ("Tebby"), and Henry, started Cronig Brothers' grocery store on Main Street in Vineyard Haven. It was a bold move for these Lithuanian Jews who spoke poor English. Their store was in competition with several long-established grocery stores on Main Street. But their dedication and their personal attention to customers soon made their venture a success.

Several other Lithuanian Jews came to Vineyard Haven during these years. Among them were Eudice and Yudl Brickman, the first Jewish married couple to move to the Island. In 1916 their daughter, Dorothy, became the first Jewish girl born on Martha's Vineyard. Eudice Brickman's brother, Essidor Issokson, arrived from Lithuania soon after. When Ida, an older daughter of the Brickmans, married David Levine in 1931, her parents bought the tiny dry-goods store owned by Mrs. H. L. Tilton and gave it to

When Benjamin and Bessie Hall of New Bedford bought an Edgartown thread shop from Martha White in 1911, they became the town's first Jewish merchants, although they stayed in New Bedford and Hall's Department Store was run by their son, Morris. Other early Jewish shopowners were the Cronigs and the Brickmans in Vineyard Haven. (MVHS Collections)

the newlyweds as a wedding present. They soon expanded it into the Vineyard Dry Goods Company.

These Jewish immigrants had broken through the WASP barrier. They formed a tightly knit, devout Jewish community in Vineyard Haven. Through the years, they moved from Orthodox to Conservative to Reform, always marrying within their faith. The small, dedicated group founded the town's Jewish cemetery (Eudice Brickman being the first person buried there) and the Hebrew Cultural Center, the Island's first synagogue.

They were not the only Jews on the Island. Benjamin and Bessie Hall of New Bedford had started Hall's Department Store on Main Street in Edgartown after buying a needle and thread shop from Martha P. White in 1911. But they hadn't moved to Edgartown; they remained in New Bedford, where they also owned a store. To run the Island store, they sent over their son, Morris.

After Benjamin Hall, the patriarch, died in 1917, his widow, Bessie, moved to Edgartown. She had bought a house on South Summer Street from Allen Mayhew a few years before. The house is still owned by the Hall family. Bessie's two sons, Morris and Alfred, went into the army in

1918 during the Great War. The war ended before they were shipped over-seas. They returned to take over the store from their mother, who had been running it in their absence.

The small Edgartown store could not support both brothers, so Alfred bought Dr. Worth's drugstore at Four Corners. He also opened a real estate office. During the 1920s he ran a brokerage house on the second floor of the drugstore building. There Edgartown's wealthy male summer residents, lounging in leather easy chairs, bought and sold stocks while Alfred posted the latest ticker-tape prices on a large blackboard. At the end of the summer of 1929 he closed down his brokerage business as usual, selling his inventory of stocks. It was a fortuitous move. The market crashed in October.

Arthur Hillman, president of the Edgartown bank, and W. Irving Bull-man of Boston joined with Alfred to form a company that bought Edgartown's movie theater, the Elms, from Richard L. Colter. Alfred had married Marjorie Pease, the daughter of Chester Pease (the town's richest man), and no doubt his father-in-law helped with the financing. Family tradition has it that an aisle seat, with the one in front of it removed, was reserved for Chester, who had a stiff leg. Within a few years the prospering company had bought all the Island's movie theaters.

Alfred Hall was a skillful entrepreneur. By 1940 he owned a third of the commercial buildings in Edgartown. He lived a long life, dying in 1992 at ninety-four.

When Bessie Hall bought the South Summer Street house in Edgartown in January 1914, she was probably the first Jew to own a house in town. And the last for a while. Discrimination against Jews continued into the 1930s. Edgartown was "the last holdout of the WASPs," according to Dorothy West, the black writer and Vineyard resident.

Discrimination against blacks was equally severe, creating a problem for the many black domestic servants who worked for the town's wealthy summer people. They had no place to relax on their days off. Restaurants and bars would not serve them. That changed when an enlightened summer resident bequeathed a small building and a plot of land on Cooke Street, opposite the Edgartown cemetery, to a black couple who had been faithful family domestics for years. The couple, Edna and James Smith, turned the house into a gathering place for blacks, and it soon took on an appropriate name: the Open Door Club. Once each summer the black domestics put on a picnic at the club to which they invited their white

Blacks pose formally in front of a rooming house at 45 Trinity Circle in the campground. They may have been one of several groups of gospel singers who performed in the Tabernacle in the late 1800s. Ads always billed them as "freed slaves." With rare exceptions, blacks were not allowed to live in the campground, although a few attended Tabernacle meetings. (MVHS Collections)

employers, thereby creating a much-talked-about integrated social event, the only such party in town.

The blacks in Oak Bluffs were not impressed with Edgartown's Open Door Club, whose members, after all, were domestics. The Oak Bluffs blacks were middle-class property owners, many with black servants of their own. Dorothy West described how they had bought their houses:

> Before World War Two, Oak Bluffs was dying and many houses were up for sale . . . and blacks bought some of these properties and improved them. Some blacks still claim they saved Oak Bluffs, because of the way they restored the dilapidated houses in the years before the war.
>
> The houses they bought were between Ocean Park and Farm Pond. Some were large houses with water views. . . . It was the "new" people who bought them. . . . The "old" black families, like mine, owned much smaller cottages in the Highlands area. [Her family had come in 1915.]

Many years later, Dorothy West wrote a column in the *Gazette* (she was its only black writer) called "Cottagers' Corner," in which she described the activities of those black summer people. The column's name came from a group that called itself the Cottagers, which had been formed in 1955 by a number of black women, all property owners. Their properties were scattered around town, as Dorothy West recalled in 1971:

> There were no separate areas [for blacks]. There were too few black vacationists to form a colony. They were Bostonians, a broad description that included blacks from Boston proper and the surrounding suburbs. [West was from Brookline.]
>
> They did not live side by side in the city and it never occurred to them to settle together here. . . . They bought the house they could afford, hoping to find one in a location to their liking.
>
> Perhaps the greatest number were on Circuit Avenue, a number not exceeding four or five. . . . There were two cottages owned by blacks, I do not think more, on what is now East Chop Drive . . . three, hardly more, in the Highlands. School Street was then exclusively year-rounders, mostly whites, a few more blacks [lived] in the little pockets of poverty on the side streets [later School Street did become mostly black].
>
> The bulk of the summer blacks began to arrive in the 1940s, the prosperous war years . . . but the peak of black participation . . . is the present [1971].

The Cottagers were an exclusive group: members had to be black, female, and owners of Oak Bluffs property. Not many could meet those requirements. Mary Louise Holman, a black working as a servant in Oak Bluffs, tried to join when it began, but she was turned down. That rankled her, as she remembered: "I couldn't join because I didn't own a house, I was working as a maid. . . . When I bought this house, they asked me to join, but I said: 'You didn't want me when I didn't have a house and I'm not going to join you now.' I never did. [But] when the NAACP came here, I joined that and I'm still on the board."

Membership in the Cottagers grew as more blacks bought property, and in 1968 the group purchased the former Cottage City Town Hall on Pequot and Grove avenues for its headquarters. The intersection soon was being called Cottagers' Corner, the name Dorothy West adopted for her column. She wrote about the activities of those middle-class black women, a subject previously unknown to outsiders.

Oak Bluffs was the only Island town where blacks could buy property. In other towns blacks and Jews were not welcome. That was especially true up-Island. The exclusion was achieved extralegally, mostly by means of summer enclaves, cooperatives of a sort. A group of whites would buy a large piece of land and invite compatible relatives, friends, or colleagues to join. These homogeneous enclaves had their own beaches and open spaces. Comfortable in their "playgrounds," the white residents spent their vacations happily in each other's company, rarely leaving their "reservation."

Of course, the desire for selectivity is not limited to whites. All humans seek out others like themselves as friends and neighbors. It is a rare group, white or black, that welcomes diversity. The Shearer Cottage in Oak Bluffs was an example of such selectivity. The rental unit was opened in 1900 and welcomed blacks, the first Island rooming house to do so, but it welcomed only a certain kind of black. Mary Louise Holman recalled: "I visited Shearer Cottage once in a while. . . . They only dealt with a certain class of blacks, like teachers and doctors and lawyers. . . . If you didn't have a degree of something, the Shearer Cottage wouldn't even rent you a room."

Doris Pope Jackson, a descendant of the founder of Shearer Cottage and its owner in 1996, confirmed the Holman observation:

> Everyone [who] came . . . all of these blacks were very, very well educated blacks . . . judges, lawyers, teachers, artists, all beautifully dressed and educated. . . . Most were New Yorkers. . . . I can remember Herbie

Tucker, the judge. His sister and he used to come up there. The Dabney family, Dr. Fuller, a renowned Boston physician. . . . Musician Harry T. Burleigh, a marvelous person, a generous man. . . . As kids, he'd take us out for ice cream and candy. He spoiled all of us.

When [I] was young the Shearer Cottage took only blacks. Times have changed. I [now] have Italian guests and Jewish guests and Irish guests.

Such restrictive enclaves go back a long way. The first was the Wesleyan Grove Campground, where only white Methodists were welcome. Its selectivity was spiritual, but it was, in fact, a protected enclave that banned Catholics and Jews; blacks were allowed in occasionally to sing their spirituals and as preachers to raise money for their churches, but not as regular worshipers. In recent years the ban has been loosened a bit.

Years after the campground was formed, nonspiritual enclaves began to be organized, most of them up-Island: Windy Gates, Barnhouse, and the Squibnocket Fish and Game Club on the south shore; on the north shore there was the oldest and largest, Seven Gates Farm.

Roger Baldwin and Evelyn Preston, his "wife" (they never were legally married), owned Windy Gates, an expanse of land along the south shore east of Squibnocket Beach. Preston was Baldwin's second "wife." (His first "marriage" had also been without legal binding; Baldwin was a free spirit.) He and Crystal Eastman, the sister of Max Eastman, who later became a Gay Head resident, were among the founders of the American Civil Liberties Union (ACLU) in 1913. Baldwin supported many unpopular causes; he defended the schoolteacher John Scopes in the historic Tennessee evolution trial, he opposed the banning of books written by James Joyce, and he protested the Great War, for which he went to prison. His activities gave Windy Gates a reputation as a haven for wild-eyed radicals. It was even said (in shocked tones) around Chilmark that Baldwin and his guests went bathing in the nude on their remote stretch of South Beach. Today he is remembered not for nude bathing, which he indeed enjoyed, but for the Chilmark Community Center, which he founded, and, of course, for the ACLU.

A similar wild reputation was bestowed on Barnhouse, founded in 1919 by Dorothy Kenyon as a summer camp for her friends, all white and, no doubt, most of them Christian. Most vocal among them was Boardman Robinson, another free spirit and an artist for the *Masses,* Max Eastman's socialist magazine.

Dorothy Kenyon and her friends bought the old Mayhew farm on

South Road. With it came a huge barn that became the group's social center; thus its name. As new members joined, space in the old farmhouse became inadequate and members renovated various chicken coops and outbuildings into sleeping rooms. Later they built upscale "chicken coops" to accommodate the still-growing membership. These coops were scattered around the property and were without electricity or running water. A communal shower and privy were provided for all. It was a no-frills vacation, and the members, who could afford better, loved it.

An aura of mystery about Barnhouse members developed among year-round Chilmarkers. Who were these well-to-do off-Islanders who came to the Island on vacation, content to live in chicken coops and mix cocktails and politics in a drafty barn? They certainly must be radicals, maybe even communists; after all, that Marxist artist "Mike" Robinson was one of them.

Thomas Hart Benton, the Island's most famous artist, and his wife, Rita, were frequent guests at Barnhouse. They would have been welcome as members, as they had "no-frills" tastes, but they had no need for a chicken coop to sleep in. They owned a nearby house.

In his book *Thomas Hart Benton: An American Original,* Henry Adams quotes Benton about Barnhouse: "We used to go over to the Barn House parties all the time in the 1920s. . . . They always had a punch made out of bathtub gin and I got quite drunk on occasion."

Benton liked his liquor and he managed to get "quite drunk on occasion," despite Prohibition. Craig Kingsbury was an up-Island supplier of illegal booze, and Benton was among his customers. Kingsbury is quoted by Henry Adams on the subject:

> I used to bring [Benton] . . . liquor from Oak Bluffs, where they had a bottling operation in the cellar of a hotel. One of the selectmen was running things and it cost a dollar a quart. . . . I used to bring it up to Tom and if we brought along our own food, Rita would cook it up for us. . . . They were some hell-raisin' parties, but if things got too rough Rita would throw us out of the house. . . . Benton was funny as hell, a rough, wild drunk, I tell you. He'd fight anybody. . . . He was so small he'd go for the belly every time. . . . I saw him beat up Max Eastman one night, but then Max couldn't fight worth a damn.

The Bentons had met in 1917, when Rita took a course in oil painting in Manhattan. A designer of women's hats, she had aspirations to become an artist. The course was taught by Tom, earning a few dollars to support himself. He was taken by her Italian beauty and used her as a model for his paintings and sculptures. One summer she and a girlfriend rented a cottage from Ella Brug on Boston Hill in Chilmark. The weather turned cold and damp and when her friend went home in disgust, Rita invited Tom to come to the Island. Tom brought his friend and agent, Tom Craven, and they stayed in the Brug barn while Tom painted Chilmark scenes and visited Rita.

The instructor-pupil relationship blossomed and in 1922 Rita and Tom were married, much to the displeasure of both sets of parents. Tom's were upset because he, coming from a famous and historic Missouri family, was marrying an Italian immigrant—a Catholic, no less. Rita's family was displeased because he was a struggling artist with no steady income and she would probably end up having to support him. Fortunately for the newlyweds, his paintings began to sell, especially those he had done on Martha's Vineyard. Tom said the Island changed his style: "Martha's Vineyard had a profound effect on me. . . . It separated me from the Bohemians of art . . . providing me with a homely subject matter and a great quiet for reflection. . . . It was in Martha's Vineyard that I first really began my intimate study of the American environment and its people."

Through the years Benton found much material for his art on the Island, as Rita was sure he would, painting many landscapes, beaches, and local people. One painting, *Picnic,* is a bold treatment of Islanders on the Menemsha Pond beach just below the camp he and Rita built in 1927 for a summer house. The cliffs at Windy Gates were another favorite subject, as were the rolling hills and plain houses of Chilmark that he painted in the bold, exaggerated style that some critics labeled caricatures.

Benton's striking portraits of craggy-faced Chilmarkers, such as Frank Flanders, Dan Vincent, and Chester Poole, helped build his reputation. Some deaf-mutes, descendants of the group that had drawn Alexander Graham Bell to the Island many years earlier, lived near Brug's barn, Tom's studio, and he painted portraits of a number of them. *The Lord Is My Shepherd* shows George and Sabrina West, both deaf-mutes, seated at a table in their home. Josie West, a deaf-mute, was another of Tom's subjects, and that portrait is now at the Martha's Vineyard Historical Society.

It is unlikely that Benton ever visited the largest of the summer enclaves, Seven Gates Farm, on the north shore. He would not have liked it; its residents were more intellectual than he preferred. Nathaniel Shaler, the Harvard geologist, had started it in the 1890s by buying up many of the abandoned farms. He had come to Martha's Vineyard to study the effects of the glacier and had fallen in love with its beauty and serenity. Sadly, he died before he could spend much time on his playground.

After Shaler died in 1906, his widow and their daughter, Mrs. Willoughby Webb, took over the enclave. Its isolation and loneliness encouraged them to invite friends to join them. The first was Russell H. Loines, a friend of Willoughby Webb. He and his family rented one of the old farmhouses in 1907. With only occasional interruptions, they returned each summer, eventually building their own house there. One of the Loines family, now Margot Willkie, is still living at Seven Gates and she recalls the early days:

> There were fewer than ten families living here (now there are thirty-one). We'd meet each morning at 11:30 at Gray's Beach. It had very high sand dunes so that you could slide down them. They weren't clay, they were sand. . . . After we swam we'd lie in the hot sun on the hind side of the dunes and talk about everything. . . . There was an old tennis court at the Chase House when we lived there. . . . My father made it better and everybody played on that court.
>
> When we went to see Mrs. Shaler, I was in a white organdy dress, white rubbers, white gloves, white everything. . . . She would be upstairs in a chaise lounge . . . we would curtsy to her and she'd ask how we were. . . . There was a sense of estate when you went to the Shalers'. . . . Everything was beautifully kept. . . .
>
> Going to the Webbs' was also very nice. . . . She was very sociable. She used to have the people from West Chop up for tea quite often. . . . We'd pull taffy and we'd wrap it up and everybody would take it home.
>
> There was this wonderful Luce's Candy Store on North Road where you turn, coming from Vineyard Haven. We used to drive to Mrs. Luce's in our pony cart. You had to ford, go through the water, to get there (there's a bridge now) and we got our ice cream. . . . Near the store, across the road, a man called Ollie Burgen "lived in sin" with a Mrs. Hall. He played the accordion very well. Norwegian folk music mostly. North Tisbury was a place of sin, we were told. . . .
>
> Then there was Nellie Vincent, who lived opposite the ice cream store. She was a gossip of the most incredible variety. . . . We boarded with her while we were building our house [at Seven Gates]. . . . She had

a party-line phone and listened on it from morning till night. . . . And we'd go to Priscilla Hancock's and buy candy there.

Mr. Burt was superintendent at Seven Gates. He was a wonderful character . . . a truly New England man, and his wife was an Islander from way back. Really good breeding. You could see it in her face. . . . They had seven children, one daughter and six sons, and every one got a college education.

Among the many proper folk summering at Seven Gates were the Dwight Morrows of Englewood, New Jersey. Morrow later became a U.S. senator from New Jersey and was ambassador to Mexico under President Coolidge. Among the children in the family was Dwight Morrow II, who married Margot Loines (later Willkie). The younger Dwight developed a serious mental illness for which no treatment was known; in 1948 living with him became so unbearable for Margot and their children that the couple divorced amicably.

During those difficult years with Dwight, Margot became very close to his sisters, Anne and Constance Morrow. By the 1940s, Anne was a well-known author and a celebrity, having married the world's most famous aviator, Charles A. Lindbergh. Margot Willkie recalls the family: "I just loved the Morrow girls, Con and Anne. . . . They were very literary and just wonderful people. Those two girls were just superb. In 1941 the Lindberghs [Anne and Charles] came and took a house here [in Seven Gates] because I was here. They took this house up on the hill, the Saltonstalls own it now. It used to be open for rental."

Years before, the Lindberghs had lived through a great tragedy when their first child, Charles Jr., was kidnapped and murdered. The arrest and trial of Bruno Hauptmann ended in his execution. During the long trial, the story made headlines around the world. When it ended the family was still unable to find privacy in New Jersey, and they moved to Long Island. But the public's continuing curiosity had so broken Anne's spirit that she decided in 1941 they must get away from New York: "I am sick of this place. We have no longer any privacy here; people telephone all day long. They even come out without calling up beforehand and look for us through the house and garden. . . . I go off to Martha's Vineyard in desperation and find a house, much too small . . . not nearly as convenient as this, but in a windy, bare, free place with a beach of its own to escape to. . . . I feel, desperately, that we must go."

In their published journals (Anne Morrow Lindbergh, *War Within and Without*, 1980, and Charles A. Lindbergh, *The Wartime Journals of Charles A. Lindbergh*, 1970), they describe how they came to love the Vineyard. Though there only about a year, they found the Island to be exactly what they needed in their search for contentment.

It was Anne's friend Margot, then living at Seven Gates, who urged them to come on a trial basis. Anne wrote to her mother, explaining the plan:

> We have taken—for two months or three—a house near Margot on Martha's Vineyard, with the idea (very much a secret) of looking around and seeing whether we could stay there all winter, maybe. We would have to move again into a house with heat, but there is one, in fact two, that would do. . . . We are trying it for late summer and autumn first, and try-ing it very lightly, too. That is, saying we are only there for a month or two . . . so that the publicity won't get out that we're thinking about it as a semi-permanent home. . . . The house we have taken is terribly small and means doubling up the children, the secretaries, etc. But it has lovely wild hills to walk over and miles of beach with practically no one on it.

On August 8, 1941, just before moving to Seven Gates, she again wrote to her mother during a flight to Cleveland with Charles. He was now deeply involved in the anti-British, anti-interventionist America First Com-mittee. (He had turned down the offer to be its first president.) There was talk that their marriage was in trouble because of America First, and Anne was eager to dispel it: "[I am] on a plane to go to Cleveland with Charles! I did not plan to . . . but the Middle West is full of rumors that C. and I are separating on his America First work. There are lots of things (and people) I don't like in the work . . . but Charles stands for integrity . . . almost more than any person I ever met. And so I stand behind him."

One week later, back at Seven Gates Farm, Anne sounded much hap-pier in another letter to her mother: "We have been here for two days and I expect C. this morning. . . . I do not feel so overcome up here . . . no tele-phone calls, no people, no dates ahead. I feel deliciously lonely and hope I stay so!" Later that day Charles arrived in the family car for his first visit to their new home. He had driven the packed car aboard the steamboat at Woods Hole like any ordinary person. During the year they lived on Martha's Vineyard, Charles Lindbergh, the world's most famous aviator, never came or went by plane, always by boat. (Of course, when war was declared in

December 1941, he had no choice. Coastal airports were closed and private planes were grounded.)

On the evening of Charles's first visit to the Vineyard, Anne wrote in her diary:

> August 15, 1941. C. arrives about noon with the car high with bags and bundles. . . . We walk over the land, finding a place for the tent. C. says it is beautiful and that he can work here.
>
> August 17. Great wind blowing, all blinds flapping. C. and I look for new site for the tent, more sheltered. . . . I walk up on the hill and lie on the ground. The security of it and the beauty make me able to think out all the things I am possessive about. The hanging-on feeling—about life itself and its passing by, of youth and romance, of time itself. . . . It is easier here to "let go.". . . I feel a new life is starting here, but I am just now at sea and do not know where it begins.

In his journal Charles put down his first thoughts about the Vineyard. He is less poetic, but impressed:

> August 15, 1941: Arrived Seven Gates Farm in time for lunch with Anne and the children. It is a very beautiful place. . . . There are all kinds of trees on Martha's Vineyard and the change of tide has little effect on the appearance of the island. But there is the sea, and there are rocks and islands in the distance. . . . Anne and I walked over the grounds and looked for a site where we can pitch our tent.
>
> Sunday, August 17: Spent first part of afternoon writing. This is an excellent place to work—quiet, stimulating, inspiring. . . .
>
> Monday, August 18: Two men came to set up the tent house on the side of a hill overlooking the sea, in a slight hollow where it will be protected from the wind.

The importance the Lindberghs placed on the tent provides a revealing insight into their lives. They both needed to be alone, not so much from each other as from everybody else. No doubt the public's curiosity that followed them everywhere was a powerful factor. Also, the new house was much too small for the couple, four children, two secretaries, a governess, and a chambermaid. It would become even more crowded when two Vineyarders, Helen and Maynard Duarte, arrived a few weeks later to be their cook and handyman. Years later in a magazine interview, Helen

offered this insight: "The Lindberghs never entertained and ate only simple food. Mr. Lindbergh always told us to call him Colonel. She was called
Anne Morrow. She had all the money."

With so many crowded into that small house, the couple's desire for a
quiet retreat is understandable, but it was more than that. Even after they
moved into a much larger house for the winter, they still spent many nights
sleeping in the tent. After losing their first child to a kidnapper, one would
think they would hover over the children, but instead they seem to have
preferred to keep them at arm's length, leaving the care and cuddling to
the nursemaids.

Their tent was not a simple canvas shelter. A photograph shows it to be
a rather large rectangular structure, apparently having a sturdy wooden
frame covered by canvas. It stood on slightly higher land above a sandy
beach a hundred yards or so from their house. Later in his journal, a grateful and admiring Charles wrote about it in detail:

> [Anne] has made even this tent beautiful and inspiring, and she does all
> this with the utmost simplicity. She has put blue print curtains on the
> windows . . . tacked up pictures of Chartres saints and angels on plywood
> boards around the walls. . . . In front of the unvarnished wood table are
> three Botticelli postcard reproductions and one Renoir. On the table are
> two very old, small brass elephants from Siam. Beside the elephants are
> a stone, a feather, and a shell.
>
> The tent is a wonderful place to work, secluded—a view to islands
> behind the sea. It is very easy to keep warm. . . . Putting an occasional
> stick of wood in the little airtight stove breaks up the monotony of too
> constant writing.

To Charles, it was "Anne's tent," and he encouraged her to spend more
time in it working on her writing, which he admired. "If anything happens
to me," he once told her, "you can make your living by your writing."

He too used the tent for his writing. He had been working on an auto-
biography, but he had put it aside for the more urgent task of writing
speeches and articles opposing going to war with Germany. As the leading
spokesman for the America First Committee, his condemnation of President Roosevelt's tilt toward England had rekindled the public's interest in
him, not totally in his favor. The America First Committee, with more than
eight hundred thousand members, held frequent rallies around the country, which provided him a national platform. He was again in the news and

suffering the penalty that came with it: "Monday, August 25: I took the 1:05 train to New York. Had to pay two fares for a drawing room! I would much prefer a coach seat, but know I would soon be recognized. . . . What wouldn't I give to be able to ride on trains and go to theaters and restaurants as an ordinary person."

Anne, too, was annoyed by the public's insatiable curiosity about herself and her family. At first she wasn't certain that Vineyard life was an improvement. A month after they moved to Seven Gates, she wrote in her diary: "Land [her son] goes with Soeur Lisi [the nursemaid] to get shoes. . . . I can never shop with my children because then they are no longer just ordinary children but become stared-at children. Now it will be even worse."

Her last sentence refers to the public's growing opposition to Charles's stand on the war. Roosevelt and Churchill had just met aboard a cruiser at sea to discuss how the United States would help England. The nation was increasingly turning against isolationists such as Charles. Things were better on the Island, but Anne wasn't optimistic, as she wrote to a friend: "I have moved from Long Island to Martha's Vineyard. It is far away, windblown, isolated and very quiet. It is better. . . . Here it is much easier to keep my sense of balance. And heaven knows things are going from bad to worse!"

She tried to concentrate on making their new life at Seven Gates Farm as normal as possible, but Charles's upcoming speech haunted her:

September 11, 1941. C. (unexpectedly) [came] for five days to write his speech. . . . The new couple [the Duartes] a little bewildered and doing nothing right. Unpack the boxes (the cook wants a potato basket). . . . The two secretaries are busy fixing up their little house, which I got them because this house is too small for a house and an office.

I try to pull the household together. If only I did not have to do it all before C.'s perfectionist eye. . . .

Then his speech—throwing me into black gloom. He names the "war agitators"—chiefly the British, the Jews and the Administration. . . . I hate to have him touch the Jews. For I dread the reaction. . . . What he is saying in public is not intolerant or inciting or bitter and it is just what he says in private. . . . Headlines will flame: "Lindbergh attacks Jews." He will be branded anti-Semitic, Nazi, Führer-seeking, etc. *I can hardly bear it. For he is a moderate.* [Italics in the original.]

I then work over the Jewish paragraph, rewriting it and putting in some of the things he believes but never says. . . . He takes almost all the suggestions. . . .

I have a sinking of heart as he goes off. It is not doubt in him, but if only people could see him as he really is. . . .

I hear C.'s speech [on the radio]—direct and honest as a clean knife. The frenzied applause of the crowd frightens me. Can he keep in control what he has in his hands? Especially since he does not really want that control, that power.

The speech was given in Des Moines, Iowa, at a huge America First rally. Charles, unlike Anne, did not seem worried about the crowd's frenzy:

Thursday, September 11: [In Des Moines] I spoke for twenty-five minutes. It seemed that over eighty percent of the crowd was with us by the time I finished. . . . When I mentioned the three major groups agitating for war—the British, the Jewish, and the Roosevelt Administration—the entire audience seemed to stand and cheer. At that moment whatever opposition existed was completely drowned out by our support.

Dozens of people came to our hotel rooms after the meeting, America First members . . . local officials, newspapermen, etc. . . . Our opposition press, of course, picks out and emphasizes the radical and fanatical types who attend.

Anne, with the children at Seven Gates, reading the papers the next day, was devastated by the headlines and turned for solace to the Island's night sky:

Saturday, September 13: I go out under the stars, which are very brilliant. I need to get calm again after the papers, which confirm my worst fears as to the reactions to C.'s speech. He is attacked on all sides . . . as openly a Nazi, following Nazi doctrine.

I lie down in the grass on the bluff and look at the brilliant spread of stars through the giant wavering grass tops which loom over my eyes. The difference between Jew and Gentile does not seem very great, looking at the stars—nor do any earthly troubles. I cannot bear to leave, to go back to the house, to go back to tomorrow—to life. . . . Lying there in bliss, I dread tomorrow's emotions with C.'s return. . . . His coming will fill the house with warmth, with fire, with wind, with life. And also with problems. . . .

[I walked] around the house with a lantern to look at the sleeping children and put on an extra cover. The miser's hour for a mother—she looks at her gold and gloats over it!

When Charles returned the next day, their conversation was emotional. Anne, though unwavering in her love and admiration for him, was torn:

I cannot explain my revulsion of feeling by logic. . . . He is incapable of being mean. How then to explain my profound feeling of grief about what he is doing? . . . He was naming the groups that were pro-war. No one minds his naming the British or the Administration. But to name "Jews" is un-American . . . because it is segregating them as a group, setting the ground for anti-Semitism. . . . I would prefer to see this country at war than shaken by violent anti-Semitism. . . . C. says that is not the choice.

To wash away those differences, they did something they rarely did: they went to South Beach, where the Atlantic's surf pounds against the land and the air is clean and invigorating. That evening they slept in a smaller tent, isolated from children and worldly concerns: "We have—in spite of the long discussion—a beautiful day on the south shore's wide, wind-swept beach, jumping the rollers with the children, C. and the boys. To sleep in C.'s little tent, staked in a hollow on the hill, under the stars."

Charles, in his journal that day, made no mention of Anne's concerns, or of the family fun on South Beach. He was so certain he was right that the gathering public storm did not worry him as he slept under the stars: "Sunday September 14. Arrived home just in time for lunch. After supper Anne and I pitched our small bug-proof tent in a hollow in the hills west of the house. It was a clear and cool night, and we could leave the top of the tent open over our heads."

The public's fury did not subside. Lindbergh's Des Moines speech caused panic at America First headquarters in Chicago. He received a telephone call from General Robert Wood, its president (also president of Sears, Roebuck): "Monday, September 15: My Des Moines address has caused so much controversy that General Wood has decided to hold a meeting of the America First National Committee in Chicago. . . . It seems that almost anything can be discussed today in America except the Jewish problem. The very mention of the world 'Jew' is cause for a storm."

Remote though Seven Gates Farm was, it could not isolate Anne from feeling the public's growing opposition to her husband. Her nights were sleepless: "The storm is beginning to blow up hard. America First is in a turmoil. . . . The Jews demand a retraction. . . . I begin to feel bitter . . . because I begin to see C. hated much as the Jews are hated, simply because he is Lindbergh. . . . We sleep again in the little tent out on the hill, with the wind blowing. C. says he sleeps deeply and well, but I lie awake and think."

For the next two months Charles and Anne did a lot of traveling, as he was the leading speaker at America First rallies. The German army was now deep inside Russia, which seemed likely to fall. Once Russia was defeated, it was certain that Germany would attack England. Should the United States stay out of the war? Lindbergh still thought so.

For the second time in a month, the Lindberghs went to the beach. The October wind was chilling, but Charles and Anne took their two older boys to Gay Head. It is the only time either of them mentioned that beautiful spot. Charles described the joyful family outing: "Saturday, October 11: Anne, Jon, Land, and I drove to Gay Head. There was a strong wind and the seas were high. Jon and I found a barrel that had been washed up on the beach. He got inside, and I rolled him down the slope to the edge of the breakers. Then we carried the barrel to the top of the bluff, and Jon, Land and I pushed it over the edge."

With winter approaching, the family moved into the larger, more comfortable, and heated Webb house, which had been Professor Shaler's home. Their decision to stay at Seven Gates through the winter confirms the couple's fondness for the Vineyard. They were virtually alone on windy Seven Gates, as most residents had left for the winter. Even Anne's sister-in-law and close friend, Margot, would soon be going to California. (Her husband's doctor had urged the move.) For the first time Anne admitted her need for a friend, someone to confide in. It would be a long, lonely winter. She tried to overcome her loneliness with her writing:

> November 1, 1941. Raining. We moved to the "Webb house" today. (Also on Seven Gates Farm.)
>
> November 6. Webb House. The children and nurse have a separate wing. The nursery is really theirs, like the nursery of the old house in Englewood. . . . I want to stop being a good housekeeper. . . . I want to go back again to being a bad housekeeper and a good writer.

Margot comes over after lunch. We talk all afternoon in front of my fire. She is moving out West with the family. There is a lump in my throat to feel I shall no longer have the exquisite luxury of sharing day-to-day life with her. Oh, I shall miss her.

The Webb house pleased them. Charles, taking a break from speaking at America First rallies, was back at writing his autobiography, *The Spirit of St. Louis*. Anne was envious. She wasn't happy being a full-time housewife and mother. Their nursemaid and housemaid had both returned to France because America's involvement in the war seemed increasingly certain.

Anne asked herself: "Can one be a good mother and write? Can one be a writer for half the day?" It seems that she preferred being a good writer to being a good mother. She looked for the silver lining:

> Work rather uninspired on "Women and a Career." I feel like the cartoon in the *Saturday Review* of the woman sitting in the middle of terrible disorder—dishes piled up unwashed, floor littered, cat into the spilled milk, baby crawling under-foot, while she, serene in the center, is typing away at an article for *Good Housekeeping*.
>
> Supper alone with C.! Wonderful! And a quiet evening in the big room which I begin to relax in and survey with satisfaction. The cheap curtains, the bedspread over the sofa, the Vlaminck on the mantel, C. at the desk, I on the chaise longue, writing letters, to the music of WQXR. Very nice.

It was November, and a cold wind whipped across Seven Gates. But it was warm in the house, "very nice," Anne thought. That was not enough for Charles. They left the children with the Duartes and headed out to the tent:

> Friday, November 21. C. suddenly decides to pitch the tent out on the bluff. It is very windy and flaps too much for me to sleep, but it is surprisingly snug and comfortable. C. says he sleeps very well after getting to sleep.
>
> Saturday, November 22. It is lovely to wake in a tent and see it get incandescent with sunlight and then know from the inside what kind of a day it is!

The incandescent loveliness of the rising sun could not erase Anne's torment: "I am—this is at the bottom of my unhappiness—angry and hurt

by two references in the paper to C. . . . I think: How badly he has
expressed himself, how inadequately I have helped him, and how basely
(chiefly this) they have abused him. . . . He is so 'idealistic,' so far into the
future, so far beyond these nose-on-their-face idealists that it will take a
generation or two before the average run of 'idealists' catch up with him."

Seeking relief from child caring, Anne went to New York City to hire a
nursemaid. Charles and the children stayed at Seven Gates with the
Duartes. He was writing a speech for a major America First rally to be held
in Boston on December 12. Anne, after interviewing potential nursemaids
for a week in New York, finally picked one, but she was not satisfied:

> And nurses—one after another until my mouth went dry—talking, trying
> to read them, endless conversations on the telephone and dreaming of
> them at night, very tired, wondering if any of them would do to put my
> tired head on their shoulder.
>
> I finally took an old Breton peasant woman very temporarily. . . . She
> had the earth quality and was gay and I hoped would do, though not per-
> fect at all.
>
> On Sunday I drove up to Woods Hole—a beautiful day, clear and cold
> and a tearing wind.

It was not just another Sunday. It was December 7, 1941, "a day that will
live in infamy." The Japanese had attacked Pearl Harbor. Anne, hearing the
news on the car radio, thought: "It is the knell of the old world. All army
officers all over the U.S. ordered into uniform. Espionage Act invoked. (If
C. speaks again they'll put him in prison, I think immediately.)"

Alone in the car, she tried to turn her mind to other things. The New
York Philharmonic was playing a Brahms concerto, but the radio program
was constantly interrupted by war bulletins. She arrived at Seven Gates
after dark: "Jon and Land run out to me in night clothes excitedly. C. says,
'Have you heard the news?' 'Yes.'"

The world had suddenly changed.

In the morning Anne took the two older children to school as though
it had not.

> I take the children to school. Land telling me the Christmas story.
> "And the angel said, 'Fear not, New York City'"! How did he get that?
> When I get back, C. is listening to the radio reports of what has hap-
> pened. . . . C. and I go out for a walk in between long-distance calls from

Chicago, New York, etc. . . . We listen to the President's declaration of a state of war over the radio at lunch at the table. . . .

America First has decided to cancel all meetings. C.'s speech is brilliant and one of his very best. I am crushed it was not given, but it is impossible now. He gives out a statement. Very good, I think.

Lindbergh's statement was published in the *Vineyard Gazette* on the front page. This seems to be the only mention the paper made of the Lindberghs during their year's stay:

The America First Committee released a statement by Charles A. Lindbergh: "We have been stepping closer to war for many months. Now it has come and we must meet it as united Americans regardless of our attitude in the past toward the policy our government has followed.

"Whether or not that policy has been wise, our country has been attacked . . . and we must retaliate. Our own defenses and our own military position have already been neglected too long. . . . When American soldiers go to war, it must be with the best equipment that modern skill can design and that modern industry can build."

Mr. Lindbergh and his family have been staying at Seven Gates Farm, West Tisbury, for several months. A meeting in Boston tonight under America First auspices, which he was to address, was cancelled by America First after the outbreak of the war.

Lindbergh's America First platform had collapsed. Only a year earlier, his support had been so strong that Senator William E. Borah, an avid America Firster, had urged him to run for president against Roosevelt, who was then seeking an unprecedented third term. Borah was sure he would win, convinced as he was that the country was turning against the war. It was not the first time that Lindbergh had been urged to run for president: "During the lunch, Borah and I discussed the coming presidential election. . . . [He] made the startling statement that he thought I might make a good candidate! . . . Many years ago—about 1927 or '28—Henry Breckinridge [at the time a leading Democrat] suggested that I lay my course toward the White House. I concluded, however (and I have never regretted it), that my happiness and usefulness lay along other routes."

His pro-Germany position now discredited, Lindbergh was eager to join the fight. It wouldn't be easy. Every time he sought a place in the military or the government, he was rejected. He turned to private industry, with the same result. Anne, alone with the children at Seven Gates, was more depressed than ever. Not only was Charles being rejected, but she learned that publishers no longer wanted her writing. She wrote in her diary on March 12, 1942: "C. is away—again looking for work. I am hurt for him when he gets another telephone call from a company which wants him but cannot afford to take him because of Administration disapproval. And I feel that his exclusion from the world of aviation is much more unfair than mine from the world of books."

That month his sympathetic relationship with Henry Ford, a known anti-Semite, was rewarded. Ford offered him a job at the new Willow Run bomber plant "to help with their aviation program." Lindbergh accepted, but he advised Ford to clear his hiring with the War Department:

> Ford was at first opposed to asking the War Department anything about it; but I reminded him that we would have to have much contact with them in the future and that a good start would be of great advantage. Ford agreed. It annoys him to think he has to ask anyone about what he wants to do in his own factory. (And, as a matter of fact, it annoys me to have to ask the government's permission to make a connection with a commercial company: it's too damn much like Russia!)

Accepting the Detroit job meant leaving the Vineyard. Anne was pregnant and eager to get settled before their child arrived. Charles, already working at Willow Run, rented a house in Bloomfield Hills, Michigan, for the family to move into. In mid-June he went to Martha's Vineyard for the last time, not without sadness: "Morning on routine—arrangements for packing, etc. Anne spent most of the morning in the tent writing. The tent arrangement has been very much worth while; she does most of her writing there. Croquet with Jon in the evening. Walk over the hills to the beach with Anne after supper. How we will miss the sea this summer! When will we find it again?"

On July 18, 1942, Anne and the children moved into the house in Michigan. She was not enthusiastic: "I feel rather depressed by all the ersatz elegance. . . . I long even for the shabbiness of Mrs. Webb's house— shabby Victorian, but it was decent."

Despite their fond memories of Seven Gates, it seems that the Lindberghs never again visited Martha's Vineyard. They began going to Maui in the Hawaiian Islands, and it was there that Charles died of cancer in August 1974. When he learned that death was near, he asked to be flown to Maui on what was the final flight for the world's most famous aviator. Anne lived until February 2001, when after a long illness she died in the Vermont farmhouse that had been her home for many years.

The *Vineyard Gazette* ignored the Lindberghs during their year at Seven Gates, but it was not because the *Gazette* didn't recognize news. Since 1920 it had been owned and edited by Henry and Betty Hough, both graduates of the Columbia School of Journalism. They knew a news story when they saw one, but they no doubt chose not to print anything about the Lindberghs out of respect for their privacy, as Anne had hoped would be the case when they moved to the Island.

The Houghs had been given the *Gazette* in 1920 as a wedding present by Henry's father, George A. Hough, editor of the *New Bedford Evening Standard*. They were the first professional journalists on an Island that had seen many newspapers come and go. Among the nonsurvivors were the *Camp Meeting Herald*, the *Island Review*, the *Cottage City Star*, the *Cottage City Chronicle*, the *Seaside Gazette*, *Chick's Vineyard Haven News*, and the *Gay Head Light*. Still publishing were the *Martha's Vineyard Herald*, the *Vineyard News*, and the *Gazette*, the *Gazette* being the oldest. Despite its longevity, the *Gazette* was not the best. When the Houghs took it over, the paper's circulation was under six hundred, and that mostly in Edgartown. The *Martha's Vineyard Herald*, published in Oak Bluffs, claimed to have more circulation, and it certainly had more news.

Henry later admitted that he and Betty both felt that what they had been given by his father wasn't much: "[Betty] was wiser than I, and with a far better sense of reality. . . . At first, we did not like the idea of taking over the *Gazette* because the whole enterprise seemed so small. . . .The population of the whole Island was fewer than 5,000 persons. Each of the three large towns had a newspaper, the oldest being the *Gazette*, the next oldest, the *Herald* [in Oak Bluffs], and the most recent was the *News* [in Vineyard Haven]."

Henry Beetle Hough had spent many summers on the remote north shore of Tisbury as a boy, but he knew nothing about Edgartown. He had little enthusiasm for their new undertaking:

> We came to Edgartown to live in 1920 and took over the *Gazette*. It was pretty primitive. All the type was hand-set. . . . The press was held together by wire. . . . It was shimmed up by pieces of wood and had to be turned by hand.

I didn't know Edgartown at all. I never spent the night here until 1920 when we came. . . . My wife had only been here a couple of times before. . . . There was an opposition paper, the *Vineyard Haven News*. There was also a paper in Oak Bluffs, the *Martha's Vineyard Herald*. . . . We traded our [old] printing press for the *Herald* [and agreed not to compete with it for job printing] and we bought out the *Vineyard Haven News* for $500. . . . There wasn't business enough for more than one paper. . . . [Our] gross business was about $5,000 a year. . . . We agreed to keep the old editor [Charles H. Marchant] on as long as he wanted to stay. He lived for about 10 years and was immensely valuable. . . . We had to have [two] Linotypes and a new press. . . . Just as we thought we were making progress then came the Depression . . . it was a hand-to-mouth existence. After that came World War II . . . with no more national advertising . . . sort of a starvation period. . . . Then gasoline rationing, some [summer people] still came because they could ride bicycles here. . . . We had the dim-out, every house had to be blacked out, the street lights were dimmed.

Henry did not like the day-to-day drudgery of being an editor. Writing, not editing, was what he enjoyed and he was very good at it. His style was more graceful than news reporting was supposed to be. So he wrote editorials, three of them a week. One major editorial success was his campaign to keep the authorities from replacing the Edgartown harbor lighthouse, damaged in the 1938 hurricane, with a flashing beacon atop an ugly steel tower. His editorials forced the authorities to relent and to replace the old light with today's much-admired and much-photographed traditional lighthouse, floated down by barge from Ipswich, where it had been discontinued in an economy move.

Henry also liked to operate the Linotypes, those huge, awkward-looking machines that arranged type matrices one letter at a time into a "line of type" on which molten lead was poured, forming a lead slug that was inked and printed by the press. The matrices were then automatically returned to their tiny bins to be used over and over. Henry was skilled at the Linotype keyboard, often writing his editorials and short articles directly on it, from his mind to type, no paper involved.

But what Henry liked most was writing books, which he did with frequency; he turned over much of the responsibility for getting the paper out to his wife, Betty, Bill Roberts, the shop foreman, and Joseph Chase

Allen, the reporter. Henry made no secret of that. He wrote about a press day in 1941:

> Betty and I were hurrying to get to the *Gazette* office as close to half-past seven as possible. It was publication day. . . . Bill Roberts and the two boys were already at the office, the typesetting machines were going, and the forms were pretty well along. Bill had made up two or three pages the evening before. About eight o'clock, Betty took what last-minute news there was from Joe Allen, our outside man, and then began to write the last of the heads. I fixed up two or three short news stories and a personal item or two on the [Linotype] machine and then helped Bill pick out the type for the first page.

Henry's first book didn't come out until 1936, sixteen years after they took over the paper. It was *Martha's Vineyard: Summer Resort,* the story of how a Methodist camp meeting, a few tents in an oak grove, had become a bustling summer resort. In some of his other books, especially *Country Editor,* he described how he and Betty ran a small-town weekly newspaper, usually giving more attention to the Island's interesting characters than to the paper. He was a keen observer of "town characters." After Betty died, he began to wonder if he might be turning into one. It was apparent that he would have enjoyed it. In *Tuesday will be Different* (1971), he quotes from a letter he wrote to a friend, Bill: "I happen to be the old guy with the torn coat and old-style cap who is—well, let me say, conspicuous—as he walks a collie dog through the streets and roundabout day after day. I don't think I'm a character as yet, though there are plenty of idiosyncrasies no one, not even Lochinvar [his collie], would be likely to tell me about. I'll have to see how things go from here on in. You don't get to be a character by trying."

The most widely read of his books is *Country Editor.* It was followed by *Once More the Thunderer.* These two wonderfully entertaining books made the *Gazette* one of the nation's best-known weekly newspapers. He also wrote a number of novels with plots set on a fictional Vineyard, but they had little success.

As one would expect, during the early years Hough did everything he could to promote the Island's tourist business, not only in the pages of the *Gazette,* but in the many articles he wrote for national magazines. His books, too, promoted the joys of the Island. There was probably nobody

Henry Hough did much to create the fame of Martha's Vineyard with his writings, not
only in the *Gazette* but in the many books he wrote. *Country Editor,* published in 1940,
was his best seller. He was unhappy about the crowds of day-trippers in Edgartown,
but economic facts forced the *Gazette* to continue its boosterism with a thick
"Invitation Issue" each year. (MVHS Collections)

who did more to make the Vineyard a nationally known summer resort than Henry Beetle Hough. And he came to regret it.

As early as 1930 he became aware of the dangers of unrestricted growth. His editorial in May 1930 was titled "Diminishing Returns":

> Everyone agrees that the Vineyard has a future. But what sort of future? Development of one sort or another the Island is to have. Every day brings fresh evidence of the march of change.
>
> The Vineyard is at a stage where its rapidly increased accessibility is just beginning to be appreciated. There is no doubt that thousands of people will wish to come here in the next few years, and it is well to bear in mind that a point of diminishing returns exists beyond which the Island will begin to lose instead of gaining. . . . We must treat conservation as of equal importance with development.

This was the first indication we have found of Hough's gradual change from boosterism to conservation. The economic downturn of the Great Depression slowed development in the 1930s and his worries lessened. Then came World War II. Thousands of servicemen from all over the country were stationed on the Island and exposed to its beauty. They spread the word, and when the war ended, the developers came back. Hough, determined to protect his Island, pushed for greater control of the wetlands, for stricter zoning, for everything that would slow down development.

But when he and Betty took over the *Gazette* in 1920, conservation had not been on their worry list. The Island was a struggling summer resort that depended almost entirely on the crowds from the mainland who came to Oak Bluffs. The rest of the Island was stagnant, still surviving, as it had for years, by fishing and farming. What was needed then was more people, more building, not less.

Oak Bluffs had electricity and gas in summer, but the other communities did not. When Oak Bluffs closed down in September so did the utilities, and they did not start up until spring. This seasonal operation brought near-disaster to Oak Bluffs on May 25, 1921, when the huge gas tank that supplied the town blew up while it was being filled for the summer.

Gas had long been used in Cottage City (now Oak Bluffs), starting as street lighting. Gas lamps came to the campground early in the 1880s. Then in 1885 the Cottage City Gas Works was formed. Some believe it may have been the first gas company organized in southeastern Massachusetts. The company bought seven lots on the edge of the village between Uncas and Wamsutta avenues for its storage tank and generating plant. They were built during the winter of 1885–86:

> Our streets present quite a cosmopolitan appearance with gangs of men at work with pick and shovel laying the wrought iron pipe mains that are to carry gas to our cottages. . . .
>
> The iron gasometer and generators, in sections, are arriving on each trip of the *Monohansett*. The vessel comes through Quick's Hole, it does not attempt Woods Hole. Now making trips every other day due to high freight volume.

The huge telescoping tank, the "iron gasometer," was supported by a separate frame. When the tank was full, it towered over the nearby shacks and gardens across Uncas Avenue. The company began distributing gas from the tank in the summer of 1886.

By 1900 electric lights had started to replace gas lamps in the homes of the wealthy summer people, and gas was relegated to cooking. Year-round residents still used kerosene lamps for illumination and woodstoves for cooking in winter, kerosene ranges in summer.

When the tank and generating plant on Uncas Avenue were being readied for the summer season of 1921, there was a huge explosion: "For several weeks repairs had been under way in preparation for the opening of summer service, and at the time of the accident, the tank was being filled with thousands on thousands of feet of gas."

The plant manager was in his office in the generator building. He heard loud noises coming from the tank. Looking out, he saw the top of the tank vibrating vigorously and immediately shut down the gas supply before running from the building. He was barely outside when the tank blew up: "The tank was tossed into the air, descending again on its side, into the receptacle which collapsed under the enormous strain. . . . The Negro settlement about the works was deserted and the surrounding fields dotted with the migrating forms of the residents."

It was a miracle that there were no injuries.

Later it was disclosed that the unpurged tank had been placed into service prematurely, which allowed gas to flow into the partly purged mains. When an "inquisitive customer" ignited a fixture to see if the gas had been turned on, the flame raced back through the main to the tank. A small explosion occurred in the meter at the Island House at the same time, but whether that was the "inquisitive customer" was not stated. The explosion brought an end to gas service in Cottage City. The crumpled tank was never replaced, and summer residents switched to kerosene for cooking.

Cottage City installed electric arc lamps on its main streets in 1895. Two companies had bid for the business. The winner agreed to operate fifty arc lamps from dusk to midnight in July, August, and September for twenty-five hundred dollars a year. Three more lights would be turned on at no additional cost "on any dark night." During the rest of the year, it would provide twenty-five arc lamps.

Arc lights are very hot, open flames that emit dangerous fumes that make them unsuitable for enclosed areas. Most were used for outdoor lighting around hotels, public squares, and the Tabernacle. With so many in use, one writer described Cottage City as the "City of Lights, a fairy land."

In Edgartown the first indoor electric lights, no doubt burning the new incandescent lamps, were installed in the public library in 1913 and a year later in the county courthouse. An article in the Town Warrant that year asked for funds to wire the Town Hall for electricity. Only the largest houses in the village center had electric lights before 1920. A few impatient homeowners, not close to any power line, installed their own generators. When electricity had not reached West Tisbury in 1920, three neighbors, Judge Everett Allen Davis, John Whiting, and Mrs. Newhall (who put up most of the money) bought a generating plant that charged one hundred batteries, enough to provide electricity for lights in their homes.

As late as 1940 the electric company's wires had not reached Chilmark. David Flanders remembers: "A lot of people up here had generators, before the electricity was put in. We didn't get our electricity in Chilmark until 1941, just before the war broke out."

It was not until years after World War II that electricity finally made it to Gay Head. It arrived when the government decided to electrify the lighthouse and equip it with an automatic beacon. Its historic Fresnel lens, a scientific marvel when it went into service in 1852, had been declared obsolete. For one hundred years it had burned whale oil, lard oil, kerosene, and finally acetylene gas to guide mariners. Now the Fresnel lens is displayed in a truncated lighthouse on the grounds of the Martha's Vineyard Historical Society in Edgartown, a priceless artifact.

Telephones came to the Island before electricity. In 1881 the first telephone line was strung between Vineyard Haven and Cottage City, connecting instruments in two hotels. During those early years telephones were placed in hotels, railroad stations, and stores. To make a call, you went to one of those places. There were few places to call, so use was limited. In 1882 there were only seven telephones in Cottage City, eighteen on the entire Island, all listed as "Public Telephone Pay Stations." A year later more pay stations opened when an underwater cable connected Vineyard Haven with the mainland, but service was undependable, often being cut off by boats snagging the cable with their anchors.

The telephone company, owned off-Island, limped along for several years. Then in 1894 Dr. Charles F. Lane of Vineyard Haven was granted permission by Cottage City to put up poles and wires from Eastville to the Edgartown road so he could set up service in Vineyard Haven. Tisbury had already agreed to its portion of the route. The Southern Massachusetts Telephone Company now had a competitor, Lane's Public Telephone Company. The *Herald* in May 1897 described how Dr. Lane was shaking things up: "The Public Telephone Company has placed telephones in the following places in Cottage City: T. D. Crowell's grocery, Allen Norton's stables, Pease's Grocery, the Pequot House and the residences of E. H. Matthews, George Burgess, and E. G. Beetle. The time is near at hand when the telephone will be as necessary in the household economy as a cook stove."

In January 1898 the *Gazette* reported that "there are now 70 Lane telephones installed around the Island." Conventional wisdom has it that Lane went into the telephone business to provide his patients with a way to call him. That was never mentioned in the news stories of his Public Telephone Company. Mrs. Elizabeth Downs of Vineyard Haven worked for Dr. Lane for years, and in an interview at the Historical Society she did not mention that patients were on his mind when he started:

> Dr. Lane had his own telephone exchange and he worked on it himself a great deal. He would climb a telephone pole with his tall silk hat. He was a difficult man to work for. Crotchety, eccentric . . . very particular about everything being clean. He was a good doctor and very dedicated. . . . I've seen him start for Gay Head in a terrible snowstorm. He would go as far as he could [in his carriage], then walk the rest of the way. He cared little for the law. He said, "I've broken all the laws." He performed abortions, he sold liquor without a license and other activities.

> The telephone exchange was a big board in one of the back rooms [in

his drugstore in Vineyard Haven] and on it were sixteen different bells with sixteen different lines that went all over the Island. We had to learn the sound of all those bells. There were no lights or anything. . . . There were several phones on a line, especially up-Island, and there was a great deal of listening. He kept the drugstore quite a long time and lived at the Mansion House with Sarah [his wife].

Lane was so filled with energy that practicing medicine wasn't enough to satisfy him. The telephone company was the outlet he needed. He sold it in 1910 to the Bell Company. Throughout his life he also worked as a carpenter, which he had done to put himself through medical school. He had built the Lane Block on Main Street in Vineyard Haven for his drugstore, doing much of the work himself. When he finally gave up his medical practice in 1926, he and his wife, Sarah, moved out of the Mansion House in Vineyard Haven, where they had lived while he was practicing, and into the Lane Block. They were living there when he died in 1931.

He was still practicing in 1922, when the Martha's Vineyard Hospital opened. It was the first time the Island's six towns, each so jealous of its own identity, had joined in a single project. It is amazing how little time it took for them to agree to create the Island's "cottage hospital." When the idea to build a hospital was first broached in 1920, committees were formed in each town and fund-raising began, headed by Mrs. James Look of West Tisbury. Mrs. Look and other energetic women around the Island wasted no time in raising enough money to buy the farmhouse of the late Captain Hiram Daggett in Eastville. Two years later the Island had its hospital.

The Reverend Newton James of West Tisbury, in his diary entry of June 9, 1922, described the new facility:

> The formal opening of the Martha's Vineyard Hospital at Eastville took place this afternoon. This building purchased by the Hospital Association has been completely remodeled and partially equipped for the benefit of the Island people. It consists of a reception room, dining room, kitchen, laundry, pantry, bathroom and two private rooms on the ground floor; nurses' room, operating room, infant room, ward for 7 or 8 patients and a toilet room, upstairs. Basement is equipped with steam-heating plant. The Hospital is very pleasantly located overlooking the Lagoon on one side and the harbor on the front. Though not large, it will be of great benefit and as funds will allow it will be increased in size. . . .

Generous donations of money and supplies were given by the large number of visitors who were very cordially received by the officials and nurses at the opening.

Long may this Institution live and increase in the healing ministry as a God-given benediction to Martha's Vineyard.

Seven years later the facility was already too small. Frank L. Norton of Edgartown was awarded the contract to build a larger hospital across the road in 1928. Soon even that new building was not large enough. It was expanded five different times before finally being replaced by the present hospital in 1974.

Islanders had never been enthusiastic Prohibitionists, but at times they did vote for candidates running on that ticket. It was not because they wanted to outlaw alcohol. On occasion, when the candidate they preferred (usually a Republican) failed to get his party's nomination, he would switch and run as a Prohibitionist. The move was not taken seriously. Anyone elected under that banner quickly forgot his adopted party's platform. (Few were ever elected.)

But in 1919 the nation and the Island were forced to take Prohibition seriously, when temperance groups persuaded voters to add the Eighteenth Amendment to the Constitution, which banned the sale of alcoholic beverages.

With Prohibition, the Island, its miles of remote beaches easily accessible to rum-running boats, discovered a new way to make money, illegal though it was. Craig Kingsbury, who knew about such things, told how easy it was:

> It was god-damned lively here during Prohibition. . . . This was a way station [for rum-runners] and we also had a lot of geniuses here cooking up their own bug juice. The old-time Portuguese were well into wine-making, also brandy. . . . There was a bunch of guys that cooked the alcohol out of a mixture of swill and molasses. . . . They put the mash in a tank, built a fire under it and the steam goes through a coil of copper tubing in a barrel of cold water . . . the alcohol vaporizes much before the other stuff and condenses and runs out the end and there's your moonshine.
>
> Making moonshine was a cottage industry on the Island. . . . One old guy peddled moonshine out of a baby carriage. My aunt used to say,

"That lovely little man, he's always wheeling his little child along the street." Silk Stocking Sam, he was called.

The Tiltons used to bring in Belgian alcohol aboard their coaster. One day I was on Church's Dock in Oak Bluffs and George Fred [Tilton] comes in: "Hey, give me a hand here," and I did. He takes two gallon cans of Belgian alcohol, I take two, walked me right up Circuit avenue to the Pawnee House. When we got back, George Fred says, "Thanks. Here's two bucks for your time, young feller." All the hotels sold booze to their guests. They wouldn't buy the local moonshine, but wanted the good stuff.

There was no problem getting a drink during Prohibition.

When the Depression hit and Franklin Delano Roosevelt was elected president, the Eighteenth Amendment was repealed. The Island hardly noticed the difference, although alcoholic beverages were—and are—sold in only two of the Island's six towns, much to the surprise of visitors even today.

The *Gazette,* of course, did little reporting on bootleggers. That was not a subject the Houghs chose to write about. They were busy making the *Gazette* an all-Island family newspaper. They had added more news from outside Edgartown with long columns of "personals" by local correspondents. There was little that escaped their reporting. If you went shopping for the day in New Bedford, everybody knew it; or if your house was shingled, you were in the news. If you were white, that is.

Rarely written about were the activities of the blacks, Portuguese, or Indians—unless they got into trouble with the law. Discrimination in the newspaper was not unique to the Island. All around the country, you had to read one of the black newspapers (published only in the larger cities) to find out what blacks were accomplishing. Any mention in the mainstream press of a nonwhite was accompanied by the adjective "colored." Most mentions were unflattering.

Dorothy West in her *Gazette* column was among the first to write about blacks in a white newspaper without labeling them colored. To her they were just people doing things, like everybody else. Skin color wasn't relevant.

In an interview in the Martha's Vineyard Historical Society's oral history program, West recalled how little Henry Hough of the *Gazette* seemed to know about the black summer residents. One day in the late 1950s, when she handed him what she had written for the week's column, Hough turned to one of his staff and said: "You know, there are so many interesting blacks on the Island and I never knew they were here." Dorothy West was shocked. "This man had been editor of the Island's oldest newspaper for thirty years and was unaware of the middle-class, successful blacks who owned summer houses in Oak Bluffs," she said. "If he saw these well-dressed blacks walking down the street, he probably thought they were Edgartown domestics on their day off."

The Houghs may have shown little interest in the blacks, but they were always eager for news about the ferry service. It was the Island's lifeline. When steam replaced sail years before, it had brought many changes that Vineyarders were slow to accept. Nantucket, perhaps because of its greater distance from the mainland, was much more ready to invest its money in steamboats. In 1833 the Nantucket Steamboat Company began running the steamboat *Telegraph* on a regular schedule between New Bedford and Nantucket, with a stop at Holmes Hole (Vineyard Haven). It made three trips a week. Various steamers, owned by mainlanders, had run between Nantucket and New Bedford before the *Telegraph,* but they were so underpowered that they were unable to operate in strong winds and rarely maintained their schedules. It was not until the new Nantucket company began operating that the steamboat was a success.

The earliest mention of the *Telegraph* we have seen is in Jeremiah Pease's diary. On May 30, 1834, he wrote of the steamer coming into Edgartown harbor on a sad trip: "Steamboat *Telegraph,* Capt. Barker, arrives from New Bedford with the body of Capt. [Jonathan] Fisher."

This was not the first time a steamboat had entered Edgartown harbor. In August 1833 Pease had reported the arrival of the steamboat *Benjamin Franklin* with 150 passengers from Providence and Newport. He didn't give the reason why such a large group had come to Edgartown, but it was probably a summer steamboat excursion, a diversion that was just becoming fashionable. Later, when the August camp meetings had become popular, many steamboats began arriving. On one day seven different steamers brought pilgrims to the camp meeting from a variety of mainland cities.

Although the Nantucket Steamboat Company was not profitable, it was determined to stay in business. In 1842 it invested in a larger vessel, the *Massachusetts,* and began making regular stops at Edgartown, and so that village had its first scheduled steamboat service.

In 1845 the New Bedford and Martha's Vineyard Steamboat Company was formed by Captain Holmes W. Smith and Jared Gabor. Captain Smith was from Edgartown. It isn't clear why he and Gabor felt another company was needed, given the financial woes of the one already operating. Perhaps it was local pride. Smith, a former whaling master, was the captain of the company's new steamboat, *Naushon*. In his diary Jeremiah Pease described how the residents of Edgartown reacted:

> August 26, 1845: Steam Boat *Naushon,* Capt. H. W. Smith, arrives from New York, having been built there for this place, she being the first Steam Boat ever owned here. Quite a rejoicing with many on the account.
>
> August 27: Steam Boat *Naushon* sails for New Bedford with 320 passengers, principally from this town.
>
> August 30: Steam Boat *Naushon* goes to New Bedford and returns at 5 P.M.
>
> September 1: Steam Boat *Naushon* commences running regularly to New Bedford.

The new steamer was scheduled to make a one-day round-trip between New Bedford and Edgartown three times a week. That required an early sailing, at 8:00 A.M., from Edgartown, something not convenient for residents of other Island towns. To get to Edgartown by that time meant a very early start if you had to come by horse and buggy from Chilmark. The competing steamer running from Nantucket to New Bedford stopped at Holmes Hole at 10 A.M., a much more convenient time and place for most Vineyarders.

Despite the handicap of schedule, the *Naushon* ran for three years, its final run being at the end of the 1847 season. It isn't clear what caused the shutdown. Some have said it was financial, but it may have been due to the poor health of her skipper and co-owner, Captain Smith. He died in January 1849 after a long illness.

In 1854 the New Bedford, Vineyard and Nantucket Steamboat Company was formed. Despite having New Bedford in its name, the company used as its terminus Fairhaven, just across the harbor from New Bedford. It began operating the steamer *Metacomet* in September 1854. The rail line from Boston ran to Fairhaven, and the *Metacomet* connected with the train, a great convenience for Vineyarders. In October 1854 Jeremiah Pease, his wife, and daughter went to Boston, taking the *Metacomet* to Fairhaven to get on the train and arriving in Boston early in the afternoon.

The *Metacomet* didn't stay in service very long. For reasons unknown, it was replaced in April 1856 by the steamer *Eagle's Wing*. Pease recorded the change:

April 14, 1856: Steamer *Metacomet* leaves this morning for the last time, the *Eagle's Wing* to take her place.

April 15: Steamer *Eagle's Wing* arrives on her first trip today.

The following winter was one of the coldest ever recorded on the Vineyard. For weeks the harbor was frozen and there was no ferry service. On January 31, 1857, Pease wrote: "This has been the most severe month I ever knew. . . . The thumometer [*sic*] has been from 4 to 12 or 13 degrees below Zero, the ice in the harbor is now 18 inches thick and extends to Cape Poge, and a great quantity floating in the Sound." The harbor was closed until mid-February, when one hundred Edgartown men went out on the ice to cut a channel so the new steamer could get through. Soon after they opened the channel, the weather moderated and the ice left the harbor.

A number of changes were made by the various steamboat companies during the next forty years in attempts to bring profits, but there was little success. Part of the reason was that there were two, sometimes three companies competing for the limited traffic. Steamboats were expensive to buy and to run. The old sailing packets made more sense economically, but there was no going back.

In 1900 the New York, New Haven and Hartford Railroad, hoping to increase its passenger business between New York and the islands by improving ferry service, bought a one-third interest in the struggling steamboat company. Ten years later it bought enough additional shares to control the operation. Still, service kept getting worse.

Summer residents on both the Vineyard and Nantucket were so disgruntled that they decided they would raise the money to buy and run the ferry themselves. Year-rounders refused to join, fearing that winter service would be cut if summer people ran the ferries. The plan of the summer people collapsed and the railroad, now securely in charge, turned the entire operation over to its subsidiary, the New England Steamship Company, the operator of the Fall River Line and other steamboat companies.

Service continued to deteriorate. By 1920 the two boats that were operating were the *Uncatena*, a paddle wheeler built in 1902, and the newer *Sankaty*, the first propeller-driven vessel on the run. Both ran from New Bedford to Nantucket with stops at Woods Hole and Vineyard Haven. The *Sankaty* was fast; it set many records and shortened travel time before it burned one night in 1924 at the wharf in New Bedford.

During the off-season the large steamers were at times taken out of

In 1922 the steamboat company, owned by a railroad, began building its "Great White Fleet," including the *Nobska*. Luxurious for passengers, the ships were not designed to handle trucks and automobiles, just then arriving at the wharf in numbers. It wasn't until the Steamship Authority took over in 1948 that ferries with large doors at each end were designed. The first began service in 1950. (MVHS Collections)

service, and the *Frances*, a small, shallow-draft steamer, was chartered to make two trips a day between Vineyard Haven and Woods Hole. It was not popular with Vineyarders; in fact, the *Gazette* seemed to consider it a joke: "It was said that *Frances* can sail up Main Street, Vineyard Haven, on a rainy day, she draws so little water. She went into service on November 1st and has already missed five trips. . . . It is impossible to total the number of persons she has made sea sick. She brings to the Island in winter, a new and fresh element of humor and a hint of uncertainty."

In 1922 the railroad made a bold move. It ordered a new steamboat, the *Islander,* to be built by the Bath Iron Works in Maine, the first of what came to be called the Great White Fleet. The handsome *Islander* looked more like a scaled-down Atlantic liner than a practical ferry boat. The designer had given little thought to automobiles and trucks. Passenger comfort was stressed:

In the lobby were rolled, wood-slatted, stationary benches on either side, with Windsor chairs placed in the center. At the base of the stanchions, brass cuspidors were conveniently located. A wide stairway led from the lobby to the saloon above. The base of the stairway was flanked to port by the men's room and to starboard by the smoking and card room. . . . On the saloon deck, forward was an open deck with solid railing enclosures, followed by the interior compartment with staterooms, or day cabins (each furnished with a couch, two chairs, a fold-away card table and a sink) and the ladies' room.

Automobiles had to be driven slowly up a narrow gangplank, through a side hatch, then jockeyed into position, sharing space with freight dollies. Unloading was equally slow. The automobile-loading problem didn't seem to be of concern to the steamship company. It ordered three more of the same sleek design, the last being the *Naushon,* launched in June 1929, which had twenty staterooms on its saloon deck and twelve more on a "hurricane" deck. Some of the staterooms even had private toilets. Nothing was overlooked, except the automobile and the future: "There was a huge glass enclosed observation room aft and she supplied her passengers with writing desks stocked with monogrammed stationery carrying the New England Steamship Company's insignia. . . . She even had her own daily newspaper."

In 2006 there remains one survivor of that Great White Fleet, the *Nobska,* floating forlornly in Charlestown Navy Yard while its admirers seek money to put the boat back in service as a memorial, it would seem, to a design that was out of date almost from its launching.

The state legislature created the Steamship Authority in 1948, taking the ferry service away from the railroad. Two years later the Steamship Authority, no longer saddled with a railroad mind-set, designed and built its first vessel, one that gave priority to loading and unloading cars and trucks. It was named the *Islander,* the third vessel to carry that name. Paul Morris and Joseph Morin offer this description in *The Island Steamers* (1977): "Designed specifically with the Vineyard service in mind . . . she looked more like a 'ferry,' than did any of the previous vessels that were built for the line. She was constructed in fact as a work horse whose basic concept would make her an economical, functional vessel, capable of decades of hard use." More than a half century later, in 2006, the *Islander* is still in service, a favorite of Vineyarders, many of whom are saddened by the plans for a replacement.

In 1927 a faster way to get to the Island began: airplanes started flying on summer weekends between Boston and Katama in Edgartown. The Katama airfield was simply a strip of flat, open grassland that a farmer, William G. Vincent, had leased to the flying service. It was an ideal natural runway with a smooth, grassy surface that did not absorb water quickly, so it remained hard after a rain.

The plane left Boston each Friday afternoon at 5:00 P.M. and landed at Katama at 6:00 P.M. after a stop at Hyannis. (It continued on to Nantucket from Katama.) Return flights left Katama at 8:20 A.M., on Monday and arrived in Boston at 9:20 A.M. Round-trip: twenty-five dollars. Two years later the Curtiss Flying Service, calling itself "the world's oldest and safest flying organization, established in 1911," took over the summer service.

Islanders had become accustomed to flying machines. The first had

The ocean was the Island's first landing strip in July 1919, when two East Chop summer residents hired a seaplane to fly them from New York on weekends and taxied up to the Wesley House beach in Oak Bluffs. Ten years later public flights began from Boston to Katama, where a strip of farmland had been turned into an airport.
(MVHS Collections)

arrived in July 1919, ten years earlier, when two navy hydroplanes from Chatham Navy Air Base landed in the Sound off Oak Bluffs and taxied up to the beach. The navy's purpose, the *Gazette* explained, was to "spur recruiting for the service and to let people see how the airplane funds have been spent." Ten days later, a private hydroplane landed in the same waters, this time taxiing through the jetties to the Wesley House pier, where its occupants went ashore: Melvin B. Fuller, Myron J. Brown, and the pilot, a Mr. Griffin. A reception was held at the Tabernacle, followed by a supper that evening in the Wesley House. It was a gala occasion.

Fuller and Brown, both East Chop summer residents, had flown from New York on a trial flight to determine whether to give up the long train and steamboat ride on weekends and come by air. We find no record of what they decided.

On Saturdays Griffin, eager to make his weekend profitable, took passengers up on sightseeing flights at ten dollars each. Two persons sat in the forward open cockpit with an unobstructed view of the Island from heights few had ever experienced. On one flight the passengers were Eugene O'Neill, a guest that weekend of Mrs. Henry Hand of East Chop, and Miss Priscilla Hand. The *Vineyard News* called O'Neill "a promising playwright from Provincetown."

A "promising playwright," indeed. The following year O'Neill's first full-length play, *Beyond the Horizon*, was awarded the Pulitzer Prize for drama.

In the summer of 1929 the Curtiss Flying Service, now providing daily flights from Boston (and bringing the Boston newspapers), opened a flying school at Katama. It advertised that one could vacation at the beach while learning to fly. Its basic ten-hour course taught the rudiments of flying; a twenty-five-hour course included navigation training; and its fifty-hour course prepared those who hoped to earn a living as pilots. The brochure did indeed make it sound like a vacation:

> A large, comfortable farmhouse, located but a short distance from the edge of the flying field, contains adequate facilities for a few students and the instructors. Completely equipped tents are located close by the house, and the students virtually live, eat and fraternize with their instructors during the entire period of their course at Martha's Vineyard. . . .
>
> A competent chef [is] in charge. . . . Milk, cream, fresh eggs and vegetables are obtained from a neighboring farm. A private bathing beach adjoins the farmhouse, and it is possible for students to enjoy a swim at

any time. . . . The students may avail themselves of all the social life to be had, including yachting, bathing, tennis, golf and other sports. . . . Arrangements are being made to provide for [guest] cards at the Edgartown Tennis Club and the Oak Bluffs Country Club, for the use of Curtiss students.

Daily flight service to Boston did not last long. We find no record of its operating after 1929. It was not a good time to introduce airplane travel. After the stock market crashed in October, there were few willing (or able) to spend money flying to the Vineyard. The train and the ferry would have to do.

Curtiss continued its Katama flying school into the 1930s, teaching the sons of well-to-do mainlanders who still had money after the crash. These young men, some driving expensive European sports cars, spent summer afternoons swimming "at the Bend" in Edgartown, today's State Beach. (South Beach bathing had not yet become popular.) The only fatality recorded at the flying school occurred when lightning struck the farmhouse dormitory, killing one student. That farmhouse, according to Mae Wannamaker of Edgartown, whose grandfather owned the Katama field, was later moved and is now the Square Rigger restaurant in Edgartown.

Mrs. Wannamaker remembered that her grandfather William G. Vincent hired many Portuguese to work on his farm. The Portuguese had been gardeners on the Island for many years. As early as 1900 some had lived in the old abandoned farmhouses at Seven Gates Farm, raising vegetables for residents. Now many more lived in Oak Bluffs.

David Welch remembered: "[They lived mostly] from Vineyard Avenue over to Wing Road . . . and along where the ballpark is. . . . All the way up to Wing Road. Up to the Lagoon Heights was all Portuguese. . . . The Portuguese Club was built probably in the thirties."

The Portuguese, more than any other minority, are essential to the story of Martha's Vineyard. Their presence began in the late 1700s, when Captain Joseph Swazey and his brother, Anthony, came to Edgartown. They were members of a distinguished Lisbon family. It was said their father was Portugal's ambassador to England at one time.

But if that was true, they were the exception. Most of the Island's Portuguese were not from mainland Europe. Instead, they were from the Western Islands, Portuguese possessions off the coast of Europe and North Africa, many miles from Portugal. The first to come to the Vineyard had crewed on whalers that stopped at those islands to fill out their crews before heading out for whales. When the whalers returned from their voyages, many Portuguese had had enough whaling and stayed in New Bedford to work in its textile mills. Later a few, unhappy with factory work, came to the Vineyard to become fishermen and laborers. That was in the mid-1800s. Those early immigrants were few compared with the many who came later, during the great emigration from Europe in the early 1900s.

The Portuguese story is complicated. Coming as they did from different islands stretching over a thousand miles of ocean from north to south, they had many differences. Those from the northern islands, Madeira and the Azores, were lighter-skinned, being mostly of European ancestry, while those from the southern islands, the Cape Verdeans, were darker-skinned, their ancestors often North African. What they had in common was their Portuguese language, not their ancestry. But to Vineyarders, they were all Portuguese or, more often than not, "Port-a-gees," a derogatory term.

Many of the Portuguese lived in shacks they had built alongside their gardens on the outskirts of Oak Bluffs. They raised vegetables and flowers that they sold door-to-door from their wagons. Later they began selling in the markets, and some became store owners as they learned the business. Through the years they became active on all economic and social levels. Today many of the Island's leading families have Portuguese ancestry. (Marianne Thomas of Edgartown has painstakingly gathered the genealogy of thousands of those families in two volumes that are available at the Martha's Vineyard Historical Society and at other libraries.) During the early years, however, they were considered second-class citizens or worse. Miriam Walker, the granddaughter of Charles Shearer of Shearer Cottage, describes how blacks, she being one, felt about the Portuguese, and vice versa: "We weren't allowed to play with the Portuguese. And the Portuguese didn't want their children to play with the black families. . . . I used to have a Portuguese boyfriend. My mother would have died if she'd known I was seeing this boy."

There were other groups who were treated as second-class. Walker tells of a conversation she had with Ida Levine, who owned the Vineyard Dry Goods Store in Vineyard Haven. Ida was proud to tell her that her son was on the board of Harvard. She said to Walker: "Can you imagine a Levine in such a position? You know what I mean."

Miriam Walker knew exactly what she meant. For Ida's son, a Jew, to be on the board of Harvard College was something neither of them could have imagined while growing up on Martha's Vineyard: "You know I know what you mean. This was a very anti-Jewish island. . . . They let the Negroes in before they let the Jews in. . . . Negroes were really accepted before the Jews."

Madison Denniston, a black whose father was then the minister at the Bradley Memorial Church in Oak Bluffs, described how the Portuguese lived when he was young: "The Portuguese were the poor of the Island at that time [early 1900s]. They raised pigs and were the swill collectors to feed their pigs. They lived in just one area, Little Portugal, you might call it. Mrs. Bradley did social work among the poor Portuguese."

Susan C. Bradley was an outstanding woman who has been forgotten in Island history. She was born Susan Clapp in 1832 in Stoughton, Massachusetts; the Clapps were an important family. She and her sister, Ruth, established a private school in Brockton and ran it for years. Always eager to help the less fortunate, Susan at the end of Civil War went to North Carolina as a representative of the American Missionary Association to run a school for freed slaves.

When she returned to Massachusetts, she settled in Cottage City and founded the Oakland Mission in her home and became a strong Prohibitionist. The Reverend Oscar E. Denniston, who became her assistant at the mission, described her work in the obituary he wrote when she died in 1908:

> She founded the Oakland Mission in 1890 and worked faithfully for more than 10 years among the colored people and Portuguese and the poor and unfortunate of the town. It was during this time that she became the wife of Stephen H. Bradley, whom she survived. . . .
>
> No one in Dukes County fought "Old King Alcohol" more severely than Susan Clapp Bradley.
>
> She was one of the most unselfish characters that labored in the cause of Christ. . . . She died in her seventy-sixth year.

Denniston knew her well, having worked for her when he came to the Island from Jamaica. He was a black minister who first heard about Martha's Vineyard from the Reverend Madison Edwards, the chaplain of the Seamen's Bethel in Vineyard Haven. Edwards had gone to Jamaica on a vacation and he and Denniston became friends, both being ministers with strong social interests. When he came north a few years later, Denniston first settled in Boston and after a year or so moved to the Island, encouraged to do so by Edwards. After working with Edwards at the Bethel for a year, he became the assistant to Mrs. Bradley at the Oakland Mission. By then she was elderly and Denniston soon took over and gradually turned the mission into a church. That was the beginning of the black Baptist church on the Island. When Mrs. Bradley died, Denniston renamed it the Bradley Memorial Mission in her honor. Under him the mission soon took the name Bradley Memorial Baptist Church.

Island blacks had preferred the Baptist faith for years, ever since it had become obvious to them that other denominations did not welcome them. The Baptist Temple on the Highlands, built in 1877, two years before the Methodist Tabernacle, at first served white Baptists only. After a few years blacks were allowed to hold their services there, led by black Baptist ministers who came over from New Bedford.

Those services were segregated, but when black choral groups from southern black colleges began touring New England giving concerts to raise money, they sang in the Temple with both whites and blacks in attendance. In 1883 a "colored quartette from Howard College" gave two concerts of "peculiar music of their section and race" in Cottage City, raising fifty dollars for their school. Singers from other black colleges gave concerts at both the Methodist Tabernacle and the Baptist Temple each summer, and attendance was racially mixed.

Denniston's church was for blacks, but it did not attract the middle-class blacks who owned summer homes in Oak Bluffs. They were "proper" Episcopalians with little desire to worship "black fashion"—to the rhythm and joyful singing of gospel hymns. They were on vacation and could wait until they got home for church. Some years later, after an Episcopal church was established in Oak Bluffs, some of those blacks worshipped there.

During the winter Denniston's congregation was small, drawn from the year-round black community. In summer it was enlarged by the many black domestic servants who came to the Island with their wealthy employers. Sunday evening services were the most crowded. Domestics had to work during the day on Sundays. That attendance pattern continued for years. As late as 1962, when the Reverend William B. Roane became the church's pastor, he described his new flock in the *Gazette*: "This church consists of 30 members who are year round and about 50 members who are here for the summer. They work here in hotels, private families and at various menial tasks and come here from all over the country. . . . The congregation is noted for its melodious voices and fervent singing in worship services."

When Denniston died in 1942, the probate record of his estate included a house on Masonic Avenue (the original Susan Bradley house) and a church building on Circuit Avenue. The Circuit Avenue building had been the Noepe movie theater. Abandoned and in great disrepair, it was bought by Denniston in the early 1900s as his summer church. Church property and his were intermingled. He was never paid a salary, but he was compensated directly by offerings from his flock each Sunday.

His life is a remarkable story. He came to Martha's Vineyard from Jamaica and soon became the leader of the black community in Oak Bluffs. There was some opposition to him and his style, especially from the summer Episcopalian blacks. All his many children finished college, some with graduate degrees. He said they did it on their own, working their way, but he and his two wives (when his first wife died, he went back to Jamaica to marry again) certainly deserve much credit.

The congregation dwindled after Denniston's death. A smaller building was needed, and in 1958 members bought the Odd Fellows Hall on Pequot Avenue. There is a wonderful symmetry here: the building had been built in the late 1800s as the town's first Baptist church (whites only, of course) and now it was again a Baptist church, this time for blacks. The old Noepe Theater on upper Circuit Avenue, which had been the summer church, was sold to Roscoe Heathman, a local contractor, who tore it down and used the lumber to build a house and workshop on the site.

In 1966 the Bradley Memorial Baptist Church disbanded. The building on Pequot Avenue was deconsecrated in April that year. Unused for a while, it again became a church, the Apostolic House of Prayer, attended by blacks and whites. It is now privately owned. But the black Baptist church, the child of the Reverend Oscar Denniston, is no more.

In 1929 the nation fell into the Great Depression. Construction on the Vineyard, as elsewhere, came to a virtual halt. Some builders went bankrupt. Carpenters and laborers, their jobs gone, turned back to the ocean for income.

Edgartown's swordfishing fleet seemed little bothered by the downturn. Swordfish was becoming popular in fancy big-city restaurants and demand was increasing. Five or six schooners from Edgartown would go out for a couple of weeks and return with a "cash crop" in their holds. After selling their catch in Boston, they would sail into Edgartown for a few days at home, their crews with fat rolls of bills stuffed in their pockets. It was a good time to be a swordfisherman, but little else.

Oak Bluffs was hit the hardest, although its hotels managed to stay open each summer despite the downturn. There was talk that they would soon have to close. The *Gazette* and Henry Hough didn't like that kind of talk. In June 1931 the paper urged optimism: "There should be a limit to all this popular worry about the depression, the depression which is, incidentally, about over. . . . The Vineyard is, in truth, one of the least expensive of the worthwhile summer resorts. . . . A vacation here is not an extravagance. . . . This is a year to come, not a year to stay away."

But happy talk didn't bring more business, nor was the Depression "about over," as Henry Hough had assured readers. It was to continue for many years. The large houses in Oak Bluffs stood unoccupied, their owners lacking funds to open them each summer. That turned out to be good news for some, as Dorothy West recalled in her book *The Richer, the Poorer*:

> The great houses stood empty, too large to run without servants, and too few, if any, families could afford a staff. The hotels and shops that struggled to stay open were barely staying alive. "For Sale" signs were everywhere, and there were no buyers.
>
> The black colony, [at first] no more than a dozen families . . . found more than they ever hoped that they would find: a place where they could stand to full size. The town was right for them, and, at the time, their coming was right for the town.
>
> They made a massive imprint. They bought the big, neglected houses and other long-empty cottages, lifted their sagging facades, put in new plumbing and wiring, scrubbed and polished and painted.

Only a few others benefited from the hard times: Mosher's Photo Shop in Vineyard Haven was one. When the Civilian Conservation Corps (CCC) set up a camp in the state forest, scores of unemployed men came to the Island. They cleared fire lanes in the forest, made roads, trimmed trees and brush. Many were from big cities and had never seen such natural beauty as the Island possessed. Eager to share their discovery with friends and family, they shot rolls of film, keeping Mosher's busy making prints for them to send home.

But the CCC men couldn't make up for the loss of business that Vineyard Haven felt when the Cape Cod Canal opened and provided a new, shorter route between Boston and ports south. Since the 1800s Vineyard Haven had been a layover port for vessels awaiting a fair wind and tide on their way to Boston. The canal changed that. First opened in the 1920s as a privately owned waterway, charging tolls, it did not do well. It was too narrow and too shallow. In 1928 the federal government bought it but did little with it until the Depression. Then the Works Progress Administration (WPA) decided it would be a good project. About fourteen hundred men were put to work creating a sea-level canal five hundred feet wide and thirty-two feet deep, said to be the largest sea-level canal in the world. When the improved canal opened in 1940, Vineyard Haven lost its shipping business. Tugs towed their barges on the shorter and more protected route via Buzzards Bay and the canal to Boston.

Somehow, even at the bottom of the Depression, Oak Bluffs managed to stay alive. Prices dropped and the crowds were smaller, but they kept coming. Guests still filled the porches of the big old hotels, rocking the hours away, entertained by the flow of vacationers and Islanders along the

Enticing every stroller on Circuit Avenue in Oak Bluffs was the sweet, buttery aroma that emanated from Darling's Popcorn Store. Most of them ended up munching on a nickel bag of popcorn. The store opened about 1900, when Carroll J. Darling started his popping. By the 1920s (shown here), he was providing all kinds of tasty temptations. (MVHS Collections)

avenue. It continued to be a joy for all who could afford to come. A nickel bag of Darling's popcorn or a cone of Rausch's homemade ice cream was enough to provide an evening's fun.

That was Oak Bluffs; the rest of the Island was less fortunate. It wasn't until World War II that the other towns began to rebound. An early taste of what was on the way came even before the war, when the army built an observation tower atop Peaked Hill in Chilmark. The tower itself wasn't a big project (it wasn't clear what it was for at the time), but a new road had to be built to get to it and that put a lot of Island men to work. A couple of years later, in 1943, with the war under way, the tower was replaced by a radar station, manned by about twenty-five soldiers. A barracks and other buildings were built, and more Island men went to work. The soldiers stationed at the radar site were in the army's Amphibian Force and wore stylish berets and high, shiny boots that impressed many young women along Circuit Avenue when the soldiers were off-duty.

With the country at war, the Island became a practice ground for mock invasions, which brought hundreds of soldiers with money to spend. One "invasion" was in early October 1942, when thousands of soldiers stormed ashore. Little was written about it in the newspapers; it was "secret," although thousands knew it was happening. To satisfy public curiosity, one week later the army put out a long press release from Camp Edwards. Here are a few excerpts:

> Thousands of Camp Edwards amphibious and amphibian troops stormed across Vineyard Sound in assault boats, and invaded the island of Martha's Vineyard, smashed enemy installations, disrupted enemy communications and forced the foe back into the sea in the most extensive land and sea maneuvers ever carried out in this section of the country. . . .
>
> The amphibious infantrymen stormed the island at three different points, parachute troops swooped down, seized the vital enemy-held airport at Edgartown. . . . Hour after hour, wave after wave, came the heavily-clad sea-going troops. . . . The main landing was in the northwest side of the island by two combat teams, with other landings at two other points so as to draw the enemy away from the main sector.
>
> The first boat struck shore exactly on schedule. Down planked the jaw-like door and onto the mushy, white sand leaped the infantrymen. . . . They were met by thunderous explosions, which shattered the mysterious stillness of the early, dreary morning. The crackle of machine

guns added to the din. An orange flash pierced the inky black sky. Another explosion. More boats landing. The incessant chatter of machine guns. More boats land. And still more.

Landings were made south of Norton Beach, southeast of Lambert's Cove, Sachem Spring and Chappaquonsett Pond, south of Paul's Point, north of Cape Higgon and North Tisbury.

Needless to say, the good guys won.

Several more such "invasions" followed. In August 1943, when amphibious forces stormed the beach at Edgartown, they brought a holiday mood. One of the invaders, PFC Robert F. Phelan of Waterbury, Connecticut, wrote home about it:

> The island is really nice this time of year and there is plenty to do. There are three towns here and I have been to two of them. We have the Brigade Band with us and they serenade us at meal time and play in town at night for our dances.
>
> A few days ago we built some tank obstacles and had some tanks test them out. One of them turned over, but no one was hurt.
>
> After the tank demonstration we had a track and field meet. . . . Jimmy Cagney and Katherine Cornell, who are vacationing on the Vineyard, [watched] the track meet. After it was over, they were invited to talk to us. Katherine Cornell didn't say very much, but we really got Cagney going. He told a couple of corny Irish jokes and then someone suggested that he sing. They hauled the band up to where he was standing . . . and he sang Yankee Doodle Dandy, A Grand Old Flag, Mary, and a few more. . . . The Fellows enjoyed him a lot.
>
> After that, we had a hot-dog roast.

There were other mock invasions, but none with such a spirited result as that one. Richard Burt, a youngster at the time, remembers watching invasions on the north shore at Seven Gates Farm, where he lived (his father was superintendent there). He recalls airplanes dropping practice bombs into ponds on the Island.

Irving Willoughby of Edgartown recalled seeing paratroopers jumping from scores of airplanes and waves of landing craft swarming up on the beaches to disgorge their troops. "It was just like a war," he said.

David Flanders saw things during the war that were not make-believe. He saw the enemy:

VINEYARD WILL SEE MANY SOLDIERS SOON, HERE FOR MANEUVERS

Public Cooperation Asked— Landing Operations Are Among War Games

Martha's Vineyard is going to see soldiers, and many of them, during the next two or three weeks.

Large scale maneuvers are to be undertaken here, and the Army is announcing the plan in order to obtain the cooperation of the public. It is important that no one should feel disturbed by the field exercises or by the appearance of troops simulating conditions of an actual campaign.

Capt. H. G. Feldman, now at Camp Edwards, has made public today the general outline of the maneuvers, the first of the kind ever held on the Vineyard. Some facts cannot be divulged, such as the number of men to be involved, their precise objectives in the exercises, and the exact time the war games will begin.

When the army prepared to make assault landings in Africa and Europe, it chose Martha's Vineyard for its practice ground. To prevent panic among residents, the army in July 1942 held a press conference to announce a series of mock invasions. The soldiers during off-duty hours brought fresh life to Vineyard businesses. (*Vineyard Gazette,* July 1942. MVHS Collections)

I've seen German submarines come up and charge their batteries during the war. They'd come up in the lee of the Island here. And the Coast Guard called in the artillery, which was over by New Bedford. There was a fort over there, Fort Rodman, and they shot at them with, I guess, five-inch guns or nine-inch guns. I never saw them get any of them, though. The guns could reach the Island but they weren't very accurate. It was about the end of their range.

And they had a lot of planes around here, you know, from the airfield, and PBY sea planes were flying around here looking for submarines.

He saw a man he believed to be a German spy one day while delivering a telegram to an up-Island beach house:

Mother had a private line for her real estate business, the only telephone up here, so she had the telegram service. They'd call from Edgartown if there was something for her up here. Mother had a little Western Union thing and she'd write it down and then type it as a telegram and she'd give it to me and I'd take it to the house.

There was a house right on the beach down here, and the guy that owned it had bought it just about the time the war started, 1941. He was in the import-export business. He came from Norway, I believe. I delivered telegrams there quite often. One time, maybe half-way through the war, 1943 maybe, I rode down on my bike and it was just coming dusk and I went to the house and nobody was there but I saw a light in the guest house. And I went down there, and then I could hear the sound of a machine, "tit-ti, tit-ti, tit-ti," the man was on a radio, he was talking. I kind of peeked in the window and his back was to me, he was sitting there and the antenna was up and he was sending.

It scared me . . . and I shouted, "Hey! Anybody here?" And he come to the door, and I gave him the telegram. So then I went back home and I told Mother that I'd seen him, he really was signaling with a teletype thing, a radio.

So she called up the number that we were supposed to call if we saw something. She told what I'd seen. . . . They sent a man named Mr. Carpenter the next day, and I had to take him over. And he wanted me to show him which house it was and describe the guy and everything. So I did. And I know they were around there for a while, but I never knew what happened.

Many years later, I was at a firemen's dinner on the Vineyard and the guest speaker was a Mr. Carpenter from the FBI. After he spoke, I went up to him and asked, "Mr. Carpenter, were you here during the war?" I told him my story and he looked at me and he says, "Yeah, you're that boy, aren't you?" I says "Yes!"

So he told me what had happened, which I was very interested in. They thought he was really talking with a submarine because they were in the area. But they didn't arrest anybody, they just followed him and looked where his contacts were and got the names and addresses of all those people. And they never did pick him up. He did get away without them knowing it. He went out on a submarine, they thought.

The Island didn't have any defense plants, but it did have the Martha's

Vineyard Shipyard in Vineyard Haven, which did defense work for the navy. It employed as many as a hundred workers, who made wooden vessels of three designs. Only one was a combat vessel: a small landing craft designed to carry up to twelve marines onto the beach.

The largest of the shipyard's vessels were "Honey barges," large, ungainly scows, about one hundred feet overall with a wide beam, used for hauling garbage out to sea from naval bases. The third design was smaller, about thirty-five feet overall, built to haul bombs and depth charges to the navy's flying boats floating on their moorings. It was rimmed with rubber fenders to prevent it from damaging the fragile aircraft during the transfer.

The shipyard was much larger than it is today, extending for hundreds of yards on both sides of Beach Road in Vineyard Haven harbor. Its effect on the Island's cash flow was great. After the war it went into a quick decline, which caused economic distress to most of its workers.

Early in the war Islanders were warned about possible enemy air attacks. Leaflets advised them what to do when one occurred. Each town set up air-raid shelters, where residents were to go during a raid. Edgartown had nine shelters; none, it would seem, afforded much protection from falling bombs. Included among the nine were the town's churches, the county jail, the public library, the school gymnasium, and the movie theater.

Air-raid wardens were appointed and provided with reporting forms to be filled out and rushed by messenger to headquarters immediately after any attack. The forms asked whether the bombs that had fallen were "High Explosive, Incendiary or Poison Gas" and solicited the approximate number of casualties ("If any trapped under wreckage, say so") and the "position of unexploded bombs." No forms had to be filled out during the war, it seems.

With such official concern about bombing and invasion, many Islanders volunteered for observation duty, looking for an approaching enemy. Some developed an irrational fear of German invasion or sabotage. From lookout posts around the Island they stared outward for hours, watching for incoming enemy, reporting lights, often imaginary, at sea and in the air.

Ensign Everett S. Allen, the son of Joseph Chase Allen, the longtime reporter and columnist for the *Vineyard Gazette*, was the officer in charge of the Naval Intelligence Office, with its headquarters on Beach Road in Vineyard Haven. He wrote in his book *Martha's Vineyard: An Elegy* that he was not impressed with what he was contributing to the war effort:

My principal duty as I saw it was to convince the Navy to close the installation. I came to that conclusion after no more than a few hours of searching for "flashing lights" that proved to have logical explanations, and "guttural accents" that derived from Hoboken, not Hamburg.

It seemed to me possible that a spy, saboteur, or traitor might show up on the Island . . . [but] if one did, he (or she) probably would not flash any lights or have a guttural accent.

Ensign Allen was flooded with reports of sightings. His favorite spotter was a woman in her sixties who "after spending twenty hours a day, looking, listening and taking notes," reported to him daily on suspicious movements of vessels and people: "She was splendid about noting the precise times at which things happened, the compass bearing, if applicable, and she recited, with what I thought considerable grace, the manners and mannerisms of her subjects. . . . I confess neither she nor I ever caught any spies or saboteurs, but I did look forward to her accounts; they sparkled and brightened otherwise dull days."

Although Allen may not have taken the threat of a German invasion seriously, others did. The coast guard manned stations along the south shore from Gay Head to Cape Poge. Men carrying rifles and accompanied by dogs patrolled the shoreline twenty-four hours a day. They were quartered in summer homes along the south shore and in the hotel, now demolished, at Gay Head.

The coast guard closely controlled the use of pleasure boats. Certain areas were declared off-limits to all private vessels, having been reserved for training exercises. Permits and passes were issued to fishermen to allow them to sail into the restricted areas. Their radios were sealed, and the seal could be broken only to report enemy activities. Of course, as the war went on and little, if any, enemy action was seen, the rules were relaxed.

Coast guardsmen were not the only ones patrolling the beaches. Island residents walked the beaches on the north shore. One volunteer was Craig Kingsbury of Tisbury:

I had East Chop night patrol as a volunteer. . . . [We used] a little house, part of the Oak Bluffs Tennis Club, that had a little four-hole golf course out there close to the lighthouse. I'd walk, checking the beach three nights a week, a guy named McDonald had three nights, and then one night each week one of the girls took over. . . . We'd go over there at 9 o'clock and come home at sunrise.

Lots of activity was going on. There were men over at Katama, practicing landings on the beach, but they didn't want civilians around. . . . There was a camp down where Katherine Cornell's place is now, on Aunt Rhody's Pond. They rebuilt the road to get their equipment down there . . . and lived in wooden tents, bolted together.

There was a heck of a bunch of [sailors] out at the airport, probably 1,800 . . . plus about a hundred soldiers scattered around the Island. . . . They'd fill the barrooms and gin mills in Oak Bluffs and Edgartown when they weren't on duty.

The airport's Naval Air Base that Kingsbury mentions was the largest wartime installation on the Island. Hundreds of navy and marine pilots and their support units came there for five or six weeks of flight training, landing and taking off on short runways that simulated an aircraft carrier's flight deck. A flagman would wave approaching planes on or off as he would aboard ship. Being waved off required the pilot to pull up and circle back. Planes occasionally stalled out and crash-landed among the forgiving small pine trees around the airport. The damaged aircraft would be hauled to the huge hangar to be repaired so they could fly again another day.

Repairing wrecked planes, maintaining the others, and keeping the base running required nearly one thousand nonflying sailors who, no doubt, enjoyed being stationed on an island, far from enemy guns. They lived in standard G.I. two-story barracks. Nearby were quarters for the officers and a recreation building, complete with slot machines, off-limits, of course, to the ordinary sailor.

As was standard in the navy, officers were well taken care of by orderlies, a company of black sailors quartered in Quonset huts across the road from the rest. Joseph Stiles was one of the orderlies. He described life at the base:

We took care of the officers' food and took care of the officers' club and their living quarters. That's as far up in the Navy a black could get at that time. Just in the kitchen.

We had to walk across the road to the nearest white barracks to take showers. The Navy was very prejudiced, we were second-class. . . . The base was so bad that we couldn't eat at the same tables with the whites.

There was a lot of racists. That's why I signed up for ship duty as soon as I could. . . . I got tired of going on liberty and having to fight my way back to camp. . . . We were scared, going on liberty at night. There was always a fight coming back.

We'd hit the night spots in Oak Bluffs, catch the last bus to camp, and we'd have fights all the way back. There'd be six or eight of us blacks and 40 of them [whites]. They'd get on the bus real drunk and some of them would come to the back, shouting, "Let's get the niggers."

All the way back there'd be fist fights. The driver tried to get to camp as fast as he could, but there was a governor on the engine. He couldn't speed it up.

That's why I asked to be transferred to a ship. It was too much for me.

Stiles never had any trouble with Vineyard residents, only with the white sailors at the airport: "There was nothing like that on the Island. The Island people were great to the blacks. That's why I came here to live afterwards, because Island people always treated us beautiful."

What happened at the air base was secret, of course, and rarely mentioned in the newspapers. It is believed that at least six navy pilots were killed when they crash-landed in the ocean off the Island because of mechanical failures. There was a period when maintenance of the aircraft was slipshod because, some said, there was too little discipline and too much alcohol. A few fires were started on the Island when planes inadvertently dropped signal flares. Sometimes bombs were dropped accidentally, but because they were usually target-practice bombs, they had little explosive power. No civilian casualties are known to have occurred. But there was damage to a few buildings, including one house on North Water Street in Edgartown.

Toward the end of the war, discipline greatly improved at the base and the number of maintenance-related accidents declined. The base's mission changed about that time to training night-attack pilots in radar guidance, a system then brand-new. The navy closed down the base in May 1946.

The army leased some land from Edward T. Vincent at Katama early in 1943, for some purpose not stated. Later that year the navy took it over and built a gunnery range on the site. The public was banned from the entire area, including the beach, where live ammunition was being used. Barracks and ammunition depots were built at a cost of three million dollars, providing more work for Islanders. The ban brought complaints from fishermen about not being able to use the beach.

The most tragic thing that happened on the Island during the war was when two sailors drowned in a tank of aircraft gasoline at the Naval Air Base. The story was covered up. Some time later the navy stated that the men had been killed by fumes while cleaning the tank. The facts were different, as we learned from Ed Krikorian, who was assigned there in January 1943 and was still there a year later when the accident happened.

He was on duty, expecting to be relieved as usual by his friend Richard Holden. When Holden failed to show up, Krikorian asked another sailor if he had seen him:

The guy said, "He's over there."

So I went over to see. There was a lot of people standing around looking down into a gas tank buried there. I was told that Holden and a fellow named Goodwin had volunteered to go down this ladder into the tank and measure it to see how much gasoline it held.

Goodwin felt a little faint and tried to climb out. The fumes got him and he fell back, pulling the ladder down with him. William Ping, a sailor from Detroit, jumped into the tank before I got there. I grabbed a rope that was on the ground and tied it around me, handed the other end to some guy standing there, and went into the tank. The gasoline was up to my chest.

I kicked around the bottom of the tank and kicked somebody. He was soaked with gasoline and heavy. I finally got him up until somebody reached down and grabbed him, shouting, "I got him." Then I passed out. They pulled me out with the rope. When I woke up, I was laying on the ground, doctors over me and the whole bit.

The guy I pulled out was Goodwin. Two guys died: Holden, my friend from Fall River, and Ping from Detroit. Goodwin was from New Hampshire. Afterwards he was real sick from swallowing so much gasoline. I wrote a letter for him to send to the Veterans Administration and he got a pension. I never applied for one.

I don't know why they had to die in that gasoline. It was a stupid order. Two men drowned in the tank. Goodwin lived and I lived, but I threw up every time I smelled gasoline for a year or so.

The Navy told the newspapers that two men had been overcome by fumes while cleaning an empty tank. That was not true. There was five feet of gasoline in the tank and the two men drowned in it.

I had just married an Island girl and was still sick in her house four days later, when a Navy man knocked on the door, carrying my sea bag that somebody had packed with my stuff. He handed me a ferry-boat ticket and off I went to Navy headquarters in Boston. They sent me to Philadelphia to a Navy school. All of us who seen what happened in that tank was shipped out right away.

Ed Krikorian was so saddened by the useless deaths of his fellow sailors that many years later he had a memorial plaque with their names on it placed at the airport, on the site of their drowning.

David Flanders of Chilmark was a teenager during those years and some of his memories of the war are happier:

My mom worked in real estate, and she rented houses to people that came from England and France during the war. The English gentlemen would send their wives and all their kids over here, to get them out of the Blitz, out of England, out of London.

I got to know a lot of the English boys and girls that came. They'd come for the whole summer, three months. I'm still in touch with some of the kids that were my age. I had a fellow call last year that I hadn't talked to since '45 or '46. He had three brothers. We used to go beach-combing every Saturday, we walked all the shore to Gay Head. And we found all kinds of stuff from boats being torpedoed. Life vests and oars and food sometimes would come on the beach, and gasoline drums filled with gas.

I remember I found some gasoline drums and my dad needed gas, awful gas shortage here. It was aviation gas, very high octane. My father had five-gallon oilcans; I siphoned the gas with a hose into the oilcans. Then I got the oilcans up on the beach and put them in the bushes. I got my bicycle, with a cart on the back, and I'd ride back and forth pulling these cans back home. I had a lot of cans full, about fifty gallons. My father diluted it, put kerosene in it. We ran the tractors on it, the cars, the boat, everything.

Not all Vineyarders had such pleasant memories of World War II. Records show that 614 Islanders served during the war: 380 were in the army; 152 in the navy; 35 in the coast guard; 34 in the marines; and 13 in the air force. Tisbury had 220, Edgartown had 181, Oak Bluffs had 173, Chilmark had 16, West Tisbury had 15, and Gay Head had 9.

The records indicate that fifteen Islanders were killed in action or died of wounds. Another seven died in the service for reasons other than enemy action. These are those who died:

KILLED IN ACTION OR DIED OF WOUNDS

Arthur C. Andrews
Douglas C. Brown (navy/marines)
Lester E. Healy
Walter Karzhewsky
William H. Monahan
Willard H. Sawyer Jr.
John P. Silva
Joseph J. Zasada

Edmund J. Berube (navy/marines)
Adelbert E. Colby
Walter H. Hermenau
Donald F. McEachern
Jean D. Ouelette
Morris Shapiro
Donald S. Swift (navy/marines)

DIED OF OTHER CAUSES

Manuel A. Enos
Robert R. Gilkes
Lawrence J. LeBlanc
Richard R. Thompson

Napoleon R. Gagnon
John D. Kelley
John A. Silvia

This list may not be complete and may have errors, but it is based on the best information we have. The navy/marines data do not indicate cause of death, so we are not sure whether those three men died as a result of enemy action.

The war had been good for business in Oak Bluffs. Not only did the men from the Naval Air Base fill its bars during off-duty hours, but family and friends who visited them kept its hotels and restaurants filled. With the war's end, things changed, as David Welch explains:

> With all the sailors and the soldiers on the Island, all their girls came and they had to have places to stay. The hotels were pretty busy. After the war, the hotels couldn't survive, there were too many of them. And the people who came then wanted motels or condominiums and beachfront rooms and stuff like that. . . .
>
> They took the top two floors off the Pawnee House and the other big hotels were torn down for the lumber. . . . There was no need for all the hotels they had.

When the big hotels were torn down, much of the joy of Oak Bluffs disappeared with them. No longer did guests sit in rocking chairs on the wide porches, watching vacationers stroll along the avenue each evening, munching on Darling's well-buttered popcorn. Gone, too, were the bands that entertained from hotel balconies. Instead of strollers filling the avenue, the automobile took over. The avenue was no longer a place for people to meander.

At the airport the Naval Air Base was turned into a chicken farm when an entrepreneur bought the abandoned barracks and filled them with thousands of cackling hens. It wasn't long before the two-story buildings began to fall apart as the hens' droppings rotted the wood: a sorry ending to a wartime chapter.

Much more than the war had ended. An era had ended with it. Henry Hough recognized that: "The end of WW II . . . [brought] a break in continuity with the long past. For 300 years the Island had been singularly homogeneous . . . a combination of farming and fishing carried on by the same people. . . . Those old traditions fitted the Island so well. . . . The Vineyard was uncrowded, there was a rhythm to the seasons."

Hough understood that rhythm well. In *Martha's Vineyard: Summer Resort,* he wrote about an Island that for two months a year took time out to be a resort. The rest of the year, it was a normal, coastal New England community where residents farmed and fished.

After World War II the nation began to discover the Vineyard. Celebrities, even a president, made it the place to be. Everything began to revolve around the business of summer.

The change was seismic. Never again would Martha's Vineyard be what it had been: a quiet island of fishermen and farmers, briefly interrupted each summer. Being a summer resort had become a full-time job.

Bibliography

Adams, Charles Francis, ed. *Familiar Letters of John Adams and His Wife Abigail Adams during the Revolution.* Freeport, N.Y.: Books for Libraries Press, 1970.

Adams, Henry. *Thomas Hart Benton: An American Original.* New York: Alfred A. Knopf, 1989.

Adams, John. *The Papers of John Adams.* Edited by Robert J. Taylor and Mary-Jo Kline. 12 vols. Cambridge: Belknap Press of Harvard University Press, 1977–2004.

Allen, Everett S. *Martha's Vineyard: An Elegy.* 1982. Rpt., Beverly, Mass.: Commonwealth Editions, 2005.

Allen, Joseph Chase. *Tales and Trails of Martha's Vineyard.* Boston: Little, Brown, 1938.

André, John. *Major André's Journal.* Tarrytown, N.Y.: William Abbatt, 1930.

Archer, Gabriel. "Relation of Captain Gosnold's Voyage" (1843). Collections of the Massachusetts Historical Society, Boston.

Bailyn, Bernard. *The New England Merchants in the Seventeenth Century.* Cambridge: Harvard University Press, 1955.

Banks, Charles E. *The History of Martha's Vineyard, Dukes County, Massachusetts.* Edgartown: Dukes County Historical Society, 1966.

Blassingame, John W., ed. *Slave Testimony: Two Centuries of Letters, Speeches, Interviews, and Autobiographies.* Baton Rouge: Louisiana State University Press, 1977.

Bradford, William. *Of Plimouth Plantation, 1620–1647.* Edited by Samuel Eliot Morison. New York: Alfred A. Knopf, 1966.

Burroughs, Polly. *Thomas Hart Benton: A Portrait.* Garden City, N.Y.: Doubleday, 1981.

Carpenter, Edmund J. *Roger Williams: A Study of the Life, Times and Character of a Political Pioneer.* New York: Grafton Press, 1909.

Chamberlain, Barbara Blau. *These Fragile Outposts.* New York: Natural History Press, 1964.

Clinton, Sir Henry. *The American Rebellion.* New Haven: Yale University Press, 1954.

Delaney, Norman C. *Ghost Ship: The Confederate Raider Alabama.* Middletown, Conn.: Southfarm Press, 1989.

Dexter, Lincoln. *The Gosnold Discoveries.* Brookfield, Mass.: Privately printed, 1982.

Dohla, Johann Conrad. *Hessian Diary of the American Revolution.* Translated and edited by Bruce E. Burgoyne. Norman: University of Oklahoma Press, 1990.

Dull, Jonathan R. *The French Navy and American Independence: A Study of Arms and Diplomacy, 1774–1787.* Princeton: Princeton University Press, 1975.

Ernst, James. *Roger Williams, New England Firebrand.* New York: Macmillan, 1932.

Flexner, James T. *George Washington in the American Revolution, 1775–1783.* Boston: Little, Brown, 1968.

Flick, Alexander C., ed. *History of the State of New York.* New York: Columbia University Press, 1933.

Forbes, Amelia. *Early History of Naushon Island.* Boston: Thomas Todd, 1935.

Freeman, James. "Description of Dukes County, 1807." *Collections of the Massachusetts Historical Society,* 1815.

Gookin, Warner F. *Capawack, Alias Martha's Vineyard.* Edgartown: Dukes County Historical Society, 1947.

Gorge, Sir Ferdinando. "Description of New England" (1837). Collections of the Massachusetts Historical Society, Boston.

Greenman, Jeremiah. *Diary of a Common Soldier in the American Revolution, 1775–1783.* Edited by Robert C. Bray and Paul E. Bushnell. DeKalb: Northern Illinois University Press, 1978.

Hale, Edward Everett. *Gosnold at Cuttyhunk.* Worcester, Mass.: American Antiquarian Society, 1902.

Hough, Henry Beetle, *Martha's Vineyard: Summer Resort, 1835–1935.* Rutland, Vt.: Tuttle, 1936.

Hutchinson, Thomas. *History of the Colony and Province of Massachusetts-Bay.* Edited by Lawrence Shaw Mayo. 3 vols. Cambridge: Harvard University Press, 1936.

Jennings, Francis. *The Invasion of America: Indians, Colonialism, and the Cant of Conquest.* Chapel Hill: University of North Carolina Press, 1975.

Kellaway, William. *The New England Company, 1649–1776: Missionary Society to the American Indians.* New York: Longman's, 1961.

Koch, Albert C. *Visit to Gay Head, 1844.* Carbondale: Southern Illinois University Press, 1972.

Lindbergh, Anne Morrow. *War Within and Without.* New York: Harcourt Brace Jovanovich, 1980.

Lindbergh, Charles A. *The Wartime Journals of Charles A. Lindbergh.* New York: Harcourt Brace Jovanovich, 1970.

Mackenzie, Frederick. *The Diary of Frederick Mackenzie.* 2 vols. Cambridge: Harvard University Press, 1930.

Mayhew, Experience. *Indian Converts: or, Some Account of the Lives and Dying Speeches of a Considerable Number of Christianized Indians on Martha's Vineyard, in New-England.* Boston: J. Osborn, 1727.

Middlekauff, Robert. *The Glorious Cause: The American Revolution, 1763–1789.* New York: Oxford University Press, 1982.

Morgan, Edmund S., ed. *The Founding of Massachusetts: Historians and the Sources.* Indianapolis: Bobbs-Merrill, 1964.

Morgan, James, ed. *Naval Documents of the American Revolution.* Washington, D.C.: Naval Historical Center, 1986.

Quinn, David B., and Alison M. Quinn, eds. *The English New England Voyages, 1602–1608.* London: Hakluyt Society, 1983.

Rose-Troup, Frances. *The Massachusetts Bay Company and Its Predecessors.* New York: Grafton Press, 1930.

Salisbury, Neal. *Indians of New England: A Critical Bibliography.* Bloomington: Indiana University Press, 1982.

Sewall, Samuel. Receipt Book, Society for Propagating the Gospel. Collections of the Massachusetts Historical Society, Boston.

Shaler, Nathaniel S. *The Geology of Martha's Vineyard.* Washington, D.C.: U.S. Geological Survey, 1888.

Sibley, John L. *Sibley's Harvard Graduates: Biographical Sketches of Those Who Attended Harvard College.* Boston: Massachusetts Historical Society, 1873– .

Society for Propagating the Gospel. "Report of the Select Committee." Cambridge, 1819–1896.

Syrett, David. *The Royal Navy in American Waters, 1775–1783.* Aldershot, U.K.: Scolar Press, 1989.

Teller, Walter M. *Consider Poor I: The Life and Works of Nancy Luce.* Edgartown: Dukes County Historical Society, 1984.

Tilley, John A. *The British Navy and the American Revolution.* Columbia: University of South Carolina Press, 1987.

Tisbury, Town of. *Records of the Town of Tisbury, 1669–1903.* Boston: Wright and Potter, 1903.

Vincent, Hebron. *History of the Camp-Meeting and Grounds at Wesleyan Grove, Ending with the Meeting of 1869.* Boston: Lee and Shepard, 1870.

———. *A History of the Wesleyan Grove, Martha's Vineyard, Camp Meeting, 1835 to That of 1858.* Boston: Geo. C. Rand and Avery, 1858.

Weeden, William B. *Economic and Social History of New England, 1620–1789.* 2 vols. Boston: Houghton Mifflin, 1890.

West, Dorothy. *The Richer, the Poorer: Stories, Sketches, and Reminiscences.* New York: Doubleday, 1995.

Williams, Roger. *The Correspondence of Roger Williams.* Edited by Glenn W. LaFantasie. Providence: Brown University Press, 1988.

Index

Page references given in *italics* indicate illustrations or their captions.

ment/building in, 298–302, 300; immigrant population of, 177; impact of development on taxes in, 258–59; industry in, 135–36, 165, 172, 185, 206–7; Jewish merchants in, 376, 376–77; Mayhew homestead in, 60; Mayhew (Matthew) as representative of, 41; Methodists in, 145, 147, 154, 162–65, 163; militia quotas in, 76; negative publicity of, 257–58, 259; newspapers in, 397; Norton farm near, 121; Oak Bluffs–Katama railroad and, 252–54, 254, 259–60; Oak Bluffs road and, 251, 253, 261–62; oystering in, 213–14; Portuguese immigrants in, 175–77; post–War of 1812 shipping in, 138; presidential election results in (1860), 201; presidential election results in (1864), 235; public library in, 348, 403; public schools in, 133; Refugee Fleet and, 115; revival meetings in, 149, 166–67; secession petition in, 151, 159; smallpox epidemic in, 114; state representative for, 262, 333–34; summer colonies in, 336; swordfishing in, 419–20; tax revenues in, 266–67, 305, 334; telephone connections in, 318, 322; transportation links with, 168–70; West Tisbury secession and, 325, 334; whaling in, 140, 141–42, 214, 228–29, 335–36, 336; during WWI, 359, 368–69; during WWII, 423–24, 426, 428, 431

Edgartown, during Civil War, 223–24; casualties from, 211, 233–34; defense efforts in, 210–11; draft failings in, 226, 228, 232; volunteer recruitment in, 211, 218, 221–24

Edgartown Board of Health, 263–64

Edgartown Finance Committee, 214

Edgartown Harbor Light, 197, 198, 299, 398

Edgartown Lyceum, 158–59

Edgartown Mining Company, 181, 182

Edgartown Playhouse, 353

Edgartown Tennis Club, 415

Edgartown Town Hall, 351, 368–69, 403

Edgartown Yacht Club, 214

education: in Cottage City, 279; employ-

ment in, 269; high school, 197; Indian, 23–24, 130–31, 133–34; rights to, 279; summer schools, 346–48

Edwards, Madison, 346, 417–18

Eldridge, Edmund G., 359

Eldridge, G. W., 323

elections: for Cottage City secession (1880), 333; presidential (1860), 199–202, 201; presidential (1864), 235; state representative (1879), 264–65; state representative (1887), 333–34

electric companies, 301, 307, 310

electric railroad, 321–22, 323

electric streetcars, 339

electricity, 274, 299, 310–12, 321–23, 401, 402. *See also specific town*

"Elephant, The" (fire engine), 279

Eliot, John, 22–23, 34

Elizabeth Islands, 7, 7–8, 26, 93, 101, 235

Elliott, Samuel K., 256–57

Ellis, George, 196

Ellis, John R., 223

Ellis, Richard, 185–86

Elm Theatre (Edgartown), 353, 377

Embargo Acts (1807–1808), 136–37

Emerson, Amelia Forbes, 85–86

Emerson, C. H., 323

Emerson, Ralph Waldo, 73

Emma Jane (whaleship), 193

employment, 267–70

Englewood, 249

Enos, Manuel A., 432

Epenow (Wampanoag Indian), 9–10, 19

Espionage Act, 394

Estaing, Charles Henri, comte d', 92, 94–96, 97–98, 99

Eunice H. Adams (whaleship), 193, 335

Europa (whaleship), 193

evangelism, 142–50

Everett, Edward, 199

Everyone Here Spoke Sign Language (Groce), 51

export economy, 207–8

Fairhaven, 100–101, 140, 169–70, 186, 409

Falcon (British warship), 75

Falmouth, 102

About the Author

Arthur R. Railton was born in Regina, Saskatchewan, in 1915 and moved to Massachusetts one year later. He studied journalism at Boston University and the University of Iowa before serving five years in the army during World War II. After the war he worked on newspapers in Wisconsin and Illinois before accepting the position of automotive editor at Popular Mechanics, where he worked for thirteen years. In 1960 he moved to Volkswagen of America, where he became vice president of corporate relations. Railton spent his first summer on Martha's Vineyard in 1923 and moved there permanently upon retirement in 1977. He has been editor of the Dukes County Intelligencer, the quarterly journal of the Martha's Vineyard Historical Society, since 1978, editing and writing more than five thousand pages of Vineyard history.

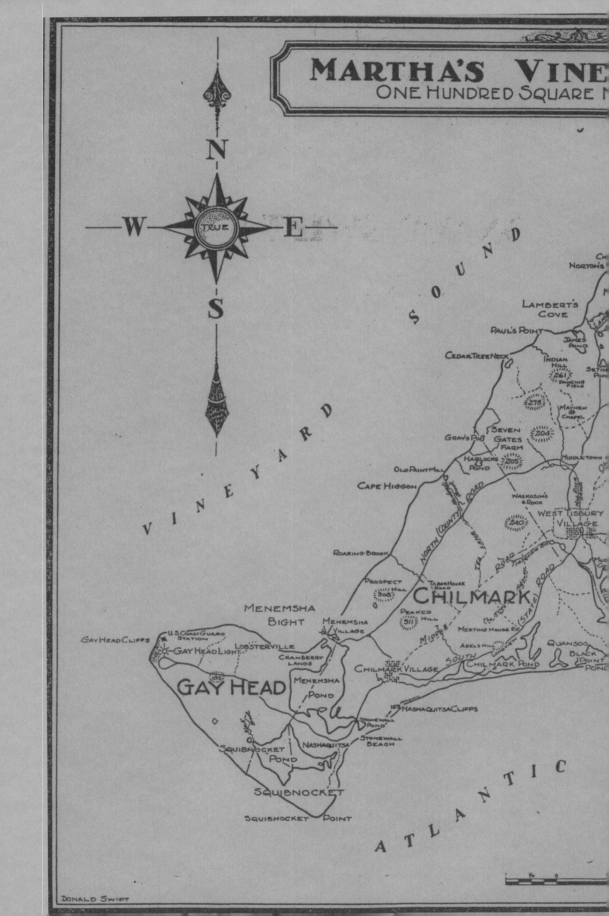

MARTHA'S VINE[YARD]

ONE HUNDRED SQUARE M[ILES]

N · **W** — TRUE — **E** · **S**

VINEYARD SOUND

VINEYARD

ATLANTIC

LAMBERT'S COVE

PAUL'S POINT

CEDAR TREE NECK

NORTON'S

JAMES POND

INDIAN HILL 261

DANCING FIELD

275

SETH[E] POND

MAYHEW & CHAPEL

204

GRAY'S POND

SEVEN GATES FARM

HARLOCK'S POND 205

MIDDLETOWN

OLD PAINT MILL

CAPE HIGGON

WASKOSIM'S ROCK

240

WEST TISBURY VILLAGE

MU[?]

ROARING BROOK

NORTH (COUNTY) ROAD

TEA LANE

PROSPECT HILL 308

TABOR HOUSE ROAD

PANHANDLE RD

CHILMARK

MENEMSHA BIGHT

MENEMSHA VILLAGE

PEAKED HILL 311

ROAD (STATE) ROAD

GAY HEAD CLIFFS

U.S. COAST GUARD STATION

GAY HEAD LIGHT

LOBSTERVILLE

CRANBERRY LANDS

MEETING HOUSE RD.

ABELS HILL

MIDDLE

SOUTH

QUANSOO

BLACK POINT POND

CHILMARK VILLAGE

CHILMARK POND

105

GAY HEAD

MENEMSHA POND

155 NASHAQUITSA CLIFFS

STONEWALL POND

STONEWALL BEACH

SQUIBNOCKET POND

NASHAQUITSA

SQUIBNOCKET

SQUIBNOCKET POINT

ATLANTIC